PUBLICATIONS
OF THE
ARMY RECORDS SOCIETY
VOL. 22

ALLENBY IN PALESTINE

The Middle East Correspondence of
Field Marshal Viscount Allenby
June 1917–October 1919

The Army Records Society was founded in 1984 in order to publish original records describing the development, organisation, administration and activities of the British Army from early times.

Any person wishing to become a member of the Society is requested to apply to the Hon. Secretary, c/o the National Army Museum, Royal Hospital Road, London, SW3 4HT. The annual subscription entitles the member to receive a copy of each volume issued by the Society in that year, and to purchase back volumes at reduced prices. Current subscription details, whether for individuals living within the British Isles, for individuals living overseas, or for institutions, will be furnished on request.

The Council of the Army Records Society wish it to be clearly understood that they are not answerable for opinions or observations that may appear in the Society's publications. For these the responsibility rests entirely with the Editors of the several works.

The Society's website can be found at
www.armyrecordssociety.org.uk

Field Marshal Viscount Allenby of Megiddo and Felixstowe painted by James McBey (1918). *(Reproduced by kind permission of the Imperial War Museum, London)*

ALLENBY IN PALESTINE

The Middle East Correspondence of
Field Marshal Viscount Allenby
June 1917–October 1919

Edited and Selected by
MATTHEW HUGHES

Published by
SUTTON PUBLISHING LIMITED
for the
ARMY RECORDS SOCIETY
2004

First published in the United Kingdom in 2004 by
Sutton Publishing Limited · Phoenix Mill · Thrupp · Stroud
Gloucestershire · GL5 2BU

British Library Cataloguing in Publication Data
A catalogue record for this book is available from the British Library.

ISBN 0-7509-3841-2

Typeset in Ehrhardt.
Typesetting and origination by
Sutton Publishing Limited.
Printed in Great Britain by
J.H. Haynes & Co. Ltd, Sparkford.

Contents

Preface and Editorial Acknowledgements

From June 1917 to October 1919, General (later Field Marshal and Viscount) Sir Edmund Allenby was Britain's supreme military commander in the Palestine theatre of operations, ultimately responsible for an immense swath of territory stretching from Egypt and Sudan in the south through the Levant and Arabia to Cilicia in southern Turkey.[1] Before coming to Palestine, he had been commander of Third Army in France; after October 1919, he was High Commissioner in Egypt, a political post he held until 1925.[2] Allenby's military command in the Middle East can be broken down into two periods: firstly, from June 1917 to October 1918, he fought Ottoman forces in Palestine at the third battle of Gaza (October–December 1917), the Transjordan raids (March–May 1918) and the battle of Megiddo (September–October 1918); secondly, from October 1918 to October 1919, he dealt with a series of low-intensity conflicts, mutinies and rebellions stretching from Egypt in the south to Cilicia in the north that spanned the political decisions being made for the post-war Middle East at the Paris Peace Conference. This volume examines Allenby's Middle-Eastern military and political correspondence as he made the shift from general to colonial administrator. It covers an immensely significant twenty-eight month period during which British-led forces under Allenby conquered the Levant and then established the basic political framework for the contemporary Middle East. Allenby's correspondence for this period is of great benefit not just for military historians interested in the First World War in general and the Palestine theatre of operations in particular, but also for scholars examining the formation of the modern Middle East in the crucial transition period between the Ottoman empire's collapse and the League of Nations Mandates for the Middle East agreed and established between 1919 and 1922.[3]

The editor would like to express his gratitude to everyone who has helped with the production of this volume. In particular, he would like to thank Dr Ahmed Aghrout, the 3rd Viscount Allenby of Megiddo and Felixstowe, Professor Martin Bull, Professor Avril Horner, Professor John Keiger, Mrs Cindy Kingham, Professor Martin Kramer, Professor Brian Longhurst, Elizabeth Lowry-Corry, Ms Patricia Methven, Ms Kate O'Brien, Dr William Philpott, Dr Yigal Sheffy, Dr Peter Stanley, Professor Asher Susser, Professor Jon Tonge, Professor David Woodward and all the academic and support staff in the School of English, Sociology, Politics and Contemporary History at the University of Salford for their help during the course of this project. The European Studies Research Institute at the University of Salford provided institutional support for archival research; the Economic and Social Research Council made possible a research trip to the Australian archives; the British Academy Elie Kedourie fund, the Moshe Dayan Centre at Tel Aviv University and the American University in Cairo all helped with research in the Middle East.

For permission to examine and reproduce papers and documents in their possession, the editor is indebted to the following: the trustees of the British Library Board; the clerk of the House of Lords Records Office; the trustees of the Imperial War Museum; the trustees of the Liddell Hart Centre for Military Archives, King's College London; the keeper of the Records of Scotland; the trustees of the National Library of Scotland; Lord Robertson for permission to quote from the papers of Field Marshal Sir William Robertson; Mrs A.E. Congreve for permission to examine the papers of General Sir Walter Congreve in the Staffordshire Record Office; Mrs Bridget Grant for permission to examine the papers of Hon. Aubrey Herbert in the Somerset Record Office; the Modern Manuscripts and Rhodes House libraries of the Bodleian, Oxford; the Middle East Centre, St Antony's College, Oxford; the National Library of Australia, Canberra; the Mitchell Library, Sydney; the Australian War Memorial, Canberra; the National Army Museum, London; the Liverpool Record Office; the Syndics of Cambridge University Library for permission to copy from the Hardinge papers; the Central Zionist Archives, Jerusalem; and the Archives and Special Collections, University of Durham. Material from the Royal Archives appears by permission of Her Majesty Queen Elizabeth II. Crown copyright material in the Public Record Office (National Archives) is reproduced by permission of the Controller of Her Majesty's Stationery Office. The maps (pp. 20–3) are reproduced by courtesy of ConstableRobinson.

If the editor has infringed the copyright of any individual or institution, he has done so unwittingly and he sincerely apologises. Having made these acknowledgements, the editor wishes to state that he alone is responsible for any errors of fact or opinion in this volume.

Matthew Hughes
Islington, London – University of Salford
October 2003

Sources and Editorial Method

Sources

The 2nd Viscount Allenby deposited his uncle's papers at the Liddell Hart Centre for Military Archives, King's College London (LHCMA) in 1976.[1] Additions to the collection were made in 1998 by the 3rd Viscount Allenby; at the same time, the papers were re-catalogued, at which time some very minor changes were made to the catalogue numbering system (a concordance is available in the holdings catalogue). A further addition was made in 2003 (see Appendix 3). This editor has used the post-1998 cataloguing numbering system for correspondence from the Allenby papers. While there are no diaries for the First World War and post-war period, there is personal correspondence for 1917 to 1919 in the form of handwritten letters from Allenby to his wife plus some letters to his mother (in 1/8–1/10).[2] There is also some correspondence to and from leading military figures during and after the Great War (2/5/1–11). The papers include notes and correspondence from the late 1930s and 1940s generated by Field Marshal Sir Archibald Wavell, 1st Earl Wavell, when he was completing his two-volume biography of Allenby (6/1–11, 7/1, 7/3). There is also some correspondence from the 1920s from General Sir Harry Chauvel, the Australian commander in Palestine, in which he questioned the part played by Colonel T.E. Lawrence at the capture of Damascus in 1918 (2/5/16–17).[3] Some photocopies of the material in the Allenby papers at the Liddell Hart Centre can be found at St Antony's College, the Middle East Centre, Oxford, including some typed extracts from Allenby's letters to Lady Allenby, and photocopies of the notes generated by Wavell for his biography. Raymond Savage, who had been on Allenby's staff during the war, did not use Allenby's papers for his 1925 biography, but later biographies by Brian Gardner (1965) and Lawrence James (1993) all made use of the papers – either through the Allenby family (Gardner) or the Liddell Hart Centre (James).[4] In Wavell's two-volume biography (1941–3), he states that Allenby left no papers, although he does acknowledge that he had access to Allenby's friends and family for his volume.[5] This is perplexing inasmuch as the notes Wavell generated for his biography ended up in Allenby's papers left to the Liddell Hart Centre; also, Wavell quoted letters from Allenby to Lady Allenby in his biography. Perhaps while Lady Allenby was still alive (she died in 1942) the status of her husband's correspondence was unclear; perhaps Wavell was ambivalent on quite what constituted personal 'papers'.[6] The holdings list for Allenby at the Liddell Hart Centre records the fact that Wavell used Allenby's papers for his biography. In his biography, Gardner points out that Wavell later left his notes to the 2nd Viscount Allenby.[7] Recent accounts examining the military and strategic aspects of the Palestine campaign have also made use of the Allenby papers.[8]

Allenby's correspondence with his wife is the most useful part of his papers for the reconstruction of his Middle East correspondence as this contains, as well as personal matters, much that is of interest to the military historian. The papers do not include letters from his wife, only those that he sent to her. The personal information in these letters has, on the whole, been omitted from this volume. None of what is left out is salacious or relevant to an understanding of Allenby's command, reflecting, rather, a deeply happy marriage, and one that went through an intense moment of grief when (Horace) Michael, the Allenbys' only child, died on active service in France in July 1917. Some of Allenby's words of comfort to his wife in the summer of 1917, as both came to terms with Michael's death, have been included in this collection to give an impression of Allenby beyond his role as commander. The personal comments in letters from Allenby to his wife reflect his interest in the local flora and fauna, the possibility of officers' wives being allowed out to Egypt, the geography of Palestine, biblical and ancient history, and the vicissitudes of various friends and acquaintances. In these letters, there is little of the gossip or invective that one finds in, say, the papers of Sir Henry Wilson (or Sir James Edmonds); nor, indeed, the sense that one is reading the papers of someone who is writing for posterity (as is the case with Sir Basil Liddell Hart).[9] In light of the relative paucity of the Allenby papers at the LHCMA, to provide a full range of his official correspondence it has been necessary to examine the private papers of a range of military and political figures as well as Allenby's correspondence (largely with the War Office) held at the Public Record Office (National Archives) (PRO) in London. Only those files in the PRO containing correspondence to/from Allenby or which have been directly used for this volume have been listed in the bibliography. To fill in some gaps in Allenby's correspondence for the summer of 1919 some of the material from the *British Documents on British Foreign Policy, 1919–39, First Series,*

Volume Four (DBFP) (London: HMSO, 1952) has been included. The editor has also made use of the earlier Army Records Society volumes on Field Marshals Sir Henry Wilson and Sir William Robertson, although readers should be aware that, in the case of the latter volume, archival re-cataloguing has taken place since the publication of the Robertson book in 1989.[10] Using these sources, this volume presents a reasonably complete set of Middle East correspondence for the period from 1917 to 1919.

Editorial Method

If a word is unclear but the editor is reasonably certain of its meaning or spelling this is noted with [?] after the word or phrase in question; if a word or phrase is indecipherable this is noted with ellipses inside brackets [. . . ?]. An endnote or comment in brackets is provided if there is a more complicated issue. Endnotes or comments in brackets are also used for any other issues requiring clarification.

Transliteration in correspondence of Arabic proper names can vary – for geographical location of places mentioned in the text, readers are advised to consult contemporary maps such as the detailed maps of Palestine in the British official history of the campaign, especially the two dedicated maps volumes and the map of Palestine in the end sleeve of part one of volume two. The problem with geographical place names is compounded by the destruction of so many Palestinian villages in 1948–9 in Israel's 'War of Independence' – what for the Palestinians was the catastrophe (*al-Nakba*) of 1948 – and their replacement with Israeli settlements bearing new Hebrew names.[11]

The Biographical Notes give details of the main individuals mentioned in the text. Otherwise, a note is provided with biographical details. If it has been impossible to locate an individual mentioned in the text this is made apparent by a note comment after the first mention of the individual in each separate piece of correspondence. However, if a minor official or junior commander is mentioned in passing and the position and role of that individual is obvious from the text then no biographical details are supplied. Ranks and honours for individuals are detailed in full in the bibliography and biographical details section at the end of the volume; if an individual is discussed in the context of the period, then ranks and honours are (usually) given as were awarded/conferred at the time. In the sender/recipient information prefixing each piece of correspondence the surname only is given (unless there is ambiguity in which case the first name/title is included).

If a piece of correspondence is available in more than one archive (or in more than one place in the same archive), this is noted in the archival reference information for each piece of correspondence. Sometimes the wording of copies can be slightly different from the original and, if this is the case, a note is made in the archival reference information suffix (this rule, obviously, does not apply if the change in wording alters the meaning of the piece of correspondence). Allenby's use of paragraph breaks is also unclear and the editor has used his best judgement on this matter. Finally, it is not always apparent in holograph copies of Allenby's letters whether he is using upper or lower case for some nouns: here too the editor has used his best judgement on the assumption that ambiguity in this matter does affect the import of the content of such letters.

Abbreviations

ADC	Aide-de-camp
AG	Adjutant General
AGM	Annual General Meeting
AIF	Australian Imperial Force
ALH	Australian Light Horse
Anzac	Australian and New Zealand
AOH	*Australian Official War History of the Palestine Campaign* (by H. Gullett)
AWM	Australian War Memorial, Canberra
ARS	Army Records Society
BC	Before Christ
BEF	British Expeditionary Force (in France)
BG	Brigadier General
BGGS	Brigadier General-General Staff
BL	British Library, London
BWI	British West Indies Regiment
CAB	War Cabinet
CB	Companion of the Order of Bath
CID	Committee of Imperial Defence
CiC/C-in-C	Commander in Chief
CIGS	Chief of the Imperial General Staff
CMG	Companion of the Order of St Michael and St George
CPO	Chief Political Officer
CRE	Chief Royal Engineers
CUL	Cambridge University Library
CUP	Cambridge University Press
CZA	Central Zionist Archives, Jerusalem
DBFP	*Documents on British Foreign Policy, First Series, Volume 4*
DFPS	*Détachement Français de Palestine et de Syrie*
DMC	Desert Mounted Corps
DMI	Director of Military Intelligence
DMS	Director of Medical Services
dob	Date of birth
DSO	Distinguished Service Order
EEF	Egyptian Expeditionary Force
ELC	Egyptian Labour Corps

FO	Foreign Office
GCB	Knight Grand Cross of the Order of Bath
GCMG	Knight Grand Cross of the Order of St Michael and St George
GCVO	Knight Grand Cross of the Royal Victorian Order
GHQ	General Headquarters
GOC	General Officer Commanding
GOC-in-C	General Officer Commanding-in-Chief
GSO	General Staff Officer
HH	His Highness
HMG	His Majesty's Government
HMSO	His/Her Majesty's Stationery Office
HoL	House of Lords Record Office, London
HW	Henry Wilson
IDF	Israeli Defence Forces
IWM	Imperial War Museum, London
KCB	Knight Commander of the Order of Bath
KCMG	Knight Commander of the Order of St Michael and St George
KM	King's Messenger
LG	Lloyd George
LHCMA	Liddell Hart Centre for Military Archives, King's College, London
LoC	Lines of Communication
MP	Member of Parliament
NAM	National Army Museum, London
NAS	National Archive of Scotland, Edinburgh
NCO	Non-Commissioned Officer
n.d.	No date
NLS	National Library of Scotland, Edinburgh
OC	Officer Commanding
OETA	Occupied Enemy Territory Administration
OH	*British Official War History of the Palestine Campaign* (two volumes by C. Falls)
OIOC	Oriental and India Office Collections, British Library, London
OPDA	Ottoman Public Debt Administration
OxBod	Oxford University, Bodleian Library
OxAnt	Oxford University, St Antony's College, The Middle East Centre
OUP	Oxford University Press
PM	Prime Minister
POW	Prisoner of War
PRO	Public Record Office, London (now the National Archives)
PS	Postscript
RA	Royal Archives, Windsor Castle
RE	Royal Engineers
RFC	Royal Flying Corps
RHA	Royal Horse Artillery

RN	Royal Navy
SAD	Sudan Archive, Archives and Special Collections, University of Durham
SNO	Senior Naval Officer
SOAS	School of Oriental and African Studies, University of London
SP	Sykes-Picot
SRO	Staffordshire Record Office
SomRO	Somerset Record Office
2i/c	Second-in-Command
UP	University Press
VC	Victoria Cross
WD	War Diary
WO	War Office

Glossary

Ahl (Al)	Family or clan
Abar (pl. of Bir)	Wells
Abu	Father (of); often – possessor (of)
Ain (pl. Ayun)	Spring
Akaba (Aqaba)	Ascent, pass
Amir	Military commander, governor, minor ruler, prince
Arish, Wadi el	River of Egypt
Bab	Gateway, door
Beersheba	Bir es Sabe (7 wells)
Beit, Beth (Heb.)	House or tent, dwelling
Beni, Bani	Sons (of)
Bethany	House of song
Bethal (Ar. Beitin)	House of God
Bir (pl. Abar, Biyar)	Well, tank, rock–cistern
Brevet	A military commission entitling an officer to assume rank above that for which s/he receives pay
Caliph	Deputy or successor to the Prophet
Custos	Keeper, custodian
Darb	Road or track
Deir	Monastery
El	Definite article (the)
Fellahin (pl)	Peasants
Gaza	The Greek form of the Hebrew 'Azzah' (fortress)
Hajj	Arabic title indicating someone who has performed the pilgrimage to Mecca.
Hijra	The flight of Muhammad from Mecca to Medina in 622 CE, the year from which the Muslim calendar commences
Jebel, (Gebel – spoken Arabic in Egypt)	Mountain, hills, desert
Jisr, Gisr	Embankment, causeway, bridge
Kaimakan (or Kaymakam)	Turkish Lieutenant-Colonel, Lieutenant-Governor or District Governor
Khan	Inn, caravanserai
Khedive	Title of Persian origin held by the Muhammad Ali dynasty in Egypt, 1867–1914

Khirbet, Kharab, Demaar	Ruin
L	Libra (Latin) £
Lajjun (or Lejjun), El	Arabic corruption of Latin 'Legio' meaning the Legion (not to be confused with Wadi Abu Lejja). The settlement of the Roman period 1 km. south of Megiddo; the site of the headquarters of the Sixth Roman Legion after the Second Jewish revolt (AD 131/2–135); often used synonymously with Megiddo
Mamour (Egyptian Ar.)	Sharif, head of police
Medina	Town
Monitor	Shallow-draft warship with one or more main guns, designed for offshore fire support
Mudir	Manager, head teacher, communal head
Mufti	A Muslim cleric or expounder of the law
Muntar, El	The watch tower
Muqatta, Nahr el	River of the ford or shallow
Nahr, Nahar	River, watercourse
Neby	A prophet
Omda	Wise or learned man, village headman
Palestine	Philistina
Pasha	Ottoman official title, usually borne by those with rank of Minister, Governor or equivalent
Qantara (or Kantara)	Bridge
Qasr, Qo(u)seir	Port or palace, castle
Quds, El (Jerusalem)	The Holy Place
Ramle(y)	Sandy plain
Ras (dim. Ruweis)	Head, cape
Sanjak, Sancak (or Mutasarrifiyya)	Ottoman administrative division, corresponding to a region or the district of a province
Senussi	Mystic Sufi brotherhood established in 1837 by Said Muhammad ibn 'Ali al-Senussi; became a religious fighting order with its base in Cyrenaica (eastern Libya)
Serai	Town hall or palace (as in Sarajevo – Seraiëvo)
Sharif	Literally 'noble'. A descendant of the Prophet (normally in the line of Hasan), especially the Sharif of Mecca.
Sheikh, Shaykh	Chief, elder, head of tribe, saint (literally 'old man')
Shellal	Cataract, waterfall
Sheria, Wadi esh	The valley of the watering place
Sirdar	A chieftain, leader or commander; (Egypt) Commander in Chief of the army
Tell (Ar.) Tel (Heb.)	Mound (especially covering ruins)
Troopers	The War Office

Um, Umm	Mother
Vali (Wali)	Provincial Governor
Vilayet (Wilayet)	Ottoman administrative division, corresponding to a province (usually governed by a Vali)
Vulgate	The Latin version of the Bible most widely used in the West
Wadi	Watercourse (normally dry), a valley
Wafk	An agreement or understanding
Wahabi	Sunni Muslim sect based in Arabian peninsula
Waqf	Charitable endowment, usually of religious land
War Cabinet	Decision-making executive headed by David Lloyd George formed in December 1916. Composed of a small core of permanent members, served by a secretariat, special advisors and specialist committees, its aim was to give purpose to British war strategy

Compiled with the help of the glossaries in Cyril Falls (with George Macmunn), *History of the Great War, Military Operations, Egypt and Palestine* (London: HMSO, 1928–30); Malcom Yapp, *The Near East Since the First World War: A History to 1995* [1991] (London and New York: Longman, 1996); and Yapp, *The Making of the Modern Near East 1792–1923* (London and New York: Longman, 1987). Modified and updated with the help of Dr Ahmed Aghrout of the University of Salford using Munir Baalbaki (ed.), *Al-Mawrid: A Modern English-Arabic Dictionary* (Beirut: Dar El-Lim, 20th edition 1986).

Introduction

Edmund Henry Hynman Allenby was born on 23 April 1861, St George's Day, on the estate of his mother's family at Brackenhurst Hall, near Southwell, in Nottinghamshire. He was the second child and eldest son of six children – three boys, three girls – of Hynman Allenby (*c.* 1822–78), a country gentleman, and his wife, Catherine Anne (*c.* 1830–1922), daughter of the Reverend Thomas Coats Cane of Nottinghamshire. Married in 1859, after the death of Hynman Allenby's father in 1861, Allenby's parents established the family home at Felixstowe House, Felixstowe, Suffolk (subsequently demolished); at the same time, they also bought an estate in Norfolk of some 2,000 acres. Brought up the son of a country squire in the countryside away from the urban sprawl of an industrialising Britain, Allenby loved nature and developed a keen knowledge of flora and fauna, a passion that would remain with him all his life, and one reflected in his correspondence: letters to his wife when he was in Palestine during the First World War are full of references to the geography, wildlife and plants of the surrounding countryside. This fascination with the outdoors remained with him until the end: in 1935, aged 74, and just one year before his death, Allenby went to Patagonia in Argentina on a final fishing trip to see if the salmon really were as big as in his beloved river Tay.

Allenby's family background and early years did not suggest a military career. After being tutored at home by a governess, Allenby went, in 1871, to Ashbocking Vicarage to be schooled by the Reverend Maurice Cowell, before going, in 1875, to Haileybury College in Hertfordshire, a former training school for the East India Company that had been resurrected as a public school in 1862. While Allenby showed no remarkable aptitude in schoolwork or sport, his schooling in the classrooms and on the playing fields of Haileybury left its imprint. Rather than intelligence, the public schools at this time emphasised courage, duty, fortitude, integrity, selflessness, self-control and a 'manly' belief in the virtues of the Christian faith as the vital attributes for 'character' and for a successful career in positions of authority.[1] While

1

there was none of the sense of divine purpose that drove on some of his generation – such as Douglas Haig – who would later rise to senior positions, the Anglican faith and tight emotional discipline of Allenby's early years gave him strength and perseverance throughout his life. His childhood and schooling formed a determined rather than an intellectual commander; a practitioner of war rather than a military thinker.

Considering Haileybury's connections with India, in 1878 Allenby decided on a career in the Indian Civil Service and went to several 'crammer' schools in London to prepare for the entrance exams. These he failed, twice. Only after this setback did he choose a career in the army. As he later recounted in a public speech, he went into the army in 1881 'because he was too big a fool for anything else.'[2] Having passed out of Sandhurst in December 1881, on 10 May 1882 Allenby was gazetted to the 6th (Inniskilling) Dragoons, a not particularly fashionable cavalry regiment. It is unclear why Allenby chose the mounted arm, but it would be as a cavalryman that Allenby would make his reputation. Military life suited Allenby. While not an automaton, he was loyal, accepted orders without question and enjoyed outdoor physical activity. When Allenby joined the army, it was beginning a period of transition as the old army gradually reformed to meet the challenges of modern, industrialised warfare. It was, however, in old-style colonial soldiering in southern Africa that Allenby served his apprenticeship as a subaltern. In 1882, he joined his regiment in South Africa before embarking in 1884 on an expedition to eject Boer lodgements in Bechuanaland (now Botswana). In 1886, Allenby returned home for a two-year stint at the cavalry depot at Canterbury, and two seasons' fox-hunting, before returning to South Africa, a captain, accompanied by some hounds, to his regiment, now on active duty in Zululand. Promoted adjutant on his return to South Africa, with this appointment there emerged a serious application to soldiering that replaced Allenby's previously good-natured insouciance. While he had seen no actual fighting in southern Africa, Allenby learned much of the basic field-craft that he would need in later wars. In this period, Allenby also became something of a martinet and, when he assumed senior command, his withering temper, imposing physical presence (matched by a voracious appetite), plus an obsession with discipline and orders, earned him the nickname 'The Bull.'

In 1890, when the 6th Dragoons returned home for garrison duties, Allenby settled into a rhythm of hunting, sport, socialising and military duties. He also married. In 1895, he had met Adelaide Mabel Chapman, daughter of Horace Edward Chapman, and, in December 1896, the two were married at the bride's home at Donhead House, Salisbury, Wiltshire. Allenby's wife shared his love of the country and the marriage was an intensely happy one, lasting until his death in 1936. Adelaide Mabel, along with Allenby's mother, to whom he wrote regularly until her death in 1922, provided a solid foundation of female support on which Allenby built his reputation as a soldier. In 1898, Adelaide Mabel gave birth to a son, (Horace) Michael, the Allenbys' only child. His death as a subaltern on the Western Front in July 1917 shattered the typically marmoreal Allenby who broke down and, inconsolable, wept in front of Sir John Shea, one of his divisional commanders in Palestine.[3]

Allenby's reticence masked considerable ambition and drive, and, in 1896, he passed, by competition, into the Staff College at Camberley, a notable achievement at a time when few cavalrymen entered Staff College except by nomination. His class included another future field marshal, Douglas Haig. The cerebral James Edmonds, another entrant of 1896, and someone who would later become an Official Historian of the Great War, recalled that Allenby was 'curiously taciturn' at Staff College and 'rather out of his depth in the very medium company' of 1896–7.[4] While it is true that Allenby was neither strikingly intellectual nor garrulous, he was more popular than other students in his cohort such as Haig, over whom fellow officers elected him to the prestigious position of Master of the Drag Hounds for the 1896–7 season. A solid rather than outstanding student at Staff College, Allenby showed himself to be tolerant and flexible and, while not a big debater, capable of interesting conversations on a range of topics. The willingness to listen to and accommodate new ideas boosted Allenby's ascent to the pinnacle of his profession.

Promoted major in 1897, in 1898 Allenby was made adjutant (equivalent to a brigade-major) to the 3rd Cavalry brigade. The next year saw the outbreak of the South African (or 'Boer') War (1899–1902) and in October 1899 the Inniskillings shipped out for service in South Africa against the Boers. This would be Allenby's first war. Given temporary command of the Inniskillings in 1900, he emerged at the war's end in 1902 with much credit, a brevet lieutenant-colonelcy, useful contacts and, in 1902, was created CB in recognition of his service. Allenby started the South African War as an unknown major; he ended it with a reputation as a competent, reliable leader, and someone marked out for possible promotion. While not a brilliant commander, Allenby had suffered no major reverses and, physically tough, had proved himself in the field on lengthy, exacting operations during which British columns swept the veldt for Boer commandos. (Allenby's officers included a

Captain Lawrence Oates, who was recommended for a VC, and who would die in an Antarctic blizzard in 1912 coming back from the South Pole.) Allenby also worked well with an attached Australian cavalry regiment, the New South Wales Lancers, a portent of future operations in Palestine during the First World War when Allenby commanded Australian and New Zealand mounted troops. After the South African War, Allenby became a full colonel and, in 1905, was made a brigadier-general and was given command of the 4th Cavalry Brigade. In 1909, he rose to the rank of major-general before, the following year, becoming Inspector-General of Cavalry, a post he held until the outbreak of the First World War. Allenby was not a reforming Inspector-General of Cavalry and Britain's cavalry force, as with much of the British army, was not best prepared for the war that came in 1914.

As he coped with the pressures of senior command before and during the Great War, Allenby became irascible, obsessive with discipline and, at times, short tempered with his subordinates. He certainly did not suffer fools gladly. Hubert Gough, Allenby's chief staff officer when he was Inspector-General of Cavalry, recalled that Allenby had a 'great regard for regulations and all sort of detail' and that if Allenby, when inspecting a unit, saw any neglect of detail or orders he was liable to explode.[5] Cavalrymen who neglected to do up their chinstraps would feel the full weight of Allenby's concern with obeying to the letter all orders. As one of his officers recalled, while Allenby had been an easy-going young officer and a good-humoured squadron leader, he was a strict colonel, an irascible brigadier and an explosive general.[6] Allenby's temper got worse once war broke out in 1914. Lieutenant-General Sir John Keir, a Western Front commander willing to withstand Allenby's tirades earned himself the sobriquet 'toreador', before being dismissed.[7] During one inspection an officer remarked 'Very good, Sir', to which Allenby barked back 'I want none of your bloody approbation.'[8] On another occasion, Allenby berated a company commander over the regulation that steel helmets and leather jerkins should be worn at all times in the trenches:

> Allenby: 'Did I or did I not issue an order that no man should go up to the front line without jerkin or helmet?'
> Company commander: 'Yes, sir.'
> Allenby: 'Then why has that man not got them on?'
> Company commander: 'The man is dead, Sir.'
> Allenby: 'Did I or did I not . . .'[9]

Nevertheless, in a war in which few generals, on any side, have fared well in the historiography, the discussion of Allenby's temper by biographers and campaign historians invariably emphasises his human side – imparting a positive spin, thus setting him apart from the real 'Blimps' of the war. Accounts of Allenby's bullying and volatile temper seem like exaggerations; apocryphal tales that are there to differentiate rather than deprecate a commander whose exploits in Palestine provided such a welcome contrast to the attritional grind in France. Allenby was a model for the sympathetic portrayal of a Great War general in C.S. Forester's post-war novel *The General* (1936) in which a product of Victorian Britain – a composite character called the 'Buffalo' in Forester's book – struggled to come to terms with a new style of warfare. Overall, Allenby has had a rather good press in the different accounts of the Palestine campaign, especially when compared to the hostility expressed towards many senior commanders of the First World War who served on the Western Front. His sharp temper was a result of having to cope with the strains of high command and war – he was, after all, a general and not a counsellor – yet he was still capable of great kindness, did not bear grudges and was willing to listen to his officers, as long as they could provide convincing evidence for their arguments. In Palestine, Sir Ronald Storrs, the Military Governor of Jerusalem, recalled how being told off by Allenby was like being 'blown from the muzzle of a gun' but when the victim regained the ground Allenby 'bore him no malice.'[10] Allenby's eruptions of temper were a response to the intense pressures of war rather than proof of a nasty streak; his willingness to listen to those under him with good ideas suggests that his outbursts were more style than substance.

On the outbreak of war in August 1914, Allenby assumed command of the Cavalry Division. While questions were raised over his handling of the cavalry during the retreat from Mons, Allenby's defence of the Messines-Wytschaete ridge during the first battle of Ypres from October to November 1914, with what was now the Cavalry Corps of two divisions, showed him at his dogged best: unflappable, reliable and determined to stick to his orders and hold his ground at all cost in the face of almost overwhelming odds. In May 1915, Allenby took over V Corps during the second battle of Ypres before taking charge of the Third Army in October 1915 with the temporary rank of general. He was also made a KCB the same year (a GCMG would follow in 1917, a GCB in 1918 and a GCVO in 1934). In the trying circumstances of the

Western Front, unable to institute manoeuvre warfare, Allenby proved himself as a competent rather than an inspiring general.

Allenby's relationship with his commander, Haig, was far from ideal. While there was goodwill between the two men, both were uncommunicative in each other's company. This made discussions of operations awkward: Allenby fumbled for words while Haig rambled through a series of unfinished sentences. In April 1917, when Allenby's opportunity to prove himself came when his Third Army attacked at Arras, the lack of communication with Haig hampered the planning and execution of operations. In the planning stages of the battle, Allenby reduced the preparatory bombardment to 24–48 hours to give his assault troops the element of surprise. But Haig vetoed Allenby's 'hurricane' bombardment in favour of a longer five-day artillery barrage and, under pressure, Allenby, who was always loyal to Haig, acquiesced in the change of plan rather than insist on the shorter fire-plan that might have yielded better results. While the longer Somme-style barrage seems to have disadvantaged him operationally, Allenby instituted a number of measures, such as using the sewers and cellars of Arras as a means of getting troops secretly to the jumping-off points, to achieve tactical surprise. The result of this planning was an impressive initial gain of almost four miles when the battle opened on 9 April 1917. Thereafter, the fighting became a series of bitter and costly attritional battles as the Third Army engaged the Germans' defence-in-depth system. Allenby's inability to convince Haig to call a halt once the battle of Arras bogged down, and his willingness faithfully to carry out orders that he must have known would achieve little except cause heavy casualties, show some of his shortcomings. As was noted in his obituary in *The Times* in 1936, at Arras 'Allenby conscientiously, if clumsily, carried out an operation which, it was recognized, could hardly be decisive, and had been continued mainly with a view to giving the French time in which to recover.'[11] The assessment of Gough, who, as commander of the Fifth Army, would himself face the sack following the first Ludendorff offensive in March 1918, was that, while Allenby was 'very just' and 'never bore any malice against subordinates who disagreed', he also had 'no ideas and when in France would apply orders rigidly without reasoning.'[12]

Allenby came unstuck after Arras and, looking for a new commander for Palestine, the British Prime Minister, David Lloyd George, dispatched him to the Middle East to command the British-led Egyptian Expeditionary Force (EEF). Theatre command in Palestine was the restorative tonic that Allenby needed to discover his skills as a general, skills that had been 'lost and forgotten in the mud and muddle of Flanders'.[13] Without the fillip of the Palestine campaign, Allenby would be remembered, at best, as another lacklustre general of the Western Front; at worst, he would have ended the war as a prematurely dismissed or castigated commander, someone who had achieved little beyond throwing away his men's lives for no apparent purpose at the battle of Arras. As it was, while Allenby was 'desolate' at being moved to Palestine – indeed, he broke down in front of Sir Julian Byng after he was told he was to go – seeing it as a demotion and punishment for failing in France, independent command in a peripheral war theatre away from the intrigues of the Western Front would make his name and, in October 1919, would culminate in a Field-Marshal's baton, a viscountcy, appointment as High Commissioner to Egypt and an award from Parliament of £50,000.[14]

When Allenby arrived in Egypt on 27 June 1917 – assuming command the following day – EEF morale had collapsed. Under the uninspiring leadership of General Sir Archibald Murray, the force had been defeated, twice, at the town of Gaza in the spring of 1917. While capable of building the communication infrastructure needed to take the EEF across the Sinai, Murray lacked the verve to move from logistics to operational success. The two defeats at Gaza, while partly the result of determined Turkish defence, were, in the main, the product of Murray's inability to control operations. This lack of grip seeped into the fabric of the EEF and Allenby's first job was to rebuild it into a force capable of successfully taking the offensive. He moved his headquarters to Khan Yunis, just behind the front line at Gaza, and embarked on a series of tours of EEF front-line troops. The tough Australian and New Zealand mounted troops that formed a mobile core to the EEF soon noticed the change in atmosphere.[15] Trooper L. Pollock, an Australian light horseman, remembered how under Murray he and his comrades were 'fed up – we considered we hadn't had the leadership we were due for and it seemed to be one blunder after another. Then the arrival of Allenby, morale rose.'[16] Allenby's impact resonated through the EEF. Richard Meinertzhagen, an EEF staff officer, recorded how the force was finally awakening from its 'lethargic sleep' under Murray, while Storrs noted that under Allenby the EEF was advancing with 'exhilaration into new hope.'[17] With the weight of the Western Front lifted from his shoulders, Allenby rose to meet the challenges of his new post. Unlike

Murray, Allenby was not an office general and, physically fit, was willing and able to travel over bumpy tracks in the stifling heat to visit units in the desert. Allenby's experience of field command of everything from a troop in southern Africa in the 1880s to an army in France gave him the standing to talk to rankers and lift their spirits. His physical and psychological presence lifted morale and, like Generals Sir Bernard Montgomery and Sir William Slim in the Second World War, he convinced the men that they now had the leadership and resources to win the impending battle.[18]

While Allenby's personality remained fundamentally the same after June 1917, the special circumstances in Palestine drew out his best qualities and emphasised a more human side to his personality.[19] The Australian Official War Historian in Palestine, Sir Henry Gullett, remembered Allenby visiting an Australian unit out in the desert where the canteen had been open for some time before Allenby arrived and, consequently, many of the men were drunk. The drunk soldiers struck matches on Allenby's car, 'almost leaned on him. The tighter they were the closer they wished to get to him.'[20] Allenby's reaction to this incident was afterwards to write an appreciative note to the unit commander. This incident provides an obvious contrast to all the talk of Allenby as a disciplinarian. Major-General Sir G. de S. Barrow, one of Allenby's divisional commanders, compared him favourably to Haig, writing how Allenby was happy to be contradicted as long as this was backed up by a cogent argument.[21] Allenby's mix of martinet, motivation and toleration infused new life into the EEF, transforming it into a fighting force capable of taking the offensive. His first battle, the third battle of Gaza, opened in October 1917 with the objective of capturing Jerusalem.

Prior to the third battle of Gaza, artillery, aeroplanes, men and equipment poured into Egypt and Palestine, turning the EEF into a well-equipped force of ten divisions – seven infantry and three cavalry. On 12 August 1917, Allenby organised these units into three corps: XX and XXI Infantry Corps, and the Desert Mounted Corps. These reinforcements were vital for the planned offensive to break the Turkish forces that stretched in a ragged line from Gaza to Beersheba. For the third battle of Gaza, Allenby adopted a plan worked out by Murray's staff before his arrival. This plan involved shifting the emphasis of attack away from Gaza, with two of Allenby's three mounted divisions, plus four of the infantry divisions available, attacking the weaker eastern extremity of the Turkish lines at Beersheba, before rolling up the enemy defences from the east. Simultaneously, intelligence deception would deceive the Turks into thinking that the attack would come, as before, at Gaza.[22] This plan worked, eventually. Australian light horse troops charged in, took Beersheba on 31 October, before moving west to join up with the force at Gaza prior to the push on Jerusalem. But the lack of water in the desiccated distance between Beersheba and Gaza hampered the advance and, as the EEF cavalry faltered for lack of water for horses and men, the Turks escaped to fight another day. Jerusalem was finally captured on 9 December 1917, the actual surrender being taken by two 'cockney' privates from the 60th (London) Division out looking for water who were accosted by the mayor of Jerusalem out looking for someone to surrender to and bearing the keys to the city.[23]

Considering the powerful punch of the EEF and the weak nature of the Turkish defences at Gaza, rather than dissipate the EEF's potential by assaulting Beersheba, would Allenby have done better to concentrate his augmented force, which included a substantial pool of medium and heavy artillery, for a direct assault on Gaza town? The presence of water and a reasonable transport system on the coastal plain of Palestine behind Gaza allowed for the rapid exploitation of any breakthrough. As it was, the gradual advance after the attack on Beersheba meant that Turkish forces escaped and regrouped. This counter-factual argument, first posited by Clive Garsia, GSO1 with the EEF's 54th Division, has led to an on-going debate that a comprehensive victory was within Allenby's grasp at the third battle of Gaza but that he threw his chance away with the decision to attack Beersheba.[24] While it is true that the decision to attack at Beersheba meant that the Turks were allowed the space to retire in good order to a new defensive line across central Palestine just north of Jerusalem from which they were not dislodged until the war's end, the third battle of Gaza revenged the two earlier defeats in 1917 and resulted in the capture of the historic city of Jerusalem. Allenby was under intense pressure to invade Palestine and take Jerusalem as quickly as possible, especially after his poor performance in the latter phases of the battle of Arras. Having examined the Beersheba plan offered to him by his staff on his arrival in Egypt, Allenby felt that the attack at Beersheba offered the best likelihood of fulfilling the wishes of his political superiors in the time allotted for the task. Under pressure at the operational level to reverse the defeats at the first Gaza battles before the winter rains arrived, he was also having to make his plans within the context of a protracted struggle between Lloyd George and elements within the British military establishment, notably the Chief of the Imperial General Staff (CIGS), General Sir William Robertson, over war strategy and whether 'side-shows' such as Palestine were worthy of support – the argument being that Robertson opposed the peripheral (or 'eastern') operations favoured by the Prime Minister. Caught in the middle of an acrimonious struggle – which culminated in Robertson's dismissal in February 1918 – Allenby had to tread carefully and please both sides as best he could.

Whether Allenby, under pressure from Robertson, produced disingenuous reports designed to scupper Lloyd George's strategy is a matter of debate. Certainly, Allenby's request on 9 October 1917 for an extra thirteen divisions to take and hold Jerusalem was, to say the least, incongruous considering his assault with ten divisions at the third battle of Gaza that took and held Jerusalem, and led some to question whether he was working in cahoots with Robertson to produce exaggerated reports that made a further offensive beyond the Jaffa-Jerusalem line seem impractical.[25] But Allenby's correspondence taken as a whole does not suggest deceit – even taking into account the secret 'R' telegram system between Robertson and Allenby – and critics of Allenby would do well to weigh up the historical evidence that points to a newly arrived, overly cautious commander responding to intelligence reports that the Turks were planning to reinforce the Palestine front and launch their own assault on the EEF. This worry of an attack by the Turks, rather than any duplicity on the part of Allenby, best explains the demand in the autumn of 1917 for extra troops for Palestine above and beyond the initial reinforcement.[26]

The capture of Jerusalem in December 1917 thrilled the British nation and Christian world (even the German press took note), and provided a welcome relief from the horrors of the third battle of Ypres that had finally petered out a month earlier with capture of the ruined Flemish village of Passchendaele. Local papers such as London's *Islington Daily Gazette* captured the popular mood, recording for its readers on 12 December 1917 how 'More than military significance attaches to the surrender into British hands of a city held in reverence by all Christendom.'[27] A week later, on 19 December 1917, the magazine *Punch* included a sketch of Richard I looking down on Jerusalem with the caption: 'The Last Crusade, Coeur-de-Lion (looking down on the Holy City). "My Dream Comes True."' With the capture of Jerusalem, Allenby became the modern-day Richard 'Lionheart', finally recapturing for Christianity the holy city lost to the Muslims in 1187. For Britain, the fall of Jerusalem was a massive propaganda coup at a difficult moment in the war; for Lloyd George, it was the Christmas present for the nation that he had demanded of Allenby before he left for Palestine.[28] Allenby's entry into the city on 11 December was a carefully stage-managed affair.[29] He entered on foot through the Jaffa Gate, having dismounted outside the walls, in a brief ceremony read out a proclamation of martial law, and then left, again on foot. This carefully contrived and understated entrance compared favourably to the German Kaiser's ostentatious entry into Jerusalem on horseback in 1898 through a hole made for him in the city walls just by the Jaffa Gate. So began thirty years of British rule in the region – Britain's 'moment' in the Middle East – that ended in Palestine with a hasty and ignoble withdrawal in 1948.[30]

Keen to push on in Palestine, in February 1918 Lloyd George sent the South African general, Jan Smuts, on a troubleshooting mission to Palestine (12–22 February 1918). Simultaneously, Robertson sent the Deputy DMO, Colonel Walter Meryyn St George Kirke, to Palestine with the job, it was later claimed, of passing on instructions from the CIGS telling Allenby that he was to ignore the Smuts Mission and was not to pursue further operations.[31] In sending Smuts to Palestine, the Prime Minister's objective was to redirect Britain's offensive punch away from France to a peripheral war zone such as Palestine. This was a strategy that Robertson strongly opposed. Prior to the Smuts Mission, Lloyd George had succeeded in getting the recently formed Inter-Allied planning forum, the Supreme War Council, to accede to Joint Note 12 that called for a defensive posture on the Western Front while an attack was delivered against Turkey.[32] But the German Ludendorff offensives on the Western Front in the spring of 1918 shattered this renewed attempt at an 'eastern' strategy. They also severely restricted Allenby's operational planning as the EEF was a potential reserve force for France. When the first Ludendorff offensive broke in March 1918, Allenby lost the bulk of his infantry and some of his cavalry that were sent to France to stem the German offensives. These losses were made good with raw Indian troops that needed time to be absorbed into the EEF. This made a rapid push forward after the taking of Jerusalem almost impossible. Nonetheless, from March to May 1918, just as his men were leaving for France, Allenby launched two Transjordan 'raids' – the official nomenclature for two multi-divisional attacks – across the river Jordan towards Amman. The objective of these failed 'raids' is not entirely clear – but seems to have been an attempt to secure Allenby's eastern flank by cutting the Hedjaz railway and uniting with allied Arab forces before a drive along the Palestine coast – and resulted in two comprehensive defeats by Turkish forces; defeats that could not be undone afterwards by disingenuous reports outlining how the raids cleverly forced the Turks subsequently to leave a large force to cover Amman.[33] These defeats constrained British policy towards local Arabs, whom Britain was keen to win over to its cause, and who now sat on the fence, seeing little gain to be had from joining a power unable to eject the Turks from Amman. This was also the only occasion during the campaign when the Turks captured EEF artillery pieces, lost in the mêlée of fighting on the eastern bank of the river Jordan – a material and symbolic triumph for Turkish forces – with the nine captured Royal Horse Artillery 13-pounder guns paraded by the Turks after the battle. These setbacks rattled Allenby and for such a circumspect commander, usually so methodical and measured, show a real loss of grip on operations.[34]

Allenby's finest hour, and the crowning triumph of the Palestine campaign, came with his final offensive against the Turkish armies in Palestine, launched on 19 September 1918, which culminated with an armistice signed at Mudros on 30 October 1918. This final battle was given the epithet 'Megiddo', as Allenby's forces pushed by the ancient settlement of Megiddo,[35] located on the Plain of Esdraelon by the Musmus Pass, the scene of many battles through history and the supposed site of the final battle (or Armageddon) revealed in the Book of Revelations (16: 16). Megiddo was a cavalry triumph: once artillery and infantry had punched a hole in the Turkish lines, Allenby's Australian, British, Indian and New Zealand cavalry swept out behind Turkish lines, captured Damascus and advanced all the way to Aleppo in northern Syria. It was an immense victory: three Turkish armies plus supporting German units routed and destroyed in addition to the entire Levant region coming under British control. Having said this, the poor condition of the Turkish forces in Palestine must be factored into any assessment of Allenby's success at Megiddo. Debilitated by a lack of men and equipment, the Turkish forces in Palestine were in a much-weakened state by September 1918. The Turkish high command from late 1917 had starved the Palestine front of *matériel*, preferring to concentrate resources on a push towards Baku on the Caspian Sea. Thus, it is argued, by the battle of Megiddo, the Turks in Palestine could do little to resist Allenby's overwhelming offensive punch. Not fully aware of the Turks' plight, Allenby's original plan at Megiddo was for a methodical push into Palestine and Syria.[36] Once he realised the extent of the Turkish collapse, he then used his cavalry force as the means to transform his original plan into something much more dramatic. This use of cavalry has aroused much interest among military historians as, while cavalry was used extensively in the Russian Civil War (and even during the Second World War), the battle of Megiddo was the last time that the mounted arm could, almost single-handedly, win such a significant battle. In this sense, the battle of Megiddo was the swansong of cavalry; the symbolic end of the era of the horse as a decisive weapon of war.

Throughout the campaign, Allenby liaised with Hashemite Arab forces allied to Britain. Directed by Colonel T.E. Lawrence ('of Arabia'), the Arabs were deployed on Allenby's right flank. While Allenby approved Lawrence's Arab operations, the considerable post-war interest in the enigmatic Lawrence should not detract from Allenby's concentration on the main push by the EEF west of the River Jordan.[37] At the battle of Megiddo, Allenby took little account of the Arab force militarily, although he accommodated the imperial need to promote the Hashemites as Britain's allies by ordering his troops to allow the Arabs into Damascus 'first', even though EEF cavalry clearly entered the city on 30 September–1 October 1918 before Arab forces arrived with the 4th Indian Division on the morning of 1 October.[38] Having said this, Allenby's correspondence does show that he was acutely aware of the wider value – both political and military – of having the Hashemites as allies, especially in a long war, and, earlier in 1918, he made much play in his reports to London of the negative impact if the Hashemites were to fight on the other side.

The war's end provided new challenges. Allenby was the military commander of a swath of territory stretching from Sudan to northern Syria before, in March 1919, becoming acting special High Commissioner for Egypt and Sudan, a post that was confirmed in October 1919 when he returned to London to be raised to the peerage and made into a Field Marshal. He chose the title 'Allenby of Megiddo and Felixstowe' in memory of his greatest victory and his childhood home. Allenby was a solid colonial administrator during a challenging period of retrenchment and change for the British empire. In early 1919, Egypt rose in revolt against British rule and Allenby had to deploy large numbers of troops to suppress, with some considerable force, the uprising that had spread across the towns and rural areas of Egypt.[39] Suppression of the Egyptian revolt was complicated by the fact that after the war the men of the EEF were clamouring to be demobilised, to the extent that some units effectively mutinied, refusing to carry out orders.[40] Once hostilities ended, there was little obvious rationale for the men to remain in uniform and, as a consequence, disorder within the

EEF became an increasing, almost endemic, problem. Service in Egypt and Palestine meant that many men had never had any leave home, and some had joined up in 1914; at the same time, there was the worry that jobs at home kept open for returning soldiers would be filled as employers looked to utilise men who had already been demobilised – typically those who had served in France. The observation among senior officers that, had the men of the EEF served in France, many would be dead, carried little weight amongst soldiers keen to return home. Trouble soon spread, compounded by the lack of amenities and an antipathy towards the local population that would today be called racism. Prejudice was especially bad among Anzac troops for whom the local Arabs were 'black and dirty, and they smelt . . . the Australians hardly thought it worth mentioning if a few were killed'.[41] In April 1915, poorly disciplined Australian troops trashed the 'Wazza' (Haret el-Wasser) red-light district of Cairo; in December 1918, Australians and New Zealanders from the Anzac Mounted Division went on the rampage through the Palestinian village of Surafend,[42] meting out brutal rank-and-file justice to the (unarmed) Arab inhabitants, some 40 of whom were beaten to death because a New Zealand trooper was found murdered near their village.[43] Surafend was then set ablaze, as was a neighbouring Bedouin village. On another occasion, a paraded Australian unit shouted Allenby 'out' in an orchestrated example of disobedience.[44] Gangs of Australians were also involved in armed robberies of rail passengers in the Cairo area.[45] Allenby was furious at these egregious acts of insubordination that offended not only his notions of discipline but also his sense of what was right and wrong. Indeed, to his credit, he paraded the Anzac Mounted Division to tell its men in no uncertain language how the Surafend murders had besmirched the glory of the Palestine campaign.[46]

Worried by the threat of mutiny by his troops and revolt by the Arabs – be it the fellahin in Egypt or the Hashemites in Damascus fearful of French imperial designs on Syria – Allenby pressed the negotiators at the Paris Peace Conference to consider carefully the consequences of their decisions for the Middle East. But the decision-makers in Paris prevaricated, partly because of the Versailles settlement with Germany that took precedence, but also because Britain was itself pressing the French to accept a truncated Syrian mandate that would allow for a British-controlled route across Arabia via the desert town of Tadmor (the ancient Palmyra). French stubbornness in the face of this attempt to extend British control delayed the agreeing of a political settlement for the Middle East. The delay bedevilled Allenby who, as has been mentioned, had an army on the verge of mutiny and an ally – Prince Feisal of the Hashemites – who was threatening to foment another Arab revolt, this time against Britain and France. Once a settlement for the Middle East was agreed at the San Remo conference in April 1920 – one that effectively ended hopes of Hashemite rule in Syria – Allenby settled in to his job as High Commissioner. Politically, this meant dealing with the demand in Egypt for independence, a perennial problem temporarily eased by the granting of some self-rule in 1922. The assassination of Sir Lee Stack, the Governor-General of Sudan, in 1924, marred the end of Allenby's tenure as High Commissioner in Egypt. Allenby never resolved the dilemma of Egypt's status and its relationship with Britain – issues that would rumble on, unresolved, into the 1930s and beyond, and not finally resolved until the Suez crisis of 1956. It was, therefore, with some relief that in June 1925 Allenby and his wife left the official residency in Cairo and returned to Britain and, finally, retirement after a long period of service as soldier and administrator.

While the King gave the Allenbys Deal Castle, by 1928 they had purchased a more manageable town house at 24 Wetherby Gardens, London SW5 on the fringes of Kensington.[47] Once retired from public duty, Allenby's chief public work was as the President of the British National Cadet Force. Otherwise, he used the time afforded by his retirement to indulge in bird watching and travelling. Indeed, it was after a trip to buy material for the aviary in his garden that Allenby died at home of a burst blood vessel in his brain on 14 May 1936. He was cremated and laid to rest (alongside Lord Plumer) in St George's Chapel in Westminster Abbey on 19 May 1936. Six years later, in 1942, Allenby's wife passed away.

Was Allenby one of the great captains of war? In his assessment of Allenby, Gullett, the Australian official historian, paints an unflattering picture:

> In any estimate of Allenby as a great General, consideration must be given to his overwhelming force and to the wretched morale and physical condition of the enemy . . . Allenby certainly made the very most of his opportunity but any general with qualities above mediocre must have won decisive success. Allenby's only claim to rank with the great captains lies in the fact that he exploited his opportunity to its extreme limit.[48]

Gullett is too harsh. Allenby was more than a cut above mediocre, especially once he was set free from the restraints of the Western Front. Too many generals of the Great War, on all sides, foundered and even cracked under the pressures of industrialised warfare. There were many commanders capable of achieving less, of breaking down under the strain, of losing the confidence of their men, even of being comprehensively defeated (and then being uninterested in the fate of their troops taken into captivity) – as happened in 1916 with General Sir Charles Townshend after defeat at the siege of Kut al-Amara in Mesopotamia. Before Allenby arrived in Palestine, Murray had achieved little beyond establishing the basic logistical infrastructure needed to take the offensive; meanwhile, on the Western Front, the rapid rotation of senior commanders reflected the immense stresses of a war that demanded the right men for the job. And it was not just the Entente powers that struggled to find the right military leaders: in Germany, the changes in supreme command from Moltke the Younger to Erich von Falkenhayn to Erich Ludendorff and Paul von Hindenburg to collapse and defeat in 1918 proved that the other side was unable to produce the winning formula when it came to leadership. Allenby did not break down, he inspired his men in the EEF and raised their morale, he husbanded his resources and built up his logistics, and, excepting the Transjordan raids, he was never defeated in battle in Palestine, instead triumphing at Jerusalem and the battle of Megiddo, and occupying for the British empire a vast stretch of territory that it could use as a bargaining tool at the Paris Peace Conference in 1919. After October 1918, Allenby proved himself a competent administrator of occupied territories[49] and he provided perspicacious advice for the decision-makers in Paris who were busy deciding the future status of the region. This is a creditable rather than mediocre record in a war in which so many commanders failed the test of the modern battlefield.

Allenby's command can be favourably compared to that of General Slim's in Burma in the Second World War as Allenby, like Slim, successfully managed an expeditionary force in a discrete theatre of operations, providing the right mix of logistics, caution and balance that led to eventual victory. Allenby's Palestine campaign, as with the Fourteenth Army's in Burma, achieved 'organisational mobility' – a style of warfare that matched operations with proper preparations to achieve operational success.[50] The result in both cases was an overwhelming theatre victory.[51] As Slim was quick to point out, it was easy to talk about dramatic pushes – or 'flings' – forward but it was often best to sit tight and work methodically against the enemy, building up supplies, morale and training before taking the offensive when the time was right.[52] This worked in Burma in 1944 when Slim resisted the calls to push forward to fight his decisive engagement with the enemy beyond the Chindwin river, instead fighting a crushing defensive battle against the Japanese Fifteenth Army at the battles of Imphal and Kohima, and in Palestine it is noteworthy that the one time that Allenby was defeated was when he pushed forward without sufficient preparation during the Transjordan raids.

As with Slim's Fourteenth Army, Allenby's EEF was a multinational, multicultural imperial effort: only two of Slim's twelve infantry divisions in 1945 were predominantly British, while in the EEF by the summer of 1918 only one division out of a total of eleven was primarily British.[53] The remainder of Allenby's force comprised Algerians, Armenians, Australians, Burmese, Egyptians, French, Hashemite Arabs, Indians, Italians, Jews, New Zealanders, Rarotongans,[54] South Africans, West Indians and others (including a Hong Kong and Singapore unit, Russian Jews, a Canadian construction battalion and former Ottoman POWs serving with Hashemite forces). There was even talk of Japan sending troops to fight with the EEF (something that Allenby encouraged, feeling that the addition of Japanese divisions would be a great benefit). These diverse national units had differing, indeed, at times, conflicting, agendas, and the management of such a disparate force – both during the war and afterwards as an occupation force – required tact and diplomacy.

The fact that, after the Ludendorff offensives in March 1918, Allenby had to absorb 54 untrained (or partially trained) Indian infantry battalions plus some 13 Indian cavalry squadrons, many of which were Muslim in terms of troop composition, as replacements for his experienced British divisions sent as reinforcements to France, compounded his predicament. These Indian troops were not only being asked to fight against a Muslim empire, but for the 29 per cent of the newly arrived force who were Sunni Muslim, their spiritual leader was the Ottoman Sultan in Istanbul.[55] Turkish intelligence was quick to exploit this situation and, in the summer of 1918, Allenby noted in his cables to the War Office the presence among his troops of seditious literature in the 'Indian vernacular'. Some Indian Pathan troops even deserted to the enemy.[56] It was Allenby's job to weld this potentially fissiparous force into one capable of taking the offensive. He succeeded. The parallel with the Burma campaign is again apparent as Slim had to contend with the lure of the Japanese-sponsored Indian National Army raised from Indian POWs in 1942 that fought for Indian independence on the side of the Japanese. Considering these challenges, Allenby's successful push on Damascus after the battle of Megiddo – and Slim's equally triumphant final offensive in 1945 towards Rangoon – are impressive achievements. Ronald Lewin's description of the 'beautiful consistency' of Slim's 'great curve' of operations that started in India and Burma and ended in the fall of Rangoon can, *mutatis mutandis*, be applied to Allenby's sweep north from the Sinai desert to southern Turkey.[57] But such a success required careful timing and preparation, and an awareness of the right moment to deliver the knockout blow. It was easy to be beguiled by the promise of quick victory – be it the Schlieffen Plan in 1914, the Dardanelles and Gallipoli in 1915, Robert Nivelle's assurances for his offensive along the Chemin des Dames in 1917 or the Ludendorff offensives in 1918 – but the Great War required a mature, methodical approach that took into account the new way in warfare. Too often, dramatic quick fixes failed. Allenby understood this and in Palestine he rarely promised what he could not deliver, either militarily or politically.

The comparison with Slim bears further examination. In Burma, Slim benefited from having Admiral Lord Mountbatten, the supreme commander in the South-East Asia theatre of operations, protecting him from unnecessary interference from Prime Minister Winston Churchill in London. This firewall gave Slim some breathing space in which to make his plans and build up his forces for the push against the Japanese. Field Marshal Sir Alan Brook as CIGS provided Montgomery with a similar service in the European theatres of operations during the Second World War. Allenby was not so lucky. Robertson as CIGS never properly shielded Allenby from Lloyd George's attempts to guide war strategy, including the direction of the war in peripheral zones such as Palestine. When General Sir Henry Wilson replaced the taciturn Robertson as CIGS in February 1918, matters failed to improve as Wilson, a natural intriguer, tried to deal with both the Ludendorff offensives and the wily Lloyd George. Consequently, Allenby was, too often, looking over his shoulder, trying to marry up contradictory instructions coming from London with the immediate military requirements in Palestine. Pulled in opposite directions, Allenby struggled with an uncertain mandate: on the one hand, Lloyd George was urging him on to achieve great things; simultaneously, Robertson and his ilk were reining him in, hoping that he would adopt, at most, an aggressive defence rather than go for the all-out attack that would take the EEF deep into enemy territory.

Allenby's cavalcade through the Holy Land in 1917 and 1918 offered such a pleasing contrast to the attritional slog on the Western Front that, after the war, there emerged a sanitised narrative of both Allenby and the Palestine campaign that has continued to this day with little interruption or upset[58] – Anthony Bruce's recent *The Last Crusade: The Palestine Campaign in the First World War* (2002) being a case in point. T.E. Lawrence's desert operations and the romanticism associated with fighting in the exotic East – as Edward Said has pointed out, the 'Orient' entered history because of the Palestine campaign[59] – have added to the appeal of Allenby's war, making it appear somehow different from other theatres of operation. This compares unfavourably with the war in France, where, in recent years, strategy, operations, tactics and leadership have come in for a raft of critical re-evaluation: some of it vitriolic and personal; most of it considered, interesting and scholarly.[60] More than ever, some reconsideration is now needed that sets out the mistakes and blunders in Palestine, contextualises operations in the light of Allenby's often overly cautious approach, critically analyses his operational method, examines the negative impact of the squabble between Lloyd George and Robertson on the Palestine campaign, and relates the campaign to British grand strategy generally.[61] This revisionism also needs to take into account Allenby's lacklustre performance in France before his departure for the Middle East in June 1917. While Allenby will never enter the pantheon of military greats – to sit alongside Alexander the Great, Hannibal, Saladin (Salah al-Din), Marlborough or Napoleon – his command in Palestine, as this introduction has attempted to show, is certainly robust enough to bear critical reappraisal, from which his reputation, warts and all, should emerge fundamentally intact.

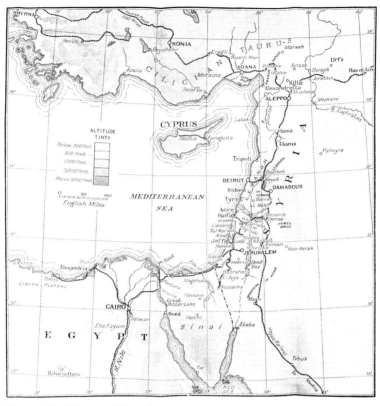

Map 1. The Theatre of Operations.

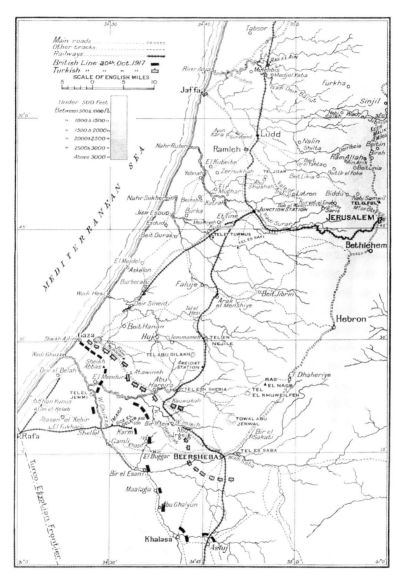

Map 2. Southern Palestine.

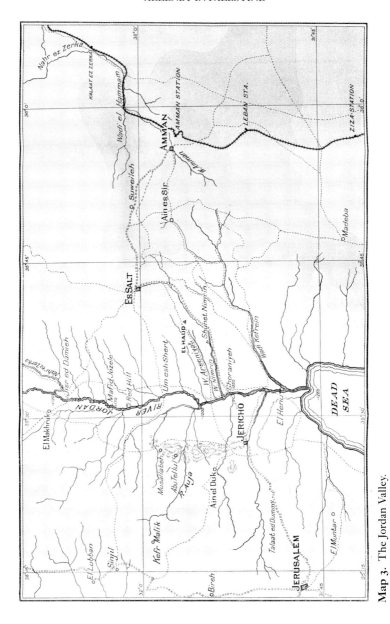

Map 3. The Jordan Valley.

22

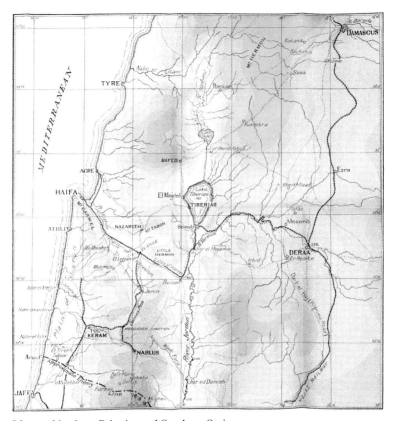

Map 4. Northern Palestine and Southern Syria.

Chapter 1
The Third Battle of Gaza and the Capture of Jerusalem, June–December 1917

I

Robertson to Allenby

[Telegram? Typescript. Partially torn]   13 June 1917
SECRET
o.1/105/303

I desire to supplement the instructions you have received to-day from the Secretary of State for War[1] on your appointment as Commander-in-Chief of the Forces in Egypt.

1. You have been furnished with figures showing the strength and composition of the forces now in Egypt, and of the drafts and units to be sent there as shipping becomes available.

2. The chief danger to the defence of Egypt is from attack by the Turkish forces in Palestine and you will realise that that danger is best removed by keeping the enemy as fully employed as possible. The collapse of Russian military power[2] for the time being has set free considerable Turkish forces, and the conquest of Palestine has, therefore, become much more difficult than appeared probable some months ago when, according to promise, we were expecting that a vigorous Russian offensive would be made during the Spring and Summer by the Caucasian Army. On the other hand, the number of men whom the Turks can maintain in Southern Palestine is limited by the state of their communications,[3] and after examination of the situation on the spot you may find it

possible to defeat the enemy south of Jerusalem and to penetrate Palestine. In formulating your plans for any such operation you should remember when considering [?] the forces which the enemy may send against you, that the situation in other theatres of war, and the precarious nature [?] of [?] our sea-communications, may make it impossible rapidly to reinforce you in the event of such reinforcements being lost [?]. I will keep you regularly informed as to the military situation in Russia.

3. Both for the defence of Egypt and for offensive operations in Palestine, the first requirements are to give the Commands, Staffs and troops a sound and definite organization, and to see that the best possible use is made of every man who can be made available for the fighting formations, by the substitution of native for white personnel in the auxiliary services where you think this is possible. You should also consider in conjunction with the High Commissioner[4] whether any further use can be made for the purpose of the war generally of the resources of Egypt and report to me in due course. I invite your early attention to these important questions.

4. I should be glad if you would keep me regularly informed as to the general military situation in your theatre, and as to the organization and condition of your troops. I also desire to have all important information about the enemy which you may obtain. A daily communiqué should be sent each evening whether there is anything special to report or not.

5. You will keep the General Officer Commanding, British Forces in Mesopotamia,[5] regularly informed as to the military situation in your theatre, and he has been instructed to send you similar information.

6. All communications regarding military operations, exclusive of 'despatches' properly so-called, should be addressed to me.

PRO: WO106/718/313–314

2
Derby to Allenby

[Telegram? Typescript] 15 June 1917
SECRET

1. You will proceed to Egypt and take over command of the forces in that theatre of war from General Sir A.J. Murray.
2. You will be responsible for the defence of Egypt both against exterior attacks and internal disorder. As regards the latter, you will keep in close touch with His Majesty's High Commissioner and will take advantage of his advice as regards all questions affecting policy in Egypt and dealing with the inhabitants. You will address the High Commissioner as regards any representations you may desire to have made to the Egyptian Government.
3. His Majesty's Government is very desirous of defeating the Turkish forces in Palestine and of effectively occupying that country. You will therefore as soon as possible after your arrival in that country report for the information of His Majesty's Government what measures you consider possible towards the attainment of that object.

PRO: WO106/718/316

3
Robertson to Allenby (CIGS to GOC-in-C Egypt)

[Telegram. Typescript] 2 July 1917
No. 37086 cipher MO

It is reported by Maude that Fahad Beg, who exercises dominant influence over Anizah, between Baghdad and Damascus, has entirely thrown in his lot with us. Maude suggests that he should send a party, with one or two British officers, across desert to country of Saba Anizah, near Sulaimiyah, 20 miles south-east of Hama, in order to cut Palestine railway, near latter place. What are your views on this proposal, and what time would be best for attempts on the railway from your point of view?

PRO: WO33/935, p. 149

4
Robertson to Allenby
[Letter. Typescript. Dictated] 4 July 1917

Lieutenant-Colonel Wavell has been appointed liaison officer between you and me. I do not know if you know him but he is quite a useful man. He is the first liaison officer I have appointed to Egypt, although I have been contemplating having one for some time past, as I have with Salonika. I wish to say, although I hope it is quite unnecessary, that he is in no way a spy. His simple duty is to help you and to help me. It is difficult to convey in telegrams or in letters exactly what one means or to give all the information that is needed. I shall be glad if you will make use of him and see that he is given the necessary facilities to carry out his work. I think he should be useful to both of us and that is the reason I have appointed him.

LHCMA: Robertson papers 8/1/62

5
Allenby to Lady Allenby
Egyptian State Railways and Telegraphs
[Letter. Holograph.] 9 July 1917

I am writing in the railway train which has been my dwelling place since the 5th of the month. I left Cairo on that day, for a tour of inspection on [sic] my Palestine front. I travelled in my own railway coach as far as the canal – near Ismailia – then changed into a special train, on this side. From railhead – which is quite close behind my front – we got about on horseback and in Ford cars. These little Ford cars, with double tyred wheels, got across country anywhere. Where the sand is very deep, we have roads made of strips of rabbit wire netting – laced together, and laid on the sand –; this makes as good a road as you want. I have gazed upon Gaza, at a few miles distance, and I have been within 8 miles of Beersheba; but we have got neither place yet. The country here – the land of the Philistines – is now parched and dry, covered with scanty grass, sandy and dusty. In the spring it is covered with verdure; fields of barly [sic], grass, flowers of many sorts – red-hot pokers, irises etc. – In the oases, and near the villages, are date palms in places; and great quantities of fig trees, apricot and almond trees. Figs are not yet ripe; but there are great patches of an inferior sort of water melon. The coast is fringed by big sand dunes, underneath which is limestone; and the low limestone rocks crop up in places along the shore. A curious feature is the occurrence of pure water wells in the limestone, within a few feet of the sea water, and practically at sea level, on the beach. The weather is pretty hot, but not unbearable, seldom over 90 degrees in the shade; and, regularly, at 10 a.m. a brisk sea breeze springs up. The wind becomes strong at about midday, and drifts the sand and dust somewhat; but it is a great boon. It drops at sunset; and the nights are still, but not very hot.

Water is none too plentiful; but we have pipelines from the Nile – 150 miles away –, and are developing the springs, and boring wells, with success. The water has, usually, a slight brackishness – something like Apollonaris [?] water – but is drinkable. Our railway uses a vast amount of the pipe-line water,[6] and our thousands of horses, mules and camels drink a lot. All the men and animals are looking well and in good condition and spirits. The men are burnt as black as Arabs. One sees them sitting in the blazing sun, often, with practically nothing on but a helmet; and apparently enjoying it. The Australians, especially, enjoy being grilled. It merely browns them – does not roast them, as it would me! On the sea coast, they bathe a great deal; and the horses and camels are also bathed, when possible, in the sea. There are a few sharks, but I don't think they bite. Beyond the villages, the country to the East, up to the desert, is cultivated by Bedouin Arabs; semi-settled. A wide acreage of barley is grown; and, in time of peace, is exported from Gaza to Scotland – to make Scotch Whisky! The Bedouin[7] are not very friendly to strangers, British or Turk; and we don't allow them near us. Of course, they are Turkish in sympathy as a rule.

You seem to have been heavily bombed by aeroplanes again; and I see that Harwich also was attacked lately. I enclose a letter[8] which I have received from the Sultan of Egypt. It is the first time I have ever had a letter from a Sultan! I've not met him yet. He is reputed as a very good friend to us. A King's messenger bag goes tomorrow; so I shall send this by it.

LHCMA: Allenby papers 1/8/6

6
Allenby to Robertson

General Headquarters, Egyptian Expeditionary Force
[Letter. Handwritten.] 11 July 1917

I came back, yesterday, from the Palestine front; and I am sending you a telegram tomorrow, with proposals and plans.

I was pleased with what I saw.

Chetwode has organised strong defensive positions, with full power to resume the offensive at will. The railway of 4'9 8½" is up to Deir el Belah – 8 miles from Gaza –, and a branch runs from Rafa to Shellal – where the Wadi Ghuzzee is bridged – and to El Gamli.[10]

Water supply is developing. Springs have been found at Shellal, and improved by the R.E. They yield, now, 250,000 gallons a day, of pure and cold water. The railway uses pipe line water, only; as the well and spring water has some salts in solution which are not good for the engines.

I went all along the front. The enemy Gaza position is now very strongly entrenched and wired. Thence, S. Eastwards, by Atawineh to Abu Hareira, there are strong entrenchments. From Abu Hareira, the fortifications turn east, along the Wadi el Sharia, to Tel el Sharia. Then there is a gap to Beer Sheba, which locality is entrenched and wired. I rode out – covered by a Mounted Division – to hill 720 (map reference Africa Sheet North H.36/E-IV and North H.36/E-III 1/125,000) some 8 miles W.N.W. of Beer Sheba; and could see the country very well. It is undulating, open, and cut by dry watercourses; offering scope for action by mounted troops. Water is scanty; except at Beer Sheba. The next plentiful water, to the North, is, I believe, at Tel el Nejileh and the Wadi el Hesy. On this flank, the Turkish positions apparently lack depth. Behind Gaza, they are organised in depth.

I think from what I have so far seen, that the Turks expect us to renew our attacks on Gaza. They probably think that we shall cling to the coast line. If we make our attack there, it will probably be costly; and, when we have broken through, we shall not have gained a flank or acquired more freedom for manoeuvre. To make the best use of our mounted troops and our mobility, it will most likely be profitable to strike further east, between Atawineh and Beer Sheba. An advance to the Wadi Imleh,[11] and an attack by three Divisions against Abu Hareira and the Sharia position, might enable the mounted troops to strike N. to Tel el Nejileh – thus turning the Gaza defences, and isolating the Beer Sheba position. Railway and water must follow rapidly after the Infantry, to Bir Afteis [?[12]]. To enable such an operation to be carried out, it will be necessary to pin the enemy to the Gaza line by strong artillery attacks, supporting raids and minor attacks by Infantry.

I estimate that not less than two Divisions would be required for such action, supported by enough heavy guns and howitzers to make the bombardments effective and thoroughly convincing. Another Division should be in reserve, South of Sheikh Abbas, while another should be available as reserve to the main attack.

This makes 7 Divisions.

The Turkish front is long. From the coast line to Atawineh is 10 miles; and from Atawineh to Tel el Sharia is another ten. The railway can feed these 7 Divisions, which number is required for the continuity of operations after hard fighting.

I think that with these 7 Divisions we can make good progress into Palestine. I propose to push on the railway, by the coast route, through Gaza, towards Jaffa; and I want also to link the Shellal branch to the Beersheba railway, near Tel el Sharia.

As we go into Palestine, I am sure that it will be necessary to double our railway line; and I want permission to begin, at once, doubling it as far as Rafa. We estimate that this will take six months, so we ought to lose no time. It will be necessary, at the same time, to double the water pipe line; as the engines cannot use the local water, and the demands of the troops will also increase.

I have supposed that the Turks will stand and fight – which is the only safe supposition – and on that I have based the calculation of my requirements.

I have every reason to believe that a success here, on a considerable scale, would raise all the Arabs of Syria in our cause.

The Western front is quiet;[13] as is, also, the interior of Egypt. I am going into the question of the reduction of garrisons, and that of manpower.

I propose to move my headquarters, as soon as possible, to about Khan Yunus – some 5 or 6 miles this side of Deir el Belah, railhead.

We are badly in need of aeroplanes of the latest types. The Turks have not many machines; but they always have a few of the newest German patterns.

We are superior in numbers, but many of our machines are obsolete.

You ought to buy the aerodrome near Aboukir.[14] Proposals have been put forward for this; but they are hung up in your Lands Department at the War Office. It is an admirable site; and, after the war, may well become the great flying school of the Empire.

Climatically and geographically, conditions are perfect. Its situation, on the coast, adjacent to the best residential suburb of Alexandria, makes the ground intrinsically valuable. If you don't buy it now, you won't get it, for ten times its present price, in a few years.

I find that the Mounted Troops here are very proud of their designation as the "Desert Column". If you make them into a Corps, as I have proposed, I hope they may keep the title and be the "Desert Corps".

LHCMA: Robertson papers 8/1/63

7
Allenby to Robertson (Chief, Egypforce to Chief LONDON)
[Telegram. Typescript.] 12 July 1917
SECRET
E.A. 40

I have just returned from the PALESTINE front, and now submit my appreciation and proposals in accordance with your instructions.

The Turkish Government appears to me to have realised that the loss of JERUSALEM, added to fall of BAGHDAD,[15] would produce disastrous results for them. They have therefore determined to oppose our further progress to the best of their power. The positions on the GAZA-BEERSHEBA line at present occupied by the Turks are of considerable natural strength, and we are, for the moment, unable to approach within striking distance, except in one small sector near the sea coast, owing to lack of water.

The position of the enemy runs from the sea at GAZA roughly along the main GAZA-BEERSHEBA road to BEERSHEBA, a distance of some 30 miles. He is therefore widely dispersed, but his lateral communications are good, and he can very quickly reinforce any threatened point. GAZA has been made into a strong modern fortress by him, heavily entrenched and wired, the centre of which is a maze of houses, gardens and cactus hedges, offering every facility for protracted defence. The remainder of his line consists of a series of strong localities, generally from 1,500 to 2,000 yards apart, viz., the SIHAN group of works, the ATAWINEH group, the BAHA group, the ABU HEREIRA trench system, and finally the works covering BEERSHEBA. It appears to me as a first impression that the sector HEREIRA-IRGEIG is probably the most vulnerable point in the enemy's line, here his works are less highly organised than those further north and here, moreover, the higher ground between IRGEIG and BEERSHEBA completely dominates his main system.

The estimate of the enemy's force in Southern PALESTINE is five divisions and one cavalry division in the front line, with at least one additional division in reserve South of JERUSALEM, representing with unattached units, a total fighting strength of roughly 46,000 rifles, 2,800 sabres, 250 machine guns and 200 guns. As regards enemy reinforcements, it is reported that the 26th Division is definitely en route to PALESTINE, also one regiment of the 46th Division.

Against this force, I have immediately available four divisions and three cavalry divisions, exclusive of the 75th Division, which will not be fit to take the field for some months, and the 60th Division, in process of equipment [sic] on arrival from SALONIKA. Units are, however, below strength, and 5,150 infantry and 400 yeomanry reinforcements are required now to complete the four divisions and mounted now in the line to full strength. The reinforcements of the infantry of the 60th Division, which is only now arriving, and of the battalion of the 75th Division now in this country, are not included in the above figures. I estimate them at about another 2,000 men.

The Turco-German General Staff do not appear to have decided whether their offensive in ASIA MINOR shall be made against BAGHDAD or on the PALESTINE front.[16] It seems that this decision is likely to be in favour of an offensive campaign against BAGHDAD. As regards Turkish intentions in PALESTINE, my opinion is that they will remain generally on the defensive, limiting any offensive that may be undertaken to an attempt to drive us back to the Egyptian Frontier, which I can frustrate. Seven divisions, three cavalry divisions and the necessary proportion of Army Troops can be supplied by the railway line east of the Canal. I could undertake an offensive with this force at the present time with a reasonable prospect of success, but the divisions must be fully equipped and maintained at full strength. At the end of this telegram are enumerated my requirements in addition to what I have now at my disposal.[17] The seven divisions referred to above do not include the 75th Division, which has as yet but nine battalions of infantry and no artillery, and which will no[t] be fit to take the field before December at the earliest, owing to the debilitated state of the battalions. With seven divisions and three cavalry divisions I should hope to be able to take GAZA and BEERSHEBA, assuming that the enemy's force in front of me is not materially increased. I might also be able to reach JERUSALEM. I shall require a considerable addition to my strength for operations beyond the JAFFA-JERUSALEM line, and possibly to maintain that line. This will necessitate the doubling of the railway east of the Canal, which should be undertaken at once. From the commencement of the work it would take about six months to double the line to RAFA. Therefore the sooner the line is doubled the better as a double line will certainly be required. The doubling of the railway line will also involve the doubling of the pipe line. It is important that I should have the troops I ask for ready for an advance in September, so as to anticipate the October rains, otherwise operations on a large scale will not be feasible before November 1st.

As regards the organisation of my PALESTINE force, I propose to form two corps and one cavalry corps, all three directly under General Headquarters. To enable me to control these corps in the field, I have decided to divide my Headquarters. The major part will move to the neighbourhood of KHAN YUNIS, while the remainder will remain in CAIRO, this will comprise representatives of Administrative Services and Departments and such portions of my Staff as are required to deal with the political and administrative questions involved in the control of EGYPT and the administration of martial law.

[There follows Allenby's requirements – see note 17 for details]

PRO: WO158/611. Slightly different copies at PRO: WO106/718/303–308 and PRO: WO33/935, pp. 167–8

8
Allenby to Robertson (GOC-in-C in Egypt to CIGS)

[Telegram. Typescript.]   16 July 1917
SECRET
E.A.61

Reference your 37086 M.O. July 2nd and my E.A.24 July 4th.

On return from his recent journey to Eastern Syria Captain Lawrence[18] submits following proposals for Arab co-operation against Syrian railway, which he is confident could be carried out, granted necessary measure of material assistance by us.

A. Akaba to be held by the Arabs as base of supply and to maintain communications thence to north of Syrian desert.

B. Arabs to occupy hill country east and south-east of Dead Sea during August thereby constituting permanent threat against Hejaz railway.[19]

C. To undertake systematic interruption of Hejaz railway between Deraa and Maan by large demolition parties, based on Azrak (one group undecipherable)r [sic] and Jafar.

D. To undertake similar action against Railway between Aleppo and Ras Baalbeck by raiding parties based on neighbourhood of Jebel Shomaris.

E. To carry out minor raids at frequent intervals on sections of railway between Ras Baal Bek and Damascus and between Kiswe and Ghazale.

F. To attempt to demolish railway bridges in Yarmuk valley between Dialha and Lake Tiberias[20] by raids based on Azrak.

G. Contingent upon the success of A. and F. above and provided C. and D. a practical success to make a general attack on Deraa and thence upon railway radiating from that point with force about 8,000 Arabs and Druses[21] from the Hauran.

2. [sic] Captain Lawrence estimates that the Arabs would be ready to commence above operations by the beginning of September, by which time the harvest will be gathered, but he considers it would be unwise to defer them until after October rains, when the majority of Bedouins habitually drift eastward for camel grazing, when tribes would be more difficult to raise.

3. There is no doubt that even the partial success of Captain Lawrence's scheme would seriously disorganize Turkish railway communications south of Aleppo, whilst its complete success would destroy effectively his only main artery of communication between northern Syria and the Palestine [2 groups undecipherable but ? Hajaz] fronts, and might further be expected to produce extensive local risings throughout the Jordan valley.

4. As regards General Maude's suggestion to send a raiding party from the Euphrates to act against northern Syrian railway in conjunction with Fahad, Captain Lawrence points out that the influence of the latter does not extend as far as the railway, and that nothing more serious could therefore be attempted from that direction than hasty raids carried out through a country which is in part potentially hostile. Such action moreover taken prematurely would certainly jeopardize the success of much larger operations outlined in paragraph 1 by putting enemy on their guard and proportionally increasing Captain Lawrence's difficulties when the time comes.

I recommend, in these circumstances, that any raiding operations undertaken in conjunction with Fahad should be arranged to synchronize with the rising of tribes in northern Syria organized by Captain Lawrence, and should then be directed exclusively against lower Euphrates lines of communication to Mesopotamia.

PRO: WO106/718/292–293. Copy at PRO: WO33/935, pp. 182–3[22]

9
Allenby to Robertson (GOC-in-C Egypt to CIGS)

[Telegram. Typescript]   19 July 1917
SECRET
EA70

Reference 38016 cypher [sic] M.O.1 of 18th.

Sir R. Wingate concurs in proposals. He is writing to you to this effect. He is also suggesting in this wire that in accordance with para. 2 War Office letter 01/85/250 of February 21st 1917

Lawrence should work under my orders during these operations. As this will take place almost entirely in the area N. of line Maan[-] Akaba I consider this arrangement essential.

I shall in any case keep in close touch with G.O.C. Hedjaz in regard to Lawrence's operations.

2. [sic] Reference my E.A.61 July 16th. Following are further remarks in Lawrence's proposals especially in relation to my telegraphic appreciation forwarded under E.A.40 July 12th.

3. I consider that the advantage offered by Arabs co-operation in lines proposed by Lawrence are of such importance that every effort should be made to reap full benefit therefrom.

4. The extent of the cooperation which Lawrence offers amounts to effective interruption at widely separated points of enemy's sole main artery of communication between his base at Aleppo and his force operating in this theatre and in the Hedjaz, while simultaneously raising against him a series of widely spread risings in amongst disaffected population of Syria and Northern Palestine, backed by considerable force of Arabs from tribes E. of the Jordan.

5. If successfully carried out such a movement in conjunction with offensive operations in Palestine may cause a collapse of the Turkish campaigns in Syria and in the Hedjaz and produce far reaching political as well as military results.

6. It is evident in the meantime that the realisation of Lawrence scheme is contingent upon the prosecution of offensive operations by me in this theatre. Although possessed of considerable fighting spirit as evidence in their recent raiding operations in neighbourhood of Maan, the Arabs are neither trained [n]or disciplined to stand against attack by regular Turkish troops whilst fear of subsequent reprisals would undoubtedly exercise powerful influence against their unwillingness to take action unless fully assured of the enemy[']s inability to take vengeance on their tribes.

7. As stated in my para.2 of my E.A. 61 Lawrence is anxious not to ? [sic] make a commencement of his operations against railway later then mid-September, as majority of Arabs upon whose support he relies are of camel breeding tribes whose

active support it would be impossible to rely on during the grazing period (November–March).

8. In view therefore of desirability of deriving utmost advantage from Arab movement, and in view of further indications that Turkish command may at an early date undertake offensive operations on a large scale on Mesopotamia front in which case an offensive in Palestine may become imperative in order to relieve pressure upon General Maude, I ought to be prepared to undertake such operations as may be possible with force at my disposal by the middle of September.

9. Whilst realising the impossibility in view of transport situation and of necessity for meeting essential demands of other theatres of immediately supplying in full the requirements of my force I would urge despatch of reinforcements (including artillery and aeroplanes) to this theatre should be hastened by all possible means in order to enable me effectively to adopt a policy of active operations within 2 months from now should the situation at that time render such action necessary.

PRO: WO106/718/289–290. Copy at PRO: WO33/935, p. 186

10
Allenby to Robertson
General Headquarters Egyptian Expeditionary Force
[Letter. Typescript. Copy]   19 July 1917
SECRET

1. I wired to you, the other day, asking for Howard Vyse[23] as B.G.G.S. of my Mounted Corps – if the formation of that Corps is approved. I am sure it would be a good thing if we can have him – or as good a man. My mounted troops are fine material, and have experience in fighting; but the higher military education of their leaders is a weak point. Chauvel is not a trained cavalry leader; and, though he has capacity for command, and fighting instincts, he would be improved by having a trained and experienced cavalryman as his B.G.G.S. Such a one I have not available. Fitzgerald, who commands the 5th Mounted Brigade,

could do it; but the Australians, including Chauvel, cannot bear the sight of him.

2. You have refused to sanction the formation of a 5th Australian Light Horse Brigade; on the score of lack of horses. If your decision could be reconsidered, it would give great satisfaction to Australia. There is a strong feeling towards having a complete Australian Light Horse Division. At one time it was proposed to make it by taking a brigade from the 1st Australian and New Zealand Mounted Division. This Division, however, objected to being broken up; on the ground that they had long campaigned and fought, together. I understood, from Birkbeck, before I left London, that he had horses in Australia; and that the monsoon was then the obstacle to bringing them over.

3. The control of Birdwood over the Australian Expeditionary Forces seems to me to be an absurdity, so far as troops here are concerned. All correspondence is sent to him; and all promotions are submitted to him for approval. This may be interesting to him; but I cannot see that the arrangement is in any way useful. Promotions are made in regiments; not through the force as a whole; therefore, here, Chauvel is the only judge – not Birdwood. Neither are there any problems of administration or pay requiring his agency. Thought [sic] no particular harm is done; yet, a useless organization is not worth retaining. I have reason to believe that the Australian authorities would be ready to approve of a change, whereby the O.C. Australian forces in this country should be authorised to deal direct with them.

4. You know my requirements and intentions, now; and I have no doubt that, what you can, you will, give me. I want to advance in Palestine, early; but I don't want to strike before I can hit hard and, moreover, follow up a success. After an initial success, I can, doubtless, afford to skin Egypt of garrisons. As it is, I am moving two garrison battalions, from the Delta (El Kantara) and the W. fronts, on to the Palestine L. of C.; and I hope to send more in that direction, before very long. They tell me that the personnel of the garrison battalions can't march, or do hard work in this country; but I think they ought to be able to hold a trench all right, and set free other troops.

5. Lawrence's activities among the Arabs promise great things; but his tribes must get going before the end of September. If they begin their raids in that month, and have success, they will go on through the rains. Normally, however, after September, they move off to the camel grazing lands in the centre of the Syrian desert, and cannot then be got back to warlike enterprises. They, naturally, won't and can't do much unless I move; and it is not much use their destroying the Turks' communications unless I take immediate advantage of such destruction. They don't care to move before September; as they will, till then, be harvesting, and retaliation by the Turks would cost them their crops. If I bring them into the fight and do not make progress myself, this will also expose them to retaliation – which to some tribes, such as the Druzes, S. of Damascus, may mean annihilation. Therefore I want to be strong enough to undertake extensive operations in September. This I shall aim at doing, anyhow, with whatever strength I may have available.

6. Bulfin will make a good Corps Commander, and I shall be glad to have him. I know him well, as a staunch fighter.

7. I look on the doubling of the railway, as far as Rafa, as very important; and I hope that it will be sanctioned at once.

LHCMA: Robertson papers 8/1/64. Holograph copy at PRO: WO106/718/195–198

11
Robertson to Allenby (Chief, LONDON to Chief, Egypforce)

[Telegram. Typescript]   Despatched 21 July 1917, received
22 July 1917

SECRET
38188 cipher

Your E.A.40 of July 12th and E.A.52 of July 14th have been considered by War Cabinet. The possibility of meeting your requirements depends upon shipping and upon getting the troops and some Artillery from SALONIKA, and they are not yet able to give a definite decision. The former is being investigated and the latter will be discussed next week at Allied Conference,[24] after which final decision will be communicated to you.

Meanwhile, however, approval is given for the doubling of the railway to RAFA, and this should be put in hand at once.

PRO: WO158/611. Slightly different copy at PRO: WO33/935, p. 195

12
Allenby to Robertson (GOC-in-C Egypt to CIGS)
[Telegram. Typescript]   26 July 1917
No. CMQT3824

Authority is requested for expenditure of up to 200,000*l.* in connection with Lawrence's proposed operations east of the Jordan. Amount required in gold.

Will you please ask treasury to instruct Egyptian Government to supply.

PRO: WO33/935, p. 203

13
Allenby to Robertson
General Headquarters, Egyptian Expeditionary Force
[Letter. Typescript]   26 July 1917
SECRET

Thank you for the way in which you are meeting my demands; and I am glad that you recognize the importance of my being able to take offensive action, if necessary, in September.

Wavell is here, and is in touch with all matters. He accompanies me tomorrow, to the Palestine front, where we shall spend a few days. I am very glad to have him, and I think that he will be able, when you see him, to give you a clear picture of the situation here and our state of readiness.

I hope to begin on the doubling of railway without any delay. The latest estimate is that it can be completed in five months. I have informed you by wire that enough water can be supplied by the doubling of the 8" pipe line if we can get the more powerful pumps asked for.

The Turks are doing a considerable amount of work on their defences, Gaza-Abu Hareira, and my policy is to encourage the belief that my attack will come against Gaza. Lately we have carried out one or two successful raids on the front of Gaza, and others are contemplated. Except near Gaza, there is as yet no great depth in the enemy system, and, though wiring is being done, the wire is not nearly so formidable as that met in France.

The Turkish cavalry, from Beersheba, push out occasionally to the line El Girbeir-El Buggar, but retire at once before our mounted troops.

The Turkish attitude is passively defensive. Beersheba is fortified; but I don't think they would stand there, if attacked. Their main line of defence turns its left back to Tel el Sharia.

I hope that you will approve of my proposal to appoint a sub-chief of the General Staff. It will be necessary, when I move my headquarters forward. I want to put G.P. Dawnay in that position. He is now B.G.G.S. to Eastern Force, with Chetwode. I shall be delighted to have Bartholomew, and I propose to put him as B.G.G.S. to Chetwode's Corps when it is sanctioned. I was offered a few days ago, a Major-General Stuart Wortley,[25] lately from France; where, apparently, they thought he lacked experience. I refused him, and, in fact, I have no vacancy for a Major-General at the moment. I would suggest that, if officers are sent here to take up active command as Major-Generals, they should be young and vigorous men with French experience – men, for example, like Loch (Lord Loch) and Cator;[26] not that I want either of these now.

A Divisional Commander in this country has more work on horseback, and lives a harder life by far, than a Divisional Commander in France.

LHCMA: Robertson papers 8/1/65. Holograph copy at PRO: WO106/718/190–192

14
Robertson to Allenby (Chief, LONDON to Chief, EGYPFORCE)

[Telegram. Typescript]   Despatched 27 July 1917, received
28 July 1917

My 38188 of July 21st.

I regret to inform you that the Allied Conference proceedings having proved abortive, no definite decision has yet been reached with respect to meeting your demands. A further conference assembles next week.

PRO: WO158/611

15
Allenby to Lady Allenby

Egyptian State Railways
[Letter. Holograph]   28 July 1917

I am on the Palestine front in my special train. The pens, in this train, will only blot the papers – or else make no mark at all – ! I have been motoring and riding round, looking at defence works and water supplies. Weather is hot but not so hot as Cairo. My train is in a siding, near a village. This evening I walked around the village with Dick.[27] Most of the people seem to be living outside it, in tents, with their camels, sheep, goats, cows etc. – in the old patriarchal manner. They all look like Biblical characters. Face, dress and everything like pictures from the Bible. Keen, handsome faces; picturesque Arab dress. Ornaments of beads, coins and enamel; much as one sees in the Egyptian Museums.

The children are beggars, all. Very pretty, some of them. All attractive, to me. I was astounded, today, to see their camels browsing on prickly pear cactus. I had always thought that the prickly pear was proof against any animal that had a palate and a tongue. But I see the camels eating it greedily, and paying no more heed to the awful spines than if they were bloom on a peach. – 29th –. I have been riding and motoring round, again, today; looking at my preparations. Strong wind, hot, and dust; till about 8p.m., when it drops. Now, the night is still and cool; my thermometer reads 78 – at 9.30 p.m. – Turkish aeroplanes came over, very high, this evening; but threw no bombs. We did a raid, night before last, and killed some 40 or 50 Turks. I heard the shooting, and saw the flashes; but was not very near. – 30th July –. I was down by the sea side, this morning. Beautiful blue and purple sea, by great sand dunes. Several ships, loaded with hay, were lying ½ a mile from shore; and surf boats were plying between them and the beach, unloading them. The sea was rather rough; and there is a curious sand bar which runs along the whole coast, some 200 yards from the beach, on which runs a heavy surf. The boats are manned by Egyptian natives, and by Raratongan [sic[28]] islanders of the New Zealand contingent.

It looks dangerous work, but I don't think any of them have been drowned. They all swim like fishes. One of the camps is in a fig and vine plantation, near the sea. Great fig trees, 100 years old, grow right up and on to the sand dunes. The vines either sprawl on the sand or cover the fig trees. Both figs and grapes are ripe. Little green, juicy figs; and little sweet grapes, green and purple. Very fresh and verdant, but very hot in the fig tree jungle. Still, hot or not, I should like to have a tent, with Waggleh,[29] in the fig groves, at the edge of the sand dunes. There is a merry bird, the Rufous warbler, who haunts the locality. I think I have already told you of him. He is pert and friendly. Looks like a big nightingale, has the manners of a robin, and flirts his tail like a red start. I saw one today attack a locust nearly as big as himself. – 31st July –. Reached the canal early this morning. I cross over, and got into another train for home. I've just had a telegram saying that the W.O. will not relax the restrictions on officers' families coming out here. I had wired and recommended that officers' wives should be allowed out; and the High Commissioner did the same. I think it is the Admiralty, who will not be responsible for their safety. Anyhow, I shall not have consented to your coming out till the submarines have been got more in hand. – Later – This evening, I have just got your wire, through the Eastern Telegraph Company.[30] My darling sweetheart, I wish I could be with you; but

I know how brave you are; and you will be strong, to bear this awful blow. You and Michael fill my thoughts, and I feel very near to you both. Every remembrance of him is a joy. From his birth to his death there is not a day that you or I would have wished changed or to have been lived otherwise than he lived it. I am glad that you had him with you so short a time ago; and I too have had much happiness in seeing him often during the war. He was always the same; keen in his work, thoughtful beyond his years, but cheerful and brave. I have never seen a boy of his age who had so mastered self. His self control was complete; and, though his quick perception was always awake to the dangers which he faced daily, his well-balanced mind never dwelt on them. This, and his real interest in his work, made his life a happy one, even in the days of terrible stress which he has had to face for so many months.

Whenever he came to stay with me, he was always the same; a friend, on equal terms; and yet, unaffectedly, he always kissed me when we met and parted – as he did when a child. He had come safely through so many dangers that I had begun to hope, more confidently, that he would . . .

[End of letter missing]

LHCMA: Allenby papers 1/8/7

16
Allenby to Robertson (GOC-in-C Egypt to CIGS)

[Telegram. Typescript]   30 July 1917
No. OCT 8883

20,000 Turkish rifles are required for arming of Syrian Arabs for special operations in September. Can these in whole or part be supplied from England or Basrah?[31] Turkish rifles are most suitable for the purpose, as Arabs understand them, and further can replenish ammunition by seizure of Turkish posts. They would be required here not later than 1st September, but earlier if possible. Alternatively, may I issue a similar number of our rifles sighted for Mark VI. ammunition? This, however, would only be in nature of an unsatisfactory makeshift, and issue would prevent return to India of 8,000 rifles released from Indian troops, see your No. 30943, A. 3/2029, 13th March, though it may be possible to secure this number later.

PRO: WO33/935, p. 212

17
Robertson to Allenby

[Letter. Typescript. Dictated. Copy]   1 August 1917
Secret and Personal

I received your letters of 11th and 19th July about two days ago. Many thanks for them. I shall do my best to send you out all I can spare in time for September as I quite realise the necessity of your being active then, with reference to your Arab bretheren [sic]. We passed four days at Paris last week arguing the point about getting you a division from Salonika, the only result being another Conference in London this week, which was to assemble to-morrow but as the French Government seem to be in prospect of falling perhaps the Conference will not take place. However, if you do not get the division in time for September I hope to send you a certain amount of heavy artillery and some more aircraft. I am always a little doubtful as to what the aeroplane situation is. Whenever I speak to Henderson he rather tends to make out that everybody has their full amount, whereas when I come to examine it I find that although they may have large numbers they are not of much use. The aerodrome question has had to be referred to the Treasury and I hope that an answer will be sent to you soon; but I understand that you already have the use of the site and after all that is the only thing that matters.

With you I think that our prospects in southern Palestine are good provided we can give you what you ask for, or something like it. The Turk has never yet had a good shelling I imagine. At the same time, and with reference to the general situation we need to be careful as to the extent to which our commitments are increased. With Russia practically out of the war we have got to consider the necessity for economising shipping and men and also for being strong on the West front. Every day points to the probability of the war being prolonged to an indefinite date and as you can easily understand shipping is the vital factor. Therefore we must economise it. Extensive operations in distant theatres mean a great strain upon shipping, and we must guard against pushing forward to localities which would put an undue strain upon us in order to maintain our position. I am therefore taking the line at present that it would be a good thing to give the Turk in front of you a sound beating, but that the extent to which we shall be justified in following him by an advance into Northern and Central Palestine is a matter which for the moment must be left open. The further we go north the more Turks we shall meet; and the greater will be the strain upon our resources. Of course if we can so knock the Turk about that he throws his hand in, nothing would be better. On the other hand it is nearly 400 miles from where you are to Aleppo and the Turks' home lies beyond Aleppo. Do not take these remarks too definitely. They are only meant to show that for the moment we must keep an open mind as to the desirability of an extensive advance northwards. (Do not treat these private letters as official instructions. After I have written them I put them away and do not again refer to them.)

We will again look into the question of the 5th Australian Cavalry Brigade, but I am afraid that we cannot possibly run to it. Maude is already short of horses because we cannot get them from Australia. The monsoon is not the obstacle stopping the sending of them over. It is the shipping.

I quite agree with you as to the absurdity of Birdwood having anything to do with your Australian forces. We have always thought it absurd and will again try to get it removed. He is the real reason for it and has a way of communicating with the Government of Australia and getting them to put forward suggestions made by him. As you can understand when they put forward suggestions we do not like to refuse them. They have always urged that Birdwood should be a sort of head man of all the Australian forces wherever they are. However, we will see what we can do. I am sure that he has more than enough to do to look after his own Corps in France.

Lawrence's scheme seems to be a good one and I hope we shall be able to take advantage of it.

P.S. – I again ask you not to take too definitely what I have said about the advance into Palestine. As you know the Prime Minister is very much in favour of it and eventually the Government may decide to do it. The only point I wish to make is that in deciding to go forward we have to bear in mind what the situation will be after we have gone forward and whether we can, having regard to all the circumstances of the war, maintain ourselves after going forward and to a useful purpose. In short one has to look not only at the feasibility of going forward but what will happen after we have gone. This is especially necessary in Eastern countries because having gone forward it is usually very detrimental to have to come back. This is all I mean by what I have said.

LHCMA: Robertson papers 8/1/67

18
Allenby to Robertson
General Headquarters Egyptian Expeditionary Force
[Letter. Typescript copy]   8 August 1917
SECRET

I am glad that you have approved of my proposals for G.H.Q. and Corps Staffs; and I note that Bartholomew and Howard Vyse will shortly arrive. A little new blood, like theirs, will do good. There is some slight tendency to put forward the local article as being the only one worth considering. Changes are always uncomfortable; but I am being firm, and any little soreness existing will soon die down.

2. [sic] So far, I have no information that you are sending me a division to make my number up to seven. I hope that you will find it possible to do so; and to give me the guns, aeroplanes etc. which I have asked for. I know that you will if you can; and I am not going to grumble if you don't. Wavell will have explained to you the need for them, if we are to do anything that will lead to big results.

3. I am applying now for gas equipment and personnel. We have no gas here; and it ought to be of great use opposite Gaza, and possibly elsewhere.[32]

4. This morning I saw Captain Lawrence, just back from Akaba.[33] He reports well on the situation there, and has schemes for further aggression against the Hedjaz railway within the next week or so. He has hopes of keeping the Arabs at this work of harassing the Turkish communications till I am ready to move, even if my start is delayed; but the sooner I can begin to deal with the enemy on my front the better, as after September it is not easy to keep the tribes together. The sight of the cruiser 'Euryalus' at Akaba gave great heart to the Arabs. I've asked the Navy to keep a ship there as along as possible. A monitor is there now. Lawrence thinks that white troops landed there would be displeasing to the Arabs, and that their support is not needed. I agree; and have no wish to make such a detachment, though it has been suggested by the High Commissioner in Egypt. I shall see H.Ey. [His Excellency – i.e. the High Commissioner?] on Friday, and shall discuss the matter with him. I get on well with him, always.

5. My intelligence have trustworthy reports that Turco-German activity is becoming more noticeable in Tripoli, in the Italian zone,[34] west of Egypt; where personnel and material arrive by submarine.

The Italians are inclined to make light of this; but I am in communication with them, and I have asked our Naval Authorities to look into the matter.

6. Do you think it would be possible to allow leave from here to men who have been here, say, for 2½ years, to England? The number would be considerable; but a lot of them are becoming tired and stale, and I think that the consequent improvement in moral tone and contentedness would compensate for the temporary diminution in effective strength.

LHCMA: Robertson papers 8/1/68. Holograph copy at PRO: WO106/718/182–187

19
Robertson to Allenby

[Letter. Typescript. Dictated]   10 August 1917
Secret and Personal

I have done my best to give you the reinforcements you asked for in order to take on the Turk. As I told you last month it is not possible to give you everything by September but I hope you will agree that we have done pretty well and I trust that you will get the balance by November. We will do our best to give you the balance before. I hope you will find the War Cabinet Instructions sufficient and clear, and if not that you will refer any doubtful point. You see it is impossible to say now what we hope to do because so much depends upon your communications, upon the Russians, and for that matter upon the Turk, and I cannot help thinking that the latter is in a pretty bad plight so far as Administration is concerned. The War Cabinet saw the draft Instructions and the result was rather amusing. Lloyd George did not think they went far enough and that I did not press you sufficiently to take advantage of any success you might gain. Others thought that I went too far and was trying to induce you to launch out into operations which we could not sustain. However, I managed to pacify both sides. I think the Instructions will be clear to you. They simply amount to doing the best you can with what you have got; to giving the Turk as hard a knock as you can; and at the same time avoiding going too far forward and getting into a position from which you can neither advance nor go back and which might involve us in commitments which we could not properly meet having regard to other places and to our resources. The paragraph about pressing the Turk early in September is intended to mean that you should be as active as you can in order to take advantage of your Arabs and also to assist Maude, while it is not intended to mean that you should make your big and deliberate attack until you are ready for it. Perhaps I had better say no more or I may confuse you. I wish you Good Luck and good weather.

LHCMA: Robertson papers 8/1/69

20
Robertson to Allenby (Chief, London to Chief, Egypforce)
[Telegram. Typescript]   10 August 1917, received 11 August 1917
SECRET

The War Cabinet has directed me to forward to you for your guidance the following instructions:

"During the coming autumn and winter it is necessary to strike the Turks as hard as possible, since a good success achieved against them will tend to strengthen the morale and staying power of this country during a season when important successes in Europe may not be feasible and it will increase the war weariness and general disaffection of the Turks with their German masters at the same time.

The Turks may shortly be free to concentrate the greater part of their forces against you and Maude in view of the Russian situation. Under these circumstances it is not now possible to assign you any geographical objective; your object will therefore be to defeat the Turks opposed to you and as the situation admits to follow up your success. In order to take advantage of the Arab situation and to relieve the pressure upon Maude by forcing the enemy to divert troops to PALESTINE, it is important that you should press the Turks opposed to you to the fullest extent of your variable resources as early as possible in September."

You should understand with reference to the above instructions, that while everything possible will be done to complete the deficiencies mentioned in my telegram 39316 of today, and to keep you up to strength and adequately supplied with munitions, that there is no prospect at present of being able to send you the further reinforcements referred to in your E.A.40 of the 12th ultimo, as being required for operating beyond the line JAFFA-JERUSALEM and perhaps for sustaining that line.

The situation of the Russians and in MESOPOTAMIA will be regularly reported to you so as to keep you informed with regard to it.

PRO: WO158/611. Slightly different copy at PRO: WO33/935, p. 239

21
Allenby to Chetwode

[Letter. Holograph]   13 August 1917

Yours of today.

I know what a valuable man Dawnay is; and, without belittling your work, do fully recognise the part he has taken in preparing the appreciation and plans. I will see that he is not overworked.

IWM: Chetwode papers, P183, folder 4

22
Robertson to Allenby (CIGS to GOC-in-C Egypt)

[Telegram. Typescript]   15 August 1917
No. 39618 cipher

Your No. E.A.153.[35] Quantities asked for cannot be sent owing to shortage of certain essentials for manufacture of smoke shells and consequent difficulty meeting requirements for France. 18–pr. shells must be shipped as deck cargo and there are limitations to that. Some have been sent every opportunity, total to date 4,000, and all possible will continue to be sent. No S.K.[36] chemical shell available, but if acceptable could send P.S.[37] 10,000 smoke shells per month could be sent, 5,000 already sailed. No prospect of being able to supply P. grenades[38] or Livens drum and projector.[39] Several gas companies could probably be sent to you at the end of October if you will inform me whether you still require them early in that month. Before then none available.

PRO: WO33/935, p. 251

23
Allenby to Robertson
General Headquarters, Egyptian Expeditionary Force

[Letter. Holograph]   21 August 1917

Wavell cabled yesterday that he starts today and brings a letter from you.

I note that my latest instructions lay stress on the desirability of my being in readiness to strike a blow at the Turks, as early as may be, next month. This, as you know, I want to do. The longer I wait, the stronger grows the Palestine defences. Moreover, I recognise fully that early action on my part may be required with a view to helping Maude and supporting the Arab movement.

I am pushing on my preparations, accordingly; and I thank you for the way in which you are acceding to my demands.

The new Corps are settling into shape; and they will, I am sure, run smoothly.

I look forward to the early arrival of Howard Vyse and Bartholomew; good men, both.

My plan is to strike rapidly at Beer Sheba, while I hold the enemy's right by an attack on Gaza. The Navy will cooperate, from the sea, against Gaza. It is there that the Turks at present expect us to attack, and I hope to keep their attention so fixed.

Bulfin, with three Divisions, will have the Gaza sector. Chetwode, with four Divisions – one of which will be in reserve, will deal with Beersheba.

The bulk of the mounted troops will turn the Turkish positions E. and N.E. of Beer Sheba.

Success depends on surprise and speed. Speed depends on transport and water supply.

There will be a wide gap between my right and left attacks. The gap is open country, without cover for a hostile movement; and though I shall hold it lightly I have no fear of serious trouble there.

All is in readiness for running out an extension of the railway from Shellal to Karm close behind the troops; and a Decauville[40] line from Gamli towards Beer Sheba, for supply of ammunition to my right.

Water is a serious problem; but I think it can be solved. Beer Sheba's water supply must be acquired. The wells will, probably, be blown in; but they can be cleared. The Mounted Corps will find some water along the Wadi es Saba[41] and Wadi el Imalah,[42] E. of Beersheba; but it is difficult to ascertain the amount, and this is the driest time of the year.[43]

Beer Sheba in my hands, I can strike N.W. against Tel esh Sharia and Tel en Nejile.

The enterprise should succeed, if well prepared. I do not want to begin it before my preparations are complete, and until my troops are up to strength and trained. The 10th Division is to come from Salonika, but I have not heard when.

The situation at Akaba is good. The presence of a Warship has given great heart to the Arabs, Lawrence has gone there, and will organise a movement, on a large scale, between Akaba and the Dead Sea. He is quite satisfied with the march of events; and he tells me that, now the Arabs are in, he can keep them in, and an early start in September by my troops is not now a necessity.

LHCMA: Robertson papers 8/1/70. Copy at PRO: WO106/718/169–170

24
Allenby to Lady Allenby

[Letter. Holograph]   26 August 1917

I don't think that Michael could have been more happily placed, than in "T" Battery; and I like your idea of applying his money for the Battery's benefit. You and I will always feel a connection with it. What a wonderful and beautiful thought yours is; that Father Knapp[44] is with our boy, and helping him to enter bravely on his new life.

Oh, my brave Darling, you are the mother of a hero. Your son could have been no other. The letter he wrote to you, on the 28th of July, is a mirror in which his whole character is shown.

Devotion to his work. Humour, dry but never cynical. Joy in all aspects of life. Wide interest in literature, sport, politics. All unaffected and honest. And, through all, beams his love for you. So, too, my own, your wide sympathy and thought for others cheers us all. God bless you my Mabel.

LHCMA: Allenby papers 1/8/12

25
Allenby to Robertson
General Headquarters, Egyptian Expeditionary Force
[Letter. Holograph]   26 August 1917

I have received your letters of the 1st and 10th [16th] inst.[45]

The War Cabinet's instructions are sufficient and clear;[46] and with your explanatory remarks, I feel that I understand exactly.

I know that you are doing everything possible to supply our needs, and I thank you.

LHCMA: Robertson papers 8/1/71

26
DMI[47] to Allenby (GOC-in-C Egypt)
[Telegram. Typescript]   [1 September 1917]
No. 40584 cipher

Following dated 21st August from two Turks who arrived in Switzerland recently:–

1. 7th Division is to be reorganized and for this purpose picked men from other divisions are being selected. 4,000–5,000 selected men are reported to have been sent already for the 7th Division from Constantinople.

2. Von Kress recently visited Constantinople and had just returned to Gaza front.

3. At the Stamboul and Haidar Pasha railway stations[48] there was considerable activity. Considerable quantities of supplies, ammunition, troops and motor transport were being moved over to Asia.

4. Army rations had been increased.

5. A number of searchlights were sent to Mosul from Constantinople at the end July in charge of 6 Turkish naval officers and 20 marines

Repeated to General Officer Commanding, Mesopotamia, and Commander-in-Chief. India.

PRO: WO33/935, p. 291

27
Allenby to Lady Allenby

[Letter. Holograph]   5 September 1917

The Turk, on my front, is quiet; and I have not begun to bother him much yet. Nevertheless, a good many deserters come over. Yesterday, a Battalion commander came across – his servant carrying his kit –. He is a fine, smart Turk; well dressed, and wearing European breeches and leggings. He gave us some useful information, as to the moral and physical condition of the Turks; but I have not heard it all yet – my investigators are still engaged with him –.

The fall of Riga[49] was a foregone conclusion, if the Boche wanted it. I suppose Petrograd will go next, and be called Petersburg[50] again. I see that the S.E. coast has had aeroplanes over it again.[51] Nevertheless, I believe that we are winning the war, but we must go on winning it, for a long time yet; and not stop till we have finished winning it. You and I, my sweet, have paid too big a price for Victory; to be content with anything short of a complete Victory.

LHCMA: Allenby papers 1/8/14

28
Robertson to Allenby

[Telegram. Typescript]   7 September 1917
R.157. Personal and Secret.

Have received your private letter of 21st ultimo and apparently you are satisfied with steps taken here to meet your demands. But as it is a little difficult for me to keep complete touch with all detailed matters I ask you to tell me if I can try to expedite anything. The balance of the heavy artillery will I hope reach you by 1st November at latest. The rate of transport of troops from Salonika is disappointing and I am trying to accelerate but doubt if I can. With respect to six-inch howitzers we have some batteries in Italy which might perhaps be set free during last fortnight of

October. Could you usefully employ more than the total you have already asked for if they can be got from Italy. [sic]

Copies to P.S. to C.I.G.S. ONLY.

LHCMA: Robertson papers 4/4/91

29
Allenby to Robertson

General Headquarters, Egyptian Expeditionary Force
[Letter. Typescript and Holograph]   12 September 1917
Sent by Colonel Wavell. Duplicate sent by K.M. bag,[52] on the 12th September 1917

1. I replied to your R. 157 cipher of 7–9–17 that I am satisfied that everything possible is being done to meet my demands; and that any 6" howitzers from Italy can be usefully employed here.

I have your letter of the 21st August, which Wavell brought out, and I know that you thoroughly understand the situation.

I see no prospect of having my preparations complete before the middle of October, and it is not my intention to undertake a big offensive until I am ready.

If circumstances necessitate a premature start, my effort will be made against the Turkish right – in co-operation with the Navy –. It is unlikely, however, that this will lead to great results. Still, it will attract the attention of the enemy to that flank; and I can carry out my original plan later, when I am reinforced up to full strength.

My aeroplanes are to be made up to 4 squadrons – 2 artillery and 2 fighting. My original demand, in my E.A. 40 of 12th July, was that I should have a total of 5 squadrons. However, I am satisfied with a total of 4, provided that I have sufficient reserve of machines. For this purpose I require, in addition to the aeroplanes of which I have been advised up to date, 12 Bristol fighters with engines. Salmond, my Flying Corps Commander, has just returned from England, and agrees with me that these machines are essential to our continued efficiency. Of artillery machines, he thinks we have enough.

2. General Bailloud, Inspector of the French troops in Eastern Theatres, has been here lately, after a tour in the Red Sea.

He is a fine old warrior, 70 years old, friendly and honest. He tells me that he thinks that the French Government can and will send one or two Divisions here, in addition to the Detachment[53] which is already with me on this front. I have told him that, so far as I am concerned, I shall be glad of them, but that the proposition must be made through the British Government. I have also informed the High Commissioner of the offer. If more troops are sent, it is all important that they be sent here and not to Akaba. The situation there is satisfactory, so far; but, as you know, the Arabs are shy and suspicious. Any landing of European Troops at Akaba now would upset everything. I mention this as I believe that General Bailloud has already sent a cable to France recommending that a Division be sent here. He recognises the inadvisability of its being sent to Akaba.

3. I have found it necessary to change the command of the 52nd Division.

I am sending its late commander – Brevet[54] Colonel and Temporary Major-General W.E.B. Smith,[55] C.B., C.M.G. – home, to report. I have replaced him by Colonel J. Hill D.S.O., A.D.C., Indian Army. Smith has not shown the necessary tactical capacity for the command he held. He might, after a rest at home, be found fit for an instructional command there.

4. Lynden Bell has for some weeks past, not been up to the mark, and I have sent him home on leave.

He tells me that his eyes have been troubling him; and he is tired, and not equal to his work.

He has given me loyal support, and has not spared himself; but the strain of prolonged service in the East has told on him.

He certainly needs two or three months rest.

Do you think that a King's Messenger service might be re-established, via Taranto?

The last letter I got from the War Office by King's Messenger bag took 30 days on the journey.

LHCMA: Robertson papers 8/1/72

30
Allenby to Robertson
General Headquarters Egyptian Expeditionary Force
[Letter. Typescript]   26 September 1917

The 10th Division has landed, with the exception of one battalion and some details. I have inspected two brigades, and I like the look of them. There is some malaria in the Division; and my D.M.S. is perturbed.[56] Longley, the Divisional Commander, on the other hand, thinks that it is not serious, and he tells me that he will guarantee Brigades at least 3,000 strong after 2 or 3 weeks in this country. I am putting the division in reserve to the XXth Corps. I was going to send the 54th Division there; but the 54th knows the Gaza Sector well, and it will be better that it should remain there. So far as I can foresee, I should be ready by the 27th October. Then the moon suits well, for night movements. Besides, my guns will have had then 6 or 7 days to settle into their positions.

You have my plans for Naval co-operation. As regards possible aid from the French Navy; I think they would do most good by threatening the Northern Coast of Syria. Excess of naval activity south of Haifa might lead the Turks to sow mines along the coast. In connection with French naval operations, manifestations of activity in Cyprus might be useful – real and simulated.

The Naval force at my disposal is, I think, sufficient for effective co-operation with the attack of the XXIst Corps on Gaza.

My intelligence locates, to-day, another Turkish division, the 24th, about Deir Sineid, N. of Gaza. We have thought that this was so, for some little time, now they – the Intelligence – are fairly sure of it.

Deir Sineid is the target for the "Tartar", the monitor with 14" guns – a railway bridge, road bridge, siding and junction.

PRO: WO106/718/98–99

31
Robertson to Allenby

[Telegram. Typescript with holograph additions]   27 September
1917

SECRET

R.165 Personal and Secret. Reference my official telegram 42057
of to-day. The twelve batteries are in Italy whence they are being
withdrawn but if you really do not need them all I would much
like to leave four in Italy and send you not more than eight as this
would allow Cadorna to train men for use next year with other
howitzers we may then send him. But as you know Prime Minister
is most anxious you should have all you want and asked me to offer
you the lot. I can hardly believe you can usefully employ as many
as twelve having regard to all circumstances and so I told him. The
howitzers will begin leaving Taranto[57] on 4th proximo. How long
do you calculate it will take to get them into action after
disembarkation. [sic] I hope it may ['it may' deleted and replaced
with following holograph addition:] these additional batteries will
not involve postponing date of your operations.

Copies to PS to C.I.G.S. ONLY.

LHCMA: Robertson papers 4/4/97

32
Allenby to Lady Allenby

[Letter. Holograph]   3 October 1917

I went out yesterday with Bols, to about 6 miles south of
Beersheba. We were covered by a Cavalry reconnaissance, and the
Turks were very quiet. A few of them were to be seen, in their
entrenched line, but they were not shooting. The day was quite
cool. Today is warm, and a strong wind is blowing.

Maude's victory, at Ramadish,[58] will have a good effect; and,
combined with the big explosion at Haidar Pasha station,[59] ought
to delay the Turkish attack to a considerable degree.

The Arab rebellion is spreading well, and the Turkish communications will be difficult to guard against their raids. The enclosed photograph[60] of the Shereef of Mecca[61] – and the proclamation by him – is one of the means we have of inducing the Arabs to desert the Turks. We drop these papers – and packets of cigarettes – over the Turkish lines, from aeroplanes. The proclamation is an appeal from the Shereef to the Arabs to leave the Turks and join in the war against them for the freedom and independence of Arabia.

A good many come in, as a result of our propaganda. I am going to stay tonight with one of my Divisions, at a distance; to inspect a Brigade thereof, tomorrow.

I shall put this in the post box, on the off chance – unlikely – of a mail going before my return.

You won't get many more letters from me, I hope, before you start, my sweetheart.[62]

LHCMA: Allenby papers 1/8/15

33
Robertson to Allenby
[Telegram. Holograph for despatch as telegram]   5 October 1917
Embossed
R170 Personal and Secret

You will understand that my 42625 of today does not originate with me because apart from the strategy I do not believe that the policy if successfully executed would have the anticipated result. However you are concerned only with framing your reply and in it you should take no chances because of the many uncertain factors. You should also remember that transport, supply water, time and space are imperfectly realised here and therefore they may need emphasising. I find it impossible to convincingly prove the great difference between the needs and facilities of Turkish and British troops in these and similar matters.

LHCMA: Robertson papers 4/4/99

34
Robertson to Allenby (Chief, London to Chief, Egypforce)

[Telegram. Typescript]   Despatched 5 October 1917, received
6 October 1917

42626 cipher.
SECRET

My 39329 August 10th and your E.A.40 July 12th.

General policy of war with special reference to desirableness of eliminating TURKEY was again discussed by War Cabinet to-day.

Her general condition, it is thought, is such that a severe defeat coupled with the effective and secure occupation of the line JAFFA*-JERUSALEM, including both those places, during the next six months might, if followed by suitable diplomatic measures, induce her to break with her Allies.

The Cabinet wish to have your military views on the matter, and your estimated requirements of troops and other resources in order to give effect to this policy if adopted. We have no information of enemy concentration towards MESOPOTAMIA, east of ALEPPO, beyond arrival of one Turkish regiment, and are therefore still in doubt whether enemy's reported contemplated offensive will be in that theatre or PALESTINE. It should also be remembered by you that two German Divisions are reported to be preparing for the East, and you should have regard to German facilities for having this force increased.

PRO: WO158/611. Slightly different copies at PRO: WO106/718/101 and PRO: WO33/935, p. 375

35
Robertson to Allenby (CIGS to GOC-in-C Egypt)

[Telegram. Typescript]   9 October 1917
No. 42857 cipher

Our Foreign Office represent that the French are very touchy on the subject of operations in their zone in Syria. French

---

*   Incorrect in cipher, but confirmation of this interpretation wired for.

Government appear only to have heard of Lawrence's operations through the French Resident in Cairo, who sent in what appears to have been a garbled account. In order to avoid this it would be advisable for you to instruct your political officer to keep his French colleague informed as soon as possible of what has taken place. Whether he is given information as to future plans I leave entirely at your discretion.

PRO: WO33/935, p. 388

36
Allenby to Robertson (Chief, Egyptforce to Chief, London)
[Telegram. Typescript]   9 October 1918
EA391 cipher
Reference 42626 cipher dated 5/10/18.

Possible Turkish divisions which might be concentrated against me in addition to the 8 1/3 divisions now facing me are – from ALEPPO 3 2/3 divisions, from CAUCASUS 2 divisions, from ROUMANIA 1 division, from CILICIA 1 division, from CONSTANTINOPLE 1 division, from SMYRNA 1 division. Total 8 1/3 + 9 2/3 divisions = 18 divisions. In addition we know that two German divisions are on their way to ALEPPO and that others may follow. Consequently, if the proposed recapture of BAGDAD is abandoned by the Germans it is possible that I may have to contend with 20 or more divisions in advancing to the line JERUSALEM-JAFFA and when holding that line. Probably, however, supply arrangements will prevent the enemy maintaining more than 12 divisions at any one time on his front, but he could replace these divisions as required.

In order to drive back an enemy of this strength, and to capture JERUSALEM-JAFFA line, I should require 20 divisions; the difference between strength of British and Turkish divisions would give me the necessary superiority of force. However, my existing lines of supply will not permit me to employ on my present front a force greater than I have now, that is, 7 divisions and 3 cavalry divisions.

By the end of December or early in January when the railway is doubled to RAFA I can supply 14 divisions and 3 cavalry divisions in my present position and further forward at the rate at which a double line of railway can be laid, which is about ¾ mile per day. I shall be able to rail up new divisions at the rate of two per month.

Therefore my total strength should be 14 divisions and 3 cavalry divisions for employment on my front and 6 more divisions to be concentrated on the Canal for purposes of replacing worn out divisions. Thus, my additional requirements in troops would be 13 divisions.

The difficulty with which I shall then be confronted is lack of rolling stock, engines and water for engines. A large demand for engines and rolling stock, which EGYPT can not [sic[63]] supply must be anticipated. Details of requirements will follow.

For the supply of this force under the altered topographical and climatic conditions consequent on my advance I should require at least 7 Auxiliary Motor Transport Companies of six sections each and a considerable number of pack mules to replace 1st Line Transport camels.

My air service should be increased to a total of five Corps Reconnaissance Squadrons, one Army Reconnaissance Squadron, two fighting squadrons and one bombing squadron.

I can procure no further supplies from EGYPT, so all additional grain, forage and fuel must come overseas. Ninety days' supplies for all divisions sent should arrive concurrently with each division.

I cannot rely on coastal sea transport to shorten or supplement my land lines of communication.

The value of the occupation of the line JERUSALEM-JAFFA would be great because when there my right would be within 40 miles of the HEJAZ railway and my flank and communications covered by the DEAD SEA and friendly Arabs.

All calculations are made on the assumption that the Arab situation will continue as satisfactory [sic] as it is at present.

Question of continued help from Arabs depends on continued belief by them that we shall keep our promises not to conclude any peace which would leave Arab territories under Turkish domination. Any idea in their minds that we intend separate peace with Turkey with possibility of their being left under Turkish rule would bring them against us and endanger my communications.

It must be understood that the bases of this appreciation may require amendment as the result of the effect of my preliminary operations, but my present opinion is that no smaller force than that estimated above would be adequate to ensure decisive victory against the numbers which the enemy might possibly concentrate against me.

PRO: WO158/611. Slightly different copies in Robertson to Secretary War Cabinet, 10 October 1917 enclosing GOC-in-C GHQ Egypt to CIGS War Office, 9 October 1917 at OxBod: Milner papers V/B/360/355–357; PRO: WO106/718/102–104; and PRO: WO33/935, pp. 388–9

37
Allenby to Robertson (GOC-in-C Egypt to CIGS)

[Telegram. Typescript]   13 October 1917
No. I.A.4191

Your No. 42857.[64] Details of Lawrence's reconnaissance in Syria north of Maan area were kept very secret in order to avoid enemy obtaining information which might handicap Lawrence's future movements and jeopardize safety of those with whom he had been in touch. His operations in Maan-Akaba area, which are outside French sphere, are regularly notified to French political officers by my political officers. So far there has been no action by Lawrence in French zone. In case of such action French Mission will be informed as fully as military exigencies permit.

PRO: WO33/935, p. 392

38
Allenby to Robertson
General Headquarters, Egyptian Expeditionary Force

[Letter. Holograph]   17 October 1917
SECRET

My preparations are getting on well. The 75th Divisions is now complete. The 10th Division lacks the "B" echelon of its

Divisional Ammn. Column; but I hope to receive it by the end of this month. There is a lot of fever in the 10th Division – some 3,000 cases –; but they came here strong, and I hope to have some 8,000 or 9,000 rifles on the day. I am in close touch with Admiral Jackson; who is, at this moment, staying with me. The Naval Captains have all been here; have reconnoitred their targets, personally, by sea and land, and know exactly what to do. My plan is just the same as I have told it to you; but my zero day will be 4 days later than the date given to you by Wavell. I thank you for the prompt way in which you have met my demands. My telegrams to you and to "Chief" always meet with quick response; but "Troopers" is usually slow. Every day's delay means more trenches and more wire on the Turkish positions.

Since I have had my new "Bristol fighters", I have brought down two hostile aeroplanes within a week. Before we had bagged none.

Lawrence is doing good work on the Hedjaz railway. I sent you a cable the other day telling you of the visit I had from the French Attaché[65] and M. Maugras[66] of the Ribot mission –. They think that a French officer should always accompany Lawrence when he is in the French zone of influence – Syria –. I told them that I recognised this, but that I did not consider it tactically advisable.

The fact is that only Lawrence can deal with the Arabs, effectively. If a French officer was sent with him, on the more adventurous expeditions, failure would be certain. As it is, Lawrence works in accord with the French representative at Akaba; but Lawrence must be the arbiter as to when and if he employs him on raids and adventures.

I told the French representatives that I would take them into my confidence whenever I could; but that I must be the sole judge of what was tactically advisable in connexion with my projected operations. At the same time, I disclaimed any right to deal with Arabs in their zone, and promised them that, if it came to treating with such people, I would at once call in their representatives. They were not pleased; but I was quite polite and firm, and we parted amicably. Still I think it likely that you will hear from the

French on this matter. Secrecy is only really important for the next 3 or 4 weeks. After that, I shall welcome the presence of a French representative on any raids or reconnaissances that may be required in their zone.

LHCMA: Robertson papers 8/1/73. Copy at PRO: WO106/718/83–85

39
Feisal to Allenby
[Letter. Typescript. Transliterated from Arabic. Copy]   Al Akaba
Moharram 1336
[17–27 October] 1917[67]

Heroic leader and dispenser of victory – General Allenby, May God keep him.

I have received your honoured letter dated Oct.13th., with great respect, in which you refer to the arrival of the Sherif Abdulla. God has made victory the ally of the armies of Right. We were much gratified at your statement that you were using every endeavour to supply the deficiencies of our army which up to now has been devoid of all the necessary equipment. Nevertheless we are continuing to make every effort to disappoint the hopes of our confederated enemies, and I have informed Major Lawrence of some of the necessaries the lack of which is still the cause of the arrest of our movement.

I trust that the supply of these necessaries will be hastened so that we may be able to do our duty. In conclusion I offer you [?] my profound respects.

General of the Northern Armies.

[Feisal's seal]

LHCMA: Allenby papers 2/5/1

40
Allenby to Robertson

General Headquarters, Egyptian Expeditionary Force
[Letter. Holograph]   19 October 1917
SECRET

This morning I received your letter of 3rd inst.

I quite understand your views on the line of action to be pursued in Palestine. You had my reply – by cable – to your "Chief, London, 42626", of 5th inst., which I received on 6th inst.; and I don't think I can put my views any more clearly.

The visit of Kaiser Wilhelm to Constantinople may mean increased attention to this part of the world; or it may be to keep the Turks' attention fixed on Baghdad – I should think probably the latter. One more Division – the 19th – is, I hear, being sent south from Aleppo; and a few more squadrons of Cavalry; but that is no great access [sic] of strength for Kress von Kressenstein – who is my vis à vis. The Turks are deserting, freely; and their morale is reported to be poor. If I can get a good success, to start with, I think it likely that Kress may have to fall back a long way; and then he may find his Turks difficult to rally. I am impressing on my commanders the importance of swift movement, and I think they are alive to it. Chetwode has made his preparations well; and his Divisional Commanders, Shea, Girdwood and Mott, are keen and wide-awake. Longley, with the 10th Division, will be in reserve on that flank. Chauvel, commanding the Mounted Corps, has had a bout of fever lately; but he is well now, and will probably be all right. If he cracks up, I have George Barrow available. Bulfin has three good Divisional Generals; Palin, Hare and Hill.

You will have noted, in my reply to your "Chief, 42626" – referred to above – my remarks on the danger of the Arabs getting any idea into their heads that we should contemplate a separate peace with the Turks, involving acquiescence in Turkish dominion over Syria and Arabia. The ex Khedive is in Constantinople, as well as the Kaiser; and he has always had ambitions to secure Arab allegiance to himself. He might be chosen to convey to the Arabs of Syria, Mesopotamia and Arabia a proposal granting self government; bribing heavily, and undermining our prestige, the while. A suggestion of our negotiating a separate peace – made by him to them – if it had any foundation of fact, would possibly do us incalculable harm. Though this is political, it is a point of vital military importance, as you will, no doubt, agree.

LHCMA: Robertson papers 8/1/75. Copy at PRO: WO106/718/79–80

41
Allenby to Robertson (Chief, Egypforce to Chief, London)
Despatched 2230. Repeated 2nd Echelon G.H.Q., General Baghdad, Britforce Salonika, High Commissioner, Rear Admiral Egypt
[Telegram. Typescript]   31 October 1917
SECRET
E.A. 475 cipher

October 31st, 2200

We completed our movements for attack on BEERSHEBA in accordance with plan by dawn today. Advanced works southwest of BEERSHEBA were captured by XXth Corps by 0840. This Corps reached all its objectives by 1305 and held whole of central sector of defences between south and west of BEERSHEBA. Meanwhile Desert Mounted which moved round to east and north of town, captured TEL EL SABA by 1600 and cleared HEBRON road as far as BIR ES SAKATY. Desert Mounted Corps, meeting considerable oppoisition [sic], was within three-quarters of a mile of town on north-east at 1630. XXth Corps was attacking works on left of its original objectives still held by Turks. We had now isolated enemy in works between XXth Corps objectives and Desert Mounted Corps. Neither prisoners nor booty yet collected but up to 1600 some 250 prisoners had been counted and some machine guns taken. Bombardment of GAZA defences has been continued by XXIst Corps. Large explosions were caused at DEIR SINEID and also at SHEIKH HASAN by naval gun fire.

Later. BEERSHEBA occupied. Some field guns besides further prisoners included in captures.

IWM: Dawnay papers 69/21/2 'Palestine 1917–18 Battle of Philistia'

42
Allenby to Lady Allenby

[Letter. Holograph]   1 November 1917

I sent you a line just before post went, telling you of Beersheba.

It was a smart little battle, achieved by careful preparation and good staff work. The Cavalry made a 25 mile night march, to turn the Turks' flank; and the Infantry did 15 miles and a battle at the end. All this was based on water supply and ammunition supply – development of wells and pumps, and pushing in of roads, trams and railways; combined with secrecy and feints. All went well. I can't tell you half of it, in a letter. I have another attack tonight, on a smaller scale.

I motored to Beersheba this a.m. It lies in a saucer of hills. A little town, with a mosque, railway station, and a dozen modern buildings – such as post office etc. Clean and rather attractive. The guarding hills were entrenched and wired; but our attack came as a complete surprise.[68] However, the Turks fought all day; and they fought well. I saw many of their dead in their trenches.

2nd November – I have your letter of 31st October. I am glad you have seen the barrage. With the Nile at flood, it must be a fine sight. I love the garden and the birds. It and the Zoological gardens are my favourite places.

Thank you for your congratulations. We took at Beersheba some 1990 prisoners, and either 13 or 15 guns. This morning, at 3 o'clock, I attacked the S.W. front of the Gaza defences. We took them; on a front of some 6000 yards, and to a depth of some 1000 to 1500 yards. We now overlook Gaza; and my left is on the sea coast, N.E. of the town. The Navy cooperated with fire from the sea; and shot well. We've taken some 300 prisoners and some machine guns, so far. I told you that you would bring me luck. You have always done so. Even at fishing; I never got a salmon unless you came down to look on. I had a kind . . .
[End of letter missing]

LHCMA: Allenby papers 1/8/27

43
Robertson to Allenby (Chief, LONDON to Chief, Egypforce)
[Telegram. Typescript] Despatched 1 November 1918, received
2 November 1918
SECRET
44428 cipher

I wish to congratulate you all concerned upon your success, which it is to be hoped you will be able to develop. At present there is no question of sending you the additional troops demanded by you in your E.A.391, Oct.9th, to carry out the policy outlined in my telegram of Oct. 5th, No. 42626. Consequently, your instructions remain as defined in my telegram of August 10th, No. 39329, namely, to press the Turks opposed to you to the fullest extent of your resources so as to force the enemy to divert troops to PALESTINE and thus relieve pressure upon Maude, and to take advantage of Arab situation.

In deciding on the extent to which you will be able to carry out safely the policy, you will be guided by the fact that an increase in the forces now at your disposal is improbable.

PRO: WO158/611

44
Allenby to Robertson
General Headquarters Egyptian Expeditionary Force
[Letter. Typescript. Copy]   3 November 1917
SECRET

I was very pleased to have your cable congratulating us on our Beersheba success – and I thank you, hereby – There was much preliminary work to be done. Water had to be developed at Khalassa and Asluj, for the cavalry; and at Esani for all arms. Material for pushing forward the broad gauge and light railways had to be accumulated at Shellal and Gamli. Reconnaissances had to be made, up to and E. of the position at Beersheba, and – as far as possible – W. of it. All this had to be done in such a way as to make the Turk – who is, really, v. Kressenstein, a Boche – think we are going to attack W. of Beersheba against the Hareira and Kanwukah positions. Von K. was deceived. My mounted troops – 2 divisions – made a night march, of 25 or more miles, to the E. and N.E. of Beersheba. These were the Anzac and Australian divisions – Chaytor and Hodgson. The 60th & 74th Divisions – Shea and Girdwood – made a 15 mile night march, and attacked the S.W. of the defences. All the Staff work – of XX Corps and Desert Mounted Corps – was good; and there was no hitch, anywhere. The Turks, though surprised, fought well. At sunset, they were still holding strong trenches, in second line, covering the town. The 4th Australian Light Horse Brigade – Br. General Grant – was ordered to clear them out. He sent the 4th Light Horse Regiment to charge them. This regiment galloped over two lines of trenches – 8 ft. deep and 4 ft[.] wide; full of Turks, shooting hard – and put a neat finish on the battle.[69] Great credit is due to Chetwode; also to Chauvel and all the higher leaders.

The water in Beersheba is not as plentiful as we had hoped or expected. However, it is being developed; and there is plenty to be obtained in time. We are pushing forward, to the N. and N.W. of Beersheba, according to plan; as fast as we can.

On the morning of the 2nd, Bulfin put in an attack, by the 54th and part of the 52nd Division, on the S.W. of Gaza. He got all his objectives, with the exception of a few yards of trench here and there. To-day has been a day of dust and haze, driven by a strong and hot south wind; and reconnaissance has been difficult. I don't really know what the Turks are doing on either flank; but they appear to be moving troops about, freely, in the back areas. My officers and men are very fit and very confident. I note that you cannot send us more divisions or more aeroplane units; and that I must cut my coat according to the cloth at my disposal. Keep me up to strength of my present establishment; and we shall get on all right, I hope. I know that you do your best for us; and I am grateful. I think I told you, last Winter, that unless you took charge of the political strategy of this war we should not win it. Recent events in Italy confirm me in that opinion. The Boche gets his hit in first every time. The trouble here, about the Italians is that the Western Arabs in their sphere [i.e. Libya] hate them and like us. If this debacle in Italy leads to trouble there, we may find ourselves in a dilemma between the Arabs our friends and the Italians our friends. Serious trouble there might seriously hamper my operations here; however, I do not think that serious trouble there is probable – anyhow, as yet. Wingate has his eye on it all, and he and I are in close agreement.

The navy have given us great help. They are making splendid practice on the Gaza defences, and the railway bridge and junction at Deir Sineid. This is the result of careful preliminary work and close collaboration between land and sea.

LHCMA: Robertson papers 8/1/79

45
Allenby to Bishop R. MacInnes[70]
General Headquarters, Egyptian Expeditionary Force
[Letter. Holograph with additions]   5 November 1917
From the Commander-in-Chief, Gen Sir Edmund Allenby. Recd a few days after the capture of Beersheba, and on the day we captured Gaza.[71]

Thank you for your letter, of the 31st October, and your kind congratulations. The Turks are fighting well, and will give us a lot more trouble yet; but we thoroughly surprised them at Beersheba. I am much obliged to you for the photographs, which will be an interesting memento of your visit to me I am very grateful for your words of sympathy in my personal sorrow. I had no idea before I lost my boy, how much sympathy does help me in trouble. And I have nothing but good memories of him. There is not a day in his 19½ years that I would have had otherwise than it was. His life was full of happiness, work and complete success.

OxAnt: J&EM LX/1

46
Allenby to Lady Allenby

[Letter. Holograph]   6 November 1917

We've had a successful day. We attacked the left of the Turkish positions, from N. of Beersheba, and have rolled them up as far as Sharia.

The Turks fought well but have been badly defeated. Now, at 6 p.m., I am sending out orders to press in pursuit tomorrow. Gaza was not attacked; but I should not be surprised if this affected seriously her defenders. I am putting a lot of shell into them, and the Navy are still pounding them effectively. There was a very wet mist, this morning; which cleared at 8 o'clock. It was in our favour, as it veiled our start; and the day has been bright and cool. I have no details, yet, of the battle; and don't know what our casualties or captures may be.

LHCMA: Allenby papers 1/8/19

47
Allenby to Wigram[72]
General Headquarters, Egyptian Expeditionary Force
[Letter. Typescript with holograph additions]   7 November 1917

I present my humble duty to the king; and I submit herewith, for His Majesty's information, a short summary of recent events in the Force under my Command.

After arriving in Egypt, in June last, I came to the Palestine front to review the situation. Thereafter, on 12th July, I sent a telegram to – "Chief, London" – wherein I stated what reinforcements I required for an active defence of Egypt and an advance to capture the line Beersheba – Gaza.

His Majesty will be familiar with the course of events, and with the disposition of my Troops, up to the end of October, by which time my preparations for an offensive were complete.

My plan was to make the enemy believe that I intended to attack via Gaza, while I prepared for a swift and sudden blow at his left, via Beersheba.

The commander of the Fourth Army;[73] General Kress von Kressenstein; has twice previously in this war been defeated owing to his making a detachment.

In each case, at Magdhaba and Rafa,[74] the detachment was surprised at dawn by Mounted Troops under General Sir Philip Chetwode. Now, again, von Kressenstein had on his left flank a detached force; at Beersheba. A gap of 8 or 9 miles separated it from the left of his main system of works at Kauwukah.

My railheads were at Shellal and Gamli, on the Wadi Ghuzzee; and at a point between Deir el Bela and Gaza. In October, the direct line towards Gaza was carried forward; up to Wadi Ghuzzee, near Sheikh Raschid. At Shellal, preparations were made to push the railway rapidly across the Wadi; and at Gamli material for light railway was stored with a view to laying a line to carry forward ammunition.

At Shellal, there are natural springs of good water. These had been developed, and yield 300,000 gallons daily. Springs at Gamli and Esani were also unostentatiously developed.

Further South, at Khalassa and Asluj, were good wells; destroyed by the Turks, but capable of development.

Zero day was fixed for October 31st. Seven days before Zero day work was begun on the railway from Shellal to Karm, and from Gamli to El Buggar, under cover of a screen of Mounted Troops, with infantry support. Detachments were also sent to Khalassa and Asluj, to develop the water supply.

The enclosed plan[75] shows the gradual concentration of troops up to Zero day. It only refers to the Mounted Corps and the 20th Corps. The 21st Corps – composed of the 52nd, 54th and 75th Divisions faced Gaza.

On Zero day – 4 day, the 27th October, a bombardment of the Gaza defences commenced, and continued without intermission. On Zero – 1 day, the 30th October, the Royal Navy began its co-operating bombardment. Monitors, with 6" guns, fired on the Gaza positions. H.M.S. "Raglan" fired, with 14" guns, on the road and railway bridges and the railway junction at Deir Sineid, as also did the French battleship REQUIN. The Naval co-operation, of which the plan had been prepared in great detail, was very effective, the shooting being extremely accurate.

On the night of the 30th/31st October, the attacking Troops moved off according to plan.

At dawn, on the 31st, the 60th and 74th Divisions – Generals Shea and Girdwood – rushed the south-western defences, after a short bombardment. Simultaneously, the Australian and Anzac Mounted Divisions attacked from the north-east. The fighting continued all day. In the evening, Turks were still holding trenches a mile east of the town. The 4th Australian Light Horse Brigade was ordered to take these trenches. Time was short, and the Brigade Commander, Brigadier-General Grant D.S.O., sent his leading regiment to charge the trenches. This Regiment, the 4th Light Horse, galloped over the trenches, which were 8 feet deep and 4 feet wide, and full of Turks. This ended all resistance, and put a neat finish to the battle.

On the 1st November, the 53rd Division – General Mott – moved up to the north of Beersheba, while a Mounted Brigade pushed up towards El Dhaheriyeh. The 53rd Division established themselves about Ain Kohleh, and the Mounted Brigade were checked some 4 miles south of Dhaheriyeh.

The wells in Beersheba were somewhat damaged, and the next three or four days were occupied in clearing them, and in moving the 74th, 60th and 10th Divisions into position for the second phase of the battle.

Meanwhile, on the morning of the 2nd November, the 21st Corps – General Bulfin – attacked the south-west and western defences of Gaza, carrying all objectives. The 54th Division – General Hare – on the left, and the 52nd Division – General Hill – on the right, carried out this operation. The Turks suffered heavily in the affair, especially in the course of unsuccessful counter-attacks.

No further action of importance took place before the 6th November, though the bombardment of Gaza continued, and some minor enterprises were carried out.

Early on the morning of the 6th, the second phase of the battle began.

The 53rd Division attacked and took Tel Khuweilfeh, north of Beersheba. The Camel Brigade[76] held the Hebron Road, south of Dhaheriyeh. The Yeomanry Mounted Division came up on the left of the 53rd Division.

This mixed force was placed under the orders of the General Officer Commanding, desert Mounted Corps – General Chauvel. The Anzac Division, of this Corps, was watering at Beersheba, the Australian Division, between Shellal and Karm, was watching the gap between 20th and 21st Corps.

General Chetwode, commanding the 20th Corps, had three divisions, 74th, 60th and 10th, on a N.E.–S.W. line, north of Irgeig, facing the flank of the Kauwukah system of works; the 74th Division – General Girdwood – on the right, the 10th – General Longley, on the left. Their attack rolled up the whole system of works; and, by nightfall, the 10th Division has [sic had] arrived within 1,000 yards of the Hareira redoubt.

The situation at 6 p.m. was that the 60th Division had swung north, towards Tel el Sheria; the 74th, on its right, was connected by the Yeomanry Mounted Division with the 53rd Division. During the whole day, the 53rd Division was heavily engaged. Von Kressenstein counter-attacked again and again with the 19th Division – newly arrived – and the remains of the 27th Division – defeated at Beersheba, against the position held by the 53rd Division, the Camel Brigade and the Yeomanry, trying to paralyse our offensive by a blow at our water supply in Beersheba. However, our troops were staunch, and he achieved nothing but heavy losses to himself.

At nightfall, the Turks were retreating in disorder, to the north. Orders were then sent to the Desert Mounted Corps to pursue. The mixed force on the Tel el Khuweileh front was placed under General Barrow, Commanding the Yeomanry Mounted Division, and General Chauvel started northwards, via Sheria, towards Jemmameh and Huj, with the Australian and Anzac Mounted Divisions.

During the night, the bombardment of the Gaza defences was violent. Early in the morning of the 7th, the 21st Corps attacked and took the whole place, with very little opposition.

The situation at mid-day, to-day, is that the bulk of the Turkish Army is retreating north, and all my available troops are in pursuit. The Atawineh works are still occupied, and are being shelled by my guns, but their garrison must surrender, and I am not wasting men by assaulting them.

I have, as yet, no definite returns as to captures or casualties. I expect that the captures will prove to be large, and I do not think that my casualties will be exceptionally heavy.

The success of these operations, which has been more rapid and complete than I had anticipated, will upset the enemy's plan of campaign, I hope, for a considerable time.

The troops, who have had careful training, marched and fought splendidly.

My Corps and Divisional Commanders have shewn [sic] marked ability.

All branches of my staff have worked with a will; no problem has been too difficult for them, and there has not been a hitch anywhere.

Royal Archive: RA PS/GV/Q2521/14[77]

48
Allenby to Lady Allenby
General Headquarters, Egyptian Expeditionary Force
[Letter. Holograph]   7 November 1917

The Turks have had an awful hammering. We attacked Gaza, early this morning; and got it, almost without opposition. A few pockets of Turks, in isolated trench systems, are holding out E. of Gaza. They will be starved out, in time; so I am only shelling them, and not wasting men in attacking them. Cavalry are pushing North of Gaza, in pursuit, and I am moving Infantry in support of them. Here and there, rearguards are making a stand and showing fight; but I think that Kress von Kressenstein's army has lost its fighting value – for some time, at any rate. I have just written a narrative for the King – my first letter to him since I came out. I'm so glad you like the horse. I've only ridden him once, but I know he is a pleasant ride.

No rain here; but the weather is perfect for campaigning, and now we have captured all the water supplies we need.

LHCMA: Allenby papers 1/8/20

49
Allenby to Lady Allenby

[Letter. Holograph]   8 November 1917

The battle is in full swing. We have driven the Turks N. and N.E.; and my pursuing troops are ten miles beyond Gaza, and travelling fast.

A lot of Turks are cut off – just N.E. of Gaza. I don't know if they will be caught; but there is no time to waste in catching them.

They pooped off a huge explosion this morning – presumably ammunition.

My army is all over the place, now; on a front of 35 miles. I am at the centre of telegraph and telephone lines, in my old headquarters. I have no idea, yet, what our captures are; but they will be something big, when all is collected. I hear that some parts of the battlefield are carpeted with dead Turks. My flying men are having the time of their lives; bombing and machine gunning the retreating columns. All my staff wear happy expressions of countenance. I fancy that Kress von Kressenstein is nearing the Jaffa-Jerusalem line, himself. I have many congratulatory telegrams – from the Sultan, the High Commissioner, etc, etc. and from General Maude – who has, himself, had another success; at Tekrit.[78]

– Later –. No more definite news, but the pursuit continues. I hear of 43 guns captured, so far; but I don't know, for certain. We ought to get a lot eventually.

LHCMA: Allenby papers 1/8/22

50
Allenby to Robertson (Chief, Egypforce to Chief, LONDON)

[Telegram. Typescript]   8 November 1917
Despatched 0115 on 9th. Repeated General BAGHDAD, Britforce
SALONIKA; High Commissioner; 2nd Echelon G.H.Q. Rear-
Admiral EGYPT
SECRET
E.A. 506 cipher

2100, November 9th. Evening report.

During the day R.F.C. dropped nearly 300 bombs on various
objectives. Troops and transport north of JULIS and FALUJEH
were bombed with destructive effect and attacked with machine-
gun fire. In JULIS station direct hits were obtained on rolling
stock. 120 bombs were dropped later in day in and around EL
TINE. Several direct hits on hangars, two of which burst
into flames. One direct hit on machine on the aerodrome. Stores
near railway and station buildings attacked with effect; troops
in neighbourhood scattered by a number of bombs dropped
among them. Our pilots then descended and machine-gunned
them.

IWM: Dawnay papers 69/21/2 'Palestine 1917–18 Battle of Philistia'

51
Allenby to Lady Allenby

[Letter. Holograph]   9 November 1917

The enclosed extract from a captured German order will amuse
you.[79] Things are going well. I have infantry already in Askalon,
and am pushing N., inland of that place. I know of 77 guns having
been taken; and 5,000 prisoners at least. I went to Gaza, this
afternoon. It is badly knocked about; as, besides the effect of our
shells, the Turks took all the wood out of the houses. Wide gardens
of fig trees, olives and such like, spread all round it; but many fine

old olives have been cut down, for railway engine fuel. There is an old and a new town, but I had not time to explore either. I went on N. of the town, to the Wady Hesy[80] at Deir Seneid. There, our naval guns had broken the railway embankment, and damaged the road bridge, badly – with 14" shells – there were overturned rolling stock, exploded ammunition stores and a dead Turk or two.

Tomorrow is likely to be a critical day, in our pursuit[.] If the Turks can't stop us tomorrow, they are done.

The King has sent me a telegram of congratulation. Please thank Mahommed[81] very much, for his kind congratulations, also; I was very pleased to have them. You will find plenty of detail, I think, in the papers. I have two press representatives at my headquarters; Reuter's man, and another for the London Press. I let them have all the information that I can, without giving away secrets. Gaza was taken by Bulfin, quite easily. The attack, on the 6th inst., went with such a rush that Gaza became untenable. Everyone has marched and fought splendidly.

LHCMA: Allenby papers 1/8/23

52
Allenby to Lady Allenby

[Letter. Holograph]   10 November 1917

Enclosed[82] is from my dear old friend the Soeur Supérieure of the Hôpital Civil, at St. Pol.[83] I have just answered it. Will you, too, write a line to the Old Lady. She knew Michael; and she once gave him a medallion of St Michael, to wear as a charm. My battle goes on pretty well. My infantry have, on the coast, got 10 miles N. of Askalon; and my Cavalry, further inland, are ahead of them. The mounted troops took some 15 guns and 700 prisoners yesterday. I've not had much news today, yet. This afternoon I went to Khan Yunis; and told the head men that they could now go out of the town, to their farms and gardens. I made a speech, in English – interpreted to them –; and the Head Sheikh made a very long speech in Arabic – also interpreted. Then about 30 of them kissed my hand, vigorously, for some time – real slobbery, smacking kisses. The villagers – some 9000 – have been kept in, by wired enclosures, up to now; as the Turks had agents there, and many warm sympathizers.

LHCMA: Allenby papers 1/8/24

53
Allenby to Robertson (Chief, Egypforce to Chief, LONDON)

[Telegram. Typescript]   10 November 1917
Despatched 0030 on 11th. Repeated General BAGHDAD, Britforce SALONIKA, Rear-Admiral, High Commissioner, 2nd Echelon G.H.Q
SECRET
E.A. 509 cipher

Further details now received of action of Warwickshire and Worcestershire Yeomanry reported on Nov. 8th. Whilst reconnoitring in an armoured car ahead of his Division, south of HUJ, G.O.C. 60th Division saw a considerable body of enemy with guns about 2,500 yards away, marching N.E. Ten troops of Warwickshire and Worcestershire Yeomanry then came up on his right. Col. Cheape, commanding Warwickshire Yeomanry, who was in command of mounted force, was ordered by G.O.C. 60th Division to charge the retiring enemy. The charge was at once carried out in face of heavy gun, machine-gun and rifle fire with gallantry and dash worthy of best traditions of British Cavalry. Captures include 12 guns, the Austrian gunners being killed or wounded at their guns, 3 machine guns and 100 prisoners. Hostile resistance was completely broken and infantry enabled to push on to HUJ as result of this action.

IWM: Dawnay papers 69/21/2 'Palestine 1917–18 Battle of Philistia'

54
Robertson to Allenby (CHIEF, LONDON to CHIEF, EGYPFORCE)

[Telegram. Typescript]   13 November 1917
Despatched 1550. Received 0400 on 14 November
SECRET & PERSONAL
45396 cipher

I should be glad to have your views and intentions as soon as you are able to estimate the full measure of your success and appreciate the situation. From prisoners and other sources you will probably be able to form a more exact estimate of the enemy's strength and condition than has yet been possible, and this information will assist War Cabinet in deciding our future policy.

I should, under the circumstances, be glad to know what you expect from the Arabs who, if they are ever going to assist us, should be inspired by your success to do something.

While it is important to lose no opportunity to weaken the enemy's offensive power and so make our position in the East secure, it is equally important that you should not be drawn into a position which you can only hold with difficulty.

The situation in EUROPE is such that it may be necessary to reduce our forces in the East to the bare minimum required for defensive purposes by the summer.

IWM: Dawnay papers 69/21/2 'Palestine 1917–18 Battle of Philistia.' Copy at PRO: WO158/611. Slightly different copy at PRO: WO33/946, p. 7

55
Allenby to Shea

General Headquarters. Egyptian Expeditionary Force
[Letter. Holograph]   15 November [1917[84]]

Thank you for your letter of the 12th inst. The fighting and marching of your division have been beyond praise. The Turks have been outmanoeuvred and outfought; and, from all accounts, the remnants of Kress' Army is quite broken and disorganised. I am very grateful to you and your Division for your kind congratulations. To your fine leading and sound judgement our success is in great measure due. I hope that very soon we shall find ourselves in possession of the line from Jericho to the Mediterranean.

LHCMA: Shea papers 4/2

56
Allenby to Robertson (GOC-in-Chief, Egypt to CIGS)
[Telegram. Typescript]   15 November 1917
MS789

High Commissioner has telegraphed to Foreign Office urging importance of concentrated efforts to secure fall of Medina and expulsion of Turks from the Hejaz.[85] Have seen his telegram, and I consider main essential is funds for liberal payment of tribesmen by Feisal operating from Akaba. It is important that I should be authorized to exceed the sum of 200,000*l.* already granted for Arab operations, and to increase it up to 500,000*l.* if necessary. Increased Arab activity now will confirm and consolidate my success in Palestine, whereas any slacking of effort on their part will render my position insecure.

PRO: WO33/946, p. 11

57
Robertson to Allenby (Chief, London to Chief Egypforce)
[Telegram. Typescript]   16 November 1917
Despatched 1550. Received 2315 on 17 November
SECRET
45777 cipher

With reference to my 44428 November 1st and 45396 November 13th, War Cabinet rather fear that the two telegrams above-mentioned may have the effect of leading you to suppose that it is not their desire that you should exploit to the utmost the successes recently gained by you. I have explained that the telegrams were not so intended and I do not think they will have the effect feared. The first telegram was sent as it was essential that you should clearly understand that at present there was no prospect of reinforcing you. The intention of the second telegram was merely to remind you of the necessity of looking well ahead and considering what might be the situation in the course of a few weeks or months, and that although it is obviously desirable that you should take every possible advantage of your successes and continue hammering the Turks, who are known to be very shaky in general; nevertheless it is also desirable not to involve yourself in future commitments which it may be difficult to meet. I send this to ensure removal of any misunderstanding in case such does exist.

Please acknowledge this telegram.

IWM: Dawnay papers 69/21/2 'Palestine 1917–18 Battle of Philistia.' Copy at PRO: WO158/611. Slightly different copy at PRO: WO33/946, p. 12

58
Robertson to Allenby
[Telegram. Holograph for despatch as telegram]   16 November 1917

R180 Personal and Secret

My 45777 of today was sent because certain members of War Cabinet have been uneasy because of my two telegrams to you. They do not understand these things. My only object was to make matters quite clear and am sure you will appreciate. I cannot think the effect feared has been produced in your mind. Also note that telegram 45396 of 13th instant asking for an appreciation when convenient was sent at a time when owing to anticipated supply and transport difficulties we here rather expected you might soon be making a halt in order methodically to prepare for the next bound. But apparently your difficulties have been overcome and your advance has certainly progressed more rapidly than we expected. You have done splendidly and at a most opportune time as Italy is causing anxiety and some depression. As a counter your blows on the Turk will upset the enemy considerably in every way.

LHCMA: Robertson papers 4/4/103

59
Robertson to Allenby (Chief, London to Chief Egypforce)
[Telegram. Typescript]   16 November 1917
Despatched 2200. Received 0700 on 17 November 1917
SECRET
45831 cipher

The Prime Minister desires that every possible precaution should be taken, if occasion arises, to secure the Holy Places, both Christian and Mahometan, from violation of any kind. I am sure the importance of this is realised by you but should be glad of an assurance which I can give War Cabinet with regard to this matter.

IWM: Dawnay papers 69/21/2 'Palestine 1917–18 Battle of Philistia.' Slightly different version at PRO: WO33/946, p. 12

60
Allenby to Robertson
[Telegram. Typescript]   17 November 1917
SECRET
Des.1.15 p.m.
Rec. 3.5 p.m. [sic]
A.M.S. 12. November 17th

Your R.180 November 16th. I quite understand your meaning. I am taking no undue risks, but am keeping up pressure on enemy. Difficulties of transport and water considerable, but hope to overcome them. Thank you for your congratulations.[86]

LHCMA: Robertson papers 4/4/104. Slightly different copy at PRO: WO158/611

61
Robertson to Allenby (CIGS to GOC-in-C Egypt)
[Telegram. Typescript]   17 November 1917
45860 cipher

Your No. M.S. 789 of the 15th. War Cabinet has agreed to increase payments to Arabs up to 500,000*l*.

PRO: WO33/946, p. 15

62
Allenby to Battine
General Headquarters, Egyptian Expeditionary Force
[Letter. Holograph]   20 November 1917

I have your letters of 22nd and 25th October. You take a wrong view of Grenfell. The destination of the letter mattered nothing. I have absolute confidence in Lord Burnham, and I would trust him with my secret; therefore, I was quite sure that he would make no use of the letter.[87] The letter was brought officially to my notice, and I had no course open to me but to take the necessary disciplinary action. I know Grenfell, and I like him; but, whatever, my personal feelings might be, I could not retain as commanding a Regiment in my Army an officer who could write such a letter. The whole letter was improper; but I could have condoned all of it except the writer's criticism of his Brigadier, and his reference to future operations in the Beersheba area. I have no ill will towards Grenfell. He has had his lesson; and I should have no hesitation in recommending him for further employment. As to what people think of my action; I care nothing. I must maintain discipline; and I shall always take whatever measures I think necessary, for the purpose. You will have seen that, up to now, we have had a considerable success. Kress von Kressenstein, for the third time in his war, left out an isolated detachment. He had done it at Magdhaba, and at Rafa; and, each time, it was snapped up by Chetwode's horse men. Now, again, he had had a detachment at Beersheba. My mounted troops made a long night march, to the

N.E.; and attacked in the early morning, simultaneously with an attack by two Divisions of Infantry on the S.W. – also, after a long night march. We fought all day; and, in the evening, a regiment of Light Horse charged the last entrenched Turks. They galloped over two lines of trenches, 8 ft deep and 4 ft wide full of riflemen; and put a neat finish to the battle. The battle turned the flank of the whole system of fortifications. The defences of Gaza were, all the time, getting it hot from my guns and the Navy; and an attack on the 2nd November brought us close in on the W. and S.W. of the inner defences. My right wing attacked again, from the W. of Beersheba, in a N.W. direction, on the 6th. Kress counterattacked, very hard, from the direction of the line Dhahariyeh-Sheria, to cut me from the water at Beersheba; but to no purpose.

By night, we had rolled up his whole system, to a depth of 9 miles; and my left – attacking Gaza, that night – went through; almost unopposed. Next day, I sent every available man, horse and gun to make for the railway junction W. of Jerusalem. The Turks fought well, and kept putting up stubborn rearguards. However, we kept one aim in view; and we gained it. The mounted troops did great good work. The regiments – the Warwicks and Worcesters, under Cheape, made a fine charge near Huj. The Bucks Yeomanry charged, with their Brigade, at Katra; and again at Abu Shusheh. They have done splendidly. It was at Abu Shusheh that Neil Primrose was killed;[88] shot through the head, in a dismounted attack. Evelyn Rothschild[89] was mortally wounded, in the head, on the Katra day. Now my mounted troops occupy Jaffa; and are pushing through the hills, to the N. of Jerusalem. Falkenhayn has gone from Jerusalem to Nablus, and Kress is at Tul Keram. We estimate that the Turks have lost, one way and another, over 28,000 men. I have taken, certainly, more than 10,000 prisoners – to date – and others are to come in. What guns we have taken, I don't know; but, I fancy, nearly 100. It has not been possible to clear the wide and deep battle area yet – indeed, I don't know when it will be possible. Enormous quantities of ammunition are left behind. The marching and fighting of my Infantry have been splendid. They have outrun their transport and supplies; but I am running forward my railway, which is already well N. of Gaza. We captured some 4 or 5 Turkish engines and some 60 or 70 trucks on their railway; so we hope to use that, to some extent, in a day or two. Its gauge is 3'5½"; and so only their stock fits it. I was in Jaffa yesterday. The bulk of the inhabitants were evacuated by the Turks; but the town seemed fairly full. There is no harbour; but a reef of rocks make a breakwater for boats, and I hope to make some use of the place for landing supplies.

The naval cooperation has been very useful to me; and their shooting, at Gaza, was accurate and destructive. A good deal of staff work, in conjunction with the Naval staff, had been done during the two months previous to the attack; and to this the efficacy of their support was greatly due. Moreover, the sea was usually calm. The weather has been good. Cool and not cold. Yesterday afternoon and night were very wet, and colder; and today is dull and showery. On clear days, Jerusalem stands out very plain on the high ridge of the mountains of Judea. From the hills near Jaffa one can see Mount Tabor, to the N., as well as the whole range of mountains till they drop towards Beersheba.

I am glad you were able to get to the Grand Fleet and see Nigel.[90] My wife is quite happy at Cairo, and very well. I have not seen her yet; and am not likely to do so soon, I fear. I get the General Staff summary, to which you refer, regularly.

Have just heard that Joe Maude is dead; but have no details.

PS: I wonder how you saw Grenfell's letter. It was stopped by me, as containing information which might be of use to the enemy – re Beersheba –. Now, on the 25th Oct. it is shewn [sic] in London; six days before my attack. If the W.O. have published it, they are culpable. If Grenfell is shewing [sic] it, he is repeating the offence for which he was rightly punished.

IWM: Battine papers 90/37/1

63
Allenby to Lady Allenby

[Letter. Holograph]   20 November 1917

Your letter of yesterday's date, says that you have our wet weather.
It is quite cold today, dull and rainy; but the rain is not heavy. It
must be very cold and wet where my advanced troops are
fighting; up in the mountains, N.W. and N. of Jerusalem. They
find the country very difficult; but they are making progress,
though news comes in very slowly. Tomorrow I shift my
headquarters forward, some 30 miles, and I shall live in a tent. Sir
R.W. [Reginald Wingate] will go forward with us, and stay a few
days more. He has gone to Beersheba today. Yesterday he and I
motored over to Jaffa, some 75 miles from here. We started at
9.a.m., and got back here at 8.30 p.m. It was interesting to see the
place. A curious old town, mixed with new. It had a population of
some 50,000; but the bulk of the upper classes were deported by
the Turks, a year or so ago. Orange gardens and fruit farms
surround it; and in the neighbourhood are many newly settled
Jewish communities; who cultivate vines, fruit trees and all sorts
of produce. The annual orange crop is valued at £250,000. There
is no harbour; but a reef of rocks makes a natural haven for
launches, boats and small craft. The ships have to lie outside in an
open road. The old town is perched on a steep limestone hill,
sloping steeply to the sea. Sir Reginald, knowing Arabic well,
could talk to the leading inhabitants; and we interviewed such
people as the Mayor, Chief of Police, chief doctor. I did not know
till today that Dalmeny had taken George, the chameleon, to
you.[91] My Australian A.D.C. has been charged with George's
education. Though young, George is a good shot at a fly; and he
has a tongue as big as himself. Sir R. is just back from Beersheba,
and has enthusiastically enjoyed his day. Naper escorted him, and
shewed [sic] him round. I'm glad your fête went off well. I know
your walk in the Jezireh gardens,[92] along the Nile, well; and the
view of the Citadel[93] in the evening. I try to imagine myself
walking there with you my dear love.

PS: I think the view is best at sunset; when the Nile is violet, and the Mokattam Hills[94] are rosy in colour.

LHCMA: Allenby papers 1/8/25

64
Allenby to Lady Allenby
[Letter. Holograph]   21 November 1917

I have moved my Headquarters, to about 20 miles N.N.E. of Gaza. We are on a ridge, whence we get a grand view of all the Judaean range.

Sir R.W. and I went, this afternoon, up to the entrance of the Vale of Ajalon – now Yalo –; and to Emmaus now Amwas. We are fighting our way up, by the road taken by Richard Coeur de Lion; and we have reached about the point at which he turned back.[95] The rain has ceased; and today has been cool, bright and clear. The roads have not been spoilt much by the rain; and the absence of dust is a great boon.

– 22nd November – I have been up to mountains today; and got to within 5 miles of Jerusalem – with Sir R.W. We could see the tops of some buildings and churches, only; not the city. It has been a bright and cool day. I have your letter of the . . .
[End of letter missing]

LHCMA: Allenby papers 1/8/28

65
Robertson to Allenby (Chief, LONDON to Chief Egypforce)
[Telegram. Typescript]   21 November 1917
Despatched 1335. Received 1800
46111 cipher

In the event of JERUSALEM being occupied, it would be of considerable political importance if you, on officially entering the city, dismount at the city gate and enter on foot. German emperor rode in and the saying went round "a better man than he walked".

Advantage of contrast in conduct will be obvious.

IWM: Dawnay papers 69/21/2 'Palestine 1917–18 Battle of Philistia.' Copy at PRO: WO33/946, p. 26

66
Wingate to Allenby

G.H.Q.

[Letter. Typescript]   22 November 1917

On the conclusion of my intensely interesting visit to your recent battlefields, I wish to thank you most sincerely for your extreme courtesy and kindness in enabling me to see so much of the conquered districts in the short time at my disposal and fact that you were able to personally explain the great events of the last three weeks added enormously to the interest.

I find it no easy matter to express my unbounded admiration first to you, General, for the magnificent strategy which enabled you to out-manoeuvre, defeat and utterly rout a brave and determined enemy – holding what the Turks and their German leaders believed to be impregnable lines which they had fortified and strengthened for months, and secondly I wish to express my admiration of the conduct of the officers, non-commissioned officers and men of your army who, with such splendid bravery, have carried out your orders to the letter.

From all I have seen I can unhesitatingly say that, on the one hand no troops ever had a more capable or efficient leader, and on the other, that no General has ever had the honour to lead to victory more gallant, devoted and well-trained troops.

Where all have done so well it would be invidious to make distinctions; but, for a cavalry learder [sic] like yourself, it must have been a supreme satisfaction to you at length to have the opportunity of employing the mounted Branches with such telling effect. The magnificent dash of the various Regiments which charged near Huj and again in the capture of the heights at Katra and in the neighbourhood north of Jerusalem are as you truly remarked, worthy of the highest traditions of the British Cavalry. The patrol and observation work of the Royal Flying Corps must have proved of the greatest possible assistance in your operations and their information of extreme value.

As a Gunner I know you will not mind my saying that the Artillery have been true to their motto "where duty and glory lead" and the prisoners' accounts of the bombardment of Gaza and the neighbourhood by your land forces, with the fine co-operation of the Navy, is the best testimony to its accuracy and intensity.

In fighting, marching and endurance the Infantry have been superb throughout and if I may be allowed to say so, I think the very greatest credit is due to one and all from the Corps Commanders, Generals of Divisions, Brigades and their respective staffs, down to the last joined recruit. As their former Sirdar, I am of course proud of the part taken in this arduous campaign by the small contingent of Egyptian troops, by the Camel Transport and Egyptian Labour Corps.

It has been my privilege to visit many of the wounded in hospital in Cairo and I have listened with intense interest to the account they gave me of their own share in helping to win this glorious victory – such pluck, endurance and grit, in the face of great pain and suffering, makes one proud indeed of being a member of the great British Commonwealth of Nations, whether it be English, Scotch, Irish or Welsh, Australians, Canadian or New Zealander, or from the East or West Indies – one and all have been actuated by that splendid British spirit which will carry us through anything and everything and bring us out conquerors in the end. Of this I am quite confident and I am equally sure that what has been carried out so successfully and so thoroughly during these last few weeks in Palestine will weigh down the scales in our favour very considerably. Your gallant army may well be proud of the splendid part it has taken in upholding the great traditions of our Empire – and its name, and that of its indomitable leader, will go down to history as having successfully accomplished one of the most difficult tasks in this great war of nations.

From the bottom of my heart, and as one who has followed every step in your heroic attack and rapid and most successful pursuit, I, as the King's representative in Egypt, beg to most heartily congratulate you, General, and every officer and man of your splendid army you have the honour to command, on your truly great achievement. I can assure you that I feel it has been a very great privilege to have been able to see with my own eyes the scenes of your splendid exploits and to address to you these few quite inadequate words before I return to Cairo. I am confident our Empire will acclaim your deeds of valour and that you will all earn the genuine thanks of a grateful nation.

You have already gone a long way in the task of reclaiming this historic land and its people from the misrule of which we have evidence on all sides, and in now bidding you good-bye, I wish you most warmly continued success and God-speed.

CUL: Hardinge papers 35, fo. 166–8

67
Robertson to Allenby
[Letter. Typescript. Dictated]   23 November 1917
SECRET

The Italians have added another disappointment to the Russian collapse.[96] If these two countries had kept their end up properly and had taken anything like a reasonable share in the war we ought to have broken the back of it this year. We have done a good deal in that respect but of course are not nearly so advanced as we ought to have been.

Russia now seems to be quite hopeless and presents us with an [sic] situation difficult to handle. We cannot treat her as though she were out of the war as that might have the effect of sending her out of it altogether, and we prefer her present condition to her making a definite peace. At the same time we feel that she will never be of much more use to us.

The Italian debacle was unpardonable and was brought about purely by the refusal of the troops to fight. They were far superior to the enemy and the latter made no really big attack. In fact downright treason started the business and then the Italian Command and Staff were unable to handle the situation. But it was a very difficult one to deal with simply because the troops and country generally have been saturated by a vigorous and invidious German propaganda which had for the moment the effect of inducing many of the troops to fight no more. However, things have improved a great deal during these last few days and the Italians are now well holding their own although the divisions we and the French have sent have not actually reached the front line. But I fear that Italy will be a burden to us to some extent for the remainder of the war. I cannot quite see that we shall be able to leave her alone ever again. I need hardly say that this is a most unwelcome addition to our task.

I cannot yet say how this new Supreme War Council[97] is going to work. There is nothing new in the idea of establishing central control. That has been talked about for practically the whole of the war. The difficulty has been to set up machinery that can be depended upon and which will be useful. On paper central control seems obviously easy and necessary. In practice it looks rather impracticable because no one country is prepared to hand itself over body and soul to the dictation of another, and quite rightly so. Further, political aims and interests are somewhat divergent and this strikes at the bottom of everything. The Military Representatives appointed to the Council seem likely to lead to dual advice, and as the Council can have no executive authority it means that so far as military advice is concerned advice will be separate from responsibility for execution, which is always an exceedingly bad principle. It is quite easy to advise. It is sometimes very difficult to execute, and therefore the man who advises should feel the responsibility of having to carry out his advice. If he has not this responsibility he is liable to put forward impracticable schemes.

Your recent successes have been splendid, and have come at an opportune time. Italy upset everybody here and made certain people look round for scapegoats, or for anything else affording shelter. The defection of Italy, the collapse of Russia, and the system of economising shipping, all make me wish to reduce your Force in the spring, and I hope this may be possible. As you know there is only one way to win this war and that is by beating the Germans. Everything seems to have gone splendidly in your operations and I imagine that you have had some difficult transport and supply problems to solve. I congratulate you heartily on what you have achieved and I hope that you are satisfied with those who helped you.

LHCMA: Robertson papers 8/1/81

68
Robertson to Allenby (CIGS to GOC-in-C Egypt)

[Telegram. Typescript]   26 November 1917
46484 cipher

Picot contends that occupied portions of Palestine should be jointly administered by us and the French, and has suggested certain French officers should be appointed for that purpose at once. You should not entertain any ideas of joint administration at any rate while operations are being conducted anywhere near Jerusalem, but should avoid any impression being gained by Picot that a British annexation of Palestine is contemplated. Picot, as French Commissioner and Representative, should join you at once and enter Jerusalem with you. He should be afforded every facility for inspection, and his ideas sympathetically received by you, but you should remember that his role is purely consultative, and not executive, which precludes his appointing any administrators. Special deference should be shown to him. He is undoubtedly discontented. The instructions already sent to you as regards treatment of Picot if operations touch French sphere still hold good.

PRO: WO33/946, pp. 35–6

69
Allenby to Robertson (Chief Egypforce to Chief LONDON)
[Telegram. Typescript with holograph additions]   26 November
1917

DRAFT
SECRET
E.A………..cipher [becomes EA 549]

Reference cipher No. 45396 of 13th November.

Ten Turkish Divisions, one Cavalry and one Depot Regiment have been opposed to me during the last 26 days. These divisions are 3, 7, 16, 19, 20, 24, 26, 27, 53 and 54, and 3rd Cavalry Division.

All these units except the Cavalry Division which has avoided battle have suffered heavily.

On 31st October I estimated the enemy's fighting strength at 41,000[98] bayonets and 300 guns. The arrival of 20th Division a few days afterwards probably brought up the total infantry and cavalry fighting strength up to 45,000.[99] Of these I have captured about 10,000 prisoners and 80 guns. I estimate the loss in killed and wounded at at least 15,000 and I believe that considerable numbers of the enemy have deserted and that there are some guns which have not yet been found. I think that of the original strength 20,000 or 15,000 remain and perhaps 200 guns.

My immediate operations are with a view to securing my right flank and capturing JERUSALEM by occupying the JERUSALEM-NABLUS road: as I do not want to fight near the Holy City I had intended to capture BIREH[100] by a rapid advance, but the difficulty of the country and the strength of the Turkish positions have not allowed me to do this, which would probably have caused the surrender of JERUSALEM. This advance, however, has brought me within a few miles of the JERUSALEM-BIREH road. I am now relieving the XXI Corps on this front by the XX Corps. When this has been finished, and the roads improved, and more guns and ammunition brought up, I intend to renew my offensive.

If I can occupy the general line JERICHO-BIREH-JAFFA, I shall be in a position to send strong raiding parties on to the MEDINA Railway east of ES SALT. These, working in cooperation, should make the supply or the withdrawal of the Turkish forces about MEDINA and MAAN very difficult.

The Turkish forces about these places are DERAA to MAAN, 6,000; MAAN area 6,000; TEBUK area 2,300; MEDINA area 15,000; total 29,300 rations strengths.

The Arabs are now doing good work in destroying bridges and breaking up the railway. Early in December the Arabs intend to cut off MEDINA by occupying an important station north of it. Arrangements have also been made for allotting certain raiding parties to definite sections of the railway. Further attacks are also intended on the railway between DAMASCUS and ALEPPO. Most of the Arab tribes are prepared to take part in these operations, but the Druses, who are the best organised, will probably wait till British forces approach NABLUS.

IWM: Dawnay papers 69/21/2 'Palestine 1917–18 Battle of Philistia.'[101]

70
Allenby to Bishop R. MacInnes

[Letter. Holograph]   28 November [1917]

I have your letter of the 25th inst.

I am not yet in Jerusalem; and, though my troops are not many miles distant from that town, it is impossible for me to say when or if we shall have access to it. Even if we get to Jerusalem, the locality will probably be – for a considerable period – the centre of military operations.

I quite understand your anxiety to go there at the first opportunity, and I will let you know when military considerations allow you to start. I am, however, afraid that it will not be very soon.

OxAnt: J&EM LX/1

71
Allenby to Lady Allenby

[Letter. Holograph]   28 November 1917

I was up on the mountains yesterday at the same place – Kuryet el Enab[102] – as I visited with H.E.[103] There is an interesting convent there, which we are using as an ambulance post. In it is a sacred well, said to have been the spot where Christ met the two men on the way to Emmaus.[104] The well is in a vaulted chapel, dating from the 5th Century. Over the chapel is a church; built by the Crusaders in the 12th Century, and restored some years ago. It is exactly in its old form, and remains of old fresco paintings are still on the walls. Two old priests look after the place. They gave us good red wine, which they make.

I am staying in camp this morning, and trying to get rid of some of my arrears of correspondence. The Turks were rather aggressive, to the N., last evening; but they gained nothing. I hear that my old opponent, Kress von Kressenstein, has been removed from the command of the 8th Army, which has been given to a Turk.[105] I fancy that there is little love lost now between Turk and Boche.[106]

LHCMA: Allenby papers 1/8/30

72
Allenby to Robertson

[Letter. Holograph]   4 December 1917
Embossed
Seen by CIGS. 1 copy to P.M. 1 copy with enclosures DMO AG to see. 22/12/17

Enclosed[107] are copies of a letter from me to the W.O., and the cabled reply. The Egyptian native personnel referred to are subject only to the Army Act. Flogging is, therefore, illegal. Everyone who knows the country considers power of flogging to be necessary. The general behaviour of the Egyptian Labour Corps is very good; but there are now and then cases for the lash. Do you think that it could be specially legalized, as asked in my letter of 29th October?

My operations have been going more slowly, lately. The pursuit was carried out by Bulfin, with 52nd and 75th Divisions; and Chauvel with the mounted troops. This was all I could keep mobile and supplied for rapid movement.

When I got on to the Railway junction-Jaffa line, I directed the Yeomanry Mounted Division on Bire – through the mountains – while the 52nd and 75th made for the Jerusalem-Nablus road, S. of Bire.[108] The rush of these three divisions carried them to the crest of the range, at a height of 2,500 feet. The mountains are bare, barren and rocky; cut by deep gorges and ravines. There is only one practicable road; the Jerusalem-Jaffa road; up which the 75th Division forced their way with great gallantry. On this account, it was impossible to get up enough guns to deal with the large number of machine guns which the Turks have there; and, after a week's hard fighting, not much progress had been made. My Divisions in the mountains had been marching and fighting, unceasingly, for four weeks; and were becoming tired. By this time, my transport and supply services enabled me to bring up Divisions from the rear; and guns.

I now have the XX Corps on my right. 60th[,] 74th and 10th Divisions for [from] Jerusalem Westwards and Northwards; 53rd Division moving N., along the Hebron road, from Beersheba. Bulfin has taken over the sector from the left of the XX Corps to the mouth of the R.[iver] Auja,[109] N. of Jaffa; and I am drawing back the mounted troops.

Thanks to the celerity with which Bulfin gained and held the hills, Chetwode has now got his Divisions into position for further attack practically without fighting. As soon as guns are in position, and registered, he will attack N. of Jerusalem; to gain the Jerusalem-Nablus road and Bire. I am purposely striking well N. of Jerusalem, lest damage be done to the Holy Places.

The mosque of Neby Samweil [?] – which is the grave of the Prophet Samuel – has been knocked about by Turkish shell. Our guns had orders to avoid it. There has been much fighting there; as it's on the dominating point, over looking the road. I want to get

Bire, before I consolidate; as it covers all the roads, and commands everything. We captured 3 or 4 engines, and 40 or 50 trucks on the Turkish light railway; and Egypt produced 3 more engines to fit it. Consequently, it has been in use; and has been of great service.

My own railway is coming along at a great rate, now; and we are also landing stores on the coast, S. of Jaffa. So the supply question is easier.

If I get Bire and the hills covering the mouth of the Auja river N. of Jaffa I shall be in a good strong position; for offence or defence. I must anyhow consolidate there, and wait till my railway is developed. I am running short of officers and some of my strengths are getting low. I know, however, that you will do what you can to keep me up to strength; and you understand its importance, as I have no reserve units. All my goods are in the shop window.

The Arab situation is, I think, satisfactory. The Hedjaz railway is constantly harried, and Medina is isolated.

LHCMA: Robertson papers 8/1/82

73
Allenby to Robertson

[Telegram. Typescript]   7 December 1917
Handed in 9.30 p.m., received 11.45 p.m.
A.14
Secret and Personal

Your R.184 Dec.4th.

I quite understand your views and I recognise that outside commitments must be cut down and reasonable risks be faced by me here.

According to the instructions given me when I was appointed Egypt Command I have conducted this campaign with a view to the defence [sic] that country entailing the defeat of Turkish army and the occupation of Beer Sheba and Gaza. That line is difficult if not impossible to hold and the only line that I can hold with reasonable security is the line Jerusalem-Jaffa with my flanks on the Dead Sea and Mediterranean.

If I can get Jerusalem-Jaffa line I ought to be able to hold it with the force I now have if my establishments are maintained.

It will not be necessary to advance further north than the consolidation of that line requires, but it will be essential to maintain that line.

Any retirement would alienate the Arabs and result in disaster.

I consider that it would not be feasible to hold that line with a less force [sic110] than that under my command and I would point out that for political as well as military reasons the majority of the troops in this country should be British.

C2 copies to: P.S. to C.I.G.S.

LHCMA: Robertson papers 4/4/108

74
Robertson to Allenby
[Telegram. Holograph for despatch as telegram]

8 December 1917
R187 Secret and Personal. Your A.14 Dec. 7th.

I note your views and if and when I send you instructions contrary to them you will have an opportunity of repeating them officially and should do so if desired. I should hope no retirement will become necessary but even if it did the disaster you fear might well be far less than one in Europe. The force you may eventually need should of course be fixed by the strength of the possible opposition rather than by the length of any given line while your fine mounted force should be a very great asset. As regards the Arabs I confess I am so far somewhat disappointed at their contribution.

Original to PS to CIGS
Desp. 11.40 a.m.

LHCMA: Robertson papers 4/4/112

75
Allenby to Lady Allenby
[Letter. Holograph]   10 December 1917
Embossed

This morning is bright and fine, after wet evening and night. I hope my roads will dry today; as they are in an awful state, and it is difficult to get food and ammunition up to my men in the mountains. All is going well there, but the difficulties of the ground and the weather make our movements slow. Consequently, we can't pursue with full effect; and events do not march with the rapidity which my impatience would desire. I hear that a lot of the Turkish transport is stuck in the mud.

I have an English mail and a letter from my mother. She is very excited and proud; and delighted with the congratulations she receives. Your mother has been writing to her; among others. I still get letters from people I have not heard from for years. I suppose that is fame! Battine is still melancholy. The Germans are pushing very hard at Byng. I wonder if the Home Authorities think they acted wisely and with dignity, in ringing the bells of St. Paul's the other day.[111] I think you will have a comfortable journey to and from Kantara in my coach. I wish I could run down and meet you; but I can't. I enclose a cutting[112] sent me by Major Austice.[113]

LHCMA: Allenby papers 1/8/31

76
Allenby to Lady Allenby
[Letter. Holograph]   11 December 1917

Jerusalem surrendered to me on the 9th. I informed the W.O., but was not allowed to publish the news before the P.M. had announced it in the House. That was done yesterday. Today I entered Jerusalem, on foot; with the French and Italian commanders – Lt.Colonel Piépape and Major Agostino – of the detachments in my Army; and the attachés and a few Staff Officers. We entered at the Jaffa Gate;[114] and, from the steps of the

Citadel,[115] – hard by –, issued a proclamation in many languages to the assembled multitude. Great enthusiasm – real or feigned – was shewn [sic]. Then I received the notables and the heads of all the churches – of which there are many, including Abyssinian. After this, we reformed our procession and returned to our horses – which we had left outside the walls. While in Jerusalem, I received the enclosed from the King;[116] and I sent a suitable reply, from the Holy City. The Turks are driven 3 or 4 miles down the Jericho road, to the East; and some 6 or 8 miles to the North. Today we occupied Bethany.[117] It was a brilliant day; hoar frost here, in the early a.m., and then iced sunshine; with no wind.

We could see, from the top of the house where I met Chetwode, the mountains of Moab;[118] deep blue and huge. The Dead Sea lay too low to be seen. Chetwode's Corps; and the Divisions of Generals Shea and Mott, in that Corps, were the lucky ones who had the honour of capturing the Holy City. You remember Mott; as a Major in the 60th Rifles, at Colchester. It was a great feat; and our losses were light. The rocky and mountainous country they fought over is indescribable. Guns could give little support; and the Turks were driven out by rifle and machine gun fire, followed by the bayonet. A great number of Turks were killed, and about 400 or 500 taken prisoner.

LHCMA: Allenby papers 1/8/32

77
Allenby to Robertson (Chief Egypforce to Chief LONDON)

[Telegram. Typescript]   11 December 1917
Repeated to High Commissioner under E.A. 593 at 1900, 11/12/17
SECRET
E.A. 591 Despatched 1400.
JERUSALEM, 1400, 11th December.

1. At noon today I officially entered this city with a few of my Staff, the commanders of the French[119] and Italian

Detachments,[120] the Heads of the Picot Mission and the Military Attaches of FRANCE,[121] ITALY,[122] and the UNITED STATES of AMERICA.[123]

The procession was all on foot.

I was received by guards representing ENGLAND, SCOTLAND, IRELAND, WALES, AUSTRALIA, INDIA, NEW ZEALAND, FRANCE and ITALY at the JAFFA GATE.

2. I was well received by the population.

3. The Holy Places have had guards placed over them.

4. My Military Governor[124] is in touch with the acting CUSTOS[125] of Latins, and the Greek representative has been detailed to supervise Christian Holy Places.

5. The Mosque of OMAR[126] and the area round it has been placed under Moslem control, and a Military cordon, composed of Indian Mahomedan officers and soldiers, has been established round the Mosque.

Orders have been issued that, without permission of the Military Governor and the Moslem in charge of the Mosque, no non-Moslem is to pass this cordon.

6. In accordance with your 46139 cipher M.O.1 of 21st November, the proclamation has been posted on the walls and from the steps of the Citadel was read in my presence to the population in Arabic, Hebrew, English, French, Italian, Greek and Russian.

7. Guardians have been established at BETHLEHEM and on Rachael's Tomb.[127] The Tomb of HEBRON has been placed under exclusive Moslem control.

8. The hereditary Custodians of the WAFK at the Gates of the Holy Sepulchre have been requested to take up their accustomed duties in remembrance of the magnanimous act of the Caliph OMAR who protected that Church.[128]

IWM: Dawnay papers 69/21/2 'Palestine 1917–18 Battle of Philistia.' Copy at PRO: WO33/946, p. 71[129]

78
War Office to Allenby (War Office to General Officer Commanding-in-Chief, General Headquarters, Egypt)

[Telegram. Typescript]   12 December 1917
No. 47761, cipher

In view of the change in position created by your recent victory over Turks, and by revised information as to enemy strength and breakdown in his transport, War Cabinet would like to have your opinion by telegram as soon as possible as to manner in which, and extent to which, it is possible to exploit your success in Palestine with forces now under your Command, plus the division under orders from Mesopotamia.

LHCMA: Robertson papers 4/5/10 (appendix I to 'Future Operations in Palestine' by Robertson, 26 December 1917). Copies at IWM: Dawnay papers 69/21/2 'Palestine 1917–18 Battle of Philistia' and PRO: WO33/946, p. 76. Slightly different copy at PRO: WO158/611 (see also PRO: WO106/718/40)

79
Allenby to Bishop R. MacInnes

[Letter. Holograph]   12 December [1917]

In reply to yours of the 9th inst. I am not likely to be in Cairo, for some weeks yet; but I shall be glad if you will write and tell me what you have to say in connection with the Relief Fund.

I entered Jerusalem yesterday, with the commanders of the Italian and French contingents; and proclaimed martial law, from the steps of the Citadel – just inside the Jaffa Gate –. The people of the city assembled in some considerable numbers, and appeared to be pleased at our arrival. I did not remain in the city, which is in charge of a military governor appointed by me. He is policing the town, and enquiring into the needs of the people.

OxAnt: J&EM LX/1

80
Proclamation of Martial Law in Jerusalem (by Allenby)
Reuters Telegrams, Cairo
[Typescript]   13 December 1917

Immediately after the entry into Jerusalem of the Egyptian Expeditionary Force the following Proclamation was issued in English, French, Italian, Hebrew, Arabic, Russian and Greek:

PROCLAMATION
OF MARTIAL LAW IN JERUSALEM

To the inhabitants of Jerusalem the Blessed and the people dwelling in its vicinity.

The defeat inflicted upon the Turks by the troops under my command has resulted in the occupation of your City by my forces. I therefore here and now proclaim it to be under Martial Law, under which form of administration it will remain so long as military considerations make it necessary.

However, lest any of you should be alarmed by reason of your experiences at the hands of the enemy who has retired, I hereby inform you that it is my desire that every person should pursue his lawful business without fear of interruption. Furthermore, since your City is regarded with affection by the adherents of three of the great religions of mankind, and its soil has been consecrated by the prayers and pilgrimages of devout people of those three religions for many centuries, therefore do I make known to you that every sacred building, monument, holy spot, shrine, traditional site, endowment, pious bequest or customary place of prayer, of whatsoever form of the three religions, will be maintained and protected according to the existing customs and beliefs of those to whose faiths they are sacred.

EDMUND HENRY HYNMAN ALLENBY, General,
Commander-in-Chief Egyptian Expeditionary Force.

December 1917

LHCMA: Allenby papers 2/5/3.[130] Copy at OxAnt Allenby papers 1/1 and CZA K12/27/3

81
Robertson to Allenby
[Letter. Typescript with holograph additions. Dictated]

14 December 1917

SECRET & PERSONAL

I have been away a good deal lately attending Allied Conferences, and helping to set up Supreme War Councils, and many other things have occupied my attention. Therefore I may seem to have neglected you recently, and more especially in not sending you a wire of congratulations on the very successful advance you have recently made. I think that the operations reflect enormously to the credit of everybody concerned in them, not least to the troops themselves who must have had a hard and trying time. Everything seems to have gone beautifully.

But as you have got on so well some Members of the War Cabinet wish to continue the operations and I have been told to consider two alternative policies:–

(a) For the complete conquest of Palestine: [sic]

(b) For an advance up to and as far as Aleppo.

These policies were under discussion two days ago in my absence and a telegram was sent to you, being drafted by a Member of the War Cabinet, asking you to report as to the extent to which you could exploit your success with the force you now have plus one division. I do not know what your answer will be as it has not yet been received, nor do I wish to influence you in any way. You know my views in general strategy and they are unchanged except that they appeal to me more strongly now than ever before. This war will be won or lost on the West front, of this I am more convinced every day. Nineteen divisions have come over from the Russian to the West front during the last month or so and we shall soon have many more over. It is not a question of our winning the war next summer, unless the German internal conditions win it for us; it may rather be a question of our holding our own during next year until the Yanks come along.

Still this has nothing to do with you. You must carry out the policy assigned to you and for that your advice as to your requirements cannot be ignored. As I say, some of the War Cabinet wish to extend your operations and this desire seems to be based on the success you have recently achieved. Some of them seem to think that we deliberately over-rated the enemy's power of resistance in order to knock out the project entirely. I am sure no such idea ever entered your mind as it never entered mine. I was opposed to an advance on Jerusalem because I felt that it might involve commitments later on which we would find it difficult to meet. I still think so, and my only hope is that the Turk may be much less formidable than we suppose and that the Germans may not be able to help him, which I rather doubt may be the case. At any rate if it is to our advantage to knock out the Turk it must be to the German's advantage to support him. It is very difficult to please Ministers sometimes, as I told the Prime Minister yesterday. If we had under-estimated the Turk and had failed we should have deserved to be hung, but because we have succeeded more easily than might have been the case does not seem to justify blaming us for taking every precaution. After all I imagine it was a very near thing your getting on as well during the first week or so as you did, and if you had not got on then you would have had a long business and you would undoubtedly have required more divisions than you now have. I feel sure that in the operations your feelings have been quite different acting under your original instructions, which left you to do more or less as much fighting as you desired, than they would have been if you had been under a definite instruction to capture Jaffa and Jerusalem.

Of course I do not think that any Members of the War Cabinet really blame us for putting views forward on the safe side. I think that what they want to do is push on north and to persuade us to do it with such forces as you now have plus a division. Whether we should be justified in advising such a policy is a matter that I have not yet fully considered. A Paper is being prepared at the present time, and I am awaiting your telegram as to your views.

Please remember on all occasions that this and other private communications are never intended in the slightest degree to influence the views you put forward. Your job is to carry out the policy given you. At the same time it is necessary you should know my views, as I am sure you will agree, otherwise you might involve yourself in operations requiring reinforcements from me which could not possibly be given. My sole reason for giving you my views is this.

[Holograph addition:] Continued good luck to you. You have done splendidly.

PRO: WO106/718/55–58

82
Allenby to Lady Allenby
General Headquarters, Egyptian Expeditionary Force
[Letter. Holograph]   14 December 1917

I went to Jerusalem on the 12th and returned yesterday. Yesterday, morning, I reconnoitred our line, N. and E. slight fighting was in progress; and a few prisoners were coming in – fine, fighting Turks; well set up and well fed –. From the highest point of the Mount of Olives, E. of the city. I got a grand panorama. We looked down on the Dead Sea and the mouth of the Jordan – 4,000 ft. below us –. Above and beyond them rose the mountains of Moab; grandly dominating and impressive. To the west, Jerusalem lay below us; and, all around, a tumbled mass of rocky mountains. The day was very bright and clear; and we could see the Turkish motor boats on the Dead Sea. Later, I went to the railway station; where we are trying to repair and reconstruct what the Turks have damaged. Then Bols and I went to Bethlehem. There we met the dignitaries of the Church of the Nativity.[131] We went quite quietly; but, directly I was recognised, they roused the town. The church bells rang, and all the populace turned out. In the church, they shewed us the grotto of the manger, and the place where the Magi[132] worshipped; the tomb of St. Jerome,[133] and that of St. Eusebius.[134] When we came out, speeches were made. All the inhabitants were in the streets; and women seized my hand, and kissed it. It was interesting. Bethlehem is a pretty town; facing east to the Desert, Dead Sea, and the mountains of Moab. The Father Superior – or Vicar – shewed [sic] me from a window the spot where the angels appeared to the Shepherds on the first Christmas Eve. He and the rest of the clergy were of a much higher class than such people are as a rule. When we came out of the grotto, into the church, the organ played "God save the King"; and did it very well. I walked through Jerusalem later. I don't allow people in the old town, yet; and I wanted to see if all was in order. Everything was quiet. The town is of great interest. I'll tell you all about it some day. We saw the old vaulted bazaars, the Jews' wailing place – where two or three women were wailing – the site of the Temple and other places; but did not go into any holy site, as I have forbidden this and have them all guarded – otherwise they would be pulled to pieces, for "souvenirs"! On my official entry, we walked into the Holy City – because the Kaiser rode in –. It was said, then, that a better [man] than he had walked. He had a gap made in the wall, for him, I went in through the Jaffa gate; not through the gap, though within 20 yards of it.

I can't say yet, my sweetheart, when I can come to Cairo; nor can I give you an appointment date. However, when I see a chance, I will give warning; and I think it possible I may be able to get away for a day or two next month.

LHCMA: Allenby papers 1/8/33

83
Allenby to Robertson

[Telegram. Typescript]   14 December 1917
No. E.A.598

Your No. 47761, cipher, 12th December. I consider it essential, at present season with rains imminent and after recent experience of effect of comparatively small rainfall, that any advance northward during next two months can only be made step by step; owing to badness of roads I must depend on the progress of my railway. After January weather will keep on improving and in this part of Palestine summer weather is more suitable for campaigning than winter. I accordingly propose first, as essential, to advance to the line of the Wadi Auja flowing east and the Wadi El Jib, Wadi Abu

Lejja, Nahr Auja, flowing west, and to consolidate on that line. Secondly, I hope to operate against Hedjaz railway during wet season, while waiting for my railway to overtake me, as there are still, 20,000 Turks south of Amman. If found practicable this seems to offer best prospect of exploiting success already gained. Thirdly, if circumstances are favourable, I may gradually push forward my left towards Tul Keram covering railway construction and perfecting preparations for offensive with naval co-operation. Either as a reinforcement on this front or in the improbable event of trouble arising in Western Desert,[135] the division from Mesopotamia[136] will be very valuable.

LHCMA: Allenby papers 2/5/6. Copy at LHCMA: Robertson papers 4/5/10 Appendix II. Abridged copy at IWM: Dawnay papers 69/21/2 'Palestine 1917–18 Battle of Philistia'; copies at PRO: WO33/946, p. 80 and OxAnt: Allenby papers, 1/1; slightly different copy at PRO: WO158/611

84
Wingate to Allenby

Cairo

[Letter. Typescript. Copy]   16 December 1917

Clayton's and Lawrence's accounts of the entry into Jerusalem were very thrilling and I am so glad to know that this great historical event passed off so satisfactorily and without any untoward incidents. Everything goes to show how sound it was to insist on the single – as opposed to joint – administration and I am sure that the Home authorities will support it, though Mark Sykes is a bit carried away with the "exuberance of his own verbosity" in regard to Zionism and unless he goes a bit slower he may quite intentionally upset the applecart. However Clayton has written him an excellent letter which, I hope, may have an anodyne effect. I have had many talks with Lawrence who is staying with me and if his plans materialise they should help your aspirations considerably. I wish one could feel that affairs in France and Italy were as satisfactory as in Palestine – evidently Byng "bit off more than he could chew", and with a longer British line to look after and numbers depleted by sending Troops to Italy, it looks as if we were in for a more strenuous time than ever – perhaps winter may help us and enable America's weight to be fully felt when Spring comes.

SAD: Wingate papers 166/3/108

85
Robertson to Allenby

[Telegram. Typescript]   18 December 1917
No. 48236, cipher

I have been asked by the War Cabinet, who attach great importance to eliminating Turkey, to submit a project for carrying out following alternative policies:–

(*a*.) To complete the conquest of the whole of Palestine and hold the country for the remainder of the war.

(*b*.) To continue the advance through Palestine and Syria to the vicinity of Aleppo so as to cause permanent interruption of railway communication with Mesopotamia.

For the purpose of (*a*) Palestine is to be considered as embracing the whole country between Dan[137] and Beersheba.

Please send me your views as soon as possible as to the execution of these policies, with your estimate as to how long you will take for each operation.

LHCMA: Robertson papers 4/5/10 (appendix III to 'Future Operations in Palestine' by Robertson, 26 December 1917). Abridged copy at IWM: Dawnay papers 69/21/2 'Palestine 1917–18 Battle of Philistia.' Copy at WO33/946, p. 87. Slightly different copy at PRO: WO158/611 dated 19 December 1918 with prefix cipher 38236

86
Allenby to Lady Allenby

[Letter. Holograph]   19 December 1917

You can't be Duchess of Jerusalem; so you must be content with being the wife of a G.C.M.G. You may address me as such. It is the highest rank of this order – higher than a K.C.M.G. – Grand

Cross; not Knight Commander. I see it in the Egyptian Gazette today. I note that you have paid £100 into the National Bank. Rain has been threatening all day; and it has rained hard in Jerusalem and the mountains; but we have had nothing but showers. I was out this morning with the Yeomanry Mounted Division – General Barrow. I presented decorations to a great number of officers and men. Afterwards, the Division marched past; and did it very well. They have done splendid work, in the pursuit and in the mountain fighting. Then I rode to Askalon, on the coast. A very interesting place. Great ruins of Crusaders' castles, mixed with marble and granite columns, of the Roman remains, of the era of Herod. Partly overblown by sand dunes. All round, fertile gardens; vines, fig trees and date palms. Then I motored to my new camp – we having shifted camp today –. I am in the mouth of the Wadi Surar (Vale of Sorek – where Samson was born) through which runs the Jerusalem railway.

LHCMA: Allenby papers 1/8/37

87
Allenby to Robertson

[Telegram. Typescript]   20 December 1917
No. E.A. 657

19th. Your No. 48236, cipher, 18th. (*a*.) Understanding Dan to be about Banias, *i.e.*, half way between Nazareth and Damascus, I calculate I might be able by June or July to place force of my present strength north of Nazareth-Haifa line, assuming enemy cannot oppose me with more than about 60,000 fighting strength and provided there are no special difficulties met with in railway construction.

(*b*.) To advance further towards Aleppo would mean to move against Damascus and Beirut. On that front enemy is served by broad-gauge railway with good lateral communications and apparently ideal ground for defence. Broad-gauge railway would put him on level with me as regards numbers that could be maintained. I should require 16 or 18 divisions besides my mounted corps to ensure success against Damascus-Beirut line if strongly held, but this is probably more than my railway could support even when doubled and when allowance is made for sea transport. My estimate is made on the supposition enemy will make use of his broad-gauge railway to its full capacity. I would point out that Aleppo is 350 miles distant and my single line of railway advances about half a mile a day. Railhead of my double line is at Bir el Mazar, but the doubling of railway has had to be stopped during my present advance. For my immediate plans see my telegram No. E.A. 598 14th December, and I think it advisable before advancing much further north to clear Turkish forces on Medina railway.

LHCMA: Robertson papers 4/5/10 (appendix IV to 'Future Operations in Palestine' by Robertson, 26 December 1917). Copy at PRO: WO33/946, p. 94; abridged copy with prefix 38236 at IWM: Dawnay papers 69/21/2 'Palestine 1917–18 Battle of Philistia.' Slightly different copy at PRO: WO158/611 dated 19 December 1918

88
Allenby to Wigram
General Headquarters, Egyptian Expeditionary Force
[Letter. Holograph]   22 December [1917]

Thank you for your letter of the 28th Nov.; and I offer my humble thanks to the King for His Majesty's kind message to me.

Since last I wrote, events have moved rapidly and widely; and His Majesty will be already acquainted with what has happened. I sent home a despatch, dated 16th inst. – covering the whole course of my campaign up to that date. After the capture of the Gaza-Beersheba line I sent the whole of my available mounted troops and two divisions of infantry to press the pursuit. This was all that I could supply; and to do this, the transport had to be taken from other troops – rendering them immobile for the time –. The direction of the pursuit was across the plain of Philistina; in a Northerly direction, towards junction station W. of Jerusalem. The Hebron road was watched by the 53rd Division, N. of Beersheba, and the Corps Cavalry Regiment of the XX Corps.

The Turks put up strong rearguard resistance; and, on the 13th, gave battle on the line El Kubeibeh-Beit Jibrin. This was a front of 20 miles, and his available force was not more than 20,000. The 75th and 52nd Divisions – XXI Corps – attacked the centre. The Australian Mounted Division on right of XX Corps, and on its left the remainder of the Desert Mounted Corps. A great feature in this battle was the capture of Katrah and El Mughar[138] position by the 52nd Division, helped by a daring dash of the 6th Mounted Brigade.

By evening, the enemy's resistance was broken; and he was falling back. Next morning, we seized junction station. A little rolling stock was captured; and this, with some available from Egypt, enabled us to make use of the Turkish narrow gauge railway. Its capacity was very limited; but it helped us a great deal, subsequently. By the evening of the 15th, the Desert Mounted Corps had occupied Ramleh and Ludd; and Jaffa was entered on the 16th. On the morning of the 15th took place a brilliant action by the 6th Mounted Brigade; who captured the ridge of Abu Shusher (Gazer[139]) by a mounted attack, followed by this mounted action. It was then that Neil Primrose[140] was killed. He is buried at Ramleh, in the grounds of the Latin Convent. It was because of immediate importance to gain the road leading N. from Jerusalem.

My supply situation would not allow me to bring up the XX Corps; so I directed the 75th and 52nd Divisions to move through the mountains by the Jerusalem main road; the only road practicable for vehicles; and the passes N. of it (Ajalon) while the Yeomanry Mounted Division took the road through Beith Sor el Tahta and Foka[141] (Betheron, lower and upper[142]). Though these Divisions had been marching and fighting for three weeks, they stormed the passes brilliantly. By evening of the 21st, we held the commanding ridge of Nebu Samwil; which proved to be the key of the mountains. It was from this point that Richard Coeur de Lion once saw Jerusalem. The Yeomanry had reached Beitunia; but opposition was too strong for them, and they had to fall back to Beit [sic] Sor el Tahta. The mountains are of the most barren and stony nature; a tangle of rocky peaks, precipices and ravines; roadless and mostly waterless. Artillery could with difficulty be moved and our infantry and dismounted cavalry could not be adequately supported thereby.

Consequently, my attack came to a standstill by the 24th; and I ordered a pause till I could bring up the XX Corps and relieve my exhausted troops on the mountains and in the passes.

By the 5th Dec. I was able to attack again, with the XX Corps. The 60th and 74th Divisions were to attack west [sic] and North West of Jerusalem, at dawn; and, pivoting on Nebi Samwil, to gain a position astride the Jerusalem-Nablus road to the N. The 53rd Division had come up the Hebron road; and was to get across the Jericho road, and to protect the right flank of the 60th Division.

The attack succeeded, according to plan, in spite of heavy and cold rain and mists. On the 9th, the Mayor of Jerusalem gave the submission of the city to the XX Corps. I established, at once, a Military Governor and Administration. Brig.-General Borton,[143] lately Postmaster General in Egypt, was appointed to this post.

On the 11th I made my official entry, on foot; accompanied by the commanders of the French and Italian Detachments and by the military attachés of France, Italy and the U.S.A. I was also accompanied by M. Picot – head of the Picot Mission –. We rode to the Jaffa gate. There we dismounted; and, forming a procession, entered the city by the Jaffa Gate. Alongside the gate, is the wide gap made in the wall for the German Emperor. This we purposely avoided. The proclamation of martial law was read out, in various languages, from the steps of the Citadel. Subsequently, I received the heads of the various churches, the Spanish Consul, and the Mayor.

Our reception was cordial everywhere; and, from the Christians, enthusiastic. A few days later I visited Bethlehem; unofficially. However, when my identity was known, the whole population turned into the streets. The Vicar of the Church of the Nativity took us into the Church. The bells were pealed; and our National Anthem was played on the organ. Outside, the populace crowded round me; shouting, "Vive les Anglais, Vive le Roi George"; and the leading inhabitants charged me to convey to His Majesty their message of gratitude and devotion to him. There was no doubt about the sincerity of the whole demonstration.

I had purposely gone unofficially, to avoid giving any offence to French or Italian susceptibilities. We have guards on all the Holy places – Moslem guards on the Mahommedan sites – and the French and Italian troops share these guards. The administration, however, is purely British; and must remain so until military conditions allow of a change. I am now engaged in widening my area, round Jerusalem and Jaffa. At present, the Turks are not more than 3 or 4 miles from Jerusalem. I must get Bireh, to the N., before I am comfortable. N. of Jaffa, the XXI Corps are now pushing the Turks N. of the R. Auja, and gaining ground in the Vale of Sharon. Both Bulfin, of that Corps; and Chetwode, of XX, have done brilliantly. Jerusalem was captured in exactly 40 days from the start of the campaign; and the day coincided with the feast of Judas Maccabeus[144] – the day he freed the Holy City from Graeco-Syrian rule. This coincidence has made a great influence on the Jewish communities, between Jaffa and the mountains, of which there are many.

The Turks have fought well, but have suffered great losses. We have taken between 12,000 and 13,000 prisoners, and get more daily. Our capture of guns is about 100, as far as I know; but probably many more are abandoned among the foothills. We have taken nearly half a million shell; 20,000,000 small arm rounds; scores of machine guns; and have accounted for over 20 enemy aeroplanes, while I have only lost one. Lately, we have been bombing Turkish depots on the Dead Sea shore; and their trading boats. Our aeroplanes, so engaged, have flown as low as 500 ft. below sea level – the Dead Sea surface being some 1300 ft below the level of the Mediterranean –. Today my bombers are pursuing retreating Turks; who are falling back N. of Jaffa, on Tabsor, before the XXI Corps. Our ships are cooperating, as are some French craft; but the Turks are careful now not to use roads along the coast where our naval guns can reach them.

I enclose one or two specimens of the maps we issue daily, shewing [sic] dispositions.

I present my humble duty to His Majesty, and remain.

PS: Excuse this scrawl; I have written it hurriedly, to catch a dispatch ride. Rain has been playing the mischief with our roads, and I have been shifting camp forward; so have been hurried. I am now in the Wadi Surar (Vale of Sorek, Samson's birthplace) a wide valley, narrowing into a defile through the mountains – through which runs the Jerusalem railway –. We are amongst the Shephelah, a foothills; rough country, like a Scottish [?] deer forest without the heather.

Royal Archive: RA PS/GV/Q 2521/15

89
Allenby to Lady Allenby

[Letter. Holograph]   30 December 1917

Twenty one years ago we were married. Since then I have had twenty one years of perfect happiness. That happiness has been marred by one great sorrow; but the remembrance of Michael will always be with us, and will be nothing but a joy. The sorrow not to have known him would be far greater than the grief of losing him for a while. For all the happiness, I thank you; my Wife.

I was up at Bire and Beitin (Bethel) today; 10 miles N. of Jerusalem. We really won a big victory. The Turks meant to retake Jerusalem. We utterly defeated them; and we gained all the ground we wanted. They lost very heavily and of their best troops. We estimate that we killed and wounded some 5,000; and we took 600 or 700 prisoners; but we have not got accurate figures yet.

LHCMA: Allenby papers 1/8/39

90
Wingate to Allenby

                                                    The Residency Cairo
[Letter. Typescript. Copy]   31 December 1917

Any telegrams which I receive from Clayton dealing purely with matters connected with the Sykes–Picot agreement[145] I send on in Clayton's name, but other telegrams I receive from him on political and administrative questions in Palestine (outside the

Sykes-Picot Agreement) I treat as coming from you on the assumption that Clayton is acting in a dual capacity, viz: as Sykes' *alter ego* on the one hand and as your C.P.O. on the other. I think that for political reasons it is important to make a distinction, and perhaps it might save misunderstandings if telegrams dealing with the political and administrative details (outside the Sykes-Picot Agreement) and which you desire to pass through me to Government, should come over your signature and not over Clayton. I do not know what your views are on the subject, but it seems to me that if Clayton (whose official status is in collaboration with Picot) takes to signing on political and administrative matters (outside the agreement), we shall be giving Picot a handle to claim a share in the administration.

SAD: Wingate papers 166/3/267–8

Chapter 2
The Transjordan Raids and the Battle of Megiddo, January– October 1918

Robertson to Allenby (Chief LONDON to Chief Egypforce)
[Telegram. Typescript]
Despatched 1915 on 2 January 1918, received 0800 on 3 January 1918
49150 cipher
SECRET

Your E.A.657, December 20th.

Question of future policy in PALESTINE has not yet been settled by War Cabinet, but I hope for a decision before long. In the meantime please send your observations on the following points:–

A. You do not say how far north of NAZARETH-HAIFA line you expect to be able to place your force by June or July. Does this mean that in your opinion you will be able to complete conquest of PALESTINE effectively by this time, taking northern frontier of PALESTINE to be in latitude of BANIAS[1] and that country to include area east of SEA of TIBERIAS to about longitude MEZERIB?

B. It is understood that you consider that PALESTINE when conquered could be held by force at your disposal including 7th Division.[2]

C. Regarding strength of the enemy, during past few weeks a large part of his force has suffered severe defeat; in all probability its morale is low; large amounts of ammunition have been lost and stores are difficult to replace and apparently transport is very short. Nevertheless, we estimate that you may possibly be opposed before long by 60,000 combatants including about 11,000 Germans, and that this force might be increased to 70,000 or 80,000 by middle of February.

We are inclined to believe that further increases would be prevented by transport difficulties and that in any case maximum force enemy could subsequently maintain in DAMASCUS area would be 100,000 combatants (-------?-------)* he would have sufficient surplus of troops to relieve from time to time some of these troops.

Please understand that all the above does not refer to the alternative policy of further advance to ALEPPO, but to the conquest and retention of PALESTINE.

IWM: Dawnay papers 69/21/2 'Palestine 1917–18 Battle of Philistia.' Slightly different copies at PRO: WO33/946, p. 121 and PRO: WO158/611

92
Allenby to Robertson (Chief Egypforce to Chief LONDON)

[Telegram. Typescript]　　　Despatched 2305 on 3 January 1918
E.A. 693 cipher
SECRET

Your 49150 cipher of 2nd.

When reference is made in my E.A. 657 cipher of 19/12/17 to "North of NAZARETH-HAIFA line" it means my occupation of defensive line only sufficiently far north to afford adequate protection to the lateral road and railway. Say a line from TIBERIAS to just north of ACRE and with right flank refused and covered by the JORDAN against possible incursion from DERAA. Even without taking into consideration stoppage of railway construction in order to operate against enemy's

---

*　Group undecipherable, reads "been".

NABLUS-TUL KERAM line, it would be May before my railhead can be far enough north to make it possible for me to operate in any force against the enemy's line south of AFULE-HAIFA.

Therefore at the earliest I could not bring up all necessary material and complete all my preparations for an advance against AFULE-HAIFA until well into June, and I could not expect to reach a line TIBERIAS – N. of ACRE until July.

With regard to "B", I consider at present that the force now at my disposal, if the 7th Indian Division is added, would enable me to hold PALESTINE up to the TIBERIAS-ACRE line, provided that the enemy cannot deploy for offensive and maintain during his offensive a force of more than 70,000 or 80,000 troops mentioned under "C" and provided my formations were constantly kept up to establishment.

With regard to your "C", I gather that you think there is a possibility that a larger force than I had been counting on may oppose my advance northwards. The question is mainly one of what the enemy can maintain on his single metre gauge railway at various points. I had been reckoning that he would not be able to maintain more than 60,000 to 65,000 fighting, or say a total ration strength of 90,000 to 95,000, south of the latitude of DERAA. But if he can oppose me by the middle of February with a fighting strength of 70,000 to 80,000, it is probable that any effective advance from my present line will be impossible without an increase in my force.

My railway will only be just far enough forward by the middle of February to allow of preparations for an operation against the NAB-LUS [sic] –TUL KERAM line.

My fighting strength in Cavalry and Infantry was about 97,000 on October 30th, it is now 69,000. In your expression "combatants" artillery is presumably included, but a sufficient margin in my favour to allow of a general offensive would not necessarily be afforded by the difference between my strength at full establishment and a combatant strength of 80,000.

I could not deploy more troops, even if I had them, until my railway line is doubled. Since operations began it has not been possible to continue the doubling of the line eastward of MAZAR, and while forward construction proceeds it will not be possible to do so.

Railway progress has been greatly delayed by wet weather and it is now much less than ½ a mile a day, and the line already in use has been greatly damaged by wash-outs, etc.

In any case I consider it essential to consolidate my position on my present line and to dislodge the enemy garrison at JERICHO and secure my eastern flank as far as the JORDAN.

IWM: Dawnay papers 69/21/2 'Palestine 1917–18 Battle of Philistia.' Copy at PRO: WO158/611. Slightly different copy at PRO: WO33/946, p. 127

93
Allenby to DMI[3] (GOC-in-C Egypt to DMI)

[Telegram. Typescript]   15 January 1918
No. 11205

Your No. 49842 of 11th January. Attitude of the Moslems hitherto for the most part non-committal, partly due to natural Moslem preference for Moslem rule and partly to fear of Turk's return.

Improvement is noticeable as this probability lessens.

Partisans of Sheriff genuinely pleased, but somewhat apprehensive of signs indicating rise of Jewish influence and possible predominance.

East of Jerusalem to Bir El Saba[4] attitude of Bedouin varies according to locality, but where it is unsatisfactory it is due to Turkish influence, the remnants of which will take time to eradicate. It is remarked that measures taken to protect Moslem sacred places caused universal satisfaction.

Occupation of Jerusalem and Palestine is welcomed by Jews as opening new era in their history.

Overjoyed at Mr. Balfour's declaration[5] which was only known authoritatively after occupation of Jerusalem. Great impetus has been given to Zionism everywhere.

Christians universally welcome occupation and freedom from enemy yoke.

Austrians and Germans are grateful for conciliatory treatment and some are even glad to be quit of Turks.[6]

See weekly telegram to Foreign Office from General Clayton.

PRO: WO33/946, p. 153

94
Allenby to Robertson

General Headquarters, Egyptian Expeditionary Force
[Letter. Holograph] 25 January 1918
SECRET

We are having a spell of beautiful weather – as an interval in the rains – and my railways and roads are being repaired and developed. My standard gauge railway is now up to Ludd, and it runs ¼ mile W. of my new Headquarters. I moved, a fortnight ago, from my camp in the Wadi Surar, to a house 2 miles W. of Ramleh – drier, warmer and healthier.

As you know, I have now a good defensive line; from N.E. of Jerusalem, to the sea N. of Jaffa. I propose to consolidate on this line, and develope [sic] my communications; which, in the rainy season, are very untrustworthy. Then I want to extend my right, to include Jericho and the N. of the Dead Sea. Later, I hope to be able to push across the Jordan, and throw a big raid, past Salt, against the Hedjaz Railway. If I could destroy 10 or 15 miles of rail and some bridges; and get [in] touch with the Arabs under Feisal – even temporarily – the effect would be great. But all depends on my communications, and on my numbers being kept up. I note that you propose to send me 19 Battalions of Indians. I don't quite understand yet whether the British battalions they replace are to be broken up to reinforce others – and, if so, whether I shall be allowed to keep those reinforcements; or whether they are meant for Europe. You will know, without my saying, that the introduction of the Indian battalions into my war-tried and experienced Divisions will, for a time, lessen their fighting value.

However, they will no doubt train into useful troops. The Turks are busied with digging, and strengthening their positions; and are not, nor can be for a long time, capable of a serious offensive. Their strength, positions and resources you know as well as I; as all our information goes to you; and you have had my views as to future possibilities.

There appears to be a desire, at home, to set up foreign administrations in this land.

I will let you know as soon as I think that such a course is possible. At present it would be very objectionable, and would hamper me greatly. When my position is secure; and when my roads and railways are working smoothly and surely – which may not be till after the rains are past – then I shall know better what to advise.

At present, I have had to send two divisions of my mounted troops and the Imperial Camel Corps[7] south of Gaza; as I can't feed them, with certainty; and, even now, a fortnight's heavy rain would bring me near starvation. I have refused to allow the Bishop in Jerusalem to come up. I have also stopped the foreign consuls, and all whose presence here is not necessary. The presence of Picot is keenly resented by the Italians; who don't believe that he is merely here to advise me in case questions arise touching Syrian Arabs – nor does Picot for that matter. He is a very pleasant fellow, and he and I are good friends; but he came out with the idea that he would have a share in the administration, and does not like his present position of nonentity. I have just cabled to you, on the subject of the French Protectorate in the Holy Land. He claims that, as French Representative, he is entitled to assume the rights and dignities enjoyed by the French Representative before the war. This includes a special dais in the Churches, at Sunday Mass; and other honours. I have told him that I shall not forbid him to assume these dignities in Church; but have asked him not to do so, as his attitude is likely to provoke ill-feeling and quarrels. He answers, in a friendly manner, that he cannot comply with my request, as it would be tantamount to resigning the position of French Representative.

The other churches, and the Italians are angry and; in Jerusalem, angry priests often come to blows in the Holy Places.

I have therefore instructed my Military Administrator to inform the Dignitaries that the status quo ante bellum must continue, during my military administration; and that I will not tolerate religious riots. That is the only attitude I can take up; though, no doubt, after the war – or even before the end of the war, when civil administration is set up – the French Protectorate may be abolished or modified. In all other ways, Picot behaves well; though he naturally tries to keep himself in the limelight as much as he can. There is nothing else for him to do in the Holy Land, but to walk round and shew [sic] himself. My only point is this; that, while military administration is required, it must be purely British, and under the British C.i.C. I can't budge an inch on that.

LHCMA: Robertson papers 7/5/84

95
Robertson to Allenby (CIGS to GOC-in-C Egypt)

[Telegram. Typescript]   28 January 1918
51182 cipher

Urgent. Foreign Office urge that it is desirable for commission[8] of Zionist leaders, with Dr. Weizmann as president to leave for Cairo about 15th February and proceed thence at your convenience to Palestine, as the present Zionist representation in Palestine is inadequate and owing to the importance of bringing their responsible leaders in touch with Arab leaders and representatives of other communities in Palestine.

Foreign Office suggest that Ormsby-Gore should be in charge of commission with temporary rank of Major, attached to Clayton's Staff and should act under your orders. There will be about seven members representing Great Britain, Russia, United States of America, France and Poland, exclusive of a secretary, a financial secretary and an agricultural expert. It may be necessary for Captain Bentwich to be attached as legal adviser.[9]

The commission would study prevention of land speculation during the war, re-opening of Jewish banks, establishment of good relations with non-Jewish elements, and the eventual laying, under British auspices, of foundation stone of Hebrew university near

Jerusalem[10] which might have far-reaching influence on Jewish world in enemy countries. The commission will have much to do in Cairo, in the first place, in connection with Arabs, Arab Bureau[11] and local Zionists.

I recommend proposal. If you concur please telegraph.[12]

PRO: WO33/946, p. 186

96
Chetwode to Allenby

Headquarters XXth Corps

[Letter. Typescript]   2 February 1918

When your Assistant Military Secretary announced that a small special list of honours for your Palestine campaign was to be submitted, he stated that we were not to send in the names of any Divisional Commanders, but that it would be better to write to you privately about them.

I therefore write to you now on the subject of the services of my Divisional Commanders.

As regards fighting the 60th Division have had slightly the most, as they fought at SHERIA and HUJ when the others were resting, the 74th and 53rd have had about the same, the 10th rather less but what the latter have done has been a very finished performance.

As regards commanders the services of Major-General Shea, C.B., D.S.O., stand out, he has fought his Division throughout with boldness, skill, and success, and has on four occasions been charged with special missions involving independent decisions, viz:–

> the conduct of the main attack by the 60th and 74th Divisions at BIR SABA,
> the advance on SHERIA and HUJ,
> the main attack on JERUSALEM, and
> the command of the right wing of the Corps (53rd and 60th Divisions) in the fighting on the 27th and 30th December

I venture to submit that he has performed exceptional services.

Major-General Longley, C.B., has shown himself to be a Commander who prepares with skill and thoroughness and executes with boldness and determination. His attack on HAREIRA and his conduct at the counter attack on the 27th to 30th December, when he commanded the left wing of the Corps, were both really good features of work. His Division is the best disciplined and his staff work the best in the Corps.

I hope you may see your way to recommend his services.

Major-General Girdwood and Major-General Mott have both done very good work, but neither are in the class of the two former Generals as Commanders.

As both of them have been recently rewarded, viz:–, Girdwood a Brevet Colonelcy and Mott a C.B., I venture to recommend that any further recommendation be reserved for the half-yearly list.

IWM: Chetwode papers, P183, folder 7

97
Robertson to Allenby
[Letter. Typescript with holograph additions. Dictated]
SECRET & PERSONAL   2 February 1918

I am sending you officially by Colonel Kirke certain documents regarding the question of offensive operations in your theatre, about which Smuts is coming to see you.[13] In your dealings with Smuts you will of course be concerned mainly with your own theatre, but it seems to me to be folly for you to try to give advice as to what can be attempted in it without having some information with respect to the main theatre the security of which is now authoritatively admitted to be vital to the Allied interests. What I mean chiefly is that you should in giving your information as to your own theatre remember what is likely to happen in others and what the effect of that may be upon you. For instance, I see no prospect whatever of sending you more divisions than you now have, except perhaps one from Mesopotamia and even this is doubtful. Similarly as regards drafts. We may expect very heavy fighting indeed on the West front this year, and to meet it we shall have to supply the necessary drafts. I see no insuperable difficulty in your going further forward for a considerable distance, but I fail to see any useful gain thereby. You need to go so far and do so much. More especially I am doubtful as to the extent to which we can continue holding on to a more advanced position for a time[14] which is quite indefinite. lastly [sic], I am doubtful of the Turk being knocked out by any effort you can make with your present force plus such small additions as we may be able to give. I have not mentioned this in the official letter I am sending you because I do not wish you to think that I am trying to tie your hands, but I do wish to prevent[15] you finding yourself in the cart later on.

LHCMA: Robertson papers 8/1/84.

98
Allenby to Battine

[Letter. Holograph]   22 February 1918

I have your letters of 14th, 15th, 16th and 28th Jan. Mails have been irregular; and come in groups, when they don't go to Davy Jones.

Robertson has now gone, and Wilson reigns in his stead. Rawly to Versailles.[16] Here my information stops. I don't know Rawly's successor. Smuts has been with me for week – in Palestine and Syria –. He has just left for home. I took him round all my front. I have done great roadmaking; and I can run in a motor car to most places, even in the mountains.

Yesterday I took Jericho, and got to the Jordan and Dead Sea. What my next step will be, I can't yet say. The country was awful, and the weather bad; but the troops fought brilliantly, as usual. I see that Repington and the Morning Post are in trouble, already. I have not heard who has replaced him with the "Times".[17]

IWM: Battine papers 90/37/1

99
Allenby to Robertson
General Headquarters, Egyptian Expeditionary Force
[Letter. Holograph]   23 February 1918

Thank you for your letter of the 26th January which I received by the last mail. I am very sorry to know that you are no longer at the W.O. Your departure[18] will be looked on, by the whole army, as a serious misfortune.

However, you will not be far away, and will be available at need. Smuts has just left the country. He spent a few days in Palestine, on my front. Then we went to Cairo, and met Gillman from Mesopotamia.[19] Smuts had a clear policy of action framed in his mind; and we merely discussed the method of carrying it out. I won't go into questions of Imperial Strategy; but from a local standpoint, the plan appears feasible.

We have pushed down into the Jordan valley, and taken Jericho, during the past week. Jericho is a typhus-haunted spot; and I don't occupy the village, but hold the heights above it. Soon, I hope to cross the river, and get to the Hedjaz railway; joining hands with the Arabs, and really breaking the line. The Arabs, led by Lawrence, have been doing pretty well; but they are an unstable lot. Lawrence has just come over to see me. He thinks the Arab movement will spread and increase now, if we continue to encourage them and to give them money; but they cannot run alone, and must have British leaders whom they know and trust. The Turks on my Northern front are quiescent, and shew [sic] signs of concentrating further back. Not many opposed me at Jericho; and they, some 2 or 3 thousand and 8 guns, have crossed the Jordan towards Es Salt. They are making some preparations to attack the Arabs, S of Kerak; but I don't anticipate much trouble there.

LHCMA: Robertson papers 7/5/86 (old number I/21/86a)

100
Robertson to Allenby

[Telegram. Typescript] 7 March 1918
No. 53711 Cipher

War Cabinet have considered General Smuts' proposals,[20] and they are of opinion that in consequence of the doubtful situation on Persian frontier, the approach of hot weather, which affects transport of troops in the Persian Gulf and the Red Sea, the advance of the Turks on the Caucasus front, the requirements of France in railway material and men, and the difficulty of providing the full amount of shipping required, some modification is necessary.

Modifications are as follows:– One Indian division and four batteries 6–inch howitzers will be transferred from Mesopotamia to you. They will begin embarkation at Basra about end of March, and should be complete in Egypt by end of May. The native battalions from India and the Indian cavalry from France will be substituted for white formations, as it will not be possible to keep the whole of your existing white formations up to full strength in any other way. By end of April the Indian cavalry should all have arrived.

It is probable that your requirements in land transport can be met, but I should like to know definitely on the above basis what these will be for your force.

As regards railway material and personnel, with track already promised you and the El Daba line we calculate you can complete doubling to Rafa and carry your standard gauge some distance beyond Haifa. Endeavours will be made to make up your locomotives to 152 and wagons to 3,245 by July, and after that date, as shipping becomes available, can send further locomotives and wagons. One Canadian construction battalion will be sent you from France as soon as arrangements for replacing it are complete. These are now in hand and will shortly be completed, and I expect in a few days' time to be able to give you date of arrival in Egypt. This will be followed later by another battalion now forming in Canada. I hope to be able to get you from Mesopotamia some railway personnel and labour, for there our policy will be an active defence with a possible extension of our sphere of operations into Persia as far as Hamadan,²¹ in order to counteract Bolshevik and enemy intrigues and enterprises.

As regards aircraft, for the present the requirements of France must have precedence, and, therefore, the most that can be given you at present is four additional squadrons during the coming summer in addition to the squadron now forming.

War Cabinet desire you to continue your operations against the Turks with all energy, which with the additions specified above, the means at your disposal admit. They attach importance to cutting the Hedjaz railway as already planned, and desire to know when you can be ready to make a northward advance.

LHCMA: Allenby papers 2/5/7. Copies at PRO: WO33/946, p. 260 and OxAnt: Allenby papers, 1/1

101
War Office to Allenby (WO to GOC-in-C Egypt)

[Telegram. Typescript]   17 March 1918
No. 54424 cipher A.G. 13

Your No. E.A. 946 of 10 March.²² In regard to men of the Jewish battalion the general policy is, that while it is undesirable to enlist Russian Jews any further, no objection exists to those or other nationalities who wish to enlist being enrolled provided they are able to produce satisfactory references. This policy is being carried out in regard to those from America. Colonel Patterson, who commanded the Zion Mule Corps²³ with success, should be able to ensure that undesirable characters do not remain undetected. If men enlisted already should not prove to be satisfactory, you should deal with them as soldiers under the military code.

PRO: WO33/946, p. 283

102
Allenby to War Office (GOC-in-C Egypt to WO)

[Telegram. Typescript]   20 March 1918
E.A.996

Reference your No. 54424, 17 March. According to Colonel
Patterson's report a certain number of Russian Jews in 38th Bn.
Royal Fusiliers consider that owing to Russian peace they should
be released from service. These Russians say that Great Britain
recognizes peace in that latterly she has refrained from calling up
Russian subjects for British Army. I recommend that an offer of
release be made to these men.

PRO: WO33/946, p. 291

103
Wilson to Allenby

London, S.W.1.
[Letter. Typescript. Copy]   21 March 1918

Last week I had two talks with General Foch about the troops that
the French insist upon sending out to you. He told me that for the
most part the troops he was sending would be good fighting
material – this I personally very much doubt – and I have asked
him to give me a programme showing in detail the troops he
proposes to send and the dates on which he sends them. If you
find that the troops he sends are of indifferent quality, or are ill-
equipped for the work in hand, send me a wire and I will at once
stop any others of that description being sent to you. As you know,
there is the political as well as the military side of this aid which
the French insist on giving us.

As regards your Yeomanry regiments set free by the arrival of the
Indian Cavalry, our present estimate is that after filling your
people up and leaving the required number over for drafts, there
will still be some 5000 Yeomanry that we can bring back to France
and turn into battalions of machine gunners. This will be a great

help on the Western Front where we are quite out-matched in Machine and Lewis guns by the Bosche.

As you will have seen by the wire we have sent you, the Man-Power question at Home keeps on being a constant source of anxiety and so long as the Government do not see their way to put in conscription on to my country it seems to me that we are bound to get shorter and shorter in men.

I heard from Shea that C.B. Thomson[24] is again rather at a loose end. If you cannot profitably use him will you let me know and I will see what can be done, either here or in some other theatre. He is much too valuable a man, as regards his brain, to be allowed to remain a C.R.E. of a Division.

Arthur Money is coming out to you as your Military Civil Governor and I am sure will do the work well. He was rather upset at the idea of going to the East again, having done 23 years in the East during his service, but he quite saw that he would be probably more use there than anywhere else, as he admitted that owing to want of opportunity he was really not fit to take command of a Division in France.

I am moving out Whigham[25] and Maurice,[26] both of whom will get Divisions in France, and taking in their places Tim Harington[27] and P. de B. Radcliffe.[28]

I am sending out Tom Bridges[29] to America to boss up all the Military Missions now there. He was a great success when he was there with Balfour and when he had two legs; he will be a colossal success with only one leg.

I think Sir Douglas [Haig] proposes to move Kavanagh[30] into an Infantry Corps, give Peyton[31] the Cavalry Corps, and make Ruggles-Brise[32] his Military Secretary.

I cannot think of any other gossip for the minute. Will you write to me whenever there is anything that you think I can do to help, and I hope to send you a letter of gossip and information much more often in future.

IWM: Wilson papers HHW2/33A/1A

104
Allenby to War Office (GOC-in-C to WO)

[Telegram. Typescript]   25 March 1918
E.A. 1015

24th, 8 p.m. Three bridges were thrown across Jordan at
Ghoraniyeh during the night of 23rd–24th March, and by 8 a.m.,
LXth Division, (?) Anzac Mounted Division and Imperial Camel
Corps Brigade were east of river: by 5.30 p.m., LXth Division
advancing in north-easterly direction had reached line Tel el
Musta to El Haud with advance guard at 127 M 27.

On the right, 2nd Australian Light Horse and New Zealand
Mounted Rifles Brigade, moving up Wadi el Kefrein and the Wadi
in 127 U 22 and U 17 had sent forward a light detachment to
secure bridge at El Howeij. On the left, 1st Australian Light Horse
Brigade had reached the vicinity of Wadi Abu Tarra. Advance
which was opposed by Turkish troops, supported by German
mass formations, was made through mountainous ground, which
greatly favoured the defence. 22nd Bn. London Regiment carried
out brilliant attacks on a hostile battery, the whole battery being
captured after our Lewis machine gunners had shot the teams.
During the days' operations 40 prisoners were taken of whom 35
were Germans, including 3 German officers, 4 field guns, 2
machine guns; advance is continuing.

PRO: WO33/946, p. 267

105
War Office to Allenby (WO to GOC-in-C Egypt)

[Telegram. Typescript]   27 March 1918
No. 55614 cipher D.M.O.

1. In continuation of my No. 54881 of 23rd March,[33] the situation
in France[34] necessitates the cancelling of instructions contained in
my No. 53711 of 7th March.[35]
2. You will adopt a policy of active defence in Palestine as soon as
the operations you are now undertaking are completed.

3. The LIInd Division (less artillery) will be sent to France as soon as shipping can be made available with the artillery of the VIIth Indian Division. It is desired be sent to France one other British division, either on arrival of IIIrd Indian Division, or before, if you consider the situation in Palestine admits of this. Which division would you send?

4. In view of change of policy, what heavy artillery can you spare? Personnel is urgently needed in France, and if you cannot spare complete batteries, could be made good later [sic].

5. Despatch of all additional transport and railway material and labour for advance to Haifa has been cancelled, but your normal upkeep will be met.

6. The despatch of four additional flying squadrons will be delayed.

7. Replacement of British by Indian units, as already notified, will be carried out.

Further details concerning this will shortly be communicated to you.

PRO: WO33/946, p. 302

106
Allenby to War Office (GOC-in-C to War Office)

[Telegram. Typescript]   30 March 1918
E.A.1034

29th, 11 p.m. East of Jordan there is no material change in the situation. Our troops, who are nearly encircling the town, were twice attacked by the enemy in Amman, but the attacks were repulsed. 5 miles of railway track south of Amman Station have now been destroyed.

We destroyed an enemy plane, which landed near the railway line. No change west of Jordan.

PRO: WO33/946, p. 307

107
Allenby to War Office (GOC-in-C Egypt to War Office
[Telegram. Typescript]   31 March 1918
E.A.1039

30th, 8 p.m. East of Jordan at 2 a.m. the 181st Infantry Brigade
and New Zealand Mounted Rifle Brigade and Imperial Camel
Corps attacked Amman, Hill 3039[36] (142 Z 7) was captured and
two lines of trenches carried south-east of village. As the enemy
hold strong positions covering station, further progress towards
Amman station was not possible.[37]

Five miles of track and culverts have been destroyed south of
Amman Station and (?) bridge at 142 X 11D has been blown up.[38]
As the capture of Amman Station would involve considerable loss
and as the object of the raid has been achieved by destruction of
railway, which will prevent traffic for a considerable period, the
raiding force will withdraw to-night to Es Salt. During operations
east of Jordan, 700 prisoners, four field guns and several machine
guns have been captured and 21 lorries which were found derelict,
were destroyed.

PRO: WO33/946, p. 312

108
Allenby to Battine
[Letter. Holograph]   1 April [1918]

Yours of 14th–18th just came. I note what you say about your
brother, but have not heard that he is coming my way. Probably, he
goes to Mesopotamia. The Germans have made a good beginning.
Now we are hoping that they are being stopped. I see that Foch
has been made C.i.C of the two armies. I've no comment to make,
on anything. Here, I have raided the Hedjaz railway, 40 miles East
of Jordan; and have done much damage. But my little show
dwindles now into a very insignificant affair in comparison with
events in Europe.

IWM: Battine papers 90/37/1

109
War Office to Allenby

[Telegram. Typescript]   2 April 1918
No. 55550 cipher M.O.2

You [sic] telegrams No. E.A.1039 of 30th March, No. E.A.1042 of
31st March, and your E.A.1046 of 1st April. Is presumption
correct that you are withdrawing completely to west of Jordan
without leaving any detachment at Es Salt?[39]

Will you please state date by which you estimate Turks can
repair railway about Amman, also possibility of further raids on
Hejaz railway through Madeba or south of Dead Sea.[40] To what
extent did the Arab Hejaz forces and Feisal co-operate during the
Amman operations?

I should like to have your views regarding situation east of
Jordan and Dead Sea generally, with special reference to Arab
situation, which does not appear to be wholly satisfactory.

PRO: WO33/946, p. 317

110
Allenby to War Office (GOC-in-C Egypt to War Office)

[Telegram. Typescript]   5 April 1918
No. E.A.1065

Your No. 55550 cipher M.O.1 [sic – 2 above], 3 April [sic – 2nd
above]. All troops have been withdrawn from Es Salt. Situation is
now as stated in my No. E.A.1053, cipher, 3rd April. I intend for
the present to maintain bridgehead at Ghoraniyeh and am
building a permanent bridge over river. Bridge in square 142 X 6
B was damaged to extent that both arches were blown down and
central pier shattered to within 3 feet of ground. A gap was made
about 25 feet depth 15 feet from rails to bottom of Wadi.
Estimated that if materials were at hand damage could be repaired
in 2 days. Reports indicate repairs have already been made.
Demolition south of Amman consisted of 4½ miles of railway
track, 3 small culvert points, 3 large culverts and crossings at

Alanda station. Engineers reckon that provided materials were forthcoming damage to line could be repaired in 3 days. Neither materials nor rolling stock are (?) immediately available from information here, but as Turks have shown great skill in repairing breaks on railway in the past it is possible that line may be open for through traffic on 7th April, but my aeroplanes should delay repairs if weather is fine. I am considering possibilities of further raids east of Jordan but this must be dependent on weather conditions and on attitude of tribes. I will let you have any further views on this later.

Turks now realise we can cross Jordan and threaten Amman and maintenance of bridgehead continued with constant patrols, pushed into Moab Mountains will probably compel Turks to maintain about Es Salt larger forces than hitherto, thereby reducing their forces north and south of this district and assisting indirectly Feisal's operations about Maan. See my telegram No. I.B. 1056[41] as regards my views generally on Arab situation.

Belga Arabs generally were found ready to co-operate with our forces, but not so ready to assist Sherif. Madea townsfolk (Christians) also entirely with us but nervous of Belga Arabs with whom they have an old feud. A section of the Beni Sakha came out further south and raided Ziza Station during Amman operations but appeared to have retired again probably owing to old feud with Belga tribes. There is no sign of Sherifian co-ordination of tribes north of Kerak at present.

PRO: WO33/946, pp. 323–4

III
Allenby to Wilson
General Headquarters, Egyptian Expeditionary Force

[Letter. Holograph]   6 April 1918

Thank you for your letter of the 21st. Since you wrote, the situation in Europe has changed; and I have your telegraphic order that my role is to be the active defensive. That I shall do my utmost to carry out. I am glad that you are insisting on the

French troops, that may be sent here, being fit to fight. They must also be mobile. I would willingly have useful Brigades and Divisions of French troops. The odd items of inefficiency [?], sent here for political reasons, merely hamper me. Under new arrangements, the new Corps etc. I was to have had has been countermanded, and Barrow remains with his Yeomanry Division. As to C.B. Thomson:– I was going to make him Chief Engineer of that Corps. He is at present C.R.E. of the 60th Division, where he has done first-rate work. He was tried in command of a Brigade, but did not quite fit that appointment; and I have no staff appointment open for him. I think it would be advisable for you to employ him in Europe, or elsewhere, as I know he is a good man, and he is somewhat wasted here. Money has arrived, and I think he will do well as Military Administrator. I am interested to hear of the changes in high places. Harington and Radcliffe will do you really well; and I am glad that de Lisle and Harper have got Corps.

We are getting to the end of the rains here; but my raid on Amman, at the end of last month, was attended by foul weather. Es Salt was gained with little trouble. Then the rain came down and cemented [?] the table land of Moab into a morass; and for three days and nights it poured with rain; freezing, in the intervals between showers. Guns, with the exception of a few mountain guns on packs, could not be brought into action, and the mass of hostile a [sic] machine guns could not be dealt with; so the big bridges and tunnels were not accessible. We did a good deal of damage, however; and killed a great number of Turks, besides getting a good bag of men and material. With my present strength and the necessity of sending [?] in men, I could not afford to maintain a garrison at Es Salt. Feisal, with his Arabs, keeps on worrying the Turk, further South; and I think he does the best he can, with the unstable people he commands.

Good luck to you, in your great task.

IWM: Wilson papers HHW2/33A/1

112
Allenby to War Office (GOC-in-C Egypt to War Office)
[Telegram. Typescript]   19 April 1918
No. E.A.1120

8 p.m. In order to locate enemy positions about Shunet Nimrim [sic – properly Nimrin] and to demonstrate in order to prevent enemy reinforcing Maan, Australian and New Zealand Mounted Division are to withdraw to bridgehead.

Hejaz operations. Arabs attacked Maan on 15th, 16th and 17th April, and occupied outer defences; 70 prisoners and two machine guns were taken. Railway station was temporarily occupied during 17th April. Arabs subsequently withdrew to outer defences, which they now occupy. Enemy's main position reported to be strongly entrenched with Hotchkiss machine-gun emplacements; until the arrival of further supplies of ammunition, therefore, general attack has been postponed.

PRO: WO33/946, p. 352

113
Allenby to Wilson
General Headquarters, Egyptian Expeditionary Force
[Letter. Holograph]   20 April 1918

It is in a mighty storm, that you have taken the helm. I am glad that you are there; and I can see, already, that you are handling affairs well. We have, it appears, checked the German rush; and latest reports are cheering.

Here, I have had some local fights; but I am no longer pushing North.

The Arabs are doing well, East of Jordan; and I have been helping them by forcing the Turks to keep a big force of all arms opposite my bridgehead on the Jordan. I hope soon to send a considerable mounted force across the Jordan, gain permanent touch with the Arabs and deny to the Turks the grain harvest of the Salt-Madeba area. They depend largely on this grain supply.

Generally, things are going well here. All good luck to you.

IWM: Wilson papers HHW2/33A/2

114
Allenby to War Office (GOC-in-C Egypt to War Office)

[Telegram. Typescript]   26 April 1918
No. E.A.1143

25th. Your No. 56766,[42] cipher, M.O.2, of 20th. The statement that I requested armistice is not correct, but is probably founded on following:–

On 11th April, Germans with Red Cross flags appeared at O 98 S 26 C; they collected dead and wounded and were not fired on. Later, 4th Welsh Regiment sent out stretcher bearers to same locality, they were, however, fired on and retired as did Germans.

On 15th April, Officer Commanding 3/3rd Gurkha Rifles sent out a Red Cross flag with two men to look for wounded. A German officer met them and a dividing line and an hour was fixed for the following day.

On 17th April a medical officer and burying party were sent out and an enemy medical officer and burying party also appeared. Proceedings watched by Officer Commanding 1/4th Bn. Wiltshire Regiment. There was no contact between parties, and except where these parties were at work no cessation of artillery or rifle fire. When burying was finished a German officer came forward under Red Cross flag and handed over pay books and identity discs of certain men of 3/3rd Gurkha Rifles whom he had buried. German officer stated Lieutenant W.F. Patton, 3/3rd Gurkha Rifles, was a prisoner and unhurt, having been stunned by a shell. Our party did not bury any enemy dead.

PRO: WO33/946, p. 362

115
Allenby to Wingate

General Headquarters, Egyptian Expeditionary Force
[Letter. Holograph]   1 May 1918

I have sent to you, today, an official letter – on the subject of enlistments for the Camel Transport Corps. We can't get the men, and we can't do without them; and I am advised that the only way to get them is compulsion – on the lines of the Corvée[43] – but paid, of course, at the present rate of wages. As you know, I am opposed to compulsion; but we seem to be between the Devil and the Deep Sea, and I don't know how to avoid it. I am carrying on some operations, E. of Jordan; and today there has been some busy fighting, in which I have lost some guns.[44] I don't mind losing them; but it is an advertisement for the Turk, which he will not fail to exploit. I was down in the Jordan valley, today. The weather was perfect, fresh and bright, after rain, and mild without heat.

SAD: Wingate papers 168/3/121. Typescript copies at SAD: Wingate papers 175/3/66, 175/3/99 and 175/3/137

116
Allenby to War Office (GOC-in-C Egypt to War Office)
[Telegram. Typescript]   2 May 1918
No. E.A.1165

1st, 8 p.m. This morning operations east of Jordan were continued; LXth Division resumed the attack on El Haud making some progress. Australian Mounted Division entered Es Salt at 4 a.m. capturing 350 prisoners, including 33 Germans; two (?) brigades we left to hold Es Salt, while two (?) brigades moved south-west to attack Paranet Minrin position from east and north-east. Enemy, estimated at 4,000 infantry, succeeded during the night of 30 April–1 May in crossing Jordan from west to east at Jisr Damie and attacked brigade protecting left flank; this brigade was forced back, and now occupies line 127 B 33 to Jordan at c 19.

During the retirement three batteries of horse artillery supporting this brigade became entangled in broken foothills of the mountains, only three guns were able to retire: the remaining nine had to be abandoned, but detachments and most horses were brought back. Reinforcements have been sent up and this line is now held by six regiments supported by two additional batteries of artillery. Operations are proceeding in accordance with plan. Enemy carried out local attacks at Abu Felah, Mezrah, Berukin and Haram Ridge (O 85 M 26) during night of 30th April–1st May; these attacks were repulsed. We withdrew posts holding Mezrah Ridge which it had not been intended to occupy permanently.

Hejaz operations – There is nothing to report.

PRO: WO33/946, p. 371

117
Wingate to Allenby

[Letter? Typescript. Copy]   3 May 1918
SECRET

Mr Gary, the new American Minister[45] (who impressed me as being genuinely anxious to act as a true ally and friend) in a recent informal talk with me made some remarks which were of such interest that I thought it well to embody them in a purely private and personal telegram to the Foreign Office. The telegram was to the following effect:–

1. Mr. Gary suggested as a means of relieving British Troops from garrison duty and of influencing Irish opinion in a new and healthy direction the despatch to Ireland of American Troops, recruited preferably from the Southern States as more dependable.

2. He gave it as his opinion that in the event of American Troops being sent to Palestine it would be desirable to include a large percentage of Jews in their ranks. Mr. Gary seemed to think it possible that we might find some active participation by America in Palestine affairs expedient and

welcome. I took care to tell Mr. Gary that I had no information on these matters but am reporting the conversation as I am inclined to think that he may open the matter with his Government.

This telegram has now been made official by the Foreign Office and in view of Mr. Gary's second suggestion I think it is well that you should know of what has passed.

When you are next in Cairo I trust I shall have an opportunity of discussing more fully with you the inwardness of this conversation.

SAD: Wingate papers 168/3/18–19

118
Allenby to Wigram
General Headquarters, Egyptian Expeditionary Force
[Letter. Holograph]   5 May 1918

I have been a bad correspondent, and I am shamed to find that my last letter to you was on the 22nd December. Events in Europe overtop the little happenings in this theatre; and we watch, with keen eyes, the gigantic struggle on the Western Front. I am kept well informed of the course of the battle, and the latest news has been good.

My own projects have been modified, and the scope of my operations limited, by the requirements of the European battlefield. I have been called upon to supply battalions for France; and have, consequently, been compelled to abandon all ideas of a vigorous offensive. However, you will know all of this. His Royal Highness, the Duke of Connaught, and General Smuts, will have given to His Majesty a full appreciation of the situation here; as it was, and is. The visit of the Duke of Connaught was a great joy to us all. He came up to Palestine, and lived with us for some days – going everywhere, and mixing with the troops; to their intense delight –. We were glad to see that His Royal Highness' health has vastly benefited by his visit to the mild climate of the Sudan; and he stood the sharp winter air of the mountains of Judea splendidly well. I had the unique honour of receiving, from the Great Master of the Order of St. John of Jerusalem, the insignia of that order in the Holy City itself; and His Royal Highness occupied, in the Kaiserin Augusta Victoria Hospice, on the Mount of Olives, the suite of rooms reserved for the Grand Master of the German Order of St. John of Jerusalem.

Since last I wrote to you, we have pushed far North of Jerusalem; and have also established ourselves in the Jordan valley, with a bridge and a bridgehead on the Jordan. On the 26th December, the Turks made a determined attempt – with fresh troops to recapture Jerusalem. It so happened that I had fixed the same day to attack with the XX Corps (Chetwode), northwards, astride of the Nablus road.

When the Turks attacked – before the hour fixed for my start – I put in movement my own attack. The result was that, by the evening of the 28th, not only had the enemy failed to take Jerusalem, but he was pushed 7 miles further from that city than when his attack started. The 60th Division bore the brunt of the attack; their right covered by the 53rd. The 74th and 10th counter attacked the Turks, from the West. We buried more than 1000 Turks, and we took nearly 800 prisoners in the three days of fighting. This gave us space and elasticity, N. of Jerusalem. Then I turned towards the Jordan valley; which it was needful to secure, for safety and freedom of action on my right flank. The grand plan consisted of a direct advance, by the 60th Division, to the cliffs overlooking the village of Jericho; while the mounted troops operated on their right flank. On their left, the 53rd Division cooperated.

This operation began on the 19th February. The chief feature of the enemy's resistance was the volume of their machine gun fire; the intricate and broken country lending itself admirably to this arm, in defence. On Feb. 21st, the Jordan was reached. During this advance, 4 officers, 140 other ranks, and 6 machine guns were captured. The enemy was now driven east of Jordan, and my right was secure.

From there, on the 12th March, the XX and XXI Corps were engaged in steady work pushing their line forward to the North.

The country was rocky and mountainous; difficult in the extreme; but hard fighting and good leading achieved success, and a good defensive line – Kh. Abu Felah-Sinjil-Medjel Yaba-Ras el Ain-Arsouf[46] – was occupied. Now I was ready to throw out a hand to our Arab ally, Feisal; who had been operating – with success – against the Hedjaz railway and the Turkish garrisons thereon, and was about to undertake a serious attack on the Turkish positions round Maan.

On the night of the 21st–22nd March, I concentrated a force West of the Jordan. This force comprised the Anzac Mounted Division, the 60th Division, the Imperial Camel Brigade; with mountain artillery, and light armoured cars. The Turks had broken the only bridge – at Ghoraniyeh – and the river was in flood and unfordable. Attempts to throw a bridge at Ghoraniyeh failed; but a bridge was thrown at Mahhadeh Hajla[47] and troops were pushed across. By 7.30 a.m. on the 23rd the Auckland Mounted Rifles, well handled, had crossed, and made northwards. They rode down the Turkish detachments, and gained ground covering Ghoraniyeh from the East. This enabled bridges to be thrown at that locality. By the evening of the 24th, the 60th Division had taken Shunet Nimrin; and the mounted troops on its flanks, were pushing on to Es Salt.

The Duke of Connaught visited the Jordan Valley, during these operations, and saw the construction of bridges at both the places of crossing. On the 25th, heavy and cold rain began to fall. Salt was reached by the 60th Division; and the Cavalry and Camels reached Naawr[48] – 14 miles S.E. of Es Salt –. On the 26th, Amman was reached; and, for four days and nights, in pouring rain, attacks were made against the strong Turkish positions covering the two big railway bridges and tunnels which were our ultimate objectives. A bridge was destroyed N. of Amman and 5 miles of track demolished S. of the town; but the positions were too strong to allow us to reach the big bridges and railway tunnel. On the evening of the 30th, I ordered a withdrawal; and by the evening of the 2nd April all the force was back on the Jordan. Adverse weather conditions prevented our objects from being completely achieved. The field guns and howitzers could not be got away, owing to heavy ground; and, without them, the many machine guns could not be overcome. Prisoners, to the number of 986, were brought back; and much Turks transport was destroyed. I had intended this raid to be a preliminary step to an advance, on the W. of Jordan to the line Nablus-Tulkeram. However, orders from the War Office, cutting down my strength and reconstituting my Divisions made such an advance impossible for the present. I pushed the right of my XXI Corps forward; improving its tactical position, at Berukin and Rafat,[49] but went no further. Towards the end of April, I had reason to believe that another raid by my mounted troops was feasible and that a successful advance on Es Salt might raise the Arabs between there and Kerak – a fertile tract, where the harvest will be of value to the Turks –. Since my last raid, the enemy had occupied Shunet Nimrin on the Es Salt road; and had strengthened this naturally strong position at the mouth of the pass. On the night of the 29th–30th, I sent two Brigades of the 60th Division to attack the position; while the bulk of my mounted troops struck N., on the E. bank of the Jordan, and made for Es Salt by the Jisr Ed Damieh-Es Salt road. A Brigade of Australian Light Horse, with three batteries R.H.A., was left to guard the road and watch the bridge at Jisr Ed Damieh. The Turks brought a reserve Division of infantry from Nablus, and the 3rd Cavalry Division also from the W. bank. They attacked and drove back my Brigade, who had to abandon 9 guns – saving, however, the detachments and teams –. During the 30th, 1st and 2nd, the Infantry fought hard to gain possession of Shunet Nimrin; while the Cavalry, from Es Salt, pressed the Turks in rear. I had hoped for Arab help in closing the alternative route, via the Wadi Sir, open to the enemy; but the Arab assistance was not forthcoming, and the Turks were able to supply Shunet Nimrin by that channel. On the 3rd, it was apparent that strong forces of the enemy were converging on Es Salt from the N. West, North and East. I ordered the Cavalry to withdraw, by the Es Salt-Umm esh Shert track; and directed them to hold a position in the foothills, linking up with the Infantry at Shunet Nimrin. This was done. On the 4th it was clear that, without permanent occupation of Shunet Nimrin, such a position was untenable. I could not afford the casualties, which would be entailed by the capture of that defile; and I, therefore, ordered a withdrawal to the line of the Jordan. There I hold the bridgeheads. Over 900 prisoners were brought back by us. The result of the raid has been that no trains have passed Amman station for five days; and the pressure of the Turks against Sherif Feisal, in the Maan district, has been much eased. The loss of my guns was annoying but not important. I have easily replaced them, from reserves. I know the Turkish losses to have been very heavy, in killed and wounded; mine are not serious.

The fact of our having undertaken this enterprise, at a time when all Egypt and Syria know that my troops are being depleted will have a good moral effect all round.

For the immediate future, my policy is to strengthen my positions W. of Jordan; to hold bridge-heads on the river; to develop my roads and railways – thus ensuring mobility and supply –; to watch for opportunity for striking a blow, or to help the Arabs. I have control, now, of the Dead Sea; and on it I keep a motorboat and three naval whalers. I want to get 2 or 3 more motorboats, as the whalers have too short a radius of action. So far, we have had no really hot weather, in the Valley of the Jordan. Later, however, military movements down there become almost impossible. Nevertheless, I can maintain my bridge-heads on the river; and I can police the Dead Sea.

The feeling of the country is very pro-British; and, if we were strong enough to advance to Damascus, we should be welcomed everywhere. I was at Hebron lately. This used to be a fanatically Moslem town, where it was dangerous for strangers to walk alone. I was received with enthusiasm; and was invited, by the Mufti, to visit the Mosque, wherein are the tombs of Abraham and Sarah.

Hitherto, strangers have not been allowed therein without a pass from the Sultan of Turkey. I went in; and the Guardian of the Tombs made a speech, in which he begged me to convey to His Majesty King George of England the delight of the inhabitants of Hebron at the coming of the British troops, and their loyal devotion to him. I believe that this feeling is genuine. We have the

Zionist Commission out here, now. The Arabs looked on it with grave anxiety and suspicion; but Weizmann, the head of the mission, has been very tactful, and has done much to allay the doubts of the natives.

I present my humble duty to His Majesty; and I offer my thanks for His gracious message, conveyed in your last letter to me.

Royal Archive: RA PS/GV/Q 2521/17

119
Wingate to Allenby

The Residency Cairo

[Letter. Typescript. Copy]   6 May 1918

I have seen Campbell and Jellicoe and have told them the result of my talks with the Sultan, Prime Minister and Advisers on the Recruitment question. They will explain the difficulties about (a) Conscription, (b) Increases of pay. If the Sultan and Ministers can be induced to agree to a system of "compulsion by persuasion" I think it would offer the best means of getting the number of men required without having recourse to the enactment of new laws which would provide fruitful soil for enemy propaganda – and the remedy might, in that case, be worse than the disease. The whole matter is even more difficult and complicated than it was last year owing to (a) the less favourable military situation, (b) the difficulty of inducing the Egyptians to ask for the withdrawal of the Proclamation which is a strong political card in their hands, and (c) the larger number of men required.

In spite of all these difficulties you may rely on me to do all in my power to help.

I have seen Dawnay and am glad the Es-Salt situation has cleared up satisfactorily.

SAD: Wingate papers 168/3/34. Abridged copy at SAD: Wingate papers 175/3/55

120
Wingate to Allenby

The Residency Cairo
[Letter. Typescript. Copy] 7 May 1918

Your very interesting letter of 5 May giving an account of your recent operations across the Jordan, crossed mine to you. I heartily congratulate you and your gallant Troops on their recent good work – the fighting must have been pretty heavy. I have just returned from a visit to No. 70 General Hospital where I saw some of the men wounded in the last days of April; they all seemed cheery but admitted there were a lot of machine guns against them. I am afraid the Arabs cant [sic] be relied upon to any great extent until they are quite certain our side is going to win – One can understand their point of view and I have had many similar experiences (on a small scale) in the Sudan – they talk a lot but when it comes to the scratch, they are apt to fail one. Feisal and his men seem to be doing well, though of course they must not be relied upon to do very much until we can make good North of the Dead Sea and there is not much chance of that at present.

SAD: Wingate papers 168/3/38–9

121
Wingate to Allenby

The Residency Cairo
[Letter. Typescript. Copy] 8 May 1918

I am fully aware of the extreme importance of maintaining the Egyptian Labour Corps and the Camel Transport Corps at full strength, and you may rest assured that I shall use every endeavour to ensure that the requisite number of recruits are forthcoming.

Immediately on the receipt of your despatch under reply,[50] I called on the Sultan, explained the seriousness of the situation and mentioned that, if other methods proved unavailing, some form of compulsory service might be necessary. His Highness expressed himself strongly opposed to the conscription of labour. In his opinion, such a step would be deeply resented throughout the country. The Prime Minister, whom I saw later, shared the views of the Sultan, and gave me to understand that the other Ministers were of the same opinion. For these and still more for other reasons, I personally feel that it would be unwise to introduce any form of conscription.

With a view, therefore, to finding what alternative measure could be adopted in order to produce the desired result immediately, I summoned a meeting at the Residency on May 5th. The following were present:–

Sir W. Brunyate, K.C.M.G.

Mr Haines

Sir M. Cheetham K.C.M.G.

Brig. General Sir G. Macauley K.C.M.G., C.B.

Mr Langley

Brig. General E. Herbert C.M.G.

As a result of prolonged discussion, we decided that the necessary result might be achieved by requisitioning labour from the villages through the Mudirs, Mamours and Omdas.[51] A corvée system of such a kind would no doubt receive the support of the Sultan and Ministers and could be introduced without causing grave discontent among the native population and, it was confidently hoped, would prove entirely successful. Mr. Haines was therefore requested to approach the Prime Minister on these lines.

I now have the honour to inform you that the Prime Minister has undertaken to send instructions to the Mudirs of such a kind as to enable them to supply the necessary number of recruits through administrative pressure.

If the Omda of every village has definite orders to produce labourers and is backed by the Mudir's approval, he can do so; and I feel that we should give this scheme a fair trial.

SAD: Wingate papers 175/3/62. Copy at SAD: Wingate papers 175/3/142

122
Wilson to Allenby

W.O.

[Letter. Holograph]   9 May 1918

My dear Allenby, What wretched weather the 60th Division seems to have had for the Amman enterprise. It really does appear to me that we have had bad luck in our weather. Mud all autumn in Flanders, no snow in Italy; heavy snow [,] rain and gales in Persia to hamper Dunsterville and fog on the Somme for Goughie and mud on the so called Amman plateau. It is odd to say the least of it. I wired a couple of days ago asking you for rather more detailed an account of what had happened over the Jordan, and then I wired later asking for an appreciation of what you saw likely in the future. The War Cabinet is, on the whole, very good but occasionally fusses rather and wants to know rather more of the inside story and your inside thoughts than appears in the usual official wires.

IWM: Wilson papers HHW2/33A/3

123
Allenby to Battine

[Letter. Holograph]   22 May [1918]

I have your letters of 18th and 25th April. I hear that the mail 25th April–5th May, hitherwards, has gone to the bottom; so I am lucky to have got yours by K.M. bag. Matters in France have steadied a bit, sine [sic] you wrote, it appears; but the Boche is, no doubt, preparing another big thing.

I see that French has arrested all the Sinn Fein leaders. What will that lead to? Nothing much doing here, for the moment; but my big raids beyond the Jordan have drawn Turks against me, and have eased pressure on the Arabs further South.

This has enabled the Arabs to put in some useful work against the Hejaz railway and its garrisons. I am glad to hear that Nigel[52] is sound and well. My wife is very fit. I was in Cairo, last week, and saw her.

IWM: Battine papers 90/37/1

124
Allenby to Shea
General Headquarters. Egyptian Expeditionary Force
[Letter. Holograph]   25 May 1918

Now that the 60th Division is being broken up and reconstituted, I want to express to you and through you to the Division my thanks and my admiration for your work up to now and my good wishes for the future.

The Battalions going to another theatre will carry with them a proud record. The Battalions staying here will – whether retaining their old formation or broken up – be the same fine fighters as ever; and they will inspire the new 60th Division with the spirit of the old.

To all; to those leaving us, whose departure I regret; to those remaining with us; I wish Good Fortune and Success.

LHCMA: Shea papers 4/2

125
Wilson to Allenby
W.O.
[Letter. Holograph]   29 May 1918

The old Boches are pushing us about rather roughly on the Aisne and Vesle and I am in hopes that his initial success may lead him to develop his attack and gradually make it his principal effort. This would be good, as we have so much more ground to give in that area than we have behind our old line. There is no doubt that we have an anxious two or three months in front of us. When we have weathered this period we shall run into smoother water. But between the time (say Sep–Oct.) when all our anxiety is removed and the time when we shall, in our turn, be in a position to say to the Boches "Now my boy I am going to show you what a hiding really means" there will be a long period, say – 12, 18, 24 months – and it is during this period that I want to exploit the outer theatres. As regards Palestine all we can do during the summer is to help you all we can with railway construction. I am going to see if I can get you some railway construction men, and I am again going into the question of tonnage to get stuff out to you. I want to see Aleppo joined to Mosul joined to Baku joined to the Urals joined to the Japanese army; and from that base an advance against the Boches.

IWM: Wilson papers HHW2/33A/3A

126
Wingate to Allenby

The Residency Cairo

[Letter. Typescript. Copy]   1 June 1918

Many thanks for yours of 30th May. By this time I suppose you are back at G.H.Q. Best congratulations on the success of the 7th Indian Division on the coast sector.

Glad you saw Ruchdi and talked over the Recruiting question with him – One or two more "incidents" have been reported, but I hope the last circular from the Interior will have some effect.

Dr. Morrison of Alexandria has handed me a copy of the letter which the Syrian doctor (lately at Kantara and now here) sent to the D.M.S. on the condition of the E.L.C. Hospital at Kantara – it is a serious indictment and I should be glad to be able to contradict it – Perhaps the D.M.S. would send the facts to Dr. Morrison. [sic]

No reply yet from the Foreign Office to my appeal. I will write as soon as it comes – Meanwhile my very best thanks.

SAD: Wingate papers 169/1/6

127
Allenby to Wilson

[Letter. Holograph]   5 June 1918
Embossed

I was glad to have, by the last mail, your letter of 9th May. The Boche has kept you pretty busy lately; but I hope that he is now held, for the present. However, he is a persistent swine; and it will

158

take you all your time to keep him quiet till the Americans can begin to pull their weight. The Western Theatre is closely watched by cities in Egypt; where, on the whole, sympathy is with the Central Powers. The departure of British units and their replacement by Indians is, naturally, much discussed in native circles. The natives regard my advance as arrested; and there is a strong feeling that the Indians will not be able to resist the German-Turk attack when it comes – as they believe, and some of them hope, that it will –.

However, the natives are behaving well; though there have been a few riots lately, owing to clumsy handling of recruiting for the Egyptian Labour Corps.

The Indians have done well, so far, but the new arrivals are short of training. There was a case of desertion to the enemy, the other day, by a post of Pathans.[53] I hope and believe it was only a sudden whim; and there have been few further signs of unrest. I put the remainder of the Company back on to the Line of Communications.

I was sorry not to be able to keep hold of Es Salt, at the beginning of May. I hoped that the Arabs S.E. of Es Salt would cooperate, and that I should be able to surround and capture the whole Turkish garrison of Shunet Nimrin – the position at the mouth of the [. . .?[54]] leading to Es Salt from the Ghoraniyeh Bridge. The Arabs, who should have blocked the track from Ain es Sir to Shunet Nimrin did not raise a finger* [see PS below]; and, though my Cavalry held Es Salt for several days and my Infantry had some success at Shunet Nimrin, the Turks were able to get ammunition and supplies by the track from Ain es Sir.

To have ejected them would have cost me too many men; and the Turks were beginning to encircle Es Salt with new arrivals of troops. I, therefore, withdrew to my bridgehead. The loss of the 9 guns opposite Jisr ed Damie was a nuisance, as it cheered the Turks and encouraged their resistance. The young Australian Brigadier, watching the Jisr ed Damieh bridge, foolishly placed

---

* This was not Feisal's fault and he was very angry with the defaulting tribe.

159

himself astride of the Jisr ed Damieh-Es Salt road, practically giving up his own communications with Ghoraniyeh.

One squadron only, on the Jordan, some miles away from the left flank, was covering this road to the South. When the attack came, this squadron was driven in, and his communications were cut.

He withdrew through the foothills, abandoning 9 of his guns. Apart from faulty tactical dispositions, there was nothing to blame. The guns, especially, fought well; and I sent them a message of congratulations.

I cannot, at my present strength, maintain troops in the mountains E. of Jordan; and I don't think it will be practicable so to do until I can reach Nablus and get control of the Nablus-Jisr ed Damieh road.

I am not strong enough to make holding attacks on both flanks, and the Turks can transfer their reserves from flank to flank as required. The Turks have more of these, the VII Army have 2400, and the VIII Army 5800, in Reserve.

	Rifles	Sabres	M. Guns	Art. Rifles
East of Jordan	8050	2375	221	30
VII Army	12850	750	289	28
VIII Army	15870	1000	314	1309
N. Palestine & L. of C.	950	–	6	–

I must maintain my hold on the bridges of the Jordan, and my control of the Dead Sea. This will cause the Turks to keep a considerable force watching me, and ease pressure on Feisal and his forces. It is absolutely essential to me that he should continue to be active. He is a sensible, well-informed man; and he is fully alive to the limitations imposed on me. I keep in close touch with him, through Lawrence. I have now in the valley two Mounted Divisions and an Indian Infantry Brigade. I cannot lessen this number yet. So far, the weather has been mild; and there have not been more than 2 or 3 really hot days. I have been 12 times to and across the Jordan, and have never struck a hot day. However, during the [. . .?] these months we shall have great heat; and fever. I am campaigning against mosquitos [sic]; draining, clearing, burning etc; and hope, in a week or two, to have improved things. Many acres of bog have already been drained and cleared, and the drains, though some are as salt [sic] as the Dead Sea, and stink of sulphur, swarm with little, active fish. These will, I hope feed on the larvae.

I wired to you, lately, asking if I could possibly have some Japanese Divisions.

If I could be reinforced by 3 or 4 good Divisions; I could, I think, really get a move on my Turks. The Divisions must, of course, be properly equipped, with transport; and thus mobile. If it can be done, I hope you will arrange it; and I should like to have the Divisions not later than in August. There must be available, I should think, lots of trained Japanese; spiriting for a fight. Meanwhile, I am planning a forward move; for the late Summer or Autumn; if I can get my Army into good form by then. My idea is to concentrate 5 Divisions and 2 Mounted Divisions on my left, and then to break through to Tulkeram. Then I should reach Messudieh[55] [Messudie railway] junction and Nablus. I believe that I can do this, provided that the Turks remain at present strength. Lately, I have advanced my left; between Ras el Ain and the Sea; with the object of preparing gun positions, in view of the above-mentioned scheme. By the late summer, the Turks will, I hope, have got used to these emplacements; and have ceased to think about them. If I could have the Japanese Divisions, too, I could do big things. As I go forward, the Arabs will all rise; and the Turks will go back, most likely, to Beirut-Damascus or further. Think of it; and [. . .?] we have them! It would be a great help to the European campaign, if I could worry the Turk really well here. Liman von Sanders is, I fancy, a much better man than my old antagonist; Falkenhayn. He knows the Turk's nature, and can get more out of him. Someday he'll attack me; and I want to attack him, first. Odds and sods, like Jewish battalions and regiments of Hottentots, are useful in a way; but they won't win wars. Americans and lame French Territorials do not make an army; and are merely an encumbrance, if immobilized by lack of transport. Give me some fighting Japanese Divisions, and I'll give you a lot of help. We are all fit and cheerful and the army is happy and confident.

The Maurice incident was amazing![56] I have not heard a word of sympathy with him.

With thanks for all your assistance and good will, and wishing you good luck.

IWM: Wilson papers HHW2/33A/4

128
Allenby to Wilson

[Letter. Holograph]   11 June 1918
Embossed

I wired, the other day, to say that I had only obsolete Tanks here; and that, in view of future possibilities, I should like a Battalion of light tanks – I think they call them Whippets –. I have received, in reply, orders to scrap the Tanks which I have here. This I will do. However, I have had no suggestion that I am to receive other tanks. If the Battalion of light tanks, for which I asked, can be provided, I hope I may have them.[57]

I want to be ready, beforehand, for the Turks; and to be a bit ahead of them – not behind them –.

I hear rumours, now, that German tanks are on their way to Aleppo; but I don't know if there is any truth in this report.

The Germans have a knack of getting in first; and are in danger of making a hobby of it. That is a bad habit, but it is sometimes annoying to us.

I am glad to see that the new attack, near Compiègne, is being well held.

IWM: Wilson papers HHW2/33A/5

129
Allenby to Wilson
General Headquarters, Egyptian Expeditionary Force
[Letter. Holograph]   15 June 1918
Embossed

[Allenby discusses the effect that the loss of his trained troops – ordered to go to France – will have on his capabilities]

The Turks opposing me are now in greater strength than hitherto – excepting just before the battle of Beersheba-Gaza –. His morale, fed on reports of European victories, has risen. The harvest is now reaped, and food is plentiful. My staff estimate that 68,000 rifles and sabres can be kept and fed on this front, during summer. As for redistributing my forces; all my goods are in the shop window. My front, from the Jordan to the Mediterranean, is 60 miles. It is, on the whole, a strong line; and I have made, and am making, roads and communications behind it. Still, it is wide – for the size of my force. It is the best line I can hold. Any retirement would weaken it. My right flank is covered by the Jordan; my left by the Mediterranean Sea. The Jordan Valley must be held by me; it is vital. If the Turks regained control of the Jordan, I should lose control of the Dead Sea. This would cut me off from the Arabs on the Hedjaz railway; with the result that, shortly, the Turks would regain their power in the Hedjaz. The Arabs would make terms with them, and our prestige would be gone.

My right flank would be turned, and my position in Palestine would be untenable. I might hold Rafa or El Arish; but you can imagine what effect such a withdrawal would have on the population of Egypt, and on the watching tribes of the Western Desert. You see, therefore, that I cannot modify my present dispositions. I must give up nothing of what I now hold.

Anyhow, I must hold the Jordan Valley. So far the weather there has not been excessively hot. I believe that the heat of the Valley and the Dead Sea has been exaggerated. Our danger is malaria. I am taking measures to deal with the mosquito – draining, clearing, burning and oiling – and I hope to minimize [. . .?58] the soil, there, as well as in the marshes of the plain of Sharon.59 Nevertheless, we have to expect much sickness from malaria; and my strength is likely to be reduced, thereby, seriously.

I know, well, the importance of concentrating all effort on the Western Front; but the addition of one Division60 will not save you there; here its absence may lose you the war. The Arabs are behaving well; but they watch us, anxiously. If we fail them, they might join the Turks. Whatever strategical purists may say about side shows, you are committed deeply here; and, if you lose Egypt, you lose the Empire which hinges thereon.

IWM: Wilson papers HHW2/33A/7

130
Wilson to Allenby

[Letter. Holograph]   21 June 1918
Embossed

I gave my opinion that we ought to withdraw both the 54th Division and the Australian Mounted Division and bring them to France. The War Cabinet, in view of the altered and altering conditions in the East thought it wiser to leave the Australians with you, and so a wire in that sense goes to you this afternoon. All this does not change my mind in the least nor my determination, later on when our anxiety in France is over, to reinforce you. But for the moment the margin is very very [sic] small. I am off to Italy early tomorrow. I want Diaz to start an offensive directly he has thrown the last Austrian on the right bank of the Piave into the river![61] The War Cabinet much appreciated the tone of your wire about withdrawing the 54th and the Australians and so did I.

IWM: Wilson papers HHW2/33A/8

131
Allenby to Wilson

[Letter. Holograph]   22 June 1918
Embossed

[Allenby discusses the reorganisation of the EEF as a result of EEF divisions going to France; also the nature of the Indian troops in Palestine – with all-Indian divisions proposed]

I shall have – when the changes in the composition of my force have been carried out – six Indian Divisions; each with three

British Battalions. Under the new proposal, each division will – in time – be composed of Indian Battalions only; each with increased British personnel, in Officer and N.C.O. rank, it is true.

The situation in Egypt is that we are surrounded by an alien and unfriendly population. The natives are nearly all anti-English. This includes many of the minorities; and the ruling family itself – with the exception of the Sultan –. Many Europeans, especially Greeks, are also ill-disposed towards us.

Anti-British propaganda is active; and is, naturally, stimulated and strengthened by the fact that the Egyptians are of the same faith as the Turks. It is fairly believed, by the majority in Egypt, that the English and French are beaten in Europe; and that those of our troops who are not removed from Egypt in time, will be made prisoners here at the end of the war. It is also believed and is being suggested to our Indian troops, that all British troops will be taken away, for safety; while Indian troops are left here, to be sacrificed. Not much of such suggestion has, I believe, yet reached Indian troops; and the situation is being carefully watched. Nevertheless, Indian troops cannot be kept entirely apart from the inhabitants of the country; whether in Egypt, or Palestine, at depots, on short leave, or in the field. Turkish agents are active; and, even in the front line, the Imams call across the line to our Moslem troops exhorting them to prayer. So far, such exhortations have had no great success; but we have had a case of desertion to the enemy, by a post of Pathans.

If we now begin to reduce the British Battalions in Indian Divisions, the propagandists will be able to say, and will say, "now has come to pass what we foretold."

I cannot urge you too strongly; not to carry out this project, in this country, at this time.

There are many details which would delay the arrival and efficiency of the reorganized battalions – such as the question of language, which most of the new officers and N.C.O.s would not be able to speak – but into these I won't go.

I want you to consider, broadly, the effect of the proposed scheme on the Egyptian mind, and that of our Arab Allies, and on the morale of the Indian troops

PS: I have only mentioned Infantry; but the reduction of British personnel in Artillery is equally inadvisable.

IWM: Wilson papers HHW2/33A/12

132
Wilson to Allenby

Written at Versailles

[Letter. Typescript. Copy]   4 July 1918
SECRET

I have just received your two letters of 5th and 15th June. I am back from Italy and on my way home got caught here for 5 or 6 days of Supreme Council Meetings! While I was in Italy the War Cabinet reversed the decision I got them to give me about the 54th Division. As you know I wanted to withdraw the 54th and also the Australian Mtd. Div. when I found I could get them, complete, to Amiens by the 17th and 21st of that month. I was allowed to bring the 54th but not the Australians, but now the 54th are to remain. When I get back I shall renew that attack if I can get the 54th back within a reasonable time, if not then I won't bother you any more. My wish and my hope is to reinforce you in the autumn after all anxiety here is past. As I often say at the War Cabinet it is a trifle to move 4 or 5 divisions from St Pol to Palestine nowadays compared to moving a few corps by march route [sic] 100 years ago from Madrid to Moscow. But I have difficulties the "Little Corporal"[62] never dreamt of! When, in March, we appointed Foch, C.inC. France [,] I urged strongly that we should agree but only on condition that we took over all the salt water and every theatre – ex. France and Italy – that lay across the salt water. I could not get L.G. or Milner to see the importance of this, and although I have repeatedly returned to the attack I have never had any success.

At the meetings now going on here this matter is being brought home to them because it is now clear that Clemenceau and Foch are going to make a bid to take over the whole war everywhere. They already issue orders in France, in Italy, in

Salonika, and in Russia. And they are asking questions about Palestine and Persia! However yesterday I got L.G. to take a stand and we gave the little Frenchmen a good shaking. This was good and will have far reaching effect. At the same time I am in this difficulty that it will severely strain the Alliance if I withdraw divisions from France to send to you, and on the other hand we have no divisions anywhere else. I have skinned Home Defence down to boys under 18½ so there is nothing there. I don't think I can withdraw anything from Italy so that it is not easy to see what can be done.

We might send you out some battalions again and strengthen you in that way but whole divisions are, of course, what you want and I must try to get them.

You will have had my letter about the Japanese. They flatly refuse to come to Europe or even Mesopotamia and there will be great difficulty in getting them into Siberia even. You see my difficulties. You will help me much if you will let me know – by private letter – what is the minimum you require in men and material (quite round numbers of course) you require [sic] for a move such as you suggest in your letter i.e. – Meesandiek Junction[63] – Nablus. That sort of thing.

I must run off to a meeting. I hope you don't get much sickness from Malaria. I am sure you are doing everything possible.

The "Affaire Maurice"[64] really was amazing and there were many mixed up in it who ought to be ashamed of themselves.

By the way, could help you in training your Native Battalions if we sent you some more officers.

IWM: Wilson papers HHW2/33A/10

133
Wingate to Allenby

Ramleh

[Letter. Holograph]   5 July 1918

Thanks for your two notes of yesterday – I think we shall manage the subsidy[65] required as well as the extra £50,000 you require[66] for Northern Operations;[67] as you will see. . . . I am urging for another £500,000 additional to the £400[,]000 en route from Australia and I am sure you will do what you can, through the W.O. to represent the importance of not risking a delay again in the payment of our Arab subsidy.

SAD: Wingate papers 169/2/103-4

134
Allenby to War Office (GOC-in-C Egypt to War Office)
[Telegram. Typescript]   7 July 1918
No. E.A.1418

Your No. 60746, M.O.2, 22nd June. Since 1st January actual number of deserters among Trans-frontier Pathans as follows:– 19th Lancers, 4, includes 2 Swatis, 2 Afudis; 28th Punjabis, 1 Jussufzai, suspected to be Trans-frontier.

[Allenby lists the distribution of the Trans-frontier Pathans – in total, 132 men in the unit]
    I have decided to withdraw them and consider that their retention in the country is undesirable. The disposal of the cavalry I suggested in my No. M.F.A.19581 of 30th June. May the infantry be sent to either France or India?

PRO: WO33/960, p. 13

135
Allenby to Wilson
[Letter. Holograph]   24 July 1918
Embossed

Thank you for your letter of 21st June. I am glad that you were able to leave the 54th Division here, and I thank you for your kind and sympathetic words and deeds.
    I am very anxious to make a move in September, on the lines which I have already indicated to you.

I think I can get to the Nablus-Tulkeram line. This will give me the railway junction at Messadieh [Messudie station?] and the road from Nablus to the Jordan at Jisr ed Damie. This, without much lengthening of my front, will give me a much better strategical position.

Nablus and Tulkeram are the Headquarters of the VII and VIII Armies, joined by a lateral line of railway. The possession by the Turks of the road Nablus-Jisr ed Damie-Es Salt is of great advantage to them; and, until I get it, I can't occupy Es Salt with my troops or the Arabs.

Another reason for moving to this line is that it will encourage both my own new Indian troops and my Arab Allies. I think, too, that I have a really good opportunity of inflicting a severe defeat on the Turks; and I may make a big haul of prisoners and guns. On the Jisr ed Damie-Nablus-Tulkeram line, I can wait as long as you like; that is, till you see your way to reinforcing me for further enterprise. I don't suppose that I shall be able to keep troops at Es Salt; but I think that the Arab may get there, and remain there. This would be an enormous gain for them, as well as for me.

The German attack, in the Jordan valley, on the 14th was a dead failure.[68] Some 1250 Germans attacked. They were feebly supported by the Turks, and were cut to pieces. We took some 370 Boche prisoners and estimate their dead at 200 or so. On one of my Brigade fronts 120 German dead were counted. This was on the right bank. On the left bank of Jordan my Indian cavalry did well. The Jodhpure[69] Lancers killed over 60 Turks with the lance and took prisoner an equal number. Old Pertap [?] Singh[70] was in the valley, with his Regiment, but did not manage to join in the charge – which has always been his ambition.

We are delighted to see how well you are all doing in France now.

IWM: Wilson papers HHW2/33A/14

136
Wilson to Allenby (CIGS to GOC-in-C Egypt)
[Telegram. Typescript]   25 July 1918

No. 63020.

Very Secret

"The question has arisen as to what form of administration would be put into force if your troops should occupy any part of the Syrian areas which are regarded as of special interest to France. The French consider that the military administration in Palestine is virtually a temporarily [sic] British civil administration, and that an extension thereof to Syria would be liable to serious misconstruction both in France and in Syria. It is very desirable from a political point of view that we should be able to assure the French that, subject to your supreme authority, French advice would be taken and French assistance accepted in regard to affairs of a purely administrative nature in areas of special interest to France if they should be occupied by your forces, but of course it is realised that in time of war military considerations are of paramount importance. I should be glad to have your personal opinion and views on this question, and hope you may be able to meet the French wishes."

PRO: WO33/960

137
Wilson to Allenby
[Letter. Typescript. Copy]   26 July 1918

Many thanks for your letters of June 19th and 22nd which only arrived yesterday. Not a very rapid post. You will have known long ago that directly we found that you and Marshall were opposed to the (India Office) proposals re reorganizing your divisions we dropped it. Also you have kept your 54th Division as well as the Australians.

This is all old history now, but it takes the heart out of one for writing letters because long before they reach you the problems have always changed.

Your E.A.1489 of 24/7/18 also came yesterday and I am pushing about to try and get you the tonnage you want and the railway engines and track you ask for. I sent you a wire today about Storrs being made a B.G. The opposition here was very great and I had to, and do, admit the force of the arguments so in the end we agreed to the pay without the rank. I hope this will satisfy you. Is'nt [sic] Foch doing well? I went to see him 3 days ago. He was in good form. It will be great fun if he pushes the old Boches back to the Aisne or even to the Vesle.

IWM: Wilson papers HHW2/33A/13

138
Wingate to Allenby

The Residency, Ramleh, Egypt

[Letter. Typescript]   5 August 1918
PRIVATE AND PERSONAL

Thanks for your two notes of yesterday. I think we shall manage the gold required, as well as the extra L500,000, additional to the L400,000 en route from Australia: and I am sure you will [do] what you can through the W.O. to represent the importance of not risking a delay again in the payment of our Arab subsidies.

The general shortening of the German lines in France seems to me to point to the adoption of a defensive policy on their Western front during the coming winter. If all we hear of troubles in the Balkans, disagreements between Turks and Germans &c &c. is true, I think it is not unlikely that the Huns may send some of their released Divisions to steady the Eastern situation – hoping that the passage of Troops through the Balkans to Constantinople and thence to Syria, may divert attention and at the same time enable them to retake the offensive in Palestine on a considerable scale. This is only a personal idea and I give it to you for what it is worth. You probably have the views of home on these points (which I have not) and are preparing for such an eventuality – but I do think the W.O. should decide – and without delay – to revert as far as possible to the scheme they contemplated when Smuts was here: anything to assure the situation in Palestine, which might become serious if strong German reinforcements are sent. I do not want to appear an alarmist, but there are many indications (amongst them the ex-Khedive's visit to Berlin) which make me feel that the coming winter will show increased enemy activity in our part of the world: and I am not sure we may not have a recrudescence of Senussi activity as well. I wish we could rely on our Italian allies to deal a little more effectively with this menace. I see that Ameglio[71] has gone and is being replaced by Garioni – does this mean that they are at last waking up to their responsibilitizs [sic] in Cyrenaica?

PS: Is there any chance of seeing you here in the near future? If not, I may if quite convenient to you, take a run up to Palestine for a weekend and have a talk.

CUL: Hardinge papers 38, fo. 162

139
Allenby to Wingate

General Headquarters, Egyptian Expeditionary Force
[Letter. Holograph]   7 August 1918

Thank you for your letter of the 5th inst. I am very glad that the gold question is settled; for this time, at any rate. I will do all that I can to represent to the W.O. the importance of not letting us run short again.

I went to the N.E. of my line, in the Jordan valley, yesterday; and looked at the ground over which the Germans attacked on the 14th July. It was a gallant attack, but had no chance of success. The weather down there is quite bearable; and, so far, malaria has not been very bad.

SAD: Wingate papers 169/3/75–77

140
Haig to Allenby

[Telegram. Typescript]   11 August 1918

Heartiest thanks for the kind message of congratulations which you have sent us from the army in Palestine. I have communicated it to the troops.

NLS: Haig papers Acc.3155/217f

141
Allenby to Wilson

[Letter. Holograph]   12 August 1918
Embossed

I wired to you, the other day, about the gold reserve. We had to raid the banks, to get the means to carry on. You know, as well as I do, that my operations depend entirely on the cooperation of the Hedjaz Arabs; and they must get their regular pay. Each fighting Arab – with camel – gets £6 a month; and that includes insurance for camel. It is low pay but numbers run into big figures. I ought to have at least one month's reserve of gold, always in hand; and I hope that you will see to this.

Will you get the French Government to hasten the supply of gun ammunition for their Detachment in this country? At present, they have batteries but no ammunition. The training of the French detachment[72] is going on well; and I am pleased with what I have seen of them. The two battalions of Tirailleurs Algériens,[73] and the two battalions of Armenians, are quite good; I propose to use them actively. The Regiment – 3 squadrons – of Cavalry is also good; and I propose to use it with my own Cavalry. The artillery is training, earnestly and efficiently, but has no ammunition.

IWM: Wilson papers HHW2/33A/17

142
Allenby to Wilson

[Letter. Holograph]   14 August 1918
Embossed

I have, today, your letters of 15th and 26th July. I quite understand the position with regard to the Divisions referred to in your letter of the 15th. I have a fair chance of getting the line Jisr ed Damie-Nablus-Tulkeram line with my present force. If the Turks are badly beaten, my Cavalry may bring off a coup and might get to Haifa. Whether or not they could stay there is uncertain. However, the Turks have lost confidence in the Germans; and, if the Germans are badly beaten in Europe, the Turks might fall back on Deraa and Damascus. Much depends on the Arabs. The King of the Hedjaz is at present inclined to quarrel with Ibn Saoud; and Ibn Saoud may, likely enough, give him a hammering. That might, conceivably, draw Feisal away South; to support his father. However, I am counting on Feisal's continued cooperation with me. Naturally, I can't push far North unless the Hedjaz railway ceases to be a menace to my right flank. I must either be able to detach a strong flank guard, or my flank must be covered by the Arabs; this, supposing always that the Turks remain strong enough and mobile enough to work on that line. Therefore, I only aim, at present, for the Jisr ed Damie-Nablus-Tulkeram line. I hope that Waterfield[74] will be able to make clear my plans to you; but I am not sure, clarity is not his strong point.

The Admiral has applied for nets, to protect the harbour of Haifa; and 'Troopers' ask me if they are really necessary. There is no doubt that, in the not remote future, Haifa will be an important harbour for me; and the nets should be ready, as they might be wanted at short notice. Thank you for your wire about gold. I know it is not plentiful; but the Arabs won't fight without it, at any rate not till I get much further forward. Good luck to you, and congratulations on your success.

IWM: Wilson papers HHW2/33A/18

143
Wilson to Allenby

[Letter. Holograph]   20 August 1918

Many thanks for yours of July 24th just received. What a long time a letter takes. Your letter however brings good news of hopeful attacks in Sep. I have just been seeing the railway people and pushing about to get as much stuff out to you as they can, and I am asking the Air Ministry this afternoon to send you out more aeroplanes if they possibly can in time for your coming operations. It would be a real good business if we gave the Turk a serious knock. Yes we are doing quite well in France now and there is no longer any doubt that the Boch of today is not the same man as he was in '14 '15 '16 and '17. Best of good fortune.

IWM: Wilson papers HHW2/33A/15

144
Allenby to Wilson

[Letter. Holograph]   21 August [1918]
Embossed

My letter will probably reach you before we kick off; but the K.M.[75] bag is the slowest mover in the whole postal world.

If we can keep our intentions and dispositions dark, I think the Turk is likely to suffer a severe defeat. I propose to use my Cavalry very boldly, and to park 3 Divisions thereof round to Afule; and thence to raid and catch the bridge over the Jordan – Jisr el Mejamie [?[76]] – if feasible. If I get Afule, I should be able also to cut off the Turks at Beisan; and this should result in disaster, on a grand scale, for the Turkish Army. I promise you nothing; but I have great hopes, if all goes even fairly well.

If my plans succeed, I can, I believe, clear Palestine up to the Vale of Esdraelon; and I may be able to hold Haifa. If I smash this Turkish Army, I can with my present force hold a good forward line. There I can wait on events. Anyhow, I think that I shall get the Jisr ed Damie-Nablus-Tulkeram line.

IWM: Wilson papers HHW/2/33A/20

145
Allenby to Wilson
General Headquarters, Egyptian Expeditionary Force
[Letter. Holograph]   11 September 1918

I congratulate you on the result of recent fighting in France, and your continued victories. You must be fairly well content. Here, my preparations are well forward; and I am hoping to start on the day fixed. So far, prospects are good.

My Arab ally, Feisal, has sent off his people to the North. Lawrence and Joyce are with them; and the intention is to raid Deraa and the railway. They will raise the Rualla Tribe, on the way; and hope to be joined by the Druses. There has been some trouble, resulting in a delayed start; but the raid will, I think, be in time to synchronise more or less with my movements.

The trouble was caused by the old King of the Hedjaz. He issued a proclamation in the "Kibla" – the official Meccan newspaper – deposing Jaafar, Feisal's C.inC. Feisal promptly resigned, and chaos ensued. In consultation with Clayton and myself, Wingate sent a series of telegrams to the King; who, obstinate at first, gradually climbed down and gave in. Now he is quite friendly, and tells me that he hopes someday to come and kiss my "intelligent forehead." He wishes me to take entire control of his northern army which is under Feisal. I think that intrigue and some jealousy of Feisal underlay it all.

IWM: Wilson papers HHW2/33A/22

146
Allenby to War Office (GOC-in-C Egypt to War Office)
[Telegram. Typescript]   12 September 1918
No. P.630.

Misunderstanding arose recently between King Hussein and Sherif Feisal which threatened at one time to stop all Arab operations east of the Jordan. King was under the impression that Gaafar Pasha had assumed the title of Commander-in-Chief of

Arab armies. He therefore published notice in the Kibla stating that Gaafar Pasha had no right to such a title and was merely one of the Arab leaders. He added that officers in the Arab Army could never have the same status as those of Ethiopian armies. When the text of this message became known at Feisal's headquarters all officers protested that they could no longer serve. Feisal supported his officers and telegraphed his resignation to [the] King. The situation was serious and operations held up. Discipline in Arab Army was threatened and even the Bedouins were affected. There was obviously misunderstanding on both sides and a series of telegrams to King and Feisal from the (?) High Commissioner and myself, respectively, resulted in clearing up matter and producing satisfactory telegrams from King to Feisal which have restored the situation. Arab operations are now proceeding according to plan.

PRO: WO33/960, p. 98

147
Allenby to Wilson
General Headquarters, Egyptian Expeditionary Force
[Letter. Holograph]   18 September 1918

Your letter of 20th August has reached me today. My preparations are as complete as I can make them, and tomorrow they will be tested. I do not think that the Turks have, so far, any inkling of my plan. Meanwhile, my Arab friends are making hay round Deraa, and have timed their raid very nicely. No harm was done by the delay which was caused by the trouble between Feisal and his father the King. I am glad that you are supporting the King of the Hedjaz, and Egypt, against India and Ibn Saoud. India's attitude, as interpreted by Philby, is dangerous and wicked. Thank you for your help, in all ways.

IWM: Wilson papers HHW2/33A/22A

148
Allenby to Lady Allenby

[Letter. Holograph]   19 September 1918

We attacked, at 4.30 a.m., today. Now – 3 p.m. – the Turks are breaking, everywhere. I left here, at 4.30 a.m., and motored to Arsuf. There, was General Shea; whose division attacked the Turkish right, on the coast. All was going well; and the head of the cavalry was just pushing along the beach, below the castle, making for the Nahr Falik.[77] Two destroyers of ours were shelling the coast road, N. of the Nahr Falik – which, you remember, is the river a few miles N. of Arsuf. Then, I motored to the Headquarters of the other Divisions; all doing well, too. Now my cavalry is many miles north of Arsuf; making for the Turks' communications in the valley of Esdraelon. His infantry and artillery are falling back;[78] hunted by my airmen, with machine gun fire and bombs. So far, many guns and 2,500 prisoners have been caught; but there will be many more. My losses are light. I bombed the Headquarters of Liman von Sanders and his two Army Commanders last night. On the E. of Jordan, the Arabs and the Druses are up; and they have cut the Hedjaz railway, N.S., and W. of Deraa. Deraa is the junction, where the railway into Palestine leaves the Damascus–Medina line; so, Liman von Sanders has lost his only railway communication with the outer world. I really don't know what he can do; and I am beginning to think that we may have a very great success. The weather is perfect; not too hot, and very clear; just right for my artillery and my aeroplanes in pursuit. My horses are very fit, and there is plenty of water on the route which they will follow; and they are in sufficient strength to be irresistible. Sir Pertap [?[79]] is with them; quite recovered from his fever, and keen as a boy. News from France, again, is capital, and in Salonika we are having success against the Bulgarians. The Austrian peace offensive has, of course, begun actively; but I hope that noone will deal with them.

LHCMA: Allenby papers 1/9/1

149
Allenby to Lady Allenby
[Letter. Holograph]   20 September 1918

My Battle is a big one; and, so far, very successful. I think I have taken some 10,000 prisoners and 80 or 90 guns, already – perhaps more –; and captures increase, hourly. My Cavalry are now in rear of the Turkish Army; and their lines of retreat are cut. One of my Cavalry Divisions surrounded Liman von Sanders' Headquarters, at Nazareth, at 3 a.m. today; but Liman had made a bolt, at 7 p.m. yesterday. We took 4 aeroplanes at Afule, in the Vale of Esdraelon. One had just flown in, with the German mails. An officer of mine, in a motor car, saw it land; and he shot the Observer and Pilot with his revolver. I was at Tulkaram today, and went along the Nablus road.[80] It is strewn with broken lorries, wagons, dead Turks, horses and oxen; mostly killed and smashed by our bombing aeroplanes.

The same bombing of fugitives, on crowded roads, continues today. I think I ought to capture all the Turks' guns, and the bulk of his Army. Rushdie Pasha saw the artillery battle, from a hill east of Jaffa, yesterday; and he will go out on to the battlefield at Tulkeram tomorrow. Today he is in Jerusalem. Mrs Gary[81] and her girl arrived, to breakfast today. They went on to Jerusalem, with Col. Finley, [?82] for a few days. I told Mrs Gary, truly, that if she had come yesterday she could have seen the battle; today is too late, as the tide has rolled far northwards. Rushdie rubbed into her the fact that he had seen it, and she had not. My losses are not heavy, in proportion to the results gained. I hope to motor out, tomorrow, to see the Cavalry in Esdraelon. The Cavalry Headquarters are at Armageddon, at the present moment. It is called by a different name on the map.

European news is good, too.

I have your letter of 19th; and have received the parcel of Ponds extracts etc, thank you.

LHCMA: Allenby papers 1/9/2

150
Allenby to Prince Feisal

GHQ, EEF

[Letter or telegram? Typescript with holograph additions]

20 September 1918

I send your Highness my greetings and my most cordial congratulations upon the great achievement of your gallant troops about DERAA, the effect of which has, by throwing the enemy's communications into confusion, had an important bearing upon the success of my own operations.

Thanks to our combined efforts, the Turkish army is defeated and is everywhere in full retreat.

This morning my cavalry occupied AFULEH, and pushed thence rapidly south-eastwards, entered BEISAN this evening, thus closing to the enemy his last line of escape.

My infantry yesterday captured TULKERAM, and are now pursuing the enemy eastwards to NABLUS.

Prisoners already counted number 8000, and we have taken over 100 guns, as well as a great mass of war material of every description, the extent of which it is not at present possible to estimate. Already the Turkish army in Syria has suffered a defeat from which it can scarcely recover. It rests upon us now, by the redoubled energy of our attacks, to turn defeat into destruction.

[Following holograph addition:]
Col Joyce
Please deliver this in suitable flowery language to Feisal. The CinC's more serious communication is under separate cover addressed to HH.
AD [Alan Dawnay?]

OxAnt: Young papers File 2

151
Allenby to King Hussein of the Hedjaz (Chief Egypforce to HH The Sultan and HH King Hussein (c/o Hedghog Cairo)
[Telegram. Typescript]   21 September 1918
O.A.M.867

I am glad to inform Your Highness that to-day my infantry reached the general line BEIT DEJAN – NEBY BELAN – JEBEL ESLAMIYEH – SAMARIA – ATTARA – BELAH and have driven the enemy into the arms of the Desert Mounted Corps operating from BEISAN and JENIN. Cavalry have occupied NAZARETH. I cannot estimate total number of prisoners, but 18,000 have been counted. Liman von Sanders fled from NAZARETH six hours before the arrival of our cavalry. Details of material captured not yet received but include more than 120 guns. The R.A.F. have dropped 9 tons of bombs from a low altitude on enemy's columns which tried to escape into the JORDAN Valley by the NABLUS – JISR Ed DAMIEH Road.

PRO: WO95/4371

152
Allenby to Lady Allenby
General Headquarters, Egyptian Expeditionary Force
[Letter. Holograph]   21 September 1918

I think that the Turkish Army is practically destroyed. We have taken well over 20,000 prisoners and some 120 or more guns. I think we shall get all guns and many more prisoners. My losses are very slight. I motored to Lejjun,[83] today; 65 miles N. of here, overlooking the plain of Esdraelon. A beautiful view across the flat vale. Nazareth, high in hills, to the N.; Mount Tabor opposite; Mount Gilboa to the E., overlooking Jezreel. Some of the Indian cavalry got into Turks with the lance, in the plain yesterday, and killed many. Liman von Sanders fled N., at 9 p.m., on the 19th. My Cavalry were round his Headquarters, at Nazareth, at 3 a.m. the 20th; so they only just missed him. I went[84] and passed through thousands of prisoners today; many of them Germans. Most of them dog tired. I should not be surprised if get 30,000 eventually; there must be hundreds scattered amongst the mountains, still, who will surrender as we push the Infantry in. All my troops have marched and fought grandly; some of the Infantry have done 20 miles, across the mountains, today. I'll ask Cheetham to come up on a visit. Rushdie returns tonight. He has thoroughly enjoyed his experience. I sent him out to the battle ground, today; as he wanted to see some "cadavers".

LHCMA: Allenby papers 1/9/3

153
Allenby to Wilson (Chief Egypforce to Troopers London)
[Telegram. Typescript]   22 September 1918
Despatched 0010 hrs on 23 September 1919
E.A.1688 [?]

The two Turkish armies west of the JORDAN have practically ceased to exist. Captures up to date are estimated at at least 25,000 prisoners and 260 guns, with the whole of the transport of the armies. Many prisoners and much material have not yet been brought in. I am now building up communications in order to exploit my success.

This morning I established a bridgehead at JIZR ED DAMIEH on the JORDAN; we took 900 prisoners and have blocked the last line of escape for the enemy.

PRO: WO95/4371

154
Allenby to Lady Allenby
General Headquarters, Egyptian Expeditionary Force
[Letter. Holograph]   22 September 1918

I have your letter of 21st. I've been out all day; motoring round, by Shechem[85] (Nablus) and Samaria (Sebustieh).[86] All goes well;

prisoners pour in. I can't get details yet; but I think that 25,000 prisoners and 200 guns is within bounds. In fact, the Turkish force W. of Jordan is practically destroyed. My losses, I hope, are under 5,000. Congratulatory telegrams are arriving; but the senders don't yet know the completeness of the victory. The Turks have lost everything W. of Jordan; Railway, rolling stock, lorries, wagons, horses, camels etc etc.

LHCMA: Allenby papers 1/9/4

155
Allenby to Wilson

[Letter. Holograph]   23 September 1918
Embossed

– 25th Sept. –

I have your H.W. wire and that from Troopers proposing a Cavalry raid to Aleppo. I don't think Aleppo possible; but am sending 3 Divisions of Cavalry, as soon as I can, to Damascus. Chaytor's Division of Anzac Light Horse is about Amman now, and will deal with enemy coming from the South. Prisoners number well over 40,000 and are still coming in. I have Australian mounted troops at the S. end of Lake Tiberias, and they are pushing to Tiberias. If I get Damascus, Beirut falls to us certainly; and I hope to push troops, Northwards, thither, by the coast-road from Haifa, feeding from the sea, stage by stage.

Wilson papers HHW2/33A/23

156
Allenby to Lady Allenby

[Letter. Holograph]   23 September 1918

I have your letter of the 22nd; also a small English mail, with a letter from my mother – of 1st inst. –. Prisoners still roll in; and the roads and defiles of the mountains are encumbered with guns, wagons, motor-lorries and all sorts of stores. It will take weeks to collect them. The Turks East of Jordan are retreating North; and I am sending all available troops from the Jordan Valley after them, via Es Salt. I've been going round hospitals today.[87] All the sick and wounded are very cheerful and content. I've told them that they've done the biggest thing in the war – having totally destroyed two Armies in 36 hours! The VII and VIII Armies, now non-existent, were the best troops in the Turkish Empire; and were strongly backed by Germans and Austrians. Old Sir Partap [?[88]] came in, today. He is suffering from fever and quite knocked up. He went right away, with his Regt., to Nazareth; a 70 mile ride, day and night. I want to send him to convalesce, at a convalescent home in Egypt, for a few days. He said to me, today, "your plan, good plan". I think it is your good magic, my Love, that has carried us through with such a rush.

I have just heard that my cavalry have taken Haifa and Acre, today. They had a bit of a fight, at Haifa; but I have no details yet. I think my Jordan troops will probably reach Es Salt tomorrow; but they won't catch many Turks there. However, my aeroplanes have been pulverising the retreating Turks in that locality.

PS: I have written to Henry Wilson about the marriages of nursing sisters.

LHCMA: Allenby papers 1/9/5

157
King George V (London) to Allenby at GHQ EEF
[Telegram. Holograph]   23 September 1918

It is with feelings of pride and admiration that we at home have received the news of the ably conceived and brilliantly carried out operations in which the British Indian and Allied forces under your command with the support of the Royal Navy have gained a complete victory over the enemy I am confident that this success which has effected the liberation of Palestine from Turkish rule will rank as a great exploit in the history of the British Empire and will stand for all time as a memorable testimony to British leadership and to the fighting qualities of British and Indian troops.

LHCMA: Allenby papers 1/9/9

158
Wilson to Allenby (Troopers London to Chief Egypforce)

[Telegram. Typescript]
Despatched 23 September 1918, received 24 September 1918
SECRET & PERSONAL
66977 cipher CIGS

Your success being so complete, I should like you to consider the possibility of a cavalry raid on ALEPPO, to be supported by infantry or not as the situation developed and as opportunities offered. Your success is taking effect in the CAUCASUS already and any further Turkish effort in North West PERSIA would be seriously crippled by even a temporary occupation of ALEPPO which might also have a considerable moral and political effect on the status of TURKEY as a belligerent.

Should you decide on such an enterprise you are authorised to start whenever you think fit and the War cabinet are prepared to accept the risks involved.

PRO: WO95/4371

159
Allenby to Lady Allenby
General Headquarters, Egyptian Expeditionary Force
[Letter. Holograph]   24 September 1918

Enclosed from the King[89] is well expressed. Will you take care of it? I have also a warmly expressed wire from the War Cabinet,[90] of which I will send you a copy. I have been out, all day, visiting hospitals and the French detachment. The French fought well, and had some 150 killed and wounded – Armenians and

Tirailleurs Algériens. Prisoners still come in. We have now taken over 40,000 and some 300 guns. Telegrams of congratulation are growing upon me. I, myself, am almost aghast at the extent of the victory! I have taken Es Salt, E. of Jordan; and, by now, my Cavalry are probably at Amman on that flank. Haifa and Acre are in my hands, and patrols are moving to Lake Tiberias.

PS: Bols motored to Haifa today and is not yet back.

LHCMA: Allenby papers 1/9/6

160
Wilson to Allenby

Embossed – War Office
[Letter. Holograph]   24 September 1918

Well done. The whole thing is really a gem. The Cabinet are sending their thanks and the King sent his yesterday. Then I have sent you two wires – a public and a private – about Aleppo. There is much talk here of the usual kind some saying you could go to Petrograd and some saying that all your force should now be transported to France, and some again who would like to see you march east to Baghdad! How dull a world it would be if we all thought the same! But as regards Aleppo I wonder what you will say. I realise of course all the difficulties and distance and time of year and so forth and yet it would be such a coup if you think it a possibility. The Cabinet, as I said in my H.W wire, is quite prepared to back you but of course there is no question of ordering or even of pressure. Of all your friends none can be more pleased than I am.

IWM: Wilson papers HHW2/33A/24

161
Allenby to Prince Feisal by way of BGGS (Bartholomew) to British Officer with Feisal

General Staff Operations, GHQ EEF

[Letter. By air. Typescript]   25 September 1918
SECRET
Z/96/027.B

British Officer accompanying Sherif Feisal
  Communicate the following message to Sherif Feisal from Commander-in-Chief, begins:–

1. There is no objection to Your Highness entering DAMASCUS as soon as you consider that you can do so with safety.

2. I am sending troops to DAMASCUS and I hope that they will arrive there in four or five days from to-day. I trust that Your Highness' forces will be able to co-operate, but you should not relax your pressure in the DERAA district, as it is of vital importance to cut off the Turkish forces which are retreating North from MAAN, AMMAN and ES SALT.

Bartholomew

[There is another copy of this message in the same PRO file addressed to Lt-Col Lawrence, C.B., D.S.O., signed by Bols and 'sent by air' with the following typescript addition: 'We took SEMAKH and TIBERIAS yesterday and British Cavalry will move on DERAA from the West starting to-day if possible. General Chaytor with the Anzac Division is at AMMAN. Our troops know your movements.']

PRO: WO95/4371

162
Allenby to Wilson (Chief Egypforce to Troopers)
[Telegram. Typescript]   25 September 1918
E.A.1696
SECRET

Operations.

1. The suggestion contained in your 66977 cipher C.I.G.S. of September 23rd has been considered by me, and I have decided that for the following reasons a cavalry raid on Aleppo is not feasible. I could not hope, even if the opposition were negligible, to reach ALEPPO, which is distant 300 miles from NAZARETH, with three cavalry divisions in less than three weeks. A march of this description would furthermore entail very heavy wastage, and the cavalry would arrive in no condition to deal with the troops in the ALEPPO-ALEXANDRETTA area. These latter now amount to 25,000 combatants, and during the next three weeks they will be augmented by reinforcements of a good quality, which are already setting out from ANATOLIA. In each succeeding week the Turkish situation will be ameliorated by the arrival of further reinforcements, which are believed to have started from CONSTANTINOPLE and the CAUCASUS.

2. I am firmly of the opinion that the only sound policy is to advance by stages as in the past, unless and until the War Cabinet is prepared to undertake a combined Naval and Military operation on a large scale at ALEXANDRETTA, and to maintain by sea the military forces employed in it.

An advance to the line DAMASCUS-BEIRUT is the first of these stages, and this I hope to begin within a few days, an infantry division marching up the coast from HAIFA to BEIRUT, while the Desert Mounted Corps, consisting of three divisions, moves on DAMASCUS. The infantry division I propose to feed, as the advance proceeds, by putting supplies from the sea into ACRE, TYRE and SIDON, and finally BEIRUT. I shall leave one cavalry division in the AMMAN area to operate against and cut off the enemy retreating Northwards from MAAN, and thereafter it will proceed to DAMASCUS and rejoin Desert Mounted Corps.

PRO: WO95/4371. Copy at PRO: WO33/960, pp. 114–15

163
Weizmann to Allenby

Paris
[Telegram. Printed]   26 September 1918

Please accept my heartfelt congratulations on your brilliant and glorious victory. I hail with joy the approaching liberation of the whole of Palestine by you.

Barzilay, Dvorah and Litvinoff, Barnet (eds), *The Letters and Papers of Chaim Weizmann, Volume 8, Series A, November 1917–October 1918* (Jerusalem & Rutgers University: Israel Universities Press & Transaction Books, 1977) p. 274

164
Note from Allenby

[Note. Typescript]   26 September 1918

I desire to convey to all ranks and all arms of the Force under my command, my admiration and thanks for their great deeds of the past week, and my appreciation of their gallantry and deter-mination, which have resulted in the total destruction of the VIIth and VIIIth Turkish Armies opposed to us.

Such a complete victory has seldom been known in all the history of war.

EHH Allenby
General
CinC

NAM: 6309/44

165
Allenby to Lady Allenby

[Letter. Holograph]   29 September 1918

I have your letter of 28th. I got back late last night and only had time to scrawl a line. Certainly, ask Sir Pertap[91] for his photograph. He would feel pleased and honoured; and he has a great admiration for you. My prisoners mount up. I hear, today, that 10,000, trying to break N., have surrendered to General Chaytor at Amman. This is probably true; but not yet verified. If true, it brings the total of prisoners to well over 60,000. I hope that my cavalry will reach Damascus tomorrow. Things are going swimmingly, too, in France and the Balkans.

I went to Haifa and Carmel yesterday. The view from the top of Carmel across the bay, is lovely; very like the bay of Naples – without Vesuvius and Capri. The bay is surrounded by mountains except where the River Kishon runs in from the Vale of Esdraelon. On Carmel is the Carmelite Monastery; where Father Knapp[92] lived, in his youth. I went in. Only 3 monks [?] remain. It is a huge building; and, if I shift my G.H.Q. to Haifa, I shall probably use it for my H.Q. offices. The Germans had done so, and have left a lot of litter behind. All the furniture, except in one or two rooms used by the staff, has been removed by them or destroyed. On the highest point on the bluff, which rises steeply to the S. of Haifa, is a monument to mark the point where the Kaiser stood, in 1898, to see the view. Nearby is a long German gun, of large calibre, which commands the bay and valley. It fired a few shots at our troops, I believe, and at the two destroyers which cooperated on the coast; but it did no harm. Carmel is a huge mass of rocky mountains; once covered with trees, but these have mostly been cut down. Now, little but scrub remains. From the northern slop[e] many good springs run out. The Kishon (or Nahr el Mokatta[93]) is dry; except for the lower 4 or 5 miles of its course where it runs through marshes to the sea. Haifa is a large, well built town, between the mountain and the southern horn of the bay. I have fixed on a comfortable villa for myself, if we go there. I have the Turkish railway running, now, from there [Haifa] to Beisan and the Jordan bridge just S. of Lake Tiberias. It won't help me much, however, south of Haifa; as I've very little rolling stock for it, and the gradients are too steep for it to pull big loads.

The enclosed snapshot was taken by Colonel Finley [?]. We had a slight shock of earthquake; at 2.30 p.m.; which shook the house, and made the doors and windows rattle for about 30 seconds.

LHCMA: Allenby papers 1/9/10

166
Allenby to War Office (GOC-in-C Egypt to War Office)
[Telegram. Typescript]   30 September 1918
No. E.A.1707

29th. Your telegram No. 67160, cipher, 25th September.[94] It is not my intention to extend the jurisdiction of the Occupied Enemy Territory Administration under General Mone[y] into the area of French influence. I shall appoint French military officers wherever administration may be necessary in the French "Blue" area.[95] They will be under my orders as Commander-in-Chief of the Allied Expeditionary Force, and shall communicate my orders to them through my Chief Political Officer. I am not extending the existing Occupied Enemy Territory Administration to places east of Jordan in the "B" area, such as Es Salt and Amman, but until such time as an Arab administration be formed later, I am merely appointing a British officer to safeguard the interests of the inhabitants. As regards the "A" area, notably the city of Damascus, I shall recognize the local Arab administration which I expect to find in existence, and shall appoint French liaison officers as required. My communication with the French Political Mission will continue to be through my Chief Political Officer. I hope by the above procedure to safeguard French and Arab interests, while ensuring that supreme control remains in my own hands as Commander-in-Chief.

PRO: WO33/960, p. 118

167
War Office to Allenby (War Office to GOC-in-C Egypt)
[Telegram. Typescript]   1 October 1918
No. 67612

You are authorized by His Majesty's Government to hoist the Arab flag in Damascus when you arrive there.

PRO: WO33/960, p. 122

168
Allenby to Wilson (Chief Egypforce to Troopers London)

[Telegram. Typescript]   1 October 1918, despatched 23.59 hrs
SECRET
E.A.1715

In continuation of my E.A. 1713 [1715?] cipher 1/10/18 to Troopers. Last night the Australian Mounted Division entered the outskirts of DAMASCUS from the N.W. The Desert Mounted Corps and the Arab Army occupied the town at 0600 to-day.

Over 7,000 prisoners have already been counted. The civil administration remains in the hands of the existing authorities, and all troops, with the exception of a few guards, have been withdrawn from the town.

PRO: WO95/4371. Slightly different copy at PRO: WO33/960, p. 125 dated 2 October 1918

169
Allenby to Lady Allenby

[Letter. Holograph]   1 October 1918

I have just cabled to the War Office that I have taken Damascus.

My mounted troops and the Arabs had surrounded the town yesterday, and it was entered this morning. I have, as yet, no details. I shall probably start, myself, for Damascus tomorrow; staying tomorrow night at Tiberias, and reaching Damascus on the 3rd. I do not propose to remain there; and shall probably be back here on the 4th.

LHCMA: Allenby papers 1/9/11

170
Allenby to King Hussein (Chief Egyptforce to HH King Hussein)

[Telegram]   1 October 1918
O.A.M.932

I am glad to inform Your Highness that our combined forces entered the City of DAMASCUS at 6 a.m. to-day. Over 7,000 prisoners were captured.

PRO: WO95/4371

171
Allenby to Lady Allenby

[Letter. Holograph]   3 September [October] 1918[96]
Embossed

I am back at Tiberias, after a long motor car journey to Damascus and back.

We left at 5 a.m.; coasted Lake Tiberias; and crossed the Jordan just south of lake Huleh – Lake Huleh[97] is just like a Scotch loch; some 2 miles long and a mile wide. Thence, up and up, to a great stony plateau; Hermon high on our left, with one tiny patch of snow near his top.[98]

Coming down from the plateau, slightly, Damascus lies – white in an ocean of verdure: gardens, graves, orchards, vineyards etc. etc. stretching for many miles. The town's disappointing, inside; but the country, for miles round, must be beautiful – in peace time –. The city lies in a plain; surrounded by mountains, near in the West, distant in the East. On arrival, I went to the Victoria Hotel. Later, the Sherif Feisal arrived; and came to see me there. He was mounted on a bay Arab; with a large escort of Arabs, all mounted. He is a fine, slim sharp featured man; of about 35. Lawrence was there too, and interpreted. I had a long and satisfactory talk with Feisal. He will take over the Administration of Damascus; in the same way as Money in Palestine; or, rather, will put in a military administration. His flag now flies over Damascus. The town is quiet now; but there was a little pillaging and shooting, the day before yesterday – quickly repressed by Lawrence. My Cavalry had some sharpish fighting, outside the town; and a good many dead Turks are still lying about; but my losses were very light. The number of prisoners is appalling; over 20,000 taken in this business, brings the total – as far as I can guess – to 80,000 or 90,000. I've only reported 71,000 officially. Barrow had to leave 2,000 behind as they could not keep up. He put them in villages and told the inhabitants to take care of them. Very likely their throats are cut, by now. Lawrence tells me that his Arabs found one village where 40 women and 20 or 30 children had been bayonetted [sic] by the Turks – in pure wantonness. After that; very few, if any, prisoners were taken by them! All my Cavalry leaders are delighted with themselves. I saw the Divisional generals, yesterday, at Chauvel's Headquarters. He is in a big house that was Jemal's[99] Headquarters standing high on the W. of the town, with a beautiful view of the whole city and its surroundings.

LHCMA: Allenby papers 1/9/12

172
Wingate to Allenby

The Residency Ramleh

[Letter. Typescript]   3 October 1918

It will be interesting to see how the Sherifian Flag and the French liaison is taken by all and sundry – I have just got the copies you kindly sent me of the wires from and to the War Office on the subject. As the political side develops we must expect difficulties with our old Meccan King and I suppose he will renew his abdication tactics – but one never really knows with these people and he may be content with the "half-loaf" offered by the S-P agreement to which H.M.G. are evidently closely adhering as far as England and France are concerned.

SAD: Wingate papers 170/2/12–13

194

173
Allenby to Wigram
[Letter. Holograph] 5 September [October] 1918[100]

I present my humble duty to the King; and I would venture to submit, for His Majesty's information, a few notes on recent events in this theatre. As you know, I made two attempts against the Hedjaz railway – at Amman – and Es Salt last spring.

These were in the nature of big raids; intended to ease pressure on the Arabs, under Feisal, further south. I could not expect to be able to maintain a hold on these localities; unless the force of Sherif Feisal could come further North, along the Hedjaz railway, and keep touch with me. The Arabs could not do this. Further, the situation in Europe led to my being reduced in numbers; and what British troops were taken from me were gradually replaced by Indians – many, quite new troops –.

Consequently, my summertime was devoted to reorganization and training; while I laid my plans for an autumn offensive.

My activities in and East of the Jordan Valley had alarmed Liman Von Sanders; and he transferred a considerable force to the left bank of the Jordan, with a corresponding weakening of the centre and right of his line. My policy, during the summer, has been to encourage him in the notion that my force was too weak for an important attack; but that, when I found myself strong enough, I should attack either East of the Jordan, in cooperation with the Arabs, or on the Nablus road Northwards. In this, I was, on the whole, successful. Incessant activity in the Jordan Valley – in which the Indian Cavalry greatly distinguished themselves – and strong and frequent raids on the Nablus front, kept the Turks nervously apprehensive.

Liman Von Sanders never seems to have comprehended the possibility of a Cavalry raid round his right; though he appears to have known that I was forming a new Cavalry Division – making four in all –. He contented himself by digging and wiring up to the sea coast. I tried to make believe that my Cavalry were all intended for the Jordan Valley; and he neglected the danger of an advance along the sea coast.

My Staff calculated for me that by the middle of September my troops would be reorganized and sufficiently trained to undertake a decisive attack, with reasonable chance of succeeding. I fixed the 19th September as the day – the moon being then just short of the full; with a short period of darkness between moonset and sunrise –.

Three Cavalry Divisions and five Divisions of Infantry were moved into position, opposite the Turkish Right, and concealed in orange and olive groves. Gun emplacements, carefully camouflaged, had been prepared many weeks before; and some 380 guns were in position, by zero day, on the front of attack. All movements were made by night, and no fires were allowed in the positions of secret rendezvous. Cooking was done on spirit stoves.

The plan of attack was that, at 4.30 a.m. on zero day, the 5 Infantry Divisions – and, on their right, the French Detachment of 4 Battalions – should attack on a front of some 10 miles. This attack was under the direction of Lieut. General Sir E. Bulfin, commanding XXI Corps. The two remaining Divisions, 10th and 53rd, formed the XX Corps under Sir P. Chetwode. He held the front thinly; and connected with the Australian and New Zealand Mounted Division, under Major General Chaytor, in the Jordan Valley. Chaytor had also under him the 20th Indian Imperial Service Brigade, two Battalions of the B.W.I. Regt., and two Jewish Battalions of the R. Fusiliers – 38th and 39th –. The 10th and 53rd Divisions were to be ready to move North by evening of zero day. The 4th and 5th Cavalry Divisions were to break through, on the coast, directly a gap was opened by the Infantry; and, followed by the Australian Mounted Division, were to cut the Turks' line of communications and retreat at Nazareth, Afule and Beisan. The only Naval cooperation deemed necessary was fire from two destroyers on the beach road, between Haifa and the mouth of the Iskanderun, to cover the sea flank of the Cavalry. At 4.30 a.m., an intense bombardment was opened by our guns.

This lasted for about 15 minutes, during which time my Infantry were moving across no man's land. Without a check, they went through the Turkish wire and front line trenches. By 6 a.m. the head of the 5th Cavalry Division – Macandrew – was through and heading for Nazareth. He was followed by the 4th – Barrow – making for Afule; then came the Australian Mounted Division – Hodgson – directed on Lejjun (which is Megiddo or Armageddon) and Jenin. The Infantry were directed on the line Shechem (Nablus) Samaria (Sebustieh) and Tulkeram. The 54th Division – Hare – on the right, with the French, took their objectives; then they formed a flank. On their left, the 3rd – Hoskins – made for Nablus. Next came the 7th – Fane – aimed at Sebustieh. The 75th – Palin –, arriving at El Tireh, stopped and fell into reserve on Palin's left, Shea – with the 60th – swung across from the coast; leaving a gap for the Cavalry; and made for Tulkeram. Everything went on oiled wheels. Staff work was perfect; there was not a hitch anywhere.

The young Indian Troops fought like old soldiers. Many marched over 20 miles, in the roughest imaginable country in the first day; and all carried on incessantly for 36 hours. When the attack was seen to be going well, Chetwode – who had, on the night of zero-1, advanced considerably on the Nablus road – ordered forward his Corps. They went at their work with equal dash and success; on both sides of the Nablus road. At 3 a.m. on the 20th Sept. Macandrew had surrounded Liman Von Sanders' Head Quarters at Nazareth. However, Liman had got away a few hours earlier. By evening of 20th Barrow was at Beisan, Macandrew at Afule, Hodgson at Lejjun and Jenin. At Jenin, the Australian's took 7,500 prisoners. By evening of the 20th, the Infantry were up to their objectives. The result was that the VII and VIII Turkish armies were completely destroyed in 36 hours; losing every gun and all their transport.

The aeroplanes cooperated splendidly, bombing and reconnoitring. The crowded fugitives, guns and transport in the defiles of the mountains suffered frightful casualties from bombs and machine gun fire. The Australian and New Zealand Mounted Division, under Chaytor, with attached Infantry then went in pursuit of the IV army on the E. bank of Jordan. Amman was taken, with many prisoners, and the remnants of the IV army fled N. towards Deraa. Barrow, from Beisan, headed off many; and, later, pursued towards Deraa and Damascus. On the 23rd Sept.

Macandrew took Haifa. There was some fighting; and the Jodhpor lancers took the town at a gallop, killing Turks with their lances, in the streets. Their Colonel was killed in this attack.

Sir Partap [?] Singh[101] had had to go back, as he was suffering from fever, or he would have been in this charge. There was no difficulty in occupying Acre.

Meanwhile, much clearing up work was being done in the mountains; and prisoners were daily being brought in by hundreds and thousands. The defeat was so complete that I decided to push the Cavalry on to Damascus. By the 27th, some sort of order was established; and the Cavalry started. Barrow went, via Jisr el Mujamieh,[102] from Biesan, on Deraa; joining hands with Feisal's Arabs near Deraa. The other two Divisions went by Tiberias (Tubaria), Safed and Kuneitra.

Barrow and the Arabs caught thousands of the retreating IV army N. of Deraa.

Chauvel, with the 4th and 5th Divisions, had a good deal of fighting; but suffered only slight casualties, the Turks being now very demoralised. German rearguards, in motor cars, fought well against him. On the 1st October, Damascus was entered by the Australians and Arabs. Prisoners taken, about Damascus, are probably some 20,000 or more; and a large number of Turks were killed. Meanwhile, Chaytor cut off and captured all the garrisons from the Maan district; who tried to escape N. along the Hedjaz railway past Amman. I went to Damascus, on the 3rd inst., and met Feisal. He has hoisted his flag their [sic], and has taken over the Civil Administration of the town and district.

It is in the French zone of interest; so a French liaison officer is appointed. He will, however, only be liaison officer between the Arab Military Governor and me, through my own political officer – Clayton –. He will have no administrative functions. While the country is under martial law, I am of course in supreme control. Now I am pushing Cavalry on towards Rayak – the road and railway junction, between Damascus and Beirut –; and I have the 7th Infantry Division moving on Beirut by the coast – fed from the sea, by ships –. Supply is going to be my difficulty now. The rains are beginning; the roads are bad; the railway is a lame one –

several important bridges in the Yarmuk valley being broken, and many gradients as steep as 1/40.

The number of prisoners, too, complicates supply and transport problems. I have, now, 71,000 prisoners; officially reported; and I believe the total is very much larger. Many are sick and starved. Barrow had to leave 2,000 behind him, as they could not walk, on his way to Damascus.

Some of the Turks, in their retreat, wantonly massacred Arab women and children; and the Arabs have got their blood up. Consequently, there will be many Turkish stragglers who will not have a pleasant time. The feeling towards the British is enthusiastic but they are not so keenly enthusiastic about our allies. I receive many protestations of loyalty to our King; and hopes that the land may be, in future, under His rule. The old King of the Hedjaz sends me many telegrams of congratulation and is evidently delighted at the course events have taken. Some 3 or 4 weeks ago, however, he was very awkward; and a strained situation arose between him and Feisal, taking a good deal of smoothing out. I hope now that the siege of Medina will be pushed by him with more vigour. The trouble is that the city is too sacred to be bombarded; and it is defended by a gallant and obstinate old Turk – Fakhredin –.

Well, things look very different now to what they did 6 months ago; both here and in Europe.

Royal Archive: RA PS/GV/Q 2521/18

174
Allenby to Wilson (Chief Egypforce to Troopers London)
[Telegram. Typescript]   6 October 1918, despatched 7 October 1918

SECRET
PARAPHRASE

SAIDA (SIDON) was occupied to-day by the 7th Division without opposition. The troops received an enthusiastic welcome from the inhabitants. The townspeople said that it was expected that Arabs would arrive and take over the Government of the town, and begged that instead, a British Governor might be appointed. I have appointed a temporary British Governor but shall replace him as soon as possible by a French Officer. The same procedure is being adopted at TYRE.

PRO: WO95/4371

175
Allenby to War Office (GOC-in-C Egypt to War Office)
[Telegram. Typescript]   6 October 1918
No. P.689

Acre has received a copy of a proclamation from Beirut of which the following are the most important points:–

1. A telegram, dated 30th September, has been received from Damascus from the chief of the temporary government of that city to the effect that a Hashemite Government is founded in Damascus in consequence of the surrender of the Turks, and the public should therefore be reassured and a new government in the name of the Arab Government be proclaimed in Beirut.

2. The late Turkish Vali[103] of Beirut handed in an official letter, dated 1st October, announcing that a critical situation had arisen in view of the proclamation issued by the Arab Government in Damascus and the chief of the municipality therefore placed in charge of the administration.

3. Here follows a list of appointments made by the new administration in Beirut.

4. Here follow various regulations for the preservation of public security.

The proclamation is signed by a certain Ar Dauk [?], who styles himself chief of the Arab Government in Beirut. Information obtained in Damascus confirms that action as indicated in the above proclamation has been taken by the Arabs. In view of paragraph 2 of the Anglo-French Agreement the unexpected action of the Arab Government, taken previous to any effective

Allied occupation of Beirut or even of Damascus, places the French representative in a difficult position. He will probably appeal to me to install a French Military Government in place of an Arab Administration and will request me to haul down the Arab flag which has doubtless already been hoisted in Beirut. As long as Beirut town and district are in military occupation by Allied forces I propose to forbid the display of any flags in the same way as I have done in Palestine. In view of the fact that I shall depend to some extent on Beirut for the maintenance of my army it is essential that I should retain supreme control. I therefore propose to appoint one of the officers of my force as Military Governor to control the local administration and ensure that military interests are safeguarded. I shall appoint a French officer to this post if I can find someone who is suitable. Except where maintenance of order may be concerned I do not propose to take part in any Franco-Arab dispute, but all developments will be cabled immediately to you.

PRO: WO33/960, p. 133

176
Allenby to War Office (GOC-in-C Egypt to War Office)
[Telegram. Typescript]   6 October 1918
No. P960

The Arabs proclaimed an Arab Government under King Hussein and hoisted the Arab flag immediately the Turkish evacuation of Damascus began, and before the Turkish troops had actually left the city an Arab Governor of Damascus was appointed. When my troops entered the city, therefore, an Arab administration was in being and the Arab flag was flying from the Government buildings.

On the 3rd October I visited the city and Sherif Feisal made his entry amid the acclamation of the inhabitants [on the] same day.

In the presence of our respective staffs I had an interview with Sherif Feisal and I informed him that I was prepared to recognize the Arab administration of occupied territory east of the Jordan, from Damascus to Maan, inclusive, as a military administration under my supreme control. I further informed him I should appoint two liaison officers between me and the Arab administration, one of whom would be British and the other French, and that these two officers would communicate with me through my chief political officer.

As long as military operations were in progress I explained that I was in supreme command, and that all administration must be under my control.

I communicated to Sherif Feisal the fact that the French and British Governments had agreed to recognize the belligerent status of the Arab forces fighting in Palestine and Syria, as Allies against the common enemy.

PRO: WO33/960, p. 133

177
Allenby to Wilson (Chief Egyptforce to Troopers London)
[Telegram. Typescript] 7 October 1918
SECRET
PARAPHRASE
E.A.1746 cipher

March of the 7th Division is being continued and it is expected that its leading troops will reach ED DAMUR to-night.

Fuller details of the occupation of SAIDA (SIDON), reported to you yesterday, have now been received. The EMIR FEISAL'S representative SAID ELIA KHORRI reached the town last night accompanied by some 50 men. It appears that the local authorities at SAIDA acting on orders telegraphed by FEISAL hoisted the Arab flag there several days ago. SAID ELIA KHORRI has been told that no flags are to be hoisted and if any are now flying that they will be taken down.

The Rear-Admiral S.N.O. Egypt and Red Sea has been informed by the French Admiral that the French Government had given him orders to enter BEIRUT as soon as possible and that he intends to do so to-morrow morning. Two French destroyers have already arrived at the Port. I have requested the French Admiral through R.N., S.N.O. Egypt and Red Sea to send a destroyer to HAIFA to embark a French detachment to take over guard duties in BEIRUT on the morning of the 11th. Col. DE PIEPAPE will be appointed Temporary Military Governor of the town.

DAMASCUS is quiet and the Arab Administration is working satisfactorily there.

PRO: WO95/4371

178
Allenby to War Office (GOC-in-C Egypt to War Office)
[Telegram. Typescript]   7 October 1918
No. P695

6th In continuation of my P.689, 5th October. The fact that Arab leaders are aware of assurances contained in Foreign Office telegram No. 753, 16th June, to High Commissioner, complicated position at Beirut; in this telegram, His Majesty's Government recognized native army and sovereign[ty] of independent Arabs inhabiting the areas emancipated from Turkish control by action of Arabs themselves during present war. Concerning areas which Allied forces occupy, His Majesty's Government drew attention to proclamations issued on capture of Baghdad and Jerusalem, and added that future government of these regions would be based principally on consent of those governed; I was not consulted before this assurance was given; further, Arab leaders have never been officially notified of terms of Anglo-French Agreement.

PRO: WO33/960, p. 136

179
Allenby to Wilson (Chief Egypforce to Troopers London)

[Telegram. Typescript]   8 October 1918, despatched 9 October 1918

SECRET
PARAPHRASE
E.A.1752

Yesterday an armoured car reconnaissance sent out from ZAHLE by the Desert Mounted Corps reached BEIRUT. They found the town evacuated by the Turks and an Arab Government under SHUKRI PASHA AYUBI[104] set up.[105] The population was quiet and orderly. A French destroyer and five French vessels had arrived in the harbour. The town was occupied by the advanced troops of the 7th Divn today, and they were accorded an enthusiastic welcome. The total of prisoners captured by the E.E.F. now exceeds 75,000, and it is estimated that of the 4th, 7th and 8th Armies and L. of C. troops not more than 17,000 have escaped, and that only 4000 of these are effective rifles. We still have at DAMASCUS at the present moment 25000 of these 75000 prisoners, and owing to their state of health and our lack of motor ambulances and lorries there is difficulty in bringing them back. Owing to an outbreak of cholera at TIBERIAS this place, which could have formed a good stop on the journey, is not available. There are 16000 sick and wounded still to be evacuated out of the total of prisoners.

DAMASCUS itself is tranquil, and the price of food has fallen 20% from what it was during the Turkish occupation.

* (Feisal has informed my Liaison officer with the Arab Administration that he will not issue any proclamation without consulting me. He is somewhat concerned as to the intentions of the French, but we are re-assuring him in every way possible).

There is some destitution and disease in AMMAN, but my Medical Authorities are dealing with these. Otherwise the situation in the AMMAN – ES SALT area is satisfactory.

* Omitted from copies given a general distribution.

PRO: WO95/4371. Slightly different copy at PRO: WO33/960, p. 140 dated 9 October.

180
Allenby to the Secretary War Office

General Headquarters
[Telegram? Typescript. Copy]   9 October 1918
SECRET

I have the honour to forward herewith copies of correspondence received from the General Officers Commanding Force in Egypt and Sollum Section, from which it appears that there is a tendency on the part of the Italian Military Authorities in Cyrenaica to establish the motor road from Sollum to Siwa as the boundary line between Egyptian and Italian territory. This motor road does not in any way mark the frontier line, which, I understand, has never been defined, and is reserved for settlement between the British and Italian Governments.

It may be considered desirable to safeguard the situation by pointing out to the Italian Government that any dividing line which it may be found convenient to establish on Military grounds between the spheres of Military action of British and Italian troops is without prejudice to future settlement of the frontier between Egypt and Cyrenaica.

SAD: Wingate papers: 132/2/106. Copy at PRO: WO95/4371

181
Allenby to Wilson (Chief, Egypforce to Troopers, LONDON repeated Britannia ISMAILIA and High Commissioner)
[Telegram. Typescript]   11 October 1918, despatched 2355
E.A.1768 cipher
Operations 2000

Advanced troops of XXIst Corps expect to reach TRIPOLI on 13th instant. BAALBEK, the first stage of its advance to HOMS, has been reached by the leading brigade of the 5th Cavalry Division.

Shukri el Ayubi has not yet been withdrawn from BEIROUT by Feisal. He has however modified his attitude so far as to instruct the heads of the Police and the President of the Municipality that they must accept my Corps Commander at BEIROUT's Orders.

The town is quiet, and the Arab flags flying here have been lowered.

The policy I am adopting is as follows:–

I am recognising Arab independence in Areas 'A' and 'B'; advice and assistance in these areas being given by French and British respectively.[106]

French interests are recognised as being predominant in the 'Blue' area.

Feisal is being warned that if he attempts to control the 'Blue' area, the settlement of which must await the Peace Conference, he will prejudice his case. He is also being told that the LEBANON's status is a peculiar one, and was guaranteed by the Powers, so that he will [be] treading on delicate ground if he attempts undue interference in that area.

LHCMA: Allenby papers 2/5/8. Copies at PRO: WO95/4371 and OxAnt: Allenby papers, 1/1. Slightly different copy at PRO: WO33/960, pp. 142–3 dated 12 October 1918

182
Allenby to Lady Allenby

Haifa
[Letter. Holograph]   17 October 1918

I got back from Damascus this evening. We started at 8 a.m.; and came by Tiberias and Nazareth, reaching here at 4.30 p.m. Lovely day. Quite cool at Damascus, but warm here. I dined last night – with Sherif Feisal and all the notabilities of Damascus. He gave me an excellent dinner; Arab dishes, but all good, served in the ordinary way of civilisation. Water to drink; but good, cool fresh water; not tepid barley water! This morning Feisal sent me a big sideboard or hall table, of the best Damascus inlaid work. The mosaic is in the finest style, and so well laid that you can't feel the least roughness with your finger. I believe it took over 3 years to manufacture. I am having it sent to Beirut; and, thence, to Cairo, by sea.

In return, I propose to give him one of my Baruch [?] photographs in your silver frame. Will you have one framed therein, and let me know when it is ready? I can't run to giving him a present of equal value to that which he gave me! I have had long talks with him, on politics etc. He is nervous about the peace settlement; but I tell him he must trust the Entente powers to treat him fairly.

I had a great reception – guards of honour of the Arab troops, cheering crowds, deputations, etc. –. You would like Feisal. He is a keen, slim, highly strung man. He has beautiful hands, like a woman's; and his fingers are always moving nervously, when he talks. But he is strong in will, and straight in principle.

LHCMA: Allenby papers 1/9/15

183
Allenby to War Office (GOC-in-C to War Office)
[Telegram. Typescript]   17 October 1918
No. I.6906/P

Have communicated the policy decided upon, as approved by High Commissioner for communication to King of Hejaz, to my French military administrator at Beirut and to Feisal with whom, yesterday, I had an interview. Feisal is very distrustful of French intentions, fearing that French military governors will take advantage of their official positions to carry on propaganda and thereby entail prejudice to an eventual settlement on a basis of real self-determination. I gave him official assurance that whatever measures might be taken during period of military administration they were purely provisional and would not be allowed to prejudice final settlement by the peace conference at which, no doubt, Arabs would have a representative. I added that instructions to military governors would preclude their mixing in political affairs and that I should remove them if I found any of them continuing [?] these orders. I reminded Feisal that the Allies were in honour bound to endeavour to reach settlement in accordance with wishes of the peoples concerned and urged him to place his trust wholeheartedly in their good faith. Feisal appeared reassured, but doubtless he is being pressed by his followers and by his father probably. The general feeling of uneasiness on the part of Arabs can only be dispelled by public declaration of policy by the French and British Governments, and any injudicious pushing by French of their own interests at the present moment will confirm suspicions of the Arabs and forfeit their confidence in the French and ourselves.

PRO: WO33/960, pp. 153–4

184
Allenby to Wilson
General Headquarters, Egyptian Expeditionary Force
[Letter. Holograph]   19 October 1918

I returned yesterday after visiting Haifa, Saida (Sidon), Beirut and Damascus. Haifa has settled down, quietly and happily, under a British Military Governor. At Saida is a French Military Governor, subordinate to the French Military Governor at Beirut. The Military Governor at Beirut is Colonel de Piépape who commands the French detachment in my force. He is a good soldier and a pleasant gentleman, but has not much idea of how to carry on a Civil Administration. I am sending Money over, from Jerusalem, to give him a little advice and help; and I have also sent Colonel Huggett [?[107]], my financial expert, to advise him on the currency question and financial administration.

I impressed on Piépape that he has nothing to do with politics; and that he is an officer of mine, responsible to me for the Civil Administration of Occupied Enemy Territory North of Palestine.

His inclination has been to congratulate the inhabitants of Syria on coming under the jurisdiction of France. This I have forbidden. My policy in Syria is the same as in Palestine; viz. – I, in Supreme Military Command, am responsible for the Civil government and Administration of all Occupied Enemy Territories. For this purpose, I have appointed Military Governors – British in the Southern Territory; French in the Northern; Arab in the Eastern. These Military Governors are my Officers, and responsible to me alone –. The French have a sort of idea that their Government has already a voice in the administration of Syria. Of this idea they must be disabused. While I command, in active operations, I must control everything, including seaports. The suggestion of a special base in Syria for the French detachment is inadmissible. That detachment is part of my Army; and I must have power to supply it anywhere, if I think it necessary.

At Damascus, the Arab Government is getting to work satisfactorily; and the Military Governor, Ali Pasha,[108] is a clear headed, hardworking man. I informed Feisal of the communication which Wingate was authorized to make to the King of Hedjaz regarding the administration of Occupied Enemy Territory; and I had some long talks with him. He, like every other Moslem in Syria, is convinced that the French mean to get hold of the country; and the fact that French military governors have been installed in coastal areas has deepened his suspicion.

I told him that these were military arrangements; and that all the present temporary organisation was liable to revision and alteration at the Peace conference – where the Arabs, as a recognised belligerent nation, would doubtless be represented –. What he feels most is that all access to the sea is barred. Haifa, Beirut, Tripoli, Alexandretta closed to the Arabs. He said – "I am in a house with no door" –. I told him to turn his mind to the administration of the great areas which have been conquered by our allied arms; and to trust, for the future, to the good faith of the British and French. I added that the French are our allies, an honourable nation, fighting for the same cause and with the same ideals.

This dislike and distrust of the French is universal among the Moslems in Syria. It cannot be abated by anything I say or do. If a statement, by the two governments French and British could be published – to the effect that, after the war, the wishes of the inhabitants would be considered in deciding on the form of government in conquered territories – it would do much to restore confidence. Cornwallis, who is my British liaison officer with Feisal, is a first rate man; wise and tactful. Captain Mercier, the French liaison officer with Feisal, has, I hear, informed his government that his position is impossible – owing to Arab obstructiveness –. I've only just heard this. It is typical of the French attitude. Mercier is, of course, my liaison officer – just as much as Cornwallis is –. He should have communicated with me. He has nothing whatever to do with the French government. I am looking into the matter; but it is only a trifle, and no trouble should ensue. Congratulations on all your victories.

IWM: Wilson papers HHW2/33A/28

185
Allenby to Wilson
General Headquarters, Egyptian Expeditionary Force
[Letter. Holograph]   22 October 1918

Thank you for yours of 24th Sept. and your kind words. I think we taught the Turks something about the proper use of Cavalry. My 5th Cavalry Division is now well N. of Hama, and making for Aleppo. My 4th near Baalbek, is very much weakened by malaria and won't be able to follow closely. However, I've sent a lot of armoured cars with the 5th; and it will have strong fire power.

Sickness is troubling us. I had the mosquitos [sic] well in hand; and soon the Jordan Valley had become almost a summer health resort. Now I'm in Turkish territory, and malignant malaria is laying a lot of people by the heels. I've a good acting D.M.S. now; one Luce;[109] and he is doing all he can, but his beds are all full. I want to send some thousands of sick to Malta; but Salonika appears to have filled up most of the beds there. My Turkish prisoners are improving in health, to some extent, and their death–

rate is diminishing. Thousands are still at Damascus, awaiting removal to Egypt, but transport is not sufficient. I am at work on the broken bridges in the Yarmuk Valley; and, meanwhile, bridging the gap by camels and motor lorries. As for roads, I propose to concentrate on the coast road from Haifa northwards, then Tripoli-Homs road, and then Beirut-Baalbek road. I hope to keep them passable during the rains; then, with my standard gauge railway to Haifa, and using the Turkish railway Haifa-Damascus-Rayak, I may keep going. The railway, N. of Rayak, is standard gauge; and sleepers are steel, so that I can't squeeze the line in to the metre gauge; therefore, I fear it is useless to me, as yet.

IWM: Wilson papers HHW2/33A/27

186
Allenby to War Office (GOC-in-C Egypt to War Office

[Telegram. Typescript]   23 October 1918
No. E.A.1808

The following instructions for the military administration of all occupied enemy territory in Syria and Palestine has been issued by me:–

"Enemy territory in occupation of Allied force of Egypt Expeditionary Force will be for the purposes of provisional military administration divided into three areas, each in charge of a chief administrator, who in all matters will be directly responsible to Commander-in-Chief.

Following are administrative areas:– First, Occupied Enemy Territory South: Chief Administrator, General Money; comprises the Sanjaks of Jerusalem, Nablus and Acre.[110]

Second, Occupied Enemy Territory east: Chief Administrator, Ali Riza Pasha el Rikabi[111] comprises all districts lying to the east of O.E.T. south and O.E.T. north up to the north [sic] limits of the (?) Threzas of Jebal Seman and El Bab. The system of administration will be in accordance with law and usages of war as laid down in Chapter 14, Section 8, manual of Military Law, and no departures from these principles will be permitted without the approval of the

Commander-in-Chief. As far as possible the Turkish system of government will be continued and the existing machinery utilized. The administration will be required to provide for all necessary government services and the extent, during a state of war, to which these services can be developed is left to the discretion of the Chief Administrator concerned. As far as possible it is desirable to retain Turkish administrative areas and in this way existing records could be utilized. The Ottoman public debt administration will, subject to general control of the Chief Administrator, be permitted to continue its functions. The Regie tobacco monopoly[112] will continue its functions under similar conditions.

All communications from Chief Administrator will be made to the Commander-in-Chief through the Deputy-Adjutant General, General Headquarters, to whom all reports should be addressed. Chief Administrators should submit reports by the 15th of each month on the general situation in their administrations.

Chief Administrators are reminded that the administration is a military and provisional one and without prejudice to future settlement of areas concerned; they are therefore instructed not to undertake, except so far as may be necessary for the maintenance of public order and security, any political propaganda or to take part in any political questions."

PRO: WO33/960, pp. 162–3

187
Wingate to Allenby

The Residency Ramleh

[Letter. Typescript]   24 October 1918

I have seen the telegrams which passed between you and London from Damascus and am in entire agreement with your views. You will also have seen my further telegram to the King of the Hedjaz and I hope it will put him off the Damascus trip for the present. When the Hedjaz Railway is in working order from Maan to Damascus, it might be possible to get him through by sea to Akaba and thence to Maan by motor – unless it be intended to admit his suzerainty over "the Blue Area" and in that case the Beyrout route would probably be more suitable.

I am delighted to see that you have put your foot down on the appellation of Picot as High Commissioner. The F.O. have not replied to my question as to the name of "the French High Commissioner in Arabia".

SAD: Wingate papers 170/2/138–9

188
DMO to Allenby (Director of Military Intelligence to GOC-in-C Egypt)

[Telegram. Typescript]   27 October 1918
No. 69503

The following point we embodied in a joint note on administration of territories of special French interest as in Anglo-French Agreement of 1916 now or hereafter occupied by Egypt Expeditionary Force. On 19th October the note was confirmed by British and ratified by French Governments:–

(*a*.) Commander-in-Chief will recognize representative of French Government as his Chief Political Adviser in these areas.

(*b*.) Latter's functions are subject to Commander-in-Chief's Supreme Authority to act as sole intermediary on political and administrative questions between Commander-in-Chief and Arab Governments in area "A" recognized by Clause I. of Agreement of 1916, subject to following provisos: Any person has right of direct access to Commander-in-Chief, Political Adviser has not the right to attend military conferences between Commander-in-Chief or staff and Arab commanders, but Commander-in-Chief shall subsequently communicate substance of official non-military conversations to Political Adviser.

(*c*.) At request of and subject to authority to Commander-in-Chief, Political Adviser will be charged with establishment of civil administration in "Blue" area in general.

(*d.*) Subject to approval of Commander-in-Chief, Adviser to supply staff for functions as in "B," European Advisory staff as Arab Governments in area "A" require under Clause I. of 1916 Agreement, personnel for civil duties in "Blue" area. Commander-in-Chief to have full powers over such staffs.

(*e.*) Adviser is responsible to Commander-in-Chief for political relations in area "A" and for political relations and provisional [sic] and administration in "Blue" area.

(*f.*) Above arrangements to remain in force until such time as reconsideration is justified by military situation. Full note follows by bag.

PRO: WO33/960, p. 168

Chapter 3
The Paris Peace Conference,
November 1918–October 1919

189
Wingate to Allenby

The Residency Cairo

[Letter. Typescript. Copy]   2 November 1918

As you rightly say in your letter of 29th October just received – "Peace is looming large on the horizons of Europe" and events are likely to move fairly quickly – You will have had the Turkish Peace Conditions last night, they seem pretty complete and savour of the "unconditional surrender" type. Your magnificent series of victories and rapid advance are, of course, the main factors which have brought about this highly satisfactory arrangement, and again I beg you will accept my most sincere congratulations.

I have wired the old King[1] and also to Aden – It will be interesting to see Hedjaz developments and how the various Turkish Commanders take their orders in Asyr[2] and Yemen – also in Tripolitania and Cyrenaica.[3] Sayed Ahmed's[4] new title – if ever he succeeds in landing – is not likely to help him much in the changed conditions.

I hope our Fleet will now knock out the German Black Sea Fleet and turn the German Eastern flank from the Crimea and Batoum.[5]

I am glad to hear from you that Sykes-Picot and Co. are coming out: their original agreement will need much alteration if not complete scrapping – when as you say they see the dangers on the spot. I get little or no war news from the F.O. I hope you are fit and well and that the sickness amongst the Troops is abating.[6] My wife joins in every kind message.

SAD: Wingate papers 170/3/19

215

190
Allenby to War Office (GOC-in-C Egypt to War Office)

[Telegram. Typescript]   4 November 1918
No. 7191/P.

3rd. Have received the following message from Feisal, dated 2nd November, No. C.196:–

"Regret to inform your Excellency that I have sure information that agents of Captain Mercier, names Michel and Joseph Kuheil, have summoned the Chief Shiekhs of the Hauran Druzes, and informed them that French Protectorate (?) anticipated will shortly be established here, and that French force will arrive in a few days. They have instructed them that all who desire French protection should immediately apply in writing in order that their applications may be forwarded to Beirut. I greatly fear that the French intend to use this as written proof Hauran inclined towards French protection, which will be, doubtless, represented as spontaneous. I continue to receive from all sides complaints of French propaganda carried out throughout Lebanon and at Beirut, and if this is now extended to area of purely Arab Government it is more than I can tolerate. I can only conclude in absence of official declaration of French intentions, for which I have repeatedly asked, that their aim is to provoke political disorder and disturbance, which they may use before the world as proof of Arab incapacity for administration and as justification to themselves to occupy country by force of arms. In this event there is no Arab force that can resist powerful nation bent on acquisition of this country by force, and we shall be left at their mercy. I have done my best to fulfil my duties, relying on your indomitable assurance, but I feel my honour is now involved, and that I cannot stay to see my country sacrificed to ambition of a nation which I do not believe has our interests at heart. In view of this situation, and of your written instructions that all your officers, whether French, British or Arab, must entirely abstain from political propaganda, I must represent that the continued presence as liaison officer in Damascus of Captain Mercier will add greatly to my difficulties in forming and maintaining efficient administration. So strongly do I feel this, that at present I do not consider myself justified in leaving Damascus, and I am therefore deferring my departure to Aleppo until I receive your reply."

I have replied as follows:–

"Following for Feisal from Commander-in-Chief: 'I have received your highly (? group omitted) telegram and you may rest assured that I shall take the question in hand. I have not sanctioned any communication to the Druze Sheikhs, and any instructions which may have been issued to them are of no effect as they do not carry my authority. I have ordered Captain Mercier to come and see me in order that he may understand quite clearly the policy which I have laid down. This will prevent any future misunderstandings. As I consider it of great importance that you should proceed to Aleppo, I hope you will start as soon as possible."

I have ordered Captain Mercier, my French liaison officer with the Arab military administration, and Captain Coulondre, acting (one group undecipherable) political adviser for French influence, to come to General Headquarters and discuss this question. I consider it important that Feisal should proceed to Aleppo at once and I have instructed my British liaison officer to proceed accompanied by a French officer whom, in Captain Mercier's temporary absence, I have detailed as acting liaison officer.

Feisal feels that unless political propaganda is checked immediately the prospects of establishment of an efficient Arab administration and the realization of Arab aspirations will be seriously prejudiced.

Possibly Druze Chiefs have exaggerated the affair, and it must be remembered that being neither pro-French nor pro-Arab they may therefore be attempting to play one party off against the other.

PRO: WO33/960, pp. 178–9

191
Allenby to Wilson

[Letter. Holograph]   9 November 1918
Embossed

I have just got your personal telegram to me – of 8th inst. – and will see that all Mark Sykes' reports and interviews are submitted to and supervised by me. He has not yet arrived. Picot has arrived; and I have had a long talk to him, in which I explained to him his position as my political adviser. He listened quite patiently, and I think he will maintain a correct attitude. I am glad that he has come; as now I have someone to whom I can talk plainly. Picot is a superficially clever man, but shallow and transparent. I know him well and he knows me.

Sykes I have never met; but I know him, fairly well, from hearsay. Colonel de Piépape is doing all right as Military Governor in the Blue Area – what I call O.E.T.A., North –. He is a gentleman and a hard worker, but with no experience of Civil Administration. However, my people have helped him to start; and I think that he'll do, all right. The administration of occupied enemy territory gives me no real trouble or anxiety, under present conditions.

The future, when martial law no longer prevails, is not so cloudless

Distrust of the French is not, in any way, abated. The Moslems are suspicious that the whole littoral will be given to the French; and I think that the French military governors think so too.

If the Arabs have no access to the sea, there will be endless trouble. Feisal has already asked to be allowed to resign. If he did so, there would be blood, fire and ruin throughout all Arabia and Syria. All communities and creeds have absolute faith in the English, and, if we act up to our declared principles regarding the rights of self-determination of peoples,[7] we shall retain that confidence. If not, there will be chaos. The military situation will be known to you, so I won't touch on it. You will bear in mind that Egypt would resent occupation by Indian or other colonial troops, even for a short period, after the war.

IWM: Wilson papers HHW2/33A/29

192
Wingate to Allenby

The Residency Cairo
[Letter. Typescript. Copy]   15 November 1918
Personal

My suspicions that the Nationalist element in Egypt would take the self-determination notice re Syria, Palestine, Mesopotamia and Arabia, as applicable also to this country, have been fully borne out and the matter is giving me no little concern, but I can tell you all about it when we meet.[8]

I was much interested in your account of your talk with Picot and need hardly say how entirely I share your views. Doubtless he and Sykes will be in constant communications and I hope their deliberations may help in sketching out a satisfactory future policy. I was glad to see Clayton.

I am glad you are hurrying off Feisal & Co., evidently His Majesty's Government are anxious that he gets to Paris in good time. When the Egyptian politicians realize that he has gone, they will become still more insistent that they should be allowed to represent their case direct to His Majesty's Government in London.

SAD: Wingate papers 170/3/211

193
Allenby to War Office (GOC-in-C Egypt to War Office)
[Telegram. Typescript]   5 December 1918
No. 21305 SH

Reference telegram No. 71693,[9] 28th November from Director of Military Intelligence to General Headquarters, Egypt, conveying message to Eder from Weizmann. Trust that will treat statements contained therein as confidential as their publication would arouse greatest apprehension here. Venture to request any further declaration Zionist policy be submitted for observations here before publication. According to Weizmann, Jewry all over the world, especially in America, is disappointed at moderation and timidity of Zionist demands. Those demands as made known in public speeches and press articles have among the non-Jewish population of Palestine sufficiently aroused distrust and apprehension and in that respect do not err on the side of moderation and timidity. Weizmann states as a whole Jewry considers Arab nations ambitions fully realized in new Arabo Syrian state. Present trend of political events is not inspiring confidence in the Arabs that their national aspirations in Syria will be realized. Apart from this it must be realized that Arab nations ambitions count for little in Palestine where non-Jewish population is concerned chiefly with maintenance in Palestine itself of a position which they consider Zionism threatens. Signing of armistice and approach of peace conference[10] and especially publication of Anglo-French declaration of 8th November,[11] have given rise to much excitement locally. Both non-Jews and Zionists consider moment has come to make their wishes widely known before definite settlement is arrived at by peace conference. It is possible that anti-Jewish action might be taken by Arabs in order to show opposition to Zionism which they cannot by other means express. In Palestine non-Jews number approximately 573,000 as against 66,000 Jews. In view of above considerations consider it essential that Zionists should avoid increasing apprehension by indiscreet declarations of policy and exaggerated demands which can only militate against their success by arousing permanent hostility and laying them open to charge of securing their arms [?aims] by force. The Zionists realize their legitimate aspirations provided that they carry out their programme patiently and show sympathy for what is to-day a very large majority of Palestine's population.

If they force the pace now (1 group undecipherable) insecure foundations will be the basis of whole structure.

PRO: WO33/960, pp. 228–9

194
Wilson to Allenby

[Letter. Typescript. Copy]   7 December 1918

Very many thanks for your letter of Nov. 16th just received and your much too flattering remarks about myself and the part I have played. It is the simple and bare truth to say that my role has been a very small one especially when it is remembered what a lot of opportunities I had for helping and how many of them I let slip.

The main credit is due to Foch, to you and to Franchet d'Esperey and the Serbs. The advent of the Americans and the blockade and work of our sailors both in the Fleet and in the Mercantile Marine were also tremendous factors. The picture of this war that I have seen for a great many years now has been this:

The Boch had set his mind on two things:

(a) Command of the sea

(b) The Near and Middle East

When in 1917 and early 1918 it became clear that he could not get command of the sea and therefore his first objective was lost to him I was always casting about in my mind how his second objective could be frustrated.

You and Franchet did that. The collapse of the main theatres followed almost automatically.

With the loss of both Prizes the Governing Class of the Boch lost heart – as well he might – and was no longer able to buoy up his Army and Navy.

Hence this indescribable crash. It is a wonderful story.

I hope Mark Sykes behaves himself. He is a good fellow but cracked and his blessed Sykes-Picot Agreement must be torn up somehow.

IWM: Wilson papers HHW2/33B/1

195
Allenby to Wavell

GHQ EEF

[Letter. Holograph]   15 December 1918

Thank you for yours of 19th Nov. and for giving my message to C.I.G.S. He has written to me; and I see, now, that Feisal is in England. He wires that he is receiving sympathetic treatment.

I'm just back from Aleppo and Beirut, and have seen both Picot and Sykes. Sykes is all for soothing the Arabs and giving them a port; and Picot is less Chauvinist than he was. I hear that they want to keep you, for the present. And I am sure that you can better work there than here; as things are at present.

LHCMA: Allenby papers 1/9/21

196
Special Order of the Day by General Sir E.H.H. Allenby, G.C.B., G.C.M.G., Commander in Chief, Egyptian Expeditionary Force

[Special order. Typescript]   [?] January 1919[12]

I wish to remind all ranks serving under my command that during the trying and unavoidably extended period that must elapse before the demobilization of the Egyptian Expeditionary Force can be completed, the good name of the British Army depends upon the individual conduct of each member of the Force in the various countries now in our occupation.

Courtesy and consideration to the inhabitants of these countries were never more essential, even during the period of active operations, than they now are, and I feel certain that I can rely on every member of this Force to maintain the traditions of the British Army in this respect.

In these countries special temptations exist with regard to Wine and Women. Both must be resisted. Our relatives and friends are anxiously awaiting our return home, and they will expect to find all those of us who have escaped wounds in action with our physical and our moral energies unimpaired. Treat all women with courtesy, but shun all undue intimacy. Remember that temptation, which when encountered is hard to resist, is often easy to avoid.

Final impressions are usually the more lasting; and on the behaviour of the troops during the present period will depend the final impression left by the British Army on the inhabitants of these countries.

The honour of the Egyptian Expeditionary Force is in your hands. I do not fear to leave it there.

EHH Allenby
General
CinC

NAM: 2001–11–125. Copy at NAM 7208–14–1

197
Wingate to Allenby
[Letter? Typescript. Copy. Dictated]   7 January 1919

My telegram of last night to the Foreign Office and repeated to you, dealing with the Lefevre-Pontalis[13] formal protest, was the outcome of an hour and a quarter's conversation with our worthy French representative here who was beside himself with annoyance and accused practically everybody but you and myself of violent Francophobe sentiments. He considered the suppression of Pichon's[14] speech,[15] which he had received from the French Foreign Office for publication in Cairo, little short of an insult. I told him that I alone was responsible for the suppression because I thought that it would probably add to your troubles in Syria, but that if you saw no objection to the publication, I should of course withdraw any opposition. I told him however that the departure of the Lebanese Deputation had brought upon you innumerable protests from other representative Syrian groups who thought otherwise and who would all demand the right to go to Paris.

It was, however, quite impossible to convince him and indeed, he went so far as to hint that the various deputations who disagreed with the departure of the Lebanese group had been put up to it by the British.

SAD: Wingate papers 172/2/16–19

198
Allenby to Wingate
General Headquarters, Egyptian Expeditionary Force
[Letter. Holograph]   15 January 1919

I arrived in Haifa, yesterday morning, after a useful tour. I visited Aleppo, Jerablus, Adana, Bozanti, Mersina, Alexandretta, Tripoli and Beirut. Things are quieter, and the situation is easier, than I had expected. Mark Sykes' influence at Aleppo has been for good. He and Picot met me there, and went with me to Jerablus; which had just been evacuated by the Turks, under orders from me. Everywhere, I received a warm reception. At Beirut, they gave me an enthusiastic official welcome; and presented me with a sword of honour – a beautiful old Damascus blade; inlaid, in gold, with texts from the Koran. Picot met me, again, there. I made the journey from Mersina, down the Syrian coast to Haifa, by sea; and was lucky in having fine, calm weather.

I've taken up my Headquarters permanently, now, in Haifa. The mission of the Lebanese to Europe has caused a lot of disquiet among the Moslems of Beirut and Syria generally. I gave Picot a serious discourse on the subject, and told him what I thought. It has done a lot of harm in Beirut. At Aleppo, he has succeeded in becoming somewhat less unpopular. The Turks are inclined to be dilatory in carrying out the terms of the Armistice.[16] I have been ordered to go to Constantinople, and insist in compliance. Please keep this information entirely to yourself; as it is essential that my coming shall be somewhat of a surprise to them.

SAD: Wingate papers 172/3/1–3

199
Allenby to mother

G.H.Q., E.E.F.

[Letter. Holograph]

19 January 1919

I am comfortably installed at Haifa. Weather is still mild, for the time of year; but yesterday we had much rain, and today is squally and showery. Mabel writes, from Cairo, that they had a regular flood of rain on the 17th – water rushing along the streets, and stopping trains and motor cars –. I see that the newspapers describe the downpour as being unprecedented. I'm afraid the letters I posted to you while I was journeying in N. Syria will be very late in reaching you. Mabel has only just got a letter I sent from Alexandretta on the 10th or 11th. – 20th Jan. – I have just got your letter of 6th Jan. – No. 1. –; and I thank you for your good wishes, and for the verse Isaiah XLII. 6; which I like to hope is true.[17] I thank you, too, for the sermon of the Archbishop of Canterbury.[18] He expresses, beautifully, what one feels and can't always put in words oneself. I like it very much. I shall be very proud to be officially received by the Felixstowe District Council when I return. The Goldsmiths' and Grocers' Companies, of London, have made me, each, an honorary freeman; and will entertain me on my return. The Warden of the Cinque Ports will do the same, at Dover. However, I don't see much chance of getting away from this country yet. I went by train, via Esdraelon and the Jordan Valley, today to the S. end of L. Tiberias; to see a regiment I have there. It was a beautiful day, and L. Tiberias was lovely; bright and blue with Lebanon – topped with snow – rising to the North. The valley of Esdraelon, especially along the River Kishon, is sprinkled with white-marianas [?[19]]; and with anemones – white, scarlet, mauve and deep purple –. There are few other flowers out, except little white star of Bethlehem.

LHCMA: Allenby papers 1/10/4

200
Allenby to Yale
General Headquarters, Egyptian Expeditionary Force
[Letter. Holograph]   28 January 1919

I am sorry to hear that you are leaving us. I take the opportunity of thanking you for the manner in which you have worked with us; tactfully, discreetly and helpfully, at all times.

OxAnt: Yale papers Box 1 File 3

201
Allenby to Wilson
[Telegram. Typescript]
Paraphrase of telegram received over telephone from London 4.40 pm 4 February 1919
SECRET
Your 74849

1. My reasons for not wishing any increase in the strength of the French detachment are as follows –
   (a) Military
   I already have sufficient troops.
   (b) Political
        Should more French troops arrive while the Peace Conference is sitting it will convey to the inhabitants, who are openly suspicious of French intentions, the impression that the future of Syria has already been decided on and that the French intend to retain permanently that part of Syria included in O.E.T. West and Silicia.[20] Anti-French feeling among Arabs, which has already been excited by French propaganda, would thus be stimulated and would prejudice a peaceful settlement of territorial questions in Syria.
2. Armenian troops[21] are unsuitable owing to the long existing feud between them and the Mahommedan population who fear reprisals for past deeds. The conduct of these troops and of the

Algerians – compared to that of Indian troops, which has been irreproachable – has lowered prestige and it is better that they should be replaced by French troops.

3. I do not recognise Monsieur Picot as having any right to give an opinion as to the number of troops necessary in my theatre of operations.

P.S. to C.I.G.S.
Copy to Prime Minister

NAS: Kerr papers GD/40/17/37/30. Copy at PRO: WO33/960, p. 290

202
Allenby to War Office (GOC-in-C Egypt to War Office)
[Telegram. Typescript]   20 February 1919
No. M.F.A.35260

There have recently occurred four cases of serious unrest: in the Royal Ordnance Department at Haifa, in the Royal Army Ordnance Corps at Kantara, Gloucestershire Yeomanry at Aleppo. Middlesex Yeomanry at Damascus. This unrest has been temporarily adjusted [sic]. The unrest in the Royal Ordnance Department and in the Royal Army Ordnance Corps was caused by doubts as to who we were entitled to bonus under Army order 14 of January, and uncertain prospects of release. In the yeomanry, the discomfort in the advanced areas resembling active service conditions, and in all cases the fact that men eligible for demobilization, though retained with and doing the same work in the same unit as men eligible for demobilization, do not draw the full bonus till after 1st May. I earnestly urge that from 1st February to date of release the full bonus be granted to all ranks serving in this force.

PRO: WO33/960, p. 307

203
Curzon (Foreign Office) to Allenby

[Telegram en clair. Typescript]   21 March 1919

Following is text of letter which has been addressed to you under date to-day, appointing you His Majesty's Special High Commissioner for Egypt and the Sudan. Letter begins:

Sir,

I have to inform you that, in view of the grave situation which has arisen in Egypt and the absence from that country of His Majesty's High Commissioner, General Sir Reginald Wingate, His Majesty the King has been graciously pleased to grant to you a Commission under the Royal Sign Manual, and Signet, constituting and appointing you His Majesty's Special High Commissioner for Egypt and the Sudan.

You are directed to exercise supreme authority in all matters Military and Civil, to take all such measures as you consider necessary and expedient to restore law and order in those countries, and to order and administer in all matters as may be required by the necessity of maintaining the King's Protectorate over Egypt on a secure and equable basis.

OxBod: Milner papers VI/D/446

204
Allenby to mother

Hotel Majestic Paris

[Letter. Holograph]   21 March 1919

I start tonight for Marseilles; where I take a passage, by Destroyer, to Malta, and thence, by Destroyer or Light Cruiser to Alexandria. I wanted to get off yesterday, but could not get clear of conferences in time.

I have had a very busy and interesting two days; and have seen everyone and had long talks with everyone – from President Wilson downwards. I have been interviewed and snapshotted, cinematographed and stared at continually. This is a huge modern hotel, near to Arc de Triomphe, taken over by the British Government for the British Delegates and those attending the conference. I have a most comfortable suite of rooms and a motor car at my disposal. I've not had a moment unoccupied, and have not been into Paris to the shops except on business.

Now I return to a restless Egypt, with full powers as High Commissioner, to tackle a difficult problem; this, in addition to my military duties.

I was brought here to discuss purely military matters connected with the Peace negociations. This Egyptian complication is a new one. Bols, my Chief of Staff, will return with me. He had intended to go on leave, for a while, to England; but that must come later. I think that my return, as Special High Commissioner, will have a calming effect; but the unrest has got a deep root, and there will be hard work to do.

I enclose some newspaper cuttings which will amuse you. I have a big luncheon party today; my guests including Sherif Feisal, the two Baronesses de la Grange,[22] Col. Lawrence – attending Feisal – Lord Robert Cecil and others.

LHCMA: Allenby papers 1/10/7

205
Wingate to Allenby
Army and Navy Club, Pall Mall, London S.W.
[Letter. Typescript]   23 March 1919

You will see, from some enclosures I send you, the action I took on being summoned to London on the 19th and on seeing the recent telegrams from Cheetham which had not been sent me during the week I was in Scotland. I only wish the authorities here had sanctioned my return to Egypt for, I think that together we could soon have evolved order of present chaos, but they assure me they consider my presence here essential, so I must bow to their decision. I have no doubt you will soon have the situation well in hand.

I do not know yet what political action His Majesty's Governt. has decided to take, or if they will adapt my idea of a very stern proclamation tempered with a promise that legitimate demands will be considered <u>when</u> the agitators have abandoned their lawless methods – but <u>not till then</u>.

When you go through the various dossiers in the Chancery you will see how earnestly I advocated in November, December & January last that some of the extremists should have been allowed to leave Egypt – Ruchdi and Adly had good reasons for urging it and had my advice been taken I think the present trouble would have been obviated – When I passed through Paris at the end of January I again urged this, and during the five weeks I was in London, I endeavoured to carry my point – finally I put up a draft telegram which I suggested should be sent to Cheetham (I enclose a copy[23]) and I think that, even at that late hour, its despatch might have averted the upset – but it was turned down, and Foreign Office telegram No. 200 to Cheetham of 26 Feb. 1919 sent instead.

Then, as I had anticipated trouble began. Much as I appreciate the difficulties with which Cheetham and Bulfin have been faced, I cannot conceive that any lasting good will result if concessions are made <u>before</u> order has been restored and a government formed.

When I failed to carry my point the psychological moment for making concessions had passed. To give way now, <u>after</u> the agitators have been guilty of every sort of breach of law & order, might produce temporary tranquility, but when the extremists know that they can terrorise our Government by lawless methods, they will unhesitatingly resort to them again whenever they cannot get their way.

It is indeed cruel to see so much of the good work which has been done during our occupation of Egypt jeopardised and our relations with the natives embittered just at a time when we might have hoped for closer union and co-operation with the sounder elements.

As is usual in countries in the condition of Egypt. It is the "tail that wags the dog" – the small and noisy clique of Nationalists have much to answer for: but had the advice of the responsible man on the spot been taken, I think this trouble might have been avoided

SAD: Wingate papers 172/7/13. Copy at OxBod: Milner papers VI/D/446 with additional preamble and final paragraphs. Copy at CUL: Hardinge papers 40, f. 143–6 (dated 23 February 1919[24])

206
Allenby to Milner

Cairo

[Telegram. Typescript]   26 March 1919

No. 442 Urgent

SIR M. CHEETHAM'S telegram No. 443

Situation up to this morning:–

South of Cairo: Dierut[25] was stated to be in the hands of the mob on 22nd, with 1,000 armed Bedouins holding up river traffic.[26]

At Assiut grave disorder occurred on 23rd and 24th, with burning and looting, notably of Coptic shops.[27] Fighting between Bedouin and natives and British troops went on during those days, and on afternoon of 24th the Mudir[28] telegraphed that ammunition was short and position dangerous. General Huddlestone's force has now been relieved. Railway and telegraphic communication with Haifa has been restored. Kena reported in a critical position and in need of troops on the 24th.

Strike is said to have occurred in Gemsa and Hurghada oil fields,[29] but another account denies this.

Minor incidents elsewhere, but order is spreading southward, and in Fayoum evacuated police outposts are being reoccupied.

Cairo: Quiet, though certain nervousness still perceptible. Lawyers' strike is thought to be wavering, and their action would probably influence that of the students. North of Cairo, West Behera, North Gharbia, and parts of Dakahlieh are still much disturbed, but numerous arrests being made in west of Behera. Troops inflicted 100 casualties in defending a construction train from attack between Zagazig and Mit Ghamr; Alexandria and Port Said quiet.

Bedouin of western desert quiet and apparently unaffected by the movement.

OxBod: Milner papers VI/D/444/3

207
Allenby to Chetwode

The Residency, Cairo

[Letter. Holograph]   29 March 1919

I was pleased to have your letter of 2nd March. I've been to Paris to talk to the swells [?] at the Conference. I was only there 2 days; and returned by swift destroyer and cruiser, making Alexandria on 25th. I find things better than they seemed; and I think they are calming down. The movement was fully National; and the nationalist feeling is [as] strong as ever, though it is curbed awhile. I have Egypt well picquetted now. Two Divs. N. of Cairo, and two south; while Stack has Soudan troops down to Assouan. I hope to get away, for a week or so, to Palestine and Syria, soon. I've not been there for some time, and its [sic] as well not to be away too long at a spell. I saw and spoke to everyone in Paris; and, though I was loath to go, I'm glad now that I went. The visit has given me a wider horizon. I was talked too [sic] and talked a great deal. Wilson and Lloyd George struck me as being the leading men, by a long way. Here, my work is going to be interesting but difficult. So far, I've had a fairly good reception; and have made a satisfactory start; I think these people trust me, on the whole; and if they were sure that the Powers supported our Protectorate, they would accept the situation. However, they still count on intervention, in their jargon, by the "League of Nations"!

You ask if I think we should intervene in Russia. I have always advocated it; but I don't think that the feeling of the people – British, French or American, – would allow effective action, even by planting troops. My wife sends kind regards. She is busy settling in, here.

IWM: Chetwode papers, P183/1, Correspondence and Appointments file (1997 additions)

208
Wilson to Allenby

[Letter. Typescript. Dictated] 2 April 1919
SECRET

I send you on a letter from Weizmann,[30] the result of a conversation I had with him a couple of days ago. I am also sending copies of this letter to the War Office so that they may see what it is that he wants and whether from their point of view, if you are agreeable, his wishes could be granted. I do not quite know what the A.G. will say about enlisting Jewish soldiers for service only in Palestine, which is what paragraph 1 of Weizmann's letter means, and it seems to me that the simplest way will be for Weizmann to get all his Jews to settle in Palestine and then to have them formed into a local corps of territorials or some such body for service in their own country. How does this smile on you?

Lawrence came to see me yesterday and told me that Feisal was going to try and see Clemenceau this week to tell him point blank that he would not have a French mandate and that if the French went in any strength [sic] he would be obliged to take active steps to stop it – not of course during your tenure of Command. Whether Lawrence's threat was only to draw fire from me I was not quite sure. It seemed rather an extraordinary a [sic] measure for a man in Feisal's position to threaten war with the French and to tell the Prime Minister so in his own capital. However, he got nothing out of me except a mental note to tell you the conversation.

I am glad to see you are getting Egypt quiet again. Someday when you have time you might write me a line of your gossip. I know how busy you must be at the present moment.

IWM: Wilson papers HHW2/33B/11

209
Allenby to mother

The Residency Cairo

[Letter. Holograph]   4 April 1919

I am late in writing you a birthday letter; but though this letter will arrive late, I wish you every good wish. We are still in turmoil. I have got the whole country occupied by my troops now; and most of the districts are, in outward appearance, quiet.

There is, however, violent agitation below the surface; and I see no sign, as yet, of it abating. El Azhar,[31] the great Moslem religious college in Cairo, is the centre of disaffection now; and owing to its sanctity, it is difficult and dangerous to deal with the agitation there preached and fostered.

It is a great nuisance, as I want to get away on a tour of inspection in Palestine and Syria. I can't well leave Cairo until there comes a change for the better.

Weather is lovely now; and the garden and river are delightful. We are both very well and busy.

Allenby papers 1/10/10

210
Allenby to Curzon

Cairo

[Telegram. Typescript]   4 April 1919
No. 499 Very Urgent

My telegram No. 496

Train left Luxor at 6 P.M. on 7th March. On board two officers and eight other ranks. At Nag Hamadi natives boarded train and insulted soldiers. Officers then took them into their first-class carriage. At Assiut three other ranks left train and Kaimakam Pope Bey, Inspector of Egyptian Prisons Department, joined it.

Train left at 4 A.M., 18th March. At every station on line large crowds had collected awaiting arrival of train, who called for 'Ingleez,' threw stones, and attempted to board train. Some stations were successfully passed. At Deirout[32] a very large crowd attacked train, drove driver from engine, and succeeded in entering first-class carriage, now solely occupied by British.

One or two were probably killed here. On train restarting many Deirout natives stayed on board as far as the next station, Der Moes. Here they were reinforced by another large crowd, who, with stones, sticks and knives, killed all the remaining British, none of whom were armed. Bodies were replaced in train, except one, which has not yet been traced, and train proceeded. At succeeding stations large crowds were collected, evidently with same object, who raised shouts of triumph on hearing English had all been killed. On arrival at Minia, bodies were taken from train, enquiry made, and bodies buried.

Steps are now being taken to exhume them. It appears that attack on train must have been prearranged, and that Egyptian and railway authorities at various stations made no effort to prevent this massacre.

OxBod: Milner papers VI/D/444/3

211
Allenby to mother

The Residency Cairo

[Letter. Holograph]   9 April 1919

We have had some trying days – Cairo seething with excitement. There have been several collisions between the people and the soldiers, due to faults and misunderstandings on both sides. I hope to have framed a Ministry by this evening; and then we may begin to get some control of public feeling. The situation has been very dangerous; and though better now, still contains many elements of danger. You may expect to see my action pretty freely criticized; but I don't mind that. I am absolutely sure that, whether successful or not, I took the right steps. I am letting some 20 Egyptians sail for Europe on the 11th and am giving leave to Saad Zaghoul[33] and his companions to join their ship at Malta. I don't suppose that the whole of British opinion will approve of this!

Weather today is somewhat sultry; with a hot wind. The garden is beautiful and a great joy.

Allenby papers 1/10/11

212
Allenby to Wingate

The Residency Cairo
[Letter. Typescript with holograph additions. Copy]
13 April 1919

I received, two days ago, your letter of 19th March and its message of welcome to Paris, for which I thank you.

We are not yet out of trouble here. As soon as I had restored some order I conceded freedom to travel and I included Zaggloul and Co. in Malta – but as private individuals only. I wish this had been done when you first advocated it. We are some months too late. – we [sic] got a Ministry but so far it has not been able to break the general strike of officials. However, Ruchdi tells me that he is more hopeful. Cairo is terrorized by students who are all on strike. They are having the time of their lives. The movement[34] has been really well organized and the whole nation is against us including the fellahin of Upper and Lower Egypt. I have little doubt that there is strong alien support below it all and there are evident signs of Bolshevism. But the signs of Bolshevism are beginning to frighten the big people and the Ministers are now working really hard for a settlement of the strike. I have refused any concessions and have warned them and the Sultan of the awful consequences to Egypt if I have to crush the strike by force. As it is, the onion crop has been lost and much irrigation water has had to be released from the Assuan Dam to let my boats up the Nile while the railways were not working. The Egyptian Army and Police have done well so far but they won't stand an indefinite strain.

With kind regards from us both to Lady Wingate and yourself.

[There is a typescript copy of this letter at SAD: Wingate papers 173/2/15 with a holograph addition from Wingate:]

'Allenby made a fatal mistake in letting Zaghlul & Co out of Malta – He knew so little of the situation that he thought the adoption of my policy of conciliation (which I had recommended <u>before</u> the troubles broke out) could be applied with success <u>after</u> the murders and revolt had taken place!'

[This letter and the one below from Allenby to Wingate of 21 April 1919 appear again at SAD: Wingate papers 162/2/29–32 with a holograph addition:]
'These letters are interesting as showing how entirely Allenby and Clayton misjudged the conciliatory attitude which they should <u>not</u> have adopted <u>after</u> the outbreak – I look on this misplaced leniency as one of the principal causes for the present situation.'

SAD: Wingate papers 173/2/8. Typescript copy of a holograph letter at SAD: Wingate papers 173/2/10

213
Allenby to Curzon

Cairo
[Telegram. Typescript]   13 April 1919
No. 571 Urgent

NO incidents have been reported in the last twenty-four hours.

I have seen Rushdy Pasha this evening. He tells me he has failed to bring about cessation of strike, but that he and his colleagues are still working hard to that end. I am under the impression that Ministry is genuinely endeavouring to arrive at a solution, and they are frightened by growing Bolshevism of national movement.

OxBod: Milner papers VI/D/444/3

214
Allenby to Curzon

Cairo

[Telegram. Typescript]   15 April 1919
No. 578. Urgent

NATIONALIST movement in Egypt is based on idea that continued agitation will result in intervention by Peace Conference.

Egyptian notables who have now been permitted to leave for Europe as private individuals are regarded by many Egyptians as a delegation, and result of their visit is awaited with universal interest. Nature of their reception in Europe therefore will have considerable effect on situation here. If some of these gentlemen can gain access to responsible Allied statesmen, and are told that allied powers are agreeable to leave control and guidance of Egypt in hands of Great Britain, effect here can only be good, especially if Allied representatives in Egypt were instructed by their Governments to repeat statements made in Paris.

On the other hand. Failure to obtain any hearing will be ascribed to British influence, and will probably lead to further endeavours to attract attention by continued agitation in Egypt, and campaigns in European and American press.

OxBod: Milner papers VI/D/444/3

215
Allenby to Wilson

The Residency, Cairo

[Letter. Holograph]   16 April 1919

Your letter of 28th March:–
I note that you received mine, with reference to Weizmann and Methuen, after I left Paris.

What you say about the possible break down of the scheme to send a Commission to Palestine, Syria etc. is very disquieting.[35] I have wired you, to that effect. Both Syria and Palestine are eagerly awaiting the Commission which has been promised to them; and, if the Commission does not come out, the Arabs will feel that we have deceived them under pressure from the French and the Jews. There is a growing feeling of opposition to Zionism in Palestine; and even now it is difficult to control the Arabs there. Very little incitement would be likely to produce attacks on Jews; and massacres would result. Likewise, in Syria, there is growing up a strong anti Christian and Xenophobic feeling, which may develope [sic] into activity.

The delay in Feisal's return to Syria is deplorable. He is the only real leading Arab personality, and the only influence which could calm a situation growing daily worse.

Here we have, outwardly, greater quiet, under the influence of my troops. Below the surface, however, the fire burns as fiercely as ever. The strike of officials has become more general. It began as a protest against Lord Curzon's speech commending the attitude of the government officials. Then it was extended; and now the strike leaders have ordered it to continue until Zaghloul and Co. are recognised as delegates to the Peace Conference. The ministry have done their best; but have no influence to stop the strike – which now threatens to paralyse the railways and the whole life of the community –. I have given them till today to do their best. They have failed, and now I must take matters in hand.

When the country is dead against us, as is Egypt at present, and when everyone is redhot with political excitement, it is likely that there will be disturbances and bloodshed. The Egyptian Army and Police have behaved well, up to now, but we can't expect them to stand firm against the fervour of a National outburst. In the circumstances, I have not enough troops for a good margin of safety. I want, in addition to the mixed Brigade from the Dobrudja,[36] a Division of British Infantry – as I have told you by wire –. My troops are behaving well; but are tired of war, and very bitter against the Egyptians for having stopped their demobilisation. The Indian troops show no sign of unrest, yet; but, if the Egyptian revolution takes a religious hue, my Moslems will be sorely tried.

This is not the moment for concessions; but it is a great pity that H.M.G. refused the Deputations last Winter. Egypt complains – with some truth – that she, who has been loyal throughout the War, is refused the right of being heard; whereas that right has been accorded to Arabs, Syrians, Palestinians, Jews and even Cypriots. Moreover, the big agitators have now at their back the whole of the Fellahin. For the first time since 1882 they are against us. Previously, the Fellahin have been our friends.

Voluntary recruiting for the Egyptian Labour Corps – carried out by press-gang methods in the provinces – is one grievance.[37]

Then again, the requisitioning of animals and supplies for military purposes; unjustly applied, in many cases. Thirdly, collections made, throughout the country, for the Red Cross Fund. This is a very real grievance. Finally the existing high prices of food – result of the war – are put down to the continued presence of the British Army.

I see that Picot is intriguing against me still. You must not let him come back to Syria with any mandate for administration. That is what he wants; and, naturally, I can't allow it. He dislikes[38] me, and fights me, for that reason.

PS: I have just got your Troopers 77112 and 77006 for which I thank you.

IWM: Wilson papers HHW2/33B/12A. Typescript copy at IWM: Wilson papers HHW2/33D/2

216
Allenby to Curzon

Cairo

[Telegram. Typescript]   19 April 1919, received 20 April 1919
No. 602.

MY telegram No. 496.

Following persons have now been identified as murdered on Assiut to Minia train on 18th March, between 8 A.M. and noon: Kaïmakam A. Pope Bey, Inspector Egyptian Government Prisons;

Major C. Jarvis, M.C., 20th Deccan Horse, I.A. Staff; Lieutenant R.F.B. Willay, General List.

361171 A.C. Q.M.S. Summersgill, A. ('812th Aerial Employment Company')

549259 A.C. Q.M.S Peacock, P.D. ('812th Aerial Employment Company')

360529 A.C. Q.M.S Culyer, A.G. ('813th Aerial Employment Company')

362433 A.C. Q.M.S Field, G.H. ('813th Aerial Employment Company')

18930 Private Redding, L.H., A.A.M.C.

Pending final establishment of facts by proper official enquiry, I send the following supplementary details obtained by personal investigation by British political officer on the spot. There had been much excitement along railway line, including greeting of train with patriotic cries, free travelling by crowds, and demonstrations of hostility to some English inspectors. Deirut[39] was reinforced from Mallawi by crowds, who remained near station till next day. Express stopped at Assiut, evidently because of rumours of trouble, and murdered men therein arrived at Assiut at 7 A.M. on 18th in local train which stopped at every station. They were all unarmed and were collected in front first-class carriage. Native ticket inspector and two native officials travelling made unsuccessful efforts to deceive and divert attention of mob, but in arrival at Deirut they battered at closed doors and windows. Kaïmakam Pope Bey and two others who got out on other side were murdered and bodies put in brake van. Though acting station-master had sent message to local police on seeing threatening attitude of mob one hour before train was due, police officer only arrived about twenty minutes after arrival of train with some six unarmed men out of forty armed men available. He did nothing and sent no warning ahead. Acting station-master, in spite of opposition, eventually got train away, natives swarming all over it, and remaining British at bay in two compartments. At Deir Moes another dense mob attacked train; two British managed to reach engine, and they and native driver tried to start train, but vacuum brake had been applied. Driver fled, and two British were overpowered and battered to death. Three remaining British gained engine and made no effort to work levers, but fought till overpowered. Five bodies battered till beyond recognition were thrown on platform, stripped and subjected to the worst indignities. Mob screamed with delight, women taking leading part in orgy. Sixty Egyptian soldiers returning from Soudan by train to join reserve leaned out of the windows cheering; their officers took no effective action. Police again arrived late and did nothing. Bodies were thrown into brake-van, and finally, after recurrent attempts at stations to stop train and see bodies, train arrived Minia, where native railway inspectors promptly had van and wrecked compartment shunted away out of reach of mob. Savagery was apparently deliberately incited by local organisations, whose agents probably travelling by train. Many railway officials and employees did all they could, but behaviour of police, native officer passengers and others seems to have been very bad.

OxBod: Milner papers VI/D/444/3

217
Allenby to Wilson

The Residency, Cairo

[Letter. Holograph]   21 April 1919

Yours of 2nd instant, enclosing Weizmann's letter. I don't quite understand his para. 1; but the time has not come for the formation of a Jewish territorial corps, nor should Jewish soldiers be enlisted for service solely in Palestine. If Jewish soldiers now in Palestine wish to settle there and are suitable and desirable men I see no objection. As regards para. 2, there is no apparent reason for prohibiting the building, on bone-fide Jewish property, such houses as may be required for the better accommodation of the proprietors and their dependants; but it would be undesirable that large numbers of houses should be built, at the present time, for the needs of prospective Jewish immigrants of whose character and capabilities nothing is yet known. At any rate, no decision should be taken until after the visit of the Commission. With regard to the purchasing of stores and material from the Army, these things are sold in open market, and the Zionists have the same opportunity of buying as have others.

I am sending Weizmann's letter to Money, at Jerusalem, for his remarks.

I am interested to hear of what Feisal said to Clemenceau. I think it is likely to be true. Unless Feisal has been converted in Paris, his dislike and distrust of the French are extreme.

The situation in Egypt has not improved. Outwardly, there is quiet; and, in the Provinces, order prevails. This is due to the presence of my troops. The strike continues, however, under terrorism. All Government offices are practically at a standstill. The law Courts are closed in Cairo. An irreducible minimum of trains are running on the main lines – worked by military staffs. I have given the ministry every chance to exert their influence, but they have none left, and have completely failed to stop the strike. I am now going to arrest the leaders of the movement – many of them lawyers and notables – and tomorrow I issue a proclamation ordering all back to work. I should have done this last week; but the week has been one of holidays, for all creeds, ending today with a big Moslem holiday. I may have to arrest 70 to 100 leaders; but it has got to be done. – 22nd April – The Prime Minister has resigned, and the fall of this ministry will possible [sic] have no bad – some good – effect. Rumours are that the officials return to work tomorrow. If so, good. If not, then I must make the arrests.

The Americans have recognised the Protectorate of Great Britain over Egypt. This was communicated to me, this afternoon, by the American Consul General; and I shall publish his letter in the papers tomorrow. The recognition will, I believe, have a calming effect on public opinion, as it was hoped and expected that Wilson (President) would support Nationalists.

I am sorry to say that some 3,000 men at the Demobilisation Camp at Kantara have refused to allow men to come on as helpers on the railways. I am working the railways by military personnel and had formed some railway companies from Kantara. Some Trade Union microbe has got into them; and they are obstinate, though polite, in their refusal. I can't shoot them all for mutiny, so I must carry on as best I can, and I must resume demobilisation. I have wired the situation to Troopers; and hope that you will hasten my promised reinforcements. One reason given by the men was that to work on the railway would be "strike breaking". However, the real reason is home sickness, and distrust of the War Office and their promises. They don't believe that reinforcements are coming; or that, if they do come, demobilisation will be resumed. – 23rd April –

Most of the government officials have returned to work this morning; and I hope the remainder will return during the day. My Proclamation; the resignation of the ministry – which had become unpopular – and Wilson's recognition of our Protectorate have all contributed to the result; and each will, probably, eventually claim the whole credit! Martial Law will have to rule the country for months to come, and I don't see much prospect of reducing the number of troops now garrisoning the country. Demobilisation must go on, or the troops will mutiny, and so I reiterate the necessity for a steady flow of reinforcements and drafts.

PS: Thanks for sending Chetwode. He will take over XXI Corps in Palestine and Syria. Bulfin commands XX Corps, in Egypt.

IWM: Wilson papers HHW2/33B/13. Typescript copies at same file reference and at IWM: Wilson papers HHW2/33D/1

218
Allenby to Wingate

The Residency Cairo

[Letter. Typescript]   21 April 1919

Symes[40] brought me your letter of 26th March and I have also yours of the 23rd with enclosures. I was much interested in reading these and I wish your first advice had been taken. It would, I think, have avoided this trouble. The Egyptians are suffering from wounded pride very keenly. I have given the Ministry a free run, and they have worked hard for a settlement, but have failed. They have now no influence on the leaders and organisers of the strike. I am therefore now going to arrest those responsible for its continuance. I think a large proportion of Government officials and employés [sic] wish to return to work but they are intimidated by threats of assassination. Black hands and red hands are enclosed in letters with these threats and there has been some vitriol throwing, a crime I have made punishable by death. The centres of agitation are the AZHAR Mosque[41] and the Ministry of Justice. All the lawyers are on strike, as are nearly all clerks and employés. We just run enough trains – with military personnel – to keep the country supplied. Moderate men and the propertied class are becoming alarmed at last and many will welcome more organisation. They begin to smell Bolshevism. – 23rd April – I issued a proclamation yesterday morning ordering all strikers back to work, under Martial Law. Concurrently the Ministry resigned, and yesterday afternoon Gary wrote to me announcing that America recognises our Protectorate. I have sent his letter to the Press and the result of these three events has been that the strikers are returning to work to-day. I hope that, for the time anyhow, we may have settled the business but the causes of unrest remain and Martial Law will have to rule for months yet. I have not made the arrests I contemplated and I hope it will not be necessary, but I shall not hesitate to take any measures that may seem desirable.

Whether we shall be able to form a new Ministry at once is doubtful. On the whole I am glad that Ruchdi [Ruschdi in holograph copy?] and Co. have fallen. They had, I fear, been making promises to the strikers; and, when they found that I would grant no concessions, were frightened for their own skins. Rushdi [sic] himself is, as you know, brave as a lion, but he found his influence gone. He has resigned on the grounds of ill-health, ostensibly. Not on political grounds. The Ministers saw the Sultan yesterday and he accepted their resignations.

SAD: Wingate papers 173/3/15. Copy at SAD: Wingate papers 162/2/31–2. Holograph copy at SAD: Wingate 173/3/17–19 (with some additional personal comments)

219
Curzon to Allenby (with alterations by Milner)
[Telegram? Typescript. Draft] [?] May 1919

Your telegram No. 630 of April 23rd.

It is not proposed to send a Royal Commission, but rather a Special Mission.[42] Although this Mission would be charged with the task of enquiring into and reporting upon recent events, its principal object would be to advise His Majesty's Government as to the future government of Egypt, and its terms of reference might be as follows:–

To enquire in to the causes of the late disorders in Egypt and to report on the existing situation in the country and the form of Constitution which, under the Protectorate, will be best calculated to promote its peace and prosperity, the progressive development of self-governing institutions, and the protection of foreign interests.

The Mission would, therefore, be entirely independent of the Residency, although Lord Milner would naturally keep in closest touch with you, and your supreme administrative authority would remain quite unaffected by his presence in Egypt.

It appears to be important to emphasise the wider rather than the narrower aspect of the work of the Mission, and to represent it as a deliberate act of policy and a necessary stage in the constitutional evolution of the country, rather than as a step that has been deliberately forced upon us by recent rising. With regard to the date of the Mission the position is as follows. Lord Milner for various reasons cannot go before September. If, therefore, in your opinion, its immediate despatch is necessary, another head must be found.

It appears to us, however, that it may be possible and even advantageous, to prepare the ground by an immediate local inquiry, instituted by yourself, into the direct causes of the recent disorders and the grievances of the fellahin in respect of forced labour, requisitions, abuses of power by local authorities, etc. On such a Commission a native official or officials might serve along with experienced British officers to investigate these questions of fact. The evidence collected by this Commission would be invaluable to the Special Mission when it reaches Egypt, while its appointment would satisfy people that something was being done.

If you agree with this policy here suggested, we would propose it in Parliament at an early date, probably next week.

OxBod: Milner papers Mss Eng.hist. c.699/117–8. Copies at OxBod: Milner papers Mss Eng.hist. c.699/111–6

220

Allenby to War Office (GOC-in-C Egypt to War Office)

[Telegram. Typescript]   2 May 1919
No. C214

Chief administrator reports with reference to impending visit of a commission to Palestine, as follows:–

"In the present state of political feeling there is no doubt that if the Zionist programme is a necessary adjunct to a British mandate the people of Palestine will in preference select the United States or France as the mandatory power or as the protecting power of an Arab administration. I do not mean by Zionist programme the interpretation of certain extreme Zionists, but the comparatively moderate programme presented to the Peace Conference.

The Palestinians desire their country for themselves and will resist by every means in their power, including active hostilities, any general immigration of Jews, however gradual.

It is thought by the people of Palestine that Great Britain is more deeply committed to the Zionist programme than either the United States or France, and during the last few months both Arab and French propaganda have been actively engaged in fostering this belief.

Egypt and India are quoted as examples of the tenacity of Great Britain's hold on countries on which she once lays her hand. More speedy autonomy is expected from United States. Moreover the people of Palestine have been greatly impressed by recent events in Egypt.

Nevertheless fear of Zionism by Moslems and Christians is the main issue, and a large majority would vote for a British mandate if this were removed.

As long as this fear exists it will be impossible for the commission to gauge the real wishes of the people, which will appear to be against the British mandate.

If a clear and unbiased expression of wishes is required, and if His Majesty's Government desire a mandate for Great Britain it will be necessary to make an authoritative announcement that the Zionist programme will not be enforced in opposition to the wishes of the majority.

In conclusion any local request for a British mandate will be precluded by the idea that Great Britain is the main upholder of the Zionist programme, and except by force and in opposition of the wishes of the large majority of the people of Palestine no mandatory power can carry through Zionist programme."

I consider above to be a true appreciation of the situation. Fear and distrust of Zionist aims grows daily, and it will not be dispelled by any amount of persuasion or propaganda.

Recently there was danger of serious disturbance in which Arabs of East Jordan were to have participated. At present the situation has been calmed by news of impending commission.

The political officers of East Jordan report violently anti-Jewish sentiment and open threats of active hostility if Zionist programme materializes.

The indefinite retention in the country of a military force following occupation of that now in Palestine will be result of a British mandate for Palestine on the lines of the Zionist programme.

PRO: WO33/981/3–4

221
Allenby to War Office (GOC-in-C Egypt to War Office)
[Telegram. Typescript]   4 May 1919
No. C.243

Your No. 77525, S.D.2, is not adequate to the situation here. If you cannot make more satisfactory arrangements to enable my troops to be demobilized and to go on leave I must warn you that, owing to the present temper of the troops, I expect serious trouble to ensue very shortly.

I feel unable for the present to reduce the strength of my forces anywhere with safety. I am, however, compelled to do so because it is safer to risk danger in this sense rather than the danger of mutinous conduct on a large scale.

In order to increase fighting efficiency I now propose to reduce the number of my units and get rid of all skeletons.

Monthly drafts must not only continue to arrive regularly but to enable my demobilization to continue at a sufficiently rapid rate they must be largely increased. Your reference to possible reinforcements for Northern Syria is not understood. In addition to troops promised from Europe, I will accept four battalions from India; these must be sent at once and up to strength, and, preferably, troops other than Mahometan. Am I to expect reinforcements for infantry of the XXVIth Division composite brigade?

I propose, if not, to convert these 700 men into a composite battalion. I must again bring to your notice the urgent necessity of sending reinforcements for technical units; the men of these units are often connected with trade unions and are liable to cause mutinous conduct among neighbouring troops. Reinforcements for the Imperial Camel Corps not being procurable, I shall replace them partly by light-armoured car patrols; for this purpose I require ample machine-gun motor car personnel. I hope to reduce numbers of British in mechanical transport by training more Egyptians and by employing more civilians to reduce the numbers in the Ordnance services. Finally, I draw your attention to the 112,000 prisoners of war and 1,150 Russian prisoners in this (? group omitted), requiring 2,000 men to staff the camp and six battalions as guards.

PRO: WO33/981, pp. 6–7

222
Allenby to Curzon

Cairo

[Telegram. Typescript]   4 May 1919, received 5 May
No. 711

My telegram No. 590.

It is clear that an attempt will be made to work up a press campaign against alleged atrocities committed by British troops in Egypt.

A printed report respecting punishment of certain villages near railway line just south of Cairo has already been published by Giza Provincial Council; it seems villages involved are Bedrashein, Azizia and Shobek. Troops are said to have burned entire villages, raped women in streets, shot and looted. In fact, after prolonged provocation, destruction of railway material, and sniping, a search was made at night for arms. Portions of villages were accidentally set on fire, women were naturally frightened, but no more. It should be noted Egyptian villages are made of mud, with roofs of dry cotton stalks, and contain nothing of value from European point of view save hoarded money and gold and silver jewellery, which natives hide in ground. Village fires are of constant occurrence, regarded as natural, if annoying features of everyday life.

Another case likely to be taken up is that of Saft-el-Meluk village, whence villagers ambushed and killed three and wounded five British troops without slightest provocation. Soldiers were naturally enraged, and were with difficulty persuaded not to take matter in their own hands. Villagers having refused to assist in identification of murderers, a number were collected in an orderly manner and flogged, this punishment undoubtedly saving them from far severer reprisals by troops.

Extremists are apparently using as models for documentary propaganda British and French Blue Books dealing with German atrocities in Belgium and Northern France, for no regret whatever was expressed at massacre in March last of unarmed British officers and men in train in Upper Egypt, British railway officials at Wasta attack on Peni Suef, and siege of British and American residents, including missionaries, women and children, at Assiut, which if successful would unquestionably have led to massacre on a large scale.

These incidents and wanton destruction of communications could only be met by forcible repression. Troops showed most praiseworthy restraint, and in opinion of foreign witnesses, and even of natives, measures taken were not sufficiently drastic. Former have expressed unstinted admiration for calmness shown by our troops under great provocation in Cairo, and Greek Minister has reported in this sense to his Government.

Total number of natives killed during whole period of disturbances is estimated at under 1,000, including casualties among Bedouins settled in Nile Valley (as opposed to tribes of the desert who behaved well), who in March started open armed insurrection in southern and western provinces.

Capital is also being made out of bombing by us from aeroplanes of certain villages where headquarters of insurgents attacking Assiut were established, and on armed bands of natives firing at Nile steamers.

These are represented as atrocities on defenceless villagers.

British casualties for period are approximately seventy-five (exclusive of Indian casualties), including a number of brutal murders of isolated unarmed British soldiers by mob of natives armed with sticks and knives, and sniping at patrols and sentries.

OxBod: Milner papers VI/D/444/3

223
Allenby to Curzon

Cairo
[Telegram. Typescript]   8 May 1919
No. 739

Your telegram No. 552.[43]

Position of British women in provinces has frequently been extremely unpleasant, but no reports, official or unofficial, of outrage or abduction have been received. Origin of rumours was probably grave anxiety at first felt as to whether nurses were on same train as officers murdered at Deirut. Wife of British railway official murdered at Wasta was hustled but not otherwise molested, and she and her children were protected by native official. There is no reason to suppose any civilians are still missing from outlying districts. Information desired as to casualties will follow.

OxBod: Milner papers VI/D/444/3

224
Allenby to Churchill

[Telegram. Typescript]   9 May 1919
No. M.F.A. 37618

See my No. M.F.A. 37593, 8th May,[44] and No. M.F.A. 37617, 9th May.[45] There is a growing danger of unrest amongst demobilizable men of the Egyptian Expeditionary Force, and it is of utmost importance that every pledge made by War Office should be fulfilled.

PRO: WO33/981, p. 16

225
Gribbon to Allenby[46]

                                            War Office, Whitehall
[Letter. Typescript]   10 May 1919

Reference attached[47] I attended the conference this morning and took Money with me, as I thought it would be a good thing for him to be au fait with these matters should I happen to be away. Ormsby-Gore, Hogarth and Toynbee from the Foreign Office attended.

The general idea was to get down to practical details which would have to be considered if Palestine is to be ready to receive the Jews. It was generally decided that the Zionist Organization should submit an outline to the War Cabinet of what it is necessary to put in hand at an early date, so as to be ready when the time comes, under the main headings of Irrigation, Land Settlement and Public Works.

The proceedings opened by a general statement of Zionist policy intentions by Weizmann. He admitted that as regards self-determination the Jews had not a leg to stand on in Palestine nor had we in Egypt. The question was whether the British Government were prepared to see their policy through in Palestine as they are in Egypt. He drew attention to the fact that Lord Robert Cecil when still a member of the Government had said "Judea for the Jews." At the same time he emphasised that the last thing the Jews meant was to oppress the Arabs in any way, though he was quite frank in saying that he hoped eventually for a Jewish Palestine.

Ormsby Gore replied by giving his personal views showing the value of the movement to the British Empire, and Hogarth then brought out the point that a practical establishment of a Jewish Palestine would involve military force.

The practical details to be considered will will [sic] be the provision of immigration facilities to the British Government after allowing for such assistance as the Zionist Organization are thus able to undertake. This will of course embrace the shipping question.

The land question will involve a decision as to whether land should be allotted to individuals or to the future Government of Palestine for them to lease as necessary.

As regards public works the main question would be what the Jews are prepared to do in the way of taking over by purchase or otherwise the existing railways and buildings which will no longer be required by our Army, and development of water power and harbours.

I suggested that, of course subject to the Adjutant General's approval, they should consider a means of helping us out of the man power question by the provision of Jewish troops for British Units, which it will be necessary to retain in Palestine.

I am asking Weizmann to send us a copy of whatever he submits eventually to the War Cabinet, who will presumably farm out the various proposals to the departments particularly concerned.

PRO: WO106/191/116–117

227
Allenby to War Office (GOC-in-C Egypt to War Office repeated FO)

[Telegram. Typescript]
Despatched 14 May 1919, received 15 May 1919
SECRET
C.602

I visited Damascus on May 12th and had long conversation with Feisal. He described the situation in Paris in respect to Arab affairs, and then asked my advice as to his attitude toward the commission. He asked if Peace Conference offered mandate for Syria to Britain whether she would exchange it. I answered I did not know. He then said that because he could not tell whether Britain would accept mandate if asked for her protection and because he could ensure greater unanimity of opinion in whole country for complete independence he had decided to ask commission for complete independence of Syria. If he got independence he would then ask British for help to govern the country. His people will ask for independence for Syria expressing at the same time the hope that it will also be given to other Arab countries. Although intending to show outward friendship to French Feisal is as bitterly opposed to them as ever and he insists that he will fight them to the last man if they remain in Syria or get any sort of mandate. He said he had heard that as British units were relieved in the north they would be replaced by French units. I said I had heard nothing of this. My answer relieved him as he said that at this report Persians [?] were already excited.

Feisal is pressing for increasing Arab army to 14,000 and gendarmerie to 6000 and asking me to supply equipment for these numbers. I said I would refer to you and will forward his arguments for increases to you. There is little doubt that his desire is to be in a stronger military position in order to threaten or fight the French. He says Lawrence told him that C.I.G.S's advice was "if you want independence recruit soldiers and be strong." I said I could not believe C.I.G.S. had said this. Feisal asked me if I would appoint to all departments of his Government British advisers. I said that under my instructions this was not possible. I saw many demonstrations while in Damascus for complete independence parading the streets in great excitement (brandishing?*) sticks [,] knives and swords all effusively friendly to myself.

PRO: WO106/191/69. Copy at PRO: WO33/981, p. 22

228
Allenby to War Office (GOC-in-C Egypt to War Office)
[Telegram. Typescript]   16 May 1919
No. E.A. 2447

In confirmation and continuation of 1st paragraph of my No. C.243 of 4th May,[48] and your No. 77880, A.G.1, of 10th May. Following request has been put forward by my Administrative Service: "Request cable be sent home and answer obtained that all 1914 men be sent home by the end of May, all 1915 men and all men over 37 years of age by the end of June, and all voluntarily enlisted 1916 men by end of August." I have 26,000 1914 men and 30,000 1915 men of all arms and 10,000 of the 1914 men belong to the Administrative Services.

The situation is most acute in all parts of my force. If above request is not favourably received I expect a refusal to work on the part of the Administrative Services and I fear this will spread to combatant units amongst whom, As you know, there is already unrest. I am convinced that these demands should be met in order to obviate mutiny on a large scale, which will have a serious effect on my Indian troops and on French and Italian feelings and on population generally. Consequently, I have decided to risk the grave danger of weak forces and to send these men home whether you can supply reinforcements or not. After the despatch of these 56,000 men I shall have in Cilicia, Syria, Palestine and Egypt, white troops and 75,000 Indian troops. The 54,000 white troops include 13,000 Australians and New Zealanders, who they say are

* Occurs in original.

255

ready to fight enemies of the Empire, but are not prepared to remain to deal with internal troubles, so they must be despatched simultaneously with British troops thereby reducing the number of white troops to 41,000 which includes 10,000 French and Armenians. My position will be dangerous but it will be safer than mutiny. I point out that unless you send me reinforcements for certain technical branches, particularly signallers and mechanical transport, those services will be inoperative on the departure of 1914 and 1915 men

PRO: WO/33/981, p. 28

229
Allenby to Wilson

[Letter. Holograph]   17 May 1919
Embossed

Egypt is quiet now; and agriculture and business are getting back to normal conditions. It will, however, be necessary to picket the country – as at present – under martial law for certainly some months to come. Meanwhile, I have been forced to resume demobilisation on a large scale.

There is great unrest and discontent [in] my army; and, in the case of the administrative services, unrest verges on mutiny. Nothing will convince the troops that military operations did not end on the signing of the armistice; and they do not think the W.[49] Office intends to deal fairly with them – by sending drafts and reinforcements which will facilitate their demobilisation within a reasonable period of time. I have, as you know, a very large proportion of /14 and /15 men. These men would, most of them, have been dead by now – no doubt – if their service had been in France – but the[y] take no comfort in that consideration. I know you are doing your best for me, and I know also your great difficulties; but it is no use my trying to hide from you the gravity of the situation as it appears here. I am thankful that you have given up the idea of our withdrawal from Syria. If I withdraw my troops, I am pretty sure that the Arabs would at once declare an independent Syria and attack the French. The Emir Feisal is as bitterly anti-French, after his stay in Paris, as he was before he left Syria for Europe. I saw him at Damascus, on the 12th inst., and had long talks with him. He told me, plainly, that he would have no French in Syria. There was a great demonstration in my honour – which practically took the form of a mass meeting. The streets were filled with procession[s] of all sorts, bands and flags, troops and civilians, pell mell, yelling and singing. Hundreds of the lower class population were armed[50] with naked swords, knives and sticks which they brandished round my car, in the wildest way, but in perfect friendliness.

My wife was with me, and thoroughly enjoyed the experience. The least hint from Feisal would turn all this mob the other way. At a big dinner given to me by him there were the leading sheikhs of all the Bedouin tribes of Syria and Trans-Jordania. He had brought them in to see him, on his return from France; and I think that, possibly, the accident of my visit prevented a Coup d'Etat and the declaration by him of the Independence of Syria. All these tribes are Feisal's men, and would obey him to the death; and they have many rifles and much ammunition. Suppose that I withdraw to the proposed strategical line Deraa[51]-Haifa, and that these Arabs were against us. My right, at Deraa, is in the air, threatened by all the Druses and Bedouin tribes – who are based in the Hauran, rich in corn and all supplies –. My long line of communication is open to attack from Es Salt, Amman, Kerak, by Arabs longing to plunder Palestine and to kill Jews who defile the Holy City of Jerusalem. Further south, the tribes of the Sinai Peninsula could attack Beersheba and El Arish; and cut my railway, or at any rate try and do so. Zionism is more and more unpopular; and I am sure that any attempt to force it on Palestine at once would result in riots and massacres. The only chance for a peaceful settlement of the Syrian and Palestinian questions lies in the speedy arrival of the promised commission from the Peace Conference. Every day it is delayed makes the situation more difficult and dangerous. Lord Curzon, I know, is trying to stop it. If it is stopped, the Arabs will have been deceived, and their anti-French sentiment will become anti-

European. The Zionists and French dislike the Commission, and so do our politicians in Mesopotamia; but it is the only solution for Syria and Palestine.

IWM: Wilson papers HHW2/33B/16. Typescript copies at IWM: Wilson papers HHW2/33D/5; NAS: Kerr papers GD40/17/38/103–6

230
Allenby to War Office (GOC in C Egypt to War Office)
[Telegram. Typescript]   21 May 1919
SECRET
OPERATIONS
E.A. 2460
Your 78044

As regards general policy (your para.C) your proposal comes as a reversal of the decision arrived at on occasion of my visit to Paris, i.e. that until the decision is made as to the future of the country allied troops should remain as at present.

Your proposal, if carried out before Peace Conference has visited this country and the decision of the Peace Conference has been given, would be interpreted as a breach of faith and grave trouble would ensue in Syria which would certainly involve Arabia and Palestine.

Moreover to withdraw British troops now would be a serious blow to British prestige in Egypt and Palestine and would affect the morale of my troops adversely.[52]

Further reasons given in my cables C.602 of May 12th, E.A.2440 of May 15th and E.A.2457 of May 21st why I regard the proposal to hand over the area N. of Damascus to French troops as inadmissible. I must point out that this is the first information I have received of any pledges given by H.M. Government to the French as regards the future of Syria or Italians as regards Cilicia: and of the nature of these pledges I am still ignorant.[53] This renders my position very difficult and lays H.M. Government in whose name I have assured inhabitants that report of Commission will settle their future Government, open to imputation of bad faith. As regards para.(1) no troops have been withdrawn owing to situation in Egypt or India.

The decision to send French troops to Cilicia was taken for the following reasons. The occupation of Cilicia was originally undertaken by French Armenian troops, and British troops were sent there only because the excesses committed by Armenian troops had caused general insecurity. The arrival of reinforcements of French regular troops gave an opportunity of relieving British troops there and thus enabling me to collect the 7th Indian Division as a central reserve in the Beirut[-]Damascus which is extremely desirable from a military point of view.

PRO: WO106/191/28–29. Slightly different copy at WO33/981, pp. 35–6

231
Allenby to Foreign Office, London
[Telegram. Typescript]
Despatched 21 May 1919, received 24 May 1919
EA2457

I have received the following from my Chief Political Officer General Clayton. Begins–

I had interview with Feisal yesterday and today. He raised the question of his policy towards the French.

He informed me that on the advice of Lawrence he had agreed verbally with Clemenceau to use his efforts with the people to secure a French Mandate for Syria on the understanding that France reognised [sic] Syrian independence. Feisal stated frankly that he had never any intention of carrying out this arrangement and that Syria was bitterly opposed to French penetration in any form whatever. He said that Great Britain would be welcomed as mandatory Power but that he was unable to ask for a British mandate as he could not ascertain whether or not Great Britain would accept a mandate if offered.

He had asked the Prime Minister this question but had received no direct reply. Feisal was obviously nervous as to the result of such an underhand policy towards the French and asked for my advice. I told him that in my opinion a policy of intrigue and deception would only recoil upon itself and might easily endanger Franco-British relations and as a consequence the relations between Great Britain and the Arabs.

Feisal has now decided to await the arrival of the Peace Conference Commission and to ask definitely for the following:

1. The independence as the ruling principle of any mandate which the Peace Conference may decide to give.

2. Advice and assistance to the Syrian state to be given by Great Britain; should they refuse, by America; if America refuses, by Great Britain, America and France; in no case by France alone. This is in accordance with the impressions I have gained when (? In Damascus on) May 12th.

NAS: Kerr papers GD40/17/38/140–1. Slightly different copy at PRO: WO106/191/33 (GOC in C Egypt to War Office)

232
Wilson to Allenby

[Letter. Typescript. Dictated] 22 May 1919
SECRET AND PERSONAL

I am sending this letter by hand[54] because I am anxious that you should understand the position we have reached here in Paris as regards Syria. This afternoon I am sending you two telegrams (Nos. 538, and 539 H.W. Personal) – one being rather fuller than the other[55] – the shorter telegram being couched in such language that I am able to send a copy to Monsieur Clemenceau. I find a certain amount of difficulty in telegraphing even this much as I rather think that my telegrams to you are sometimes tapped. I hope therefore that my two telegrams sent this afternoon will not confuse you. I did not like to refer in either of these two telegrams to the fact that I am sending you out an officer.[56]

Now the position we have reached as regards Syria is this. We have had two rather hectic meetings between the French, and ourselves, President Wilson being also present, but no Italians. About a week ago the Prime Minister nominated me to discuss with M. Tardieu, who had been nominated by M. Clemenceau, the relief of British troops by French in Syria. I at once decided that it was impossible to carry out such a relief until the frontier line had been established between the French area and our own. On that, in my office here, we drew up what we considered a reasonable line of demarcation and the map which I am sending by the same officer as this letter will show you the line we traced. At my first meeting with Tardieu I showed him this map and gave him the reasons why we thought the line ought to be traced as shown. He produced a counter-proposal and I have also traced the French line on this same map. You will see that our line keeps further north in Palestine and includes Tadmur. The French line takes in Hauran and Tadmur in their area. I then refused to consider any question of the relief of your British troops by French troops until the two Prime Ministers (Lloyd George and Clemenceau) had come to an agreement on the line of demarcation. Mr Lloyd George entirely endorsed my proposals and at the two meetings with M. Clemenceau and President Wilson he urged in the strongest possible way that that line should be adopted. Clemenceau flatly refused to agree. At the meeting this morning there was a good deal said about the Sykes-Picot Agreement and our Prime Minister made it quite clear that either the Sykes-Picot must remain in its entirety or be torn up. He said it was intolerable that such portions of the Sykes-Picot as were agreeable to the French should be claimed by them as having been agreed to by us and that such portions as did not suit them should be left out of the account. On the whole Clemenceau agreed that the Sykes-Picot was dead but his whole mind was coloured by the Sykes-Picot and in his arguments advancing his claims he constantly kept either referring directly to it or basing claims by inference upon it. The Prime Minister made it quite clear to Clemenceau that he would not budge an inch from the line which we claim, and Clemenceau made it equally clear that he would not accept it. We have therefore reached an <u>impasse</u>, and it was because last night we saw this <u>impasse</u> coming that a telegram was sent to you to occupy Tadmur if you could do so.

At the meeting this morning when it was clear that no further progress could be made in reaching a decision by common consent the Prime Minister proposed that the Commission should at once go out to Syria. Clemenceau did not respond in any way, and President Wilson said that his two men were going out in any case and would report to him on the situation which they found out there and on the facts of the case. I will have another word to say later in the letter about these Americans. Before the meeting broke up I asked the Prime Minister if it was quite clear that as no agreement had been reached, your position as Supreme Military Commander would remain the same as it has been all along. He emphatically replied that that was so. I then in the presence of Clemenceau said that I would wire to you and ask you if you wished any more French troops sent out and that if you did not M. Clemenceau would doubtless prevent their despatch. I have now written to M. Clemenceau to make that position quite clear, viz, that you are the sole judge and adviser as to the number of troops required, and the sole military authority over their distribution in your Command.

IWM: Wilson papers HHW2/33B/14. Copy at IWM: Wilson papers HHW2/33E/4A

233
Wilson to Allenby

[Telegram. Typescript]   22 May 1919
SECRET

538. May 22nd
The question of the future of Syria is now being discussed but it seems possible that no final decision may be reached for some little time. That being so you will remain as heretofore the only military judge and adviser as to the number of troops and the only military authority as to the distribution of troops. Do you wish any more troops sent out? I am sending a copy of this telegram to Monsieur Clemenceau.

NAS: Kerr papers GD40/17/38/116

234
War Office to Allenby (GOC-in-C Egypt)

[Telegram. Typescript]   23 May 1919
No. 78285

1. On the understanding that France will receive the mandate for Northern Syria it is necessary to decide on the most desirable frontiers (from a military point of view) between the French area and (*a*) Palestine and (*b*) Mesopotamia.

2. We are working in Paris to secure acceptance by the French of the following frontier (reference Asia 1 : 1,000,000) Nahr-ez-Zaharani to the north of Zaharani – northwards along Jebel Libnan to about Point 1680 – thence eastwards including Jeb Jenin, round Mount Hermon, including Rasheya – Sasa – Deir Ali – Point 594 – northwards through El Maksura – Jebel et Turfa – Jebel el Wustani – Point 490 – Jebel Dabbas – Jebellel Beshri – El Munkara, inclusive – El Hawi – northwards along Khabur Su and Jagh Jagh [sic] Su – Nisibin, exclusive – Midiat – Khandik.

3. The frontier suggested above has been selected, after consideration of the whole question from the widest Imperial point of view, with a view to:–

(*a*) Restricting the length of the strategic defensive frontier of Egypt and advancing it from the point of view of their defence.

(*b*) Inclusion of the greater part of the Hejaz railway south of Damascus and all the headwaters of the Jordan.

(*c*) Strong natural features such as Mount Hermon and inclusion of the lower waters of the River Litani.

(*d*) Inclusion of potential railway, pipe-line and air routes between Palestine and Mesopotamia, viâ the Euphrates.

4. The political province of Lebanon is excluded, and it would be useless to press for the inclusion of the City of Damascus itself.

5. With a view to the establishment of the above line the Prime Minister has decided to stake our claim by the occupation of Palmyra[57] as soon as possible, if you consider this operation feasible.

6. Marshall will be asked to establish a post near El Munkara under an experienced political officer, at the same time as you Palmyra, so as to prevent the French coming too far down the Euphrates.

7. You should remember in replying that above line has been selected as the best compromise between the requirements of Imperial defence and the local claims of French, Arabs and Jews.

8. The Palmyra force should be accompanied by wireless in order to maintain touch with Marshall.

9. Please telegraph a summary of your plans for carrying out the required operations and date by which it can be executed, and communicate directly with Marshall with a view to concerted action.

PRO: WO33/981, pp. 38–9

235
Wilson to Allenby
[Letter. Typescript. Dictated]   23 May 1919
SECRET

I take the opportunity of Nugent going out to you with my other letter to write you a line about the position of your Force in Egypt, Palestine and Syria. As you know we are in real difficulties at home in regard to finding troops for the different theatres and more especially for the technical services. I confess I get very confused with the A.G's returns about the effectives in Egypt, and Winston, who is over here, and I have been going into the A.G's figures and have had to ask him a number of fresh questions. What struck both of us was whether you could economise both in officers and, especially, in transportation services, if you organised your forces more on the basis of a mobile police against internal disorders than on the divisional and corps organization which is more fitted to compete with regular armies in the field.

IWM: Wilson papers HHW2/33B/15. Copy at IWM: Wilson papers HHW2/33D/4

236
Lee Stack to Allenby

[Letter or telegram? Typescript]

Erkowit
24 May 1919

SINCE I reported to you in my telegram of the 30th April the incident that occurred at Port Soudan when the Egyptian army details returning from Egypt made a slight demonstration at that place, and subsequently on the train to Atbara, there have been two incidents of a similar nature at Port Soudan and Atbara.

At Port Soudan, the arrival of the Coptic[58] bishop from Egypt on his way to Khartoum was the occasion. A few railway battalion men and young Egyptians from the town gathered in front of his house, and subsequently paraded the streets waving flags and shouting. No action was taken beyond telling the demonstrators to go home, which they did.

The Coptic bishop refused to address the gathering, and told the Governor afterwards confidentially that the Copts were only forced into an attitude of sympathy with the Moslems by reason of the smallness of their numbers, and that he personally was most anxious to avoid such displays of feeling as this in the Soudan.

The Atbara affair was on a somewhat larger scale. Large numbers of Egyptian employees and railway battalion soldiers demonstrated in a peaceful but very noisy manner on two successive nights in the streets of the town. The excitement was caused by the spreading of a strong rumour that the British Government had communicated to Rushdy Pasha an announcement of the independence of Egypt.

There has been no attempt at violence on any of these occasions, and the attitude of the Sudan natives has been one of indifference and even disgust.

OxBod: Milner papers VI/D/444/3

237
Allenby to Foreign Office[59]

Cairo
[Telegram. Typescript]   24 May 1919
URGENT
Private

I have carefully considered arguments you have sent me in favour of postponement of mission until early autumn.

Conditions here have altered since my last telegram to you; it has now been possible to form a Ministry and I now consider it desirable to give this Ministry time to settle down and prove their worth. If arrival of mission is delayed until September the new Ministry should have established itself firmly and would be of assistance to mission in bringing before that body carefully considered and matured views as to future Government of Country.

I have consulted both Sultan and Prime Minister and they both agree with me as to this. I therefore recommend that mission should not arrive in this country until September; in the meantime I am appointing a committee here to collaborate and collect such evidence as may be useful when it arrives.

OxBod: Milner papers VI/D/452/152

238
Prince Feisal to Allenby
[Letter. Typescript]   28 May 1919

I have returned from Europe after the Peace Conference had decided to send an International Commission to the Arab country, especially to Syria, in order to ascertain the desire of the peoples and ask them about their future.

I had informed you, when I had the pleasure of meeting you, of all that had happened in Paris, as well as of the present conditions in the country owing to the delay of the Commission. The people have long been waiting for its coming, and their long waiting has led them to perplexity which has caused confusion in the regular trade and living and other vital operations, besides confining the Arab Government to the Turkish regulations, the influence of which is well-known in the country, because the Arab personnel, by dint of the military state, are not able, in any way, to carry out any urgent reform and improvement. What makes the responsibility lain upon me greater and of more grave nature, is, [sic] the fact that the peoples of all denominations, creeds, religions, and countries, have stated either themselves or through their representatives, openly in private and public meetings, that they had entrusted unto me their affairs, and given me full authority to look after their foreign interests. As I am the representative of Hejaz, and plenipotentiary of Syria, and Deputy for all the Arab countries, which have acknowledged my representing them in several ways, it is therefore incumbent upon me to submit the case to your Excellency as you are the Commander-in-Chief of the Allied Forces in this zone, and beg you to furnish me with the latest news you have regards the said Commission, and what became of them, so that the people might know how they really stand. They have decided amongst themselves to ask for their national rights and defend their national being with all the powers they have of legal means. The country will not withdraw the aim they cherish, and on which they have set their hearts, and will not accept any other decision besides the first one. The country will not accept any judgment passed in its regards unless it be in agreement with its aspirations. I, with my countrymen, consider ourselves not responsible for any consequence that might ensue in case anything happens which contradicts our desires. I have presented, enclosed herewith,[60] a letter with the same meaning to the Peace Conference as I had informed your Excellency by wire. This is passed for your information.

IWM: Wilson papers HHW2/33B/20[61]

239
Allenby to War Office (GOC-in-C Egypt to War Office)

[Telegram. Typescript]   29 May 1919
No. E.A. 2480

Your No. 78285,[62] C.I.G.S., paragraphs 5, 6 and 9.

(*a*) Palmyra is nearly 150 miles from Damascus and 90 from Homs. Roads are bad and the maintenance even of a very small force at Palmyra would strain to the utmost my transport resources, which are being cut down by demobilisation to a minimum, in fact, it would require careful examination to decide whether, with my existing transport, it is practicable to feed a force there at all.

(*b*) From a military point of view the situation of a small force at Palmyra would be indefensible, it would be out of reach of support and the Arab tribes, who are under no control, could cut its communications at any time.

(*c*) The despatch of British troops there could have no military justification and would be viewed with deep suspicion by both French and Arabs, and might cause active hostility on the part of the latter.

As Commander-in-Chief of Allied Forces, I have always been careful not to use troops for political purpose.

Royal Air Force have already made arrangement to establish a landing ground at Palmyra, and only difficulties of transport have prevented the stocking of it with petro [sic] and oil, which the local Sheikh has agreed to guard. I will now push on the landing ground and arrange for visits by aeroplane. I will also examine feasibility of sending a political officer there on an occasional visit.

With regard to the first part of your telegraph, you know my views regarding the political danger and economic disadvantages of separating Palestine and Syria, which is contrary to the wishes and interests of the great majority of the population. I also think that from a military point of view the old frontier of Egypt, with rectifications which have already been suggested to you, gives a better frontier for defence than any in northern Palestine. I would point out that there is no practicable route from Palestine or Syria to Palmyra without passing through what will be French sphere according to boundary given in your telegram.

PRO: WO33/981, pp. 43–4

240
Allenby to Balfour (addressed Troopers, repeated Foreign Office)

[Telegram. Typescript]   30 May 1919
Decypher [sic] of telegram from General Allenby, Cairo, to Balfour (addressed Troopers, repeated Foreign Office)
No. E.A. 2484

[This telegram begins with copies of two telegrams that Allenby has received from Feisal saying that trouble will ensue if the French are allowed to occupy Syria. Allenby has passed on the warning from Feisal with the following message:]

I look on the situation as extremely grave. Unless you [Wilson or Balfour] can at once enable me to reassure Feisal and tell him that the Commission is coming out and will decide the future of the country it is certain that he will raise the Arabs against the French and ourselves. This will jeopardise position of my troops in Syria and will seriously endanger the whole situation in Syria and Palestine. A word from Feisal will bring against us all the warlike Bedouins from the East of Jordan, on whose friendly attitude depends the safety of Palestine and the security of my long lines of communication.

A rising of these Bedouins would bring against us also the tribes of the Sinai Peninsula and serious trouble will certainly break out in Egypt and the Soudan.[63] In such a case I shall be totally unable to handle the situation with the troops at my disposal.

HoL: Lloyd George papers F/205/3/12. Copies at NAS, Kerr papers, GD40/17/1341/1; NAS: Kerr papers GD40/17/38/131–3; PRO: WO32/5580; and PRO: WO33/981

[In NAS: Kerr papers GD40/17/1341/2–3 and GD40/17/38/144–5 there are two replies from London (see below) to Allenby's EA2484 above and sent to Allenby but not signed. Both are dated 31 May. Different versions of these replies can be found in DBFP.]

1. With reference to your telegram E.A.2484, you may announce that the Commission which is to investigate the problems connected with the political future of the people of Syria, Palestine and Mesopotamia will arrive in the East almost immediately. The American representatives have already started. We have long been prepared and anxious to send ours. It is not yet certain whether the French will consent to send their Commissioners to the East at all.[64] If they do not we think it for obvious reasons inexpedient to send ours. But in that event we authorise you to announce that the British Government is prepared to give the fullest weight to the advice which the Council of the Principal Allied and Associated Powers will receive from the American Commissioners. His Majesty's Government rely upon you to see that the Commissioners are given every facility in prosecuting their enquiries.[65]

2. With further reference to your telegram E.A. 2484 you appear to think that the Commission will decide the future of the various ex-Turkish territories. That is not correct. They will have no power to decide, but after examining all the facts of the case will tender their advice to the Council of the principal Allied Powers, who will have to take the final decision.[66]

241
Allenby (Cairo) to Balfour (Paris)

[Telegram. Printed]   31 May 1919, received 1 June 1919
EA 2487

In continuation of my E.A. 2479 of May 30 I at once sent the following telegram to Feisal. Begins: Your C.721 and 722.[67]

As follows for Feisal from C.-in-C., begins:

With reference to information cabled to you by memoir in Paris. I have no knowledge whatever of such a decision.

Your telegrams Nos. C.721 and C.722 of May 29 have been repeated to War Office and Foreign Office and I have requested an early reply. I count upon you in the meantime to maintain order and discipline, and to restrain any action that might endanger future of your country. Any hasty action that would bring you into conflict with my troops would put an end to all your national aspirations at once.

Addressed Troopers, repeated War Office.

DBFP, pp. 259–60

242
Allenby to War Office (C. in C. Egypt to War Office)
[Telegram. Typescript]   2 June 1919
SECRET
E.A.2403

Following for Sir H. Wilson. Nugent arrived yesterday with maps [,] letters and papers and has explained your views. My telegram E.A.2460 [,] E.A.2480 and 2484 will have given you my views and I see no reason to modify them. As regards Tadmor I propose to use it as an intermediate depot for aeroplanes and I have ordered a detachment of the Arab troops under my command to occupy it and it will be visited often by my armoured cars. I believe that the partition of Syria by either of lines marked on your map will be violently resented by all Syrian Arabs. Feisal and entire population of both Syria and Palestine have since the original announcement of the Inter-Allied Commission been counting on the arrival of an authoritive [sic] body through whom they can state their case to the Peace Conference before a final decision is made.

With reference to my E.A.2484 I have since learnt that Feisal on the receipt of the telegram from his Agent in Paris was about to proclaim the independence of Syria and attack the French. With difficulty he was dissuaded by my political officers at Damascus. For the time being the news department [sic] of the American

271

delegates has restored situation. I have to-day received letter from Chief Administrator O.E.T.A. South reiterating in strongest terms that it is not (group omitted) that nonfulfilment of promise to send Commission may result in serious situation in that country. Disregardment of the pledges made to our Arabs in (1 gr. omitted) will certainly lead us into grave troubles. I urge most strongly if it has been definitely decided to partition Syria that Feisal should be recalled to Paris and there told what is intended.

PRO: WO 106/192/71. Copy at WO33/981, p. 51

243
Allenby to Wilson

[Letter. Holograph]   3 June 1919
Embossed

I am sorry that you are cutting Syria into French and British areas. I am convinced that acute trouble will follow. Feisal is absolutely determined not to have any French control, and is bitterly opposed to a division of Syria. I have pointed out all this, in letters and telegrams. It looks to me as if you are reviving the Sykes-Picot agreement, in its worst form; and settling the future of Syria without reference to the will or wishes of the inhabitants. It will make no difference to the Arabs whether you settle on your line of demarcation or Tardieu's. The Arabs will accept neither line. Much better let the French have all Syria, and do their own fighting, than act as cats paw to them.

IWM: Wilson papers HHW2/33B/18. Typescript copy at IWM: Wilson papers HHW2/33D/7

244
Allenby to Curzon

Cairo

[Telegram. Typescript]   4 June 1919
No. 909

NEW Ministry was formed on 21st May under Mohammad Said Pasha,[68] who was Prime Minister under Lord Kitchener[69] and Sir E. Gorst.[70] He is of Turkish extraction, and passes as a strong man with a greater knowledge of the provinces than Rushdy Pasha, and likely to keep order with a strong hand. Sirry,[71] Wahba[72] and Ziwar[73] Pashas are again in Ministry, the other appointments being new ones. Extremists are very angry at formation of a Ministry, and especially at Said Pasha's appointment, which they regard as a severe blow to their cause. Apart from possible danger of assassination, Ministry appears fairly firm on its seat and is doing well.

Extremists are endeavouring to get up another strike of Government officials and lawyers, but it is impossible that their efforts will succeed, as country is growing tired of disorders. Situation will not, however, improve until a peace is signed, as great hopes are set on Germany's refusal to sign.

Strike continues on canal, but of a peaceful character. Otherwise, situation is to all intents and purposes normal. Trial of villagers involved in murder of British officers in Luxor express is proceeding, and is likely to involve punishment of a large number of persons. This will give further material for atrocity campaign, which Egyptians at Paris are carrying on with great zeal.

OxBod: Milner papers VI/D/444/3

245
Wilson to Allenby

[Letter. Typescript. Dictated]   5 June 1919
SECRET & PERSONAL

Your letter of the 17th May reached me two or three days ago and everything you say in it has been confirmed by your telegrams since that date. The real fact of course is that we are in a horrible mess. It is quite clear that in your opinion any line of demarcation such as I have proposed, or as Tardieu has submitted, is impossible without our having a row with the Arabs, the Arabs with the French, and possibly ourselves with the French also. Clemenceau is hardening in his attitude about this Syrian affair. As you know he flatly refused to allow any Frenchmen to form part of the Commission, and he appears now to be going to go back and stand on the Sykes-Picot Agreement, calling on us to honour our signatures. As during all these months I have never been able to get the Sykes-Picot formally torn up I think that Clemenceau will be within his rights if he harks back and claims to stand on that Agreement. This of course would be the devil for us because not only does it divide up the Arabs very much in the manner of the proposals that I sent you out by Nugent, but it gives the French Mosul and the upper waters of both the Rivers.

IWM: Wilson papers HHW 2/33B/17. Typescript copy at IWM: Wilson papers HHW2/33D/6

246
Allenby to Wilson

[Letter. Typescript. Copy]   6 June 1919

It does not matter which line cuts Syria in two – yours or Tardieu's. If Syria is divided, and the fate of the peoples decided without reference to them – in spite of all the pledges given – you will light a fire that will blaze for years.

The situation in the Hedjaz aggravates the difficulty of the problem. This Wahabism is of the nature of the fanatical Puritanism of the Cromwellians. It is extremely contagious; and is attractive to the wild, illiterate Arab, who sees his opportunity of gaining a martyr's crown. The movement may well spread to Syria, if it is successful in the Hedjaz. I am suggesting that Feisal shall send some officers and some machine guns to help his father. He may do so; but, if Ibn Saud really means business, I doubt if they could be in time to save Mecca.

Feisal has wired today, to his father, that he may come to his help. He says "but in that case we shall lose Syria", so I don't suppose he will go. I think it likely that he or the King of the Hedjaz will ask the French to send Moslem troops to help in the defence of Mecca. What are you going to do then? I am told, from F.O., that Indian troops are not to be used there; but I presume that it would not advance our prestige if we left the salvation of Mecca and Medina to the French.

IWM: Wilson papers HHW2/33B/20. Typescript copy at IWM: Wilson papers HHW2/33D/9. Slightly different copy at HofL: Lloyd George papers F/47/8/22

247
Allenby to Curzon

Cairo

[Telegram. Printed]　　　　12 June 1919, received 20 June 1920
E.A.2529

I have received the following from Feisal from Aleppo. Begins:–

Will Your Excellency very kindly find out from Commission or elsewhere whether League of Nations is prepared to put into force recommendations made by Commission and whether Commission is authorized to recommend the giving of Mandate to any power wanted by great majority of population. Unless this be known the people of Syria will be severely handicapped in approaching Commission. If they ask for Britain and Great Britain is unable to take mandate they will run grave risks of getting power which is only desired by very small minority as it will be only (?other) competing. If they knew Britain is not to be available they can inform Commission accordingly that is to say the vast majority of Syrians want Great Britain. Failing that they wish for complete independence although they well know difficulties and dangers of latter course but they prefer them to France. If they knew England was not going to accept a mandate and League would not allow complete independence Syria would ask for America in preference to France. Your Excellency can well understand although these are real sentiments of people it is quite impossible for all these alternatives to be appointed and sufficiently clearly expressed by people for Commission to be justified in afterwards making really confident recommendations to League. It is only fair to Syria that it should know what is possible and what is impossible. The only result of keeping Syria in the dark will be a (?mixed) opinion, some asking for England, some for America, some for France and some for complete independence, and Commission might then report that opinion is so divided that France will be as acceptable as any other Power. This Your Excellency well knows will be a complete misunderstanding of situation. I beg you in fairness to the country you have liberated to help it obtain what it now wants for its future peace and development. I have been told that Commission is only a show and that fate of country has been already decided. I feel sure this is incorrect but at this crisis in history of Syria a clear pronouncement (on) that point is of greatest importance.

Besides communicating them to me will Your Excellency be pleased to issue answers to these questions in as public a manner as possible to enable Syria to state its mind to Commission with freedom and confidence.

If you approve I should like to meet Commission myself at earliest date possible. Can this very kindly be arranged? I await Your Excellency's answer by telegraph at Aleppo.

Please accept my humblest apologies for giving Your Excellency this trouble. Ends.

I have replied as follows. Begins: Following for Feisal from Commander-in-Chief. The Commission will advise Council of Allied and Associated Powers as to wishes of people with regard to future form of Government or mandate.

His Majesty's Government have expressed unwillingness to accept a mandate for Syria but will give fullest weight to advice of Commission in the Council of Allied and Associated Powers.

General Officer Commanding-in-Chief has not yet seen Commission which landed in Jaffa on 10th but Clayton is with Commission in Palestine. He returns probably tomorrow and will then be able to report programme and itinerary of Commission. You will be informed when Commission visits Syria and when and where you will be able to meet it. Ends.

DBFP, pp. 275–6

248
Balfour to Allenby (Cairo)

Paris
[Telegram. Printed]   18 June 1919
No. 58

Dr Weizmann has asked that following message may be delivered to Friedenwald, Zionist Commission, Jaffa, through General Clayton.

'Present our case before American Commissioners with firmness, moderation and dignity on lines submitted by us to Peace Conference. Inform them our co-operation with Feysal and our desire to work harmoniously with Arab population for good of Palestine. Draw their attention to achievements Jewish colonisation under difficult circumstances and great possibilities now when greatest majority Jewish people all over world resolutely supports Zionist aims and considerable numbers waiting first opportunity settle Palestine. Wire position. Weizmann.'

DBFP, p. 278

249
Balfour to Allenby (Cairo)

Paris
[Telegram. Printed]   26 June 1919
No. 59

General Clayton's telegram No. 2536.[74]

Feisal has based his message on a misunderstanding of your reply quoted in No. E.A.2529. Feisal's view apparently is that while H.M.G. are reluctant to be mandatory for Syria, they would

277

accept position if American Commission advised that this was in accordance with the wishes of the people concerned.

This however is a mistake. H.M.G. have not departed from view expressed orally by Prime Minister, I think in your presence, to M. Clemenceau in the presence of Signor Orlando and myself that in no circumstances would Great Britain become mandatory for Syria; and this has been explicitly repeated in telegram No. 16 to General Clayton which runs as follows:

'You can only reply to Feisal that His Majesty's Government are determined not to take a mandate for Syria.'

I feel confident that Feisal was told the same thing when he was here though I can find no record of this having been done.

It is evident he is unwilling to accept even the most direct statement as conclusive, but it is all important that he should be made to understand that whatever else happens Great Britain must refuse to take any leading part in guidance or control of Syrian affairs, and that he is quite without justification in thinking that this refusal constitutes an abandonment either of himself or of the Arab cause. We earnestly desire to support both, but for reasons with which he is perfectly well acquainted we cannot add to the other responsibilities which we have undertaken on behalf of the Arab race, the position of Mandatory of Syria.

Repeated to Foreign Office No. 1092.

DBFP, pp. 298–9

250
Allenby to War Office (GOC-in-C Egypt to War Office)
[Telegram. Typescript]   7 July 1919
No. E.A.2578

I visited Damascus on 30th June and saw the American Commissioners. They are now at Beirout and thence go to Tripoli, Homs and Aleppo and then return to Constantinople. They are making good progress. I was favourably impressed by their earnest ability and impartiality. They hope to complete their work in Syria and Palestine by about the third week in July. I also saw Feisal who enquired about the advisability of his returning to Paris. I advised him to go there in 3 or 4 weeks['] time when Commission had finished its tour. He understands that Great Britain will not accept a mandate for Syria. I told him I thought he had no cause for fear but could give him no definite assurance. On 1st July motored from Homs to Tadmor and remained there two nights. Landing ground at Tadmor was used by several aeroplanes during my tour. There will be a permanent gendarmerie there. A depôt of petrol and oil will be established shortly there and a hangar erected. Natives appear quiet and content, but parties of Shammar Arabs from Mesopotamia had been raiding in the neighbourhood. There was a fight on day of my arrival some 20 miles west of Tadmor and I was met by Bedouins of Roalla tribe bringing in prisoners and camels of raiders whom they had defeated, killing or capturing the whole band. General Barrow who has lately visited Urfa, Jerablusy and Cilicia, is quite satisfied with the situation there.

PRO: WO33/981, p. 73. Copy at PRO: WO32/5580

251
Allenby to Cheetham
The Residency Ramleh Egypt
[Letter. Holograph]   18 July [1919?]

I was glad to have your letter of the 29th, and to hear you[r] news. I hope that, by now, you will have seen Curzon. Here, things are improving. The Ministry is, I think, gaining strength; but there was nearly a big crisis the other day. However, that has passed over. We have got through with the murder trials – of Dierut [?75] etc. –; and, now, I have closed the Special Military Courts, and have handed over the remaining cases connected with recent disturbances to the Civil Courts. I have also – on the occasion of signing of Peace Treaty, taken off censorship; and I have released Political prisoners. Dunlop and Haines are both resigning; and I have obtained sanction to replace them by Pattison and Clayton.[76]

Hope Vere[77] is with us now; and is a hard working and useful man. Dalmeny returns to England early in August; and my wife goes about the same time. I hope to get away, towards end of August, if things run smoothly here. Hedjaz and Syria are both centres of possible trouble, and might stop me.

I am sorry to hear that you and Lady Cheetham have not been well. My wife joins me in best wishes and remembrances.

OxAnt: Cheetham papers, file 5, DT82.5.GY

252
Allenby to Curzon
Ramleh

[Telegram. Printed]   30 July 1919, received 31 July 1919
No. 1177

Following from Policy [Political Office] Egypt Expeditionary Force. Begins.

An article has been submitted to a Jewish paper in Palestine by Zionist organization. . . .[78] Purporting to come from London *Daily Telegraph* correspondent Percival Landon,[79] to the effect that Zionists in Paris have won 'Tremendous victory at Peace Conference', that they are to be given great powers in Administration of Palestine and that they are busy with plans for re-population and intensive cultivation. Unrestricted immigration is implied.

If such articles find their way to Palestine they will inflame an already excited population. I urge that Zionists in London and Paris should be told to restrain the exuberance of their press supporters and to be moderate and cautious in their views. Ends.

DBFP, pp. 324–5.

253
Allenby to Churchill
General Headquarters

[Letter. Printed]   6 August 1919

Mr. Justice Brandeis, who sailed for Europe on the 26th July, will no doubt discuss at some length with you the impressions he has gained and the conclusions he has come to as the result of his visit to Palestine.

On his arrival in Egypt I pointed out to the Judge, in a lengthy interview between us, the peculiar local difficulties besetting the Zionist programme in Palestine, the opposition to it on the part of the non-Jewish elements of the population – which at present constitute a large majority – and the fact that my administration, being a purely military one, can only act in strict adherence to the laws and usages of war. I laid stress on the fact that scrupulous fairness characterised the dealings of my administration with all classes and creeds, and I pointed out that His Majesty's Government's policy, contained in the Balfour Declaration, though fully appreciated by myself and my subordinates, did not entitle me as a military administrator to grant to the Zionists privileges and opportunities denied to other members of occupied enemy territory. Mr. Justice Brandeis, who appears to me to consider the future of Zionism in a statesmanlike and broad-minded manner, at first gained the impression, I believe, that I was unduly apprehensive, and consequently rigorous in my control of the actions of the Zionist Commission. On his return from his tour, however, he admitted that my review of the position was in no wise [sic] exaggerated, and that he found the difficulties more numerous and serious than he had anticipated. At the same time his visits, which included twenty-two colonies and all the towns where important Jewish influence exists, confirmed and strengthened his opinion as to the wisdom and practicability of the establishment of a National Home for the Jews in Palestine. He agrees with me that the only policy to be followed at present is one of great patience and moderation, and that every care should be taken to avoid exciting, by threats of expropriation and subjection to Jewish dominion, the enmity and fear of the non-Jewish elements.

It is a matter for regret that the same sane spirit and sound vision does not characterise the leading articles of Zionist publications in Europe, most of which find their way into the chief centres of Palestine and are the primary cause of the bitter antagonism at present shown to the Zionist programme.

Mr. Justice Brandeis was accompanied by the Zionist Commission during his tour, but Major Waley[80] also travelled with him and ensured his coming into close contact with such sections of the community as cause a bad impression and represent the unsatisfactory aspect of Zionism. His demeanour towards local leaders was exceptionally dignified, and on several occasions he administered rebuke to those who had caused trouble by immoderate conduct and self-advertisement, thus giving proof to Palestinian Jewry that the real leaders of the movement appreciate the pettiness and undesirability of local disputes and intrigues. The Zionist Commission, on the other hand, has not always been firm enough with the unruly spirits of the community, and has made promises of concessions impossible to be carried out. This has resulted in a loss of authority and prestige.

During his tour various grievances against my administration were laid down before Mr. Justice Brandeis. It was alleged that there had been unfair restrictions on Jewish development, amounting to contravention of His Majesty's Government's policy, and that this was due to anti-Semitic prejudice on the part of Government officials.

I have enquired fully into the alleged anti-Semitic attitude of the administration, and am satisfied that any such complaints are without foundation. I understand that Mr. Justice Brandeis on the conclusion of his visit held the same opinion. There have certainly been some misunderstandings between the administrators and the Jewish leaders, and it has been and will continue to be necessary for questions of public security or military exigency to take precedence, a necessity which the Zionists are naturally sometimes unable to appreciate. The chief administrator has, however, invariably been ready to receive the representatives of the Zionist Commission at any time, and if those grievances had always been brought before him they would have been carefully considered. The Zionist Commission has, however, not always adopted this policy, and has referred complaints direct to its organisation in Europe. Such procedure makes difficult the relations between the Chief Administrator and the Zionist Commission.

Mr. Justice Brandeis fully appreciated this and has explained to the present leaders of the Commission his views as to the correct method of procedure.

On his departure the Judge expressed his gratitude for the sympathetic reception by the authorities and for all the facilities afforded him during his stay.

DBFP, pp. 338–9

254
Allenby to Shea

The Residency Ramleh Egypt

[Letter. Holograph]   7 August 1919

My sincere thanks for your letter of 5th instant, with its welcome message of congratulations, and for the kind words in which it is expressed. I owe my success in no small measure to you, and I am very grateful for all you have done. I am glad to hear that things in Syria are quiet.

LHCMA: Shea papers 4/2

255
Allenby to mother (256)

[Letter. Holograph]   8 August 1919

I see, by the late telegrams, that I am to be made a Viscount – which is a respectable title. Mabel wired congratulations yesterday, from Marseilles; so she should be home by tomorrow, and I hope she will go straight to Felixstowe.

You seem to be full of economic and Bolshevistic troubles, especially in Yorkshire and at Liverpool.

Here we are quiet, now; and hope that the Volcano is extinct. If things remain tranquil, I hope to come home early in September for a few weeks.

I shall try to return early in October; in time for Milner's Commission, which is timed to come out about mid-October. My discontents threaten to renew troubles and strikes when this Commission comes out; as a protest; but we are better prepared, this time, and I doubt if anything will happen.

[End of letter missing]

LHCMA: Allenby papers 1/10/12

256
Allenby to Kenyon

The Residency Ramleh Egypt

[Extract from letter. Typescript]   11 August 1919

As regards SmithDorien [sic] & Le Cateau: – I went to see himat [sic] 1 a.m. & told him that unless his troops continued the retreat before daylight they could not get away, as the Germans were close on their billets and bivouacs. He consulted Hubert Hamilton[81] & ForestierWalker[82] [sic]: & they reported the troops as unable to start before daylight, owing to fatigue. Smith-Dorrien, therefore, decided to fight; & I think that, under the circumstances, he could not have done otherwise.[83]

[Below the above there is a handwritten note as follows:]

75 St. George's Road SW1

May 23. 1920

My dear Fred,

Above is an extract I promised to read you. It is in a private letter to myself and is an answer to a question I asked as to his opinion. It seems to me a valuable piece of evidence, well worth preserving as the question of Le Cateau will be much discussed in years to come; but of course it cannot be published in Allenby's lifetime without his consent.

Your affectionate brother,

Edward R. Kenyon

The original is in my copy of French's Despatches 1914–16, opposite page 11.

BL: Smith-Dorrien papers Add.Mss.52777 f. 13

257
Allenby to Wingate

The Residency Cairo

[Letter. Holograph]   16 August [1919]

Things are quieter now, and I hope that we shall soon have a new Ministry that will carry on satisfactorily. I want the Commission to come out not much later than next month; and, if Milner is not available, I hope a capable substitute will replace him. I am just back from a tour of inspection to Jerusalem, Damascus, Beirut and Haifa.

I found Feisal as bitterly anti French as ever; and I fear great trouble if the French get a mandate for Syria. In Palestine the anti Jewish feeling is now very acute. Muslims and Christians are united in their opposition to the Jews, and the latter have not been displaying the greatest tact.

I hope the mixed commission for Syria, Palestine, etc. will not long be delayed. It is eagerly expected; and its non arrival or unduly delayed arrival will be sure to cause outbreaks – anti Zionist and anti European – in both Palestine and Syria.

SAD: Wingate papers 174/2/26

258
Allenby to Lady Allenby

The Residency Ramleh

[Letter. Holograph]   23 August 1919

Enclosed is a letter to Garter King of Arms.[84] He wants to know my title; and desires that I, or a representative, shall call at the College of Arms to see him.

Will you read the letter and send it on to him? I don't think I can do better than "Allenby of Megiddo." Megiddo was the crucial point of last year's campaign; and is the base of the name "Armageddon", which means "Place of Megiddo".

Alternatives are Esdraelon, or Aleppo; and I like neither.

[End of letter missing]

LHCMA: Allenby papers 1/10/14

259
War Office to Allenby (War Office to Field Marshal C-in-C Egypt)

[Telegram. Typescript]   28 August 1919
No. 80841 M.I.2

It has been proposed by Dr Weismann [sic] that (*a*) in view of the necessity for a future garrison in Palestine the Jews should take a larger share in producing the man power. In his opinion it would be possible to recruit 10 to 15 thousand Jewish volunteers of good physical standard principally from Georgia, Transylvania, Czecho-Slovak prisoners in Siberia and Polish-Jew prisoners of war in Italy.

(*b*) In order to facilitate dealing with questions regarding Jewish battalion a Jewish liaison officer should be attached to your headquarters. For this duty he recommends Colonel F.D. Samuel.[85]

PRO: WO33/981, p. 100

260
Curzon to Allenby (Cairo)

Foreign Office
[Telegraph. Printed]   29 August 1919
No. 986

Your telegram No. 1071[86] (of 6th July – French troops for the Hejaz).

French Chargé d'Affaires states that Hussein has asked for the despatch of four French tanks for the protection of pilgrims on the Medina road. Have you any confirmation of Hussein having made such a request to the French?

DBFP: p. 365

261
Allenby to Curzon

Ramleh

[Letter. Typescript]   31 August 1919, received 17 September 1919
No. 411

WITH reference to your telegram No. 445 of the 9th April last and my despatch No. 351 of the 31st ultimo, I have the honour to forward to your lordship herewith a copy of a confidential memorandum by the General Staff Intelligence Department on the subject of Bolshevistic propaganda in this country.

You will observe that a prominent part is being played by an Italian named Pizzuto,[87] who is connected with the organisation of various workmen's syndicates.

It should be noted that, according to Pizzuto's own statement, funds are brought for Bolshevistic propaganda here by Scandinavian sailors on their way to the Far East. I am accordingly causing an enquiry to be held secretly, the result of which will be reported to your Lordship in due course, and careful supervision over all suspects to be exercised at Port said and Suez.

I have the honour to request that a similarly strict supervision may be instituted in the United Kingdom and other ports upon vessels sailing for Egypt.

It would also be of considerable assistance to me in combating this insidious form of subversive propaganda if your Lordship could cause to be sent out to Egypt a reliable Intelligence Officer who has dealt with these matters either in Scandinavia or those foreign countries where the Bolsheviks have their central organisation, in order that he may be able to assist in controlling the movements of their agents through the Canal, and keep me informed of any relevant measures adopted by His Majesty's Government.

OxBod: Milner papers VI/D/444/4

262
Allenby to Lady Allenby

The Residency Ramleh[88]

[Letter. Holograph]   10 September 1919

I am writing from the Normandy Hotel, Deauville. We had a calm and pleasant voyage; reaching Marseilles on the morning of the 8th. I came on to Paris that evening, arriving yesterday.

There I found that I was to come to Deauville, to see the P.M. I lunched with Mr Balfour in Paris, yesterday; and came on in the afternoon by train. It is almost 4 hours by train.

Mr Lloyd George is staying at a beautiful villa, some 2½ miles from here. I dined there last night, and had a long talk with him. He tells me that I shall not be able to get away before next Tuesday. It is an awful nuisance. I had hoped to be in London by last night. However, I can see the importance of my being here just now; so I try not to cry, though I am very disappointed. We shall go back to Paris, tomorrow or next day; as there are big talks coming off. I have been interviewed once, at Marseilles; but have dodged other interviews, so far.

In Paris, snapshotters and cinematographers purs[u]ed me. They motor on, ahead; then jump out, and take their shots; then repeat the process, till they are tired. Shea, who is with me, beamed with pride; as you may suppose! We had a big dinner party, last night, at the P.M's villa. Bonar Law, Hamar Greenwood,[89] Auckland Geddes,[90] and others; also Mrs Waldorf Astor,[91] Miss Bonar Law[92] and other ladies.

[End of letter missing]

LHCMA: Allenby papers 1/10/15

263
Allenby to Congreve

9 Upper Cheyne Row, Chelsea

[Letter. Holograph]   3 October [1919?]

I am glad to hear that things are going pretty well in Egypt. I am to have a talk with Curzon and Milner on Wednesday next and I hope that I may learn then what H.M.G. really propose with regard to Egypt's future. From what I have heard, from H. Wilson and W. Churchill, there is no desire in the W.O. to reduce the garrison of Egypt greatly at present; or to remove it to Kantara. I hope to get back towards the end of this month. Shipping is difficult; and, now, it has been settled that we leave on the 17th by Orient-Express for Constantinople. Thence, the Admiralty will send us on; by the 'Surprise'; to Egypt – arriving about the 24th inst. at Alexandria.

I am interested, but not surprised, to hear of the French belief in our intrigues against them. . . .

SRO: Congreve papers D1057/M/U/11/11

264
Allenby to Wingate

9 Upper Cheyne Row, Chelsea
[Letter. Typescript. Copy]   16 October 1919

It has now been intimated to me that I am appointed High Commissioner. It is with mixed feelings that I hear this; as it means the termination of our happy association in the East. I must take this opportunity of thanking you once more for all the support you gave me, and for your advice and help, in the difficulties I encountered during the period I had the honour and pleasure of working with you. I shall always remember it with gratitude. I am, as at present arranged, to remain C.inC. of the E.E.F. Egypt is, from the latest accounts, fairly quiet; but till Europe settles down and till peace with Turkey is signed, there will I fear always be simmering trouble. In Syria the danger lies.

Feisal is still here; but no real solution has been found to his difficult problem, and his attitude towards the French is almost as unconciliatory as ever. I came over hoping to have 3 or 4 weeks of restful leave; but have not, so far, had much rest.

SAD: Wingate papers 175/1/91. Copy at OxBod: Milner papers VI/D/446/305–6. Holograph copy at Wingate papers 175/1/93–94

265
Allenby to Curzon

Hotel Majestic Paris

[Letter. Holograph]   31 October 1919

I have seen Lord Derby, twice; and I have met Gouraud and Berthelot.[93] Gouraud appears to be an honest man; and has that reputation. Today, Berthelot called on me; having asked for an interview. We talked about Syria. He expressed regret that some French Newspapers took the view that Feisal should turn to the French for sympathy, rather than to the English; and he declared himself to be of the opinion that the result of the negotiations, now in progress with the Emir, would cause him to understand that French and British alike were to be trusted to uphold the interests and rights of the Arabs. He discussed the diverse views of the British Prime Minister and of Clémenceau, at length. I told him that I was not concerned with the political aspects of the controversy; but that I would act in loyal cooperation with General Gouraud, to carry out the orders relating to the relief of my troops by the French, and also by the Arabs – in their respective zones.

Berthelot assured me that the French government had entire confidence in myself and Gouraud. He declared, moreover, that he would deal tactfully and patiently with the claims and propositions which the Emir Feisal was still putting forward. There was, however, – he said – a limit which must bound the Pan Arab claims – and added that this limit was to be recognized, in the interest of all parties.

On the whole, I considered the attitude of Monsieur Berthelot to be favourable and conciliatory. Nevertheless, I fear that he – like other statesmen – [. . .?] the peril of an Arab revolt against a settlement which might be considered unjust – and as endangering the future of the Arab nation.

OIOC: Curzon papers Mss Eur F112/208A/16–18

Appendix 1
Allenby and Zionism

Report on meeting between Allenby and Weizmann
[Report. Typescript]   Sometime after 3 April 1918

REPORT on Dr. Weizmann's visit to General Allenby at General Headquarters on Wednesday, the 3rd April 1918.

Dr. Weizmann left Cairo on Tuesday, April 2nd, and arrived at Bir Salem Station on Wednesday morning, where he was met by Major Ormsby-Gore and Captain James de Rothschild.

Major Ormsby-Gore informed Dr. Weizmann that his impression of General from the Zionist point of view quite satisfactory. On the other hand, the General was anxious to administer the country fairly with justice to all groups and nationalities and was most desirous of "getting on with the War."

Major Ormsby-Gore then left Dr. Weizmann and went on to Jaffa, where, he said, the Community were preparing a big demonstration to receive the Commission.[1] He was of the opinion that the time was not opportune for such a demonstration and he desired therefore to go to Jaffa to prevent it being held.

Dr. Weizmann replied that whilst he did not desire flag-waiting [sic], he certainly did not wish that the Commission should be hushed up. However, as he was now taken over by two Aidesde-Camp [sic] and Lord Dalmeny, he could not continue the conversation.

These having left him, Capt. James de Rothschild took upon himself the task of explaining to Dr. Weizmann the situation as it appeared to him. His impression was the position was very serious and that Dr. Weizmann must be very careful and tentative in what he was going to say to the General. In fact, the attitude of Captain James de Rithschild [sic] implied fear. He volunteered the opinion that he was quite sure our line would not advance any further, as in view of the critical position in France, a number of troops had been taken away from Palestine, and the arrival of the Commission was rather an inopportune moment. It was natural therefore that Dr. Weizmann should feel greatly displeased, which, added to a long and wearisome night journey, made him feel that he would be placed at a disadvantage when meeting the General.

On the other hand, Lord Dalmeny was extremely agreeable to Dr. Weizmann personally, and displayed a great enthusiasm about the aims and aspirations of the Commission. He informed Dr. Weizmann that Lady Crewe had written a great deal to him about Zionism, and he had been most interested to meet Dr. Weizmann.

Dr. Weizmann was then presented to the Commander-in-Chief, General Allenby, who immediately put him at his ease. Dr. Weizmann's impression of General Allenby was that he is a charming and intelligent man, understanding his task and meaning to carry it to a successful issue.

Dr. Weizmann handed the General leave letters for him from the Prime Minister and Mr. Balfour.

The General mentioned that he had a discussion with Major Ormsby-Gore on the aims of Zionism and the work of the Commission, and, as far as he was concerned, he was in full sympathy with our aims and would do whatever he could to help us in our work.

On the other hand, he was responsible to the British government for the fate of Palestine and he would like to hand over Palestine at the end of the War in a good condition, having done justice to all and having avoided friction wherever it was possible. The General thought that the Zionists were misunderstood by the Arabs, who were ignorant of the principles of Zionism.

Dr. Weizmann then gave the General a short exposé of Zionism, to which he added that the fate of Palestine would eventually be determined on the principle of self determination, which meant not only the desires of the Jews of Palestine, but also the Jews all over the world. Indeed the opinions of Jews would have to determine many questions at the end of the War. The power of the Jews in America was very great and men such as Brandas [presumably Justice Louis Dembitz Brandeis], Baron Edmond de Rothschild will wield a great influence. Dr. Weizmann spoke on the Zionist influence in London as evidenced by the letters which General Allenby had received. It was to be remembered that millions of Jews were now under German rule, and Germany would attempt to use them as a powerful German factor. This could only be counteracted if the attention of these Jews were focussed on a Jewish Palestine, and if Palestine was also a British Palestine, a powerful pro-British factor would be created. Dr. Weizmann then dealt with the relative merits of the Arabs and the Jews in relation to Palestine. He pointed out that whilst the

Arabs might possibly be an asset now, they may be a liability tomorrow. On the other hand, the Jews were a permanent asset to Great Britain, an asset which was constantly operating.

General Allenby did not venture an opinion on this comparison. After the interview had ended, Dr. Weizmann saw General Clayton who stated that General Allenby had expressed pleasure and satisfaction at the conversation he had had with Dr. Weizmann.

Dr. Weizmann was then invited to dinner by the Commander-in-Chief. During dinner General Allenby discussed the activity of Mr. Picot. He informed Dr. Weizmann that Picot had been instructed by him to carry out the instructions of G.H.Q., as otherwise he must return to France.

Dr. Weizmann gave it as his opinion that the France which was represented by M. Clemenceau and M. Pichon were ignorant of Mr. Picot, and did not have any interest in the future of Palestine. Mr. Picot had been brought into the Palestinian problem by some outsiders. In any case, the Zionists could only negotiate with the British Government. It was only in so far as Zionist propaganda was concerned that we could work in each country.

During the dinner, General B[o]lls [sic – Bols], Chief of the Staff, who sat on the other side of Dr. Weizmann, stated that the Military Authorities had apprehended three Russian Jews for spying, whom they had caught red-handed. This came as a shock to Dr. Weizmann, who did not pursue the matter any further during dinner. It was evident to all those in the immediate neighbourhood that Dr. Weizmann was greatly perturbed.

Capt. James de Rothschild supplemented this information by saying that three Russian Jews were to be hanged in the morning. Dr. Weizmann replied that, should this be true, the Commission would have no alternative but to return to England, as it could not work in Palestine in the face of suspicion and hostility which such an act would create.

However, in the morning, Captain de Rothschild visited Dr. Weizmann and told him that he had been mistaken in his information.

Dr. Weizmann perceived the unfavourable impression of the activities of Capt. De Rothschild whilst in General Headquarters.

The next morning was spent in conversation with General Clayton and Colonel Deedes,[2] who appeared to be satisfied with the visit of Dr. Weizmann to G.H.Q.

CZA: Z4/170

Allenby to Methuen

General Headquarters EEF

[Letter. Typescript]   25 February 1919

Brigadier-General Storrs has sent me on your letter to him of the 3rd February on the subject of Maltese emigration to Palestine. The question is a very delicate one and likely to cause considerable agitation if raised now – at a time when the future status of Palestine is awaiting the decision of the Peace Conference. As you are perhaps aware, H.M.G. have given certain pledges to the Zionists in regard to a National Jewish Home in Palestine. It remains to be seen how far the peace conference will support the Zionist policy of the eventual establishment of a Jewish Palestine, but this policy, as formulated by the Zionists, includes Jewish immigration on a large and organised scale. It is obvious, therefore, that any premature scheme of immigration for the benefit of the Maltese or any other class of person, would excite great uneasiness in Zionist circles, and might also prejudice the whole case of Palestine before the Peace Conference. An article in Number 26 Vol.IV, dated 1st February, of "Palestine" (an official Zionist publication, which has just reached me [)], shows that considerable feeling has already been aroused. I would observe that the remarks made to you by Lieut. Colonel Gabriel* regarding the undertaking of extensive works at Haifa are quite unauthorized. At present the future of Palestine is undetermined and the present military administration can only undertake those works which are of immediate and urgent necessity.

PRO: FO371/4167/801

Allenby to War Office

[Telegram. Typescript]   6 June 1919 (received 13 June 1919)
EA 2501 6th.
Your 78549 MO2.

I am strongly opposed to any increase of Jewish troops in Palestine. The measure would be interpreted as a preparation to enforce the claim of the Jewish minority on the rest of the population. The present distrust of Zionist aims among non-Jewish population would be greatly increased.

---

*   Of the Indian Army and, supposedly, anti-Zionist.

There have already been incidents between Jewish soldiers and non-Jewish inhabitants especially Moslems and an increase in number of Jewish troops would certainly lead to riots and wide spread trouble with the Arabs.

PRO: FO371/4181/2117

Report on meeting between Allenby and Rosoff[3]
[Report. Typescript] Sometime after 16 June 1919

On Monday, June 16, 1919, at 10.30 a.m. Major Waley informed Mr. Rosoff that General Allenby wished to see him. Interview at Residency, Cairo, Monday, June 16, 1919, 11.45 a.m. Present General Allenby, Major Waley, Mr. Rosoff and Capt. Levin.

General Allenby began by asking what the news from Paris was. Mr. Rosoff replied that it is quite settled in Paris that Palestine is to be the national home of the Jewish people, and he referred to the letter of President Wilson to Mr. Frankfurter. General Allenby pointed out that he is in charge of affairs in Palestine, not as High Commissioner, but as Military Governor, that in this position he is a trustee and cannot take sides, cannot now act on the assumption that Great Britain is to receive a mandate for Palestine as the Jewish homeland. He added that Zionism was meeting with opposition in Palestine, that even Jewish people were opposing it. He said that at present the visiting Zionists in Palestine must confine themselves to making plans, preparations; that projects could not now be carried out. Mr. Rosoff replied that this was well understood. General Allenby inquired if Justice Brandeis knew this; and he was assured that Justice Brandeis was acquainted with this situation. Mr. Rosoff said that in Paris, Emir Feisal had expressed himself as being in accord with the Zionist aims. General Allenby said that Emir Feisal does not possess quite as much influence with the Arabs as he thinks he has. Major Waley added that when Emir Feisal speaks to the Zionist leaders in Paris he gets a different story from what is told to the Arabs by the Jews in Palestine. Mr. Rosoff pointed out that the position of Jews in Russia was so serious that the Zionist Organization must take all necessary steps to prepare Palestine for a large Jewish immigration and that he was now going to Palestine to see what is to be done. General Allenby acquiesced.

CZA: L3/427. Copy at CZA AK297/7

Allenby to Lloyd George

Residency Cairo

[Letter. Copy. Typescript]   24 December 1919

Dr. Weizmann, the bearer of this letter, is leaving Egypt tomorrow after a prolonged visit to Palestine. He will no doubt explain to you the state of Zionism in Palestine. I should like to add that Dr. Weizmann has been of great assistance to my administration: his moderate views having gone a long way to ameliorate the political condition in Palestine and restore the confidence of the Arab in the Jew. Dr. Weizmann has prepared a comprehensive programme for the preliminary work necessary to inaugurate the Jewish National Home and I trust he will return to Palestine at no distant date to give me the benefit of his further advice.

CZA: AK 207/2. Copy of letter at HoL: Lloyd George papers F/49/13/2

Allenby to Lloyd George

Residency Cairo

[Letter. Copy. Holograph]   14 April 1920

I hope that you will be able to see Dr. Weizmann, who brings this. His schemes for the future of Zionism are bold and progressive; but, as outlined to me, they appear practicable if not hurried or brought in before the country is settling down after the signature of the Peace Treaty with Turkey. On one point I differ with Dr. Weizmann; and that is, in not sharing his views that our Military Administration has been unsympathetic with and – perhaps subconsciously – opposed to Zionism. It has, I believe, carried out its duties loyally and impartially. Dr. Weizmann'[s] own influence has been entirely for good and he has always been helpful to me.

CZA: AK 207/2. Copy of letter at HoL: Lloyd George papers F/49/13/2

Appendix 2
General Sir Harry Chauvel's Notes on Lawrence and the Capture of Damascus

Chauvel to Allenby

Department of Defence. Inspector-General. Army Headquarters.
Melbourne

[Letter. Typescript]   22 October 1929

I have just had sent to me, through the Australian Official Historian, the proof copies of the last eleven Chapters of the Official History of the Campaign in Egypt and Palestine. I am much concerned about the acceptance of so much of Lawrence's production, "Revolt in the Desert". The Official Historian seems to have swallowed it whole. The proofs I have just been dealing with are teeming with quotations from it or statements which could come only from that source. I have commented on some of these but there are others which, however sure I may be that they have little or no foundation on fact, I am not in a position to criticise.

I am naturally most concerned about Lawrence's absurd claims re the administration of Damascus and have written, as you will see from the enclosure, the full history of it.[4]

LHCMA: Allenby papers 2/5/16.

Copy of Record written by Lt.Gen. Sir H.G. Chauvel. Meeting of Sir Edmund Allenby and the Emir Feisal at the Hotel Victoria, Damascus, on Oct. 3rd, 1918

[Typescript with holograph additions]   22 October 1929
                                                       Confidential

I got a message on the afternoon of the 2nd October, from the Chief of Staff to say that the Commander in Chief would visit me on the

297

following day (October 3rd), would arrive at Damascus at 1 o'clock and wished to stay at the Hotel Victoria.

On the early morning of October 3rd, Lawrence informed me that the Emir Feisal would arrive at Damascus that afternoon and that he wishes to have a triumphal entry, at 3 p.m., galloping in like an Arab Conqueror of old at the head of about 300 horsemen. Seeing that he, Feisal, had very little to do with the "conquest" of Damascus, the suggested triumphal entry did not appeal to me very much but, having in view the fact that the Arabs were to have the Administration of the City, I thought it would not do any harm and gave permission accordingly.

Later on, on the morning of the 3rd, I got a further message from the Chief of Staff to say that Sir Edmund Allenby would not stay the night at Damascus as he wished to get back to Tiberias on the night of the 3rd, and would therefore have to leave Damascus on the return journey not later than 3 p.m.

Accompanied by my B.G.G.S., Brigadier-General C.A.C. Godwin, I motored to Kaukab to meet Sir Edmund. On meeting him I asked him if I had done right in agreeing to Shukri Pasha being Governor of Damascus. Sir Edmund told me I had done quite right but that there were some complications in that the French were to have the Mandatory power over Syria and that he wanted to see Feisal at once. I told him that Feisal would not be in until 3 p.m. when he was to have a triumphal entry. The Chief said "I cannot wait till 3. You must send a car out for him and request him to come in and see me at once. He can go out again for his triumphal entry."

Accordingly, on arrival at Damascus, I despatched my A.D.C., Captain W.G. Lyons, in my own car to meet Feisal, with a note explaining the circumstances and asking him to come in the car. He did so. Arriving at the Hotel Victoria about 2.30 p.m. and there was a conference at once at which the following were present:– Sir Edmund Allenby, General Bols, myself, General Godwin, the Emir Feisal, Lt-Col Lawrence, the Sherif Nasir and Nuir Bey.*

The Chief explained to Feisal:–

(a) That France was to be the Protecting or Mandatory Power over Syria.

---

* [Holograph addition:] There were others present i.e., Stirling and, I think, Cornwallis,[5] but I did not record them.

(b) That he, Feisal, as representing his Father, King Husein, was to have the Administration of Syria (less Palestine and the Lebanon Province) under French guidance and financial backing.

(c) That the Arab sphere would include the hinterland of Syria only and that he, Feisal, would not have anything whatever to do with the Lebanon, which would be considered to stretch from the Northern boundary of Palestine (about Tyre) to the head of the Gulf of Alexandretta.

(d) That he was to have a French Liaison Officer at once, who would work for the present with Lawrence, who would be expected to give him every assistance.

Feisal objected very strongly. He said that he knew nothing of France in the matter; that he was prepared to have British assistance; that he understood from the adviser that Sir Edmund Allenby had sent him that the Arabs were to have the whole of Syria including the Lebanon but excluding Palestine; that a Country without a Port was no good to him; and that he declined to have a French Liaison Officer or to recognise French guidance in any way.

The Chief turned to Lawrence and said: "But did you not tell him that the French were to have the Protectorate over Syria?" Lawrence said: "No Sir, I know nothing about it." The Chief said: "But you knew definitely that he, Feisal, was to have nothing to do with the Lebanon". Lawrence said: "No Sir, I did not."

After some further discussion the Chief told Feisal that he, Sir Edmund Allenby, was Commander in Chief and that he, Feisal, was at the moment a Lieut-General under his Command and that he would have to obey orders. That he must accept the situation as it was and that the whole matter would be settled at the conclusion of the War. Feisal accepted this decision and left with his entourage (less Lawrence) and went out of the City again to take on his triumphal entry which I am afraid fell rather flat as the greater bulk of the people had seen him come in and out already!

After Feisal had gone, Lawrence told the Chief that he would not work with a French Liaison Officer and that he was due for leave and thought he had better take it now and go off to England. The Chief said: "Yes! I think you had!", and Lawrence left the room.

The Chief afterwards relented about Lawrence and told me to tell him that he would write to Clive Wigram about him and arrange for an audience with the King, also, that he would give him a letter to the Foreign Office in order that he might explain the Arab point of view.

Sir Edmund Allenby left shortly afterwards for Tiberias.

Lawrence left Damascus next morning for England.

Neither my Chief of Staff nor I knew at the time that Feisal had already taken steps to proclaim the Hedjaz authority in the Lebanon and, I presume with Lawrence's knowledge, had already despatched Shukri Pasha (whom I had installed as Governor in Damascus and which Sir Edmund Allenby had confirmed) to Beirut to take over the administration thereof.

We did not discover this until the 7th and in the meantime had got ourselves mixed up in it through Macandrew's impulsiveness. On the 6th October, Macandrew who had reached Rayak, asked for permission to send an Armoured Car Reconnaissance to Beirut. I concurred very reluctantly, as I looked upon the coast as entirely Bulfin's sphere and knew that he was due at Beirut on the 8th. I only agreed when Macandrew pointed out the necessity, on account of our supply difficulties, of ascertaining as soon as possible if the road and rail between Damascus and Beirut were all right. Macandrew took upon himself to send Major Hyler Holden, who was mistaken for one of my Staff, with the Armoured Cars. Holden unfortunately arrived at the Serai at Beirut just as Shukri was unfurling the Hedjaz flag and proclaiming King Husein. The fat was in the fire. The whole thing was reported at once to the French and to Bulfin and I got the credit of supporting Feisal in his action, because one of my Staff was there by Shukri's side!

Bulfin, on arrival on the 8th made Shukri remove his flags and himself from the Serai and put in Col. Piepape as Military Governor of the Lebanon. I had no difficulty in explaining my share of it to General Bulfin but, up to the time I left the Country, I never succeeded in persuading Col. Piepape that I was not backing Feisal in his attempt to annex Lebanon.

H.G.C. 22.10.29.

LHCMA: Allenby papers 2/5/17

Appendix 3
Allenby Additional Accession[6]

Allenby to mother
[Letter. Holograph. Transcribed]   22 December [1917?]

I have had a considerable success. N. of Jaffa, and the Turks have fallen back some miles. It was a very fine performance by my troops. Rain ceased last night – and today has been very fine. However, the barometer is low. I rode this afternoon, on to the clump of rocky hills whereon stands Abu Shusheh (Gezer[7] – which was built by King Horam in Joshua's time; and was a Canaanite stronghold, till Pharaoh killed them off and gave the place as a dowry to Solomon with his daughter; I Kings IX.16)

It is a collection of limestone hills, stony and barren; with fertile fields between them, and good springs of water. The hills are honeycombed with caves – natural, some of them; others cut in the limestone – of great age. There are some remains of Crusaders' buildings, but not much. The value of the sight [*sic* – site?], of old was that it lies opposite the opening of the valley of Betheron, Ajalon and Sorek [?] which are the main approaches to Jerusalem and Jericho. My cavalry took it, before they could Ramleh, as it dominates the Jaffa Road. It was here that Neil Primrose[8] – Darling's [?] brother[9] – was killed. From the top of the hills, one sees Carmel, far away North; and all Philistine and the plain of Sharon, as well as the whole range of the Judean mountains.

LHCMA: Allenby papers 1/8/41–3

Allenby to mother
[Letter. Holograph. Transcribed]   28 December [1917?]

This Christmas day is one of wind and rain. For three days we have had a gale, with rainstorms. Last night was wet and windy; and today, there is a heavy and persistent and heavy downpour. It is cold, too. Some of my

Roman Catholic officers were going to attend the Christmas Mass at Bethlehem. The weather conditions up there must be horrible, and the roads will be bad for locomotion. I was at Jaffa yesterday; I went North, to the [. . . ?] of last week's battle on the R.Auja. The Turkish position was very strong; commanding ones [?], at the river – 15 yards wide, 15 ft deep – runs along its front. The stream is sluggish; and 3 [?] battalions of mine crowded, on rafts, at midnight. The Turks were completely surprised. We took over 300 prisoners, and killed as many – our losses were exactly 100. The Turks must have lost half their [there follows a short gap in the transcription] in that section. They are now back to a line 12 miles from Jaffa; which has given us elbow room and freedom of movement. The orange season is in full swing, now. All the gardens about Jaffa are full of oranges; millions of them; and everyone there is either; selling, buying or eating oranges. They are mostly the big, rather wax orange; but there are also tangerines of good quality. The quantity of fruit is doing my men a lot of good; as they were suffering from a shortage of fresh vegetables. During the summer and autumn, they were much troubled by septic sores on their hands, these followed by [?] little scratch or cut like the Veldt-sores we used to get, in winter, in South Africa. Now these are disappearing. You may have seen the enclosed[10] Reuter Telegram. Mabel called my attention to it. I still receive thanks and congratulations from all parts of the world. As I write the weather has [....?] in a great thunder storm. This I hope may finish the spell of storm and rain.

LHCMA: Allenby papers 1/8/41–3

Allenby to mother

[Letter. Holograph. Transcribed]   31 December [1917?]

I have your letter, No 18 of 4th inst. I hear that most of the mails of 1st–5th Dec. from England have gone to the bottom of the sea, in the "Aragon" [?]; so I am lucky for this one. I am glad that you received my Christmas cheque all right. During the last 4 days I have won a considerable victory over the Turks N. of Jerusalem. I was going to attack them on the 27th. Luckily, they decided to do the same to me. They put in a very strong attack with their whole available force, against me; from the N. and N.E. Their intention was to retake Jerusalem. I held them in front and put in a strong counter attack from the W. By the evening of the 29th, I had driven them back 10 miles N. of Jerusalem; beyond Beilin [presumably Beitin] (Bethel). I was up there yesterday; barren country of mountains and loose rocks. Bethel is a small village, on a strong ridge, surrounded by bald rocky mountains, which run up to 3,300 ft for 4 or 5 miles N.E. of Bethel. We killed a great number of Turks and took 600 or 700 prisoners. My troops were very pleased with themselves, and our losses were not very heavy. I went to the Kaiserin Augusta Victoria Sanatorium, on the Mount of Olives, after I came back from Beitin. It was built by the Kaiser and his wife and just finished before the war. It is a vast hotel-like building, of stone, on the highest point of the Mount of Olives. A high tower with peal of bells in it, gives a wonderful view over Jerusalem, the Dead Sea to Jordan and the mountains of Moab. There is a magnificent Chapel in the Building, richly decorated with mosaics and paintings. One of the roof paintings depict[s] the Kaiser and his Consort bigger than life size, in their imperial crown and robes, holding between them a model of the building. There is a very fine organ in the Chapel. A private soldier was playing on it beautifully. He told me that he was the organist in a Congregation Church in N. London. I'm afraid the flint implement picked up on the Wadi Ghuzze was not Thor[']s hammer; but the discarded tool of an old flint-using, stone-age savage. I used it as a paper weight and my servant lost it, on my last flight of Headquarters. It was some 4 inches long and 2½ inches wide, with no hole in it – something like this [a small rough sketch follows]. No German would respect the owner of it! I am interested in hearing you are researching the writings of the prophets – major and minor [?]. I have been reading Isaiah; and I have been following the campaigns of Joshua. I have fought over much of his country. In Makkadah, where he hanged the five kings of the Amorites, was Magra; where my Bucks Yeomanry rode a fine charge in the middle of November. I have just had a letter from the Belgian officer de liaison, at our Headquarters in France telling me the King of the Belgians has conferred on me the Croix de Guerre. I shall be pretty well hung with ribbons soon.

LHCMA: Allenby papers 1/8/41–3

Notes

Publication details of works mentioned in the Notes are given in the Bibliography.

Preface and Editorial Acknowledgements

1 In this volume the terms 'Turkey' and 'Ottoman' will be used interchangeably. This is, strictly speaking, incorrect inasmuch as the modern republic of Turkey was not formed until 1922–3 when the Ottoman empire finally disappeared.

2 Allenby was not alone in finding new employment as a colonial administrator in the Middle East. Field Marshal Sir Herbert (later Viscount) Plumer, for instance, became High Commissioner for Palestine in 1925. While Allenby was acting High Commissioner from March 1919, he was not formally appointed as such until October 1919.

3 In a meeting with the French at Deauville on the French coast, 6–15 September 1919, the British agreed to evacuate Syria and Lebanon. This ended any real hope of a Hashemite regime in Syria. Then, in 1920, at the San Remo Inter-Allied Conference (19–26 April), the British and French agreed the framework for the mandates for the Middle East that was formally approved by the League of Nations in 1922. In July 1920, French forces invaded and occupied Syria, defeating a small Hashemite force at Maysalun before occupying Damascus. Feisal was then forced to flee to Egypt, eventually being established as the ruler of Iraq (former Mesopotamia) following the Cairo Conference of March 1921.

Sources and Editorial Method

1 The death of the 1st Viscount Allenby's son, Michael, on the Western Front in 1917 meant that Allenby's nephew (Dudley Jaffray Hynman Allenby) succeeded to the viscountcy by special remainder in 1936. The current Lord Allenby (the 3rd Viscount Allenby), Michael Jaffray Hynman Allenby, the son of the 2nd Viscount Allenby, succeeded to the viscountcy in 1984. The current Lord Allenby is one of the 92 hereditary peers still allowed to sit in the House of Lords.

2 In the late 1990s, the 3rd Viscount Allenby deposited Boer War diaries for his great uncle at the Liddell Hart Centre for Military Archives (LHCMA).

These were catalogued in 1998. Lady Allenby (Allenby papers 7/2/3) noted that her husband's diaries had been lost when moving house. The current Lord Allenby has confirmed to this editor that all papers and diaries in his possession have now been passed to the Liddell Hart Centre. The lack of any letters from Lady Allenby to her husband suggests that while she kept his letters to her, he lost the ones that she sent to him.

3 Chauvel's letter and notes on Lawrence are included as Appendix Two to this volume.

4 In the author's note to Raymond Savage's biography, he acknowledged that Allenby had 'no knowledge' of the contents of his biography: Savage, *Allenby of Armageddon* (1925) p. 7.

5 Archibald Wavell, *Allenby: A Study in Greatness* (1941) p. 7. The 1993 Gregg Revival reprint of Wavell's biography includes a useful introduction by Brian Holden Reid.

6 Comparing Allenby's letters in the LHCMA with the extracts quoted in *Allenby: A Study in Greatness*, it as apparent that Wavell, at times, conflated passages from letters and paraphrased sentences (see, for instance, p. 192).

7 Brian Gardner, *Allenby* (1965) p. xviii.

8 Anthony Bruce, *The Last Crusade: The Palestine Campaign in the First World War* (2002); Matthew Hughes, *Allenby and British Strategy in the Middle East, 1917–1919* (1999); Jonathan Newell, 'British Military Policy in Egypt and Palestine, August 1914 to June 1917' (Doctoral thesis: University of London, 1990); Newell, 'Allenby and the Palestine Campaign' in Brian Bond (ed.), *The First World War and British Military History* (1991); Newell, 'Learning the Hard Way: Allenby in Egypt and Palestine 1917–1919', *Journal of Strategic Studies*, 14/3 (1991), pp. 363–87; Yigal Sheffy, *British Military Intelligence in the Palestine Campaign 1914–1918* (1998). Thomas Pakenham also made use of the Allenby papers for *The Boer War* (1979).

9 C.E. Callwell published extracts from Wilson's diaries in his two-volume biography, *Field-Marshal Sir Henry Wilson: His Life and Diaries* (1927). Keith Jeffery edited Wilson's correspondence in an earlier Army Records Society volume: *The Military Correspondence of Field Marshal Sir Henry Wilson* (1985). Liddell Hart's papers form the backbone of the immense collection of military papers held at the Liddell Hart Centre for Military Archives, King's College London.

10 Ibid. and David Woodward (ed.), *The Military Correspondence of Field-Marshal Sir William Robertson* (1989).

11 See the entries in Walid Khalidi (ed.), *All That Remains: The Palestinian Villages Occupied and Depopulated by Israel in 1948* (1992); Benny Morris: *The Birth of the Palestinian Refugee Problem, 1947–49* (1987); and Morris, *1948 and After: Israel and the Palestinians* [1990] (1994). For a trenchant argument supportive of the Israeli position, see Efraim Karsh: *Fabricating Israeli History: The 'New Historians'* [1997] (2000).

Introduction

1 Lawrence James, *Imperial Warrior: The Life and Times of Field Marshal Viscount Allenby, 1861–1936* (1993) p. 6. The other biographies are Raymond Savage's sycophantic *Allenby of Armageddon* (1925), Archibald Wavell's *Allenby: A Study in Greatness*, two volumes (1941–3) and Brian Gardner's *Allenby* (1965).

2 Savage, *Allenby of Armageddon*, p. 24.

3 General John Shea, Imperial War Museum London (hereafter IWM) Sound Archive, 4227, typescript of oral recording, 5, pp. 41–2.

4 Gardner, *Allenby*, p. 23.

5 Quoted in ibid., p. 62.

6 Wavell, *Allenby*, 1, p. 114.

7 Diary, 7 August 1916, Haldane papers, NLS, Ms. 20249.

8 Diary, 8 November 1916, Haldane papers, NLS, Ms. 20249.

9 Ibid.

10 Ronald Storrs, *Memoirs* [1937] (1972) p. 270.

11 Obituary of Lord Allenby, *The Times* (15 May 1936), 18. Many senior officers preferred the longer bombardment at Arras. See Noel Birch to Falls 22 November 1937 Public Record Office (hereafter PRO) CAB45/116; Charles Fergusson to Falls, 14 May 1937, PRO: CAB45/116.

12 Talk with David Lloyd George and Hubert Gough, 28 November 1935, Liddell Hart papers, Liddell Hart Centre for Military Archives (hereafter LHCMA), King's College London, 11/1935/107.

13 John Connell, *Wavell: Soldier and Scholar* [1964] (1966) p. 124.

14 Gardner, *Allenby*, p. 113; Snow to Wavell, 29 April 1937, Allenby papers, LHCMA, 6/7/55–56.

15 Allenby's Australian and New Zealand 'cavalry' were usually classified as 'mounted' rather than 'cavalry' troops because they were not armed with the sword or the lance.

16 Trooper L. Pollock, IWM, Sound Archive, 4220.

17 Meinertzhagen diaries, 15 July 1917, Rhodes House library, Oxford; Storrs, *Memoirs*, p. 270.

18 Matthew Hughes, *Allenby and British Strategy in the Middle East, 1917–1919* (1999) pp. 14–17

19 This is a point made by Cyril Falls in his entry for Allenby in the 1949 *Dictionary of National Biography*. Allenby's entry for the *New DNB* (2004) (edited by Brian Harrison) has been comprehensively revised by this editor.

20 'Murray', Gullett papers, Australian War Memorial (hereafter AWM), Canberra, Australia, AWM, 40/69.

21 George de S. Barrow, *The Fire of Life* (1942) p. 46.

22 For discussion of the intelligence dimension at the battle, see Yigal Sheffy, 'Institutionalised Deception and Perception Reinforcement: Allenby's Campaign in Palestine', in Michael Handel (ed.), *Intelligence and Military*

Operations (1990) and Sheffy, *British Military Intelligence in the Palestine Campaign, 1914–1918* (1998).

23 James, *Imperial Warrior*, p. 140. Some accounts have two sergeants taking the surrender and photographs of the surrender show two sergeants with the dignitaries of the city.

24 See Clive Garsia to S.W. Hare 8 June 1920, Hare papers, IWM, 3rd Gaza Folder, 66/85/1; Garsia to Historical Section CID, 10 October 1928, PRO, CAB45/78, authors A–D, p. 3; Garsia to Liddell Hart, 28 April 1934, Liddell Hart papers, LHCMA, 1/306/1; and Garsia, *A Key to Victory: A Study in War Planning* (1940). The 'Gaza School' debate is discussed in Hughes, *Allenby*, pp. 43–59.

25 See David Woodward, *Lloyd George and the Generals* (1983) pp. 206, 231 and Hughes, *Allenby*, pp. 35–40.

26 For more on Allenby's relationship with Robertson and British strategy with regard to Palestine generally, see David Woodward, *Field Marshal Sir William Robertson: Chief of the Imperial General Staff in the Great War* (1998) ch. 9.

27 Held at Islington Central Library, Fielding Crescent, London N1.

28 David Lloyd George, *War Memoirs* (1938) 2, pp. 1089–90.

29 Jonathan Newell, 'Learning The Hard Way: Allenby in Egypt and Palestine 1917–19', *Journal of Strategic Studies*, 14/3 (September 1991) p. 372.

30 Elizabeth Monroe, *Britain's Moment in the Middle East: 1914–1956* (1963).

31 Kirke to Wavell, 1 March 1939, Allenby papers, LHCMA, 6/9–10/31 and Résumé of Kirke's Career, Kirke papers, IWM, volume 7, p. 6.

32 A copy of Joint Note 12 can be found in PRO: WO106/729 (also in PRO: CAB25/68 dated 19 January 1918). There is a published copy of Joint Note 12 in *History of the Great War: Belgium and France, 1918, Appendices* (1935) appendix.

33 See Hughes, *Allenby*, pp. 71–88.

34 For Allenby's shock at the failure of the Trans-Jordan raids, see Shea to Archibald Wavell, 10 May [1939?], Allenby papers, LHCMA, 6/9–10/40–1.

35 Scholars generally explain 'Armageddon' as a Greek translation of the Hebrew phrase *har megiddo* ('the mountain of Megiddo'): see Bruce M. Metzger and Michael D. Coogan (eds), *The Oxford Companion to the Bible* (1993) p. 56. There is no mountain of Megiddo – this is perhaps a reference to the 60–metre mound of Megiddo, the site of settlements built one on top of another. Megiddo is also sometimes referred to as El Lajjun (or Lejjun) as the Roman HQ of the Sixth Legion (Lajjun being Arabic for Legion) lies 1 km. to the south of the main Megiddo site: see Kay Prag, *Blue Guide: Israel and the Palestinian Territories* (2002) pp. 351–4.

36 Hughes, *Allenby*, p. 97.

37 For Allenby's approval of Arab operations to take Damascus, see Alan Dawnay to Pierce Joyce, n.d, Joyce papers (formerly the Aqaba papers), LHCMA, I/M11. Jeremy Wilson, *Lawrence of Arabia: The Authorised*

Biography (1990) p. 1102, endnote 24 gives a date of 20 September for this message.

38 The issue of who entered Damascus first is discussed in Elie Kedourie, 'The Capture of Damascus, 1 October 1918', *Middle Eastern Studies*, 1/1 (October 1964), pp. 66–83 (reprinted and expanded in Kedourie, *The Chatham House Version and other Middle-Eastern Studies* [1970] (1984), pp. 33–51).

39 For repression of the revolt see PRO; FO371/3715–20, also court transcripts in FO371/3722.

40 Hughes, *Allenby*, pp. 141–3.

41 Bill Gammage, *The Broken Years: Australian Soldiers in the Great War* (1974) p. 144. See also Suzanne Brugger, *Australians and Egypt, 1914–1919* (1980) p. 80 (also ch. 8).

42 Or Sarafend. There were two villages of Surafend – 'greater' and 'smaller' Surafend. The killings of 1918 seem to have occurred in 'smaller' Surafend. Located close by the modern-day Israeli town of Rishon le Zion, both villages were destroyed and their Arab inhabitants forced to flee in the first Arab-Israeli war of 1948–9. See Walid Khalidi (ed.), *All That Remains: The Palestinian Villages Occupied and Depopulated by Israel in 1948* (1992) pp. 411–13 and Benny Morris: *The Birth of the Palestinian Refugee Problem, 1947–49* (1987) map. 2 & pp. xvi–xvii. Today, an Israeli military base covers much of the area.

43 For more on the 'Wazza' disturbances, see Kevin Fewster, 'The Wazza Riots, 1915', *Journal of the Australian War Memorial*, 4, April 1984, pp. 47–53. For details of the murders at Surafend see WD, 3rd Australian Light Horse Regt, 11 December 1918, AWM, 2[10/8], roll 158 and Bean papers, AWM, 38/3DRL/7953/item 8. Trooper G.T. Birkbeck noted that 36 Arabs were killed: diary, 10 December 1918, Birkbeck papers, Mitchell Library, Sydney, Australia, MSS810. For a sympathetic view of why the Anzacs thought it acceptable to beat to death civilians, see C. Guy Powles, *The New Zealanders in Sinai and Palestine, Volume III of the Official History of New Zealand's Effort in the Great War* (1922) pp. 265–7 (also the account in AOH, pp. 788–90). A.J. Hill's more recent, *Chauvel of the Light Horse: A Biography of General Sir Harry Chauvel* (1978) pp. 192–3 does little beyond briefly describing the Surafend incident. Finally, see also anon., 'The Surafend Incident. Why Allenby Ignored The Anzacs', *The New Zealand Returned Soldiers' Association Review*, 15, February 1939, pp. 17–18 and anon. 'The Surafend Incident, Further Light on Same', *The New Zealand Returned Soldiers' Association Review*, 15, May 1939, pp. 26–7.

44 A.F. Nayton describes the shouting 'out' incident in a letter to *The Times* (29 May 1964) (not A.F. Naylor as noted by James, *Imperial Warrior*, p. 262, note 22).

45 Report by GHQ, EEF to General Staff, War Office, 22 April 1919, PRO: WO106/191/161.

46 A.J. Hill, *Chauvel of the Light Horse: A Biography of General Sir Harry*

Chauvel (1978) pp. 192–3.

47 Marked with a commemorative Blue Plaque, Allenby's London home at Wetherby Gardens is now divided into apartments.

48 'Allenby', Gullett papers, AWM, 40/77.

49 For a less flattering portrayal of Allenby as High Commissioner in Egypt, see Elie Kedourie, *Politics in the Middle East* (1992) pp. 163–4.

50 For the comparison with Slim, the author is indebted to General Sir Rupert Smith 'Should Generals be Slim Today?' Talk given at the British Commission for Military History AGM, Imperial War Museum, 9 February 2002.

51 Williamson Murray and Allan R. Millet, *A War to be Won: Fighting the Second World War* (2000) pp. 350–1.

52 William Slim, *Defeat Into Victory* (1956) p. 291.

53 Cyril Falls, *Official History, Military Operations, Egypt and Palestine* (1928 & 1930) 2, pp. 418, 421.

54 One of the Cook Islands in the Pacific, Rarotonga is sometimes spelt (incorrectly it seems) as Raratonga. The Rarotongans came to Palestine with New Zealand forces.

55 GHQ Egypt to War Office, 1 July 1918, Milner papers, Bodleian library Oxford, III/B/140.

56 Allenby to Wilson, 5 June 1918, Wilson papers, IWM, HHW2/33A/4. See also Oriental and India Office Library, British Library, London, files at L/MIL/17/5/3919–3920.

57 Ronald Lewin, *Slim: The Standardbearer* [1976] (1990) p. 192.

58 An exception to this, and reflective of a new critical approach to Allenby and the Palestine campaign, is the work of Jonathan Newell: 'Learning The Hard Way: Allenby in Egypt and Palestine 1917–1919', *The Journal of Strategic Studies*, 14/3, September 1991, pp. 363–87; 'Allenby and the Palestine Campaign', in Brian Bond (ed.), *The First World War and British Military History* (1991). See also Hughes, *Allenby*.

59 Edward W. Said, *Orientalism: Western Conceptions of the Orient* (1991) p. 240.

60 Such as John Terraine, *The White Heat: The New Warfare 1914–1918* (1982); David Woodward, *Lloyd George and the Generals* (1983); Peter Simkins, *Kitchener's Armies: The Raising of the New Armies 1914–1916* (1988); John Laffin, *British Butchers and Bunglers of World War One* (1988); J.M. Bourne, *Britain and the Great War, 1914–1918* (1989); Tim Travers, *The Killing Ground: The British Army, the Western Front and the Emergence of Modern Warfare, 1900–1918* (1990); Brian Bond (ed.), *The First World War and British Military History* (1991); Denis Winter, *Haig's Command: A Reassessment* (1991); Robin Prior & Trevor Wilson, *Command on the Western Front: The Military Career of Sir Henry Wilson* (1992); Tim Travers, *How the War was Won: Command and Technology in the British Army on the Western Front, 1917–1918* (1992); Martin Samuels, *Doctrine and Dogma: German and British Infantry Tactics in the First World War* (1992); Martin

Samuels, *Command or Control? Command, Training and Tactics in the British and German Armies, 1888–1918* (1995); Bill Rawling, *Surviving Trench Warfare: Technology and the Canadian Corps, 1914–1918* (1995); 'Haig the Unknown Soldier' (BBC TV: Timewatch, 3 July 1996); Paddy Griffith (ed.), *British Fighting Methods in the Great War* (1996); Shane Schreiber, *Shock Army of the British Empire: The Canadian Corps in the Last 100 Days of the Great War* (1997); Ian Brown, *British Logistics on the Western Front, 1914–1919* (1998); John Mosier, *The Myth of the Great War: A New Military History of World War One* (2001); and Gary Sheffield, *Forgotten Victory. The First World War: Myth and Realities* (2001). David French has also produced two relevant studies: *British Strategy and War Aims, 1914–1916* (1986) and *The Strategy of the Lloyd George Coalition 1916–1918* (1995).

61 Similar comments could be made about the limited historiography dealing with the war in Mesopotamia, Italy, the Russian Front, Africa and Asia – reflective of a Eurocentric (or, more precisely, Western Front) approach to the First World War. Hew Strachan's recent *The First World War. Volume 1: To Arms* (2001) dealing with the opening period of the war helps redress this imbalance with an extensive analysis of the war outside of Europe.

Chapter 1

1 Edward George Villiers Stanley, 17th Earl of Derby (1865–1948).

2 Allenby assumed command in the period between the spring and autumn revolutions in Russia. Russia's collapse led to the withdrawal of Russian forces from the Caucasus and eastern Anatolia region. As a consequence, the Turks retook the territory lost to Russia, 1914–17, and launched their own attack that culminated in the capture of Baku on the shores of the Caspian Sea in September 1918. The British feared (incorrectly) that Turkish military resources released by Russia's collapse would be directed towards offensive operations in Mesopotamia or Palestine.

3 Turkish communications with Palestine relied on a 1,275 mile single-track railway from Istanbul to Palestine with breaks in the Taurus and Amanus mountains in Cilicia where tunnels had yet to be completed. These tunnels were not finished until October 1918 when, at the war's end, the first through trains finally ran. There was also a break from standard to narrow gauge at Rayak in Lebanon. Thus, before October 1918, goods for the Palestine front had to be loaded on and off the train at least five times. In addition, there was a shortage of fuel for the locomotives that resulted in the cutting down of olive and orange trees, and Lebanon's cedar forests (at times even camel dung was used to fire the boilers). Precedence given to de luxe trains carrying senior officers compounded the delays on this overstretched line of communication. See W.R. Stanley, 'Review of Turkish Asiatic Railways to 1918: Some Political-Military Considerations', *Journal of Transport History*, 7, 1966 [published 1970] pp. 189–203; Matthew Hughes,

Allenby and British Strategy in the Middle East, 1917–1919 (1999) p. 54; and 'Translation of Turkish Document, 5 February 1918, "Memorandum for the Journey Constantinople-Aleppo"', Chetwode papers, IWM, PP/MCR/C1, folder 6. The Ottoman genocide against the Armenians also adversely affected the running of the railway as many skilled railway workers were Armenian.

4 General (or Sirdar) Sir Reginald Wingate (1861–1953).

5 Lieutenant-General Sir Frederick Stanley Maude (1864–1917). Maude died of cholera in November 1917 and was replaced by Lieutenant-General Sir William Marshall (1865–1939).

6 The British built a pipeline parallel to the military railway across northern Sinai to take drinking water to the troops and water for railway locomotives. Initially 6-inches in diameter, it was upgraded using 12-inch pipe alongside, in places, 10-inch pipe (8-inch pipe also seems to have been used). Remnants of the British railway are still visible in the Sinai today, although the Israelis ripped up parts of the line to use as construction material for their 'Bar-Lev' defensive positions on the east bank of the Suez canal built after the 1967 Arab-Israeli war.

7 The British viewed the nomadic Bedouin population of the Sinai as pro-Turk and categorised them as suspects, POWs or civilians who had committed a hostile act (Provost Marshal reports for Australian/New Zealand and Australian divisions in PRO: WO154/164 and 167). Those caught by EEF troops (including women and children) were concentrated in wired, guarded enclosures ('Light Horse', Gullett papers, AWM, 40/68). EEF instructions were that Bedouin who committed hostile acts should be treated as civilians (i.e. were liable to be shot) (Political Intelligence GHQ EEF, POW report, 16 June 1917, AWM, 4[1/10]).

8 Not here.

9 This '4' is partly obscured by a hole punch.

10 Qamle in the British Official History (OH) of the campaign.

11 Wadi Imleih in the British OH.

12 Presumably Bir Ifteis on the Wadi Imleih just east of the junction with the Wadi Sheria (see A.P. Wavell, *The Palestine Campaign* [1928] (1933) map XI on p. 134).

13 Earlier in the war, the British had clashed with the Senussi tribespeople of the Western Desert of Egypt close to the border with Italian Libya. The Senussi, whose home spanned the Libyan-Egyptian border, had resisted Italian occupation from 1911–12 when the Italians first invaded; thereafter, Istanbul infiltrated Ottoman officers (some by submarine) into Libya to foment discontent among groups such as the Senussi against Italian and Britain occupation.

14 The bay to the east of the city of Alexandria in Egypt.

15 Baghdad fell to British-led forces on 11 March 1917.

16 In 1917, the Turks and Germans organised a military force, codenamed

Yilderim by the Turks and Army Group (*Heeresgruppe*) F by the Germans, to be deployed for offensive use in the Middle East. In the end, the strength of this force was more nominal than real, but reports of its formation caused consternation for the British. An account of the activities of the force from the Turkish side can be found in Hussein Husni Amir Bey's unpublished *Yilderim* (Turkish General Staff, n.d.) (Translated by G.O. de R. Channer) (copy in AWM45). See also Edward Erickson, *Ordered to Die: A History of the Ottoman Army in the First World War* (2001) p. 159.

17 The additional needs were 2 fully trained divisions plus artillery, full divisional artillery complements for all EEF divisions, 14 heavy artillery pieces for each division, 5 squadrons of aircraft for the EEF, 2 corps signal coys, 1 heavy artillery signal section, 2 wireless sections of corps signal coy, RE services and 10 hospitals, Casualty Clearing Stations and sanitary sections.

18 On 6 July 1917, Hashemite Arab forces, accompanied by T.E. Lawrence, British political liaison officer with the Hashemites, captured the Turkish-held port of Akaba. Lawrence then travelled back to Egypt across the Sinai, a journey of some 160 miles, arriving in Cairo at noon on 10 July 1917, where, soon after, he met with Allenby and discussed the future of the Arab revolt. The precise date of the meeting with Allenby is unclear although in Lawrence's account in *Seven Pillars of Wisdom* [1935, privately printed 1926] (1962) (pp. 329–30) he states that it was very soon after arriving in Egypt. For more on the meeting between Allenby and Lawrence see Jeremy Wilson, *Lawrence of Arabia: The Authorised Biography* [1989] (1990) pp. 418–24. Lawrence James gives a date of 12 July for the meeting between Allenby and Lawrence: *Imperial Warrior: The Life and Times of Field Marshal Viscount Allenby 1861–1936* (1993) p. 124.

19 Completed in 1908 with engineering assistance from Germany, the Hedjaz railway from Amman to Medina via Maan, built with the financial help of donations from Muslims across the globe, facilitated the passage of pilgrims going on the Hajj to Mecca and Medina. The railway also served the purpose of extending Ottoman central control over western Arabia (see Strategical Part I, May 1906 [1910?], PRO: WO106/42, C3/14b). The sleepers on the Hedjaz railway were made of German steel (and stamped as such with the German foundry maker) because of the fear that local people would knock out wood sleepers for use as domestic fuel. An extension to the railway from Medina to Mecca was planned but never completed (hence the Turks had an ample stock of spare sleepers and rails, to be used for the extension to replace track damaged by Hashemite Arab raids, 1916–18). Because of damage to the line during the war by British and Hashemite Arab forces, the line never functioned properly after 1918. For more information on the Hedjaz railway, see W.P. Pick, 'Meissner Pasha and the Construction of Railways in Palestine and Neighbouring Countries', in G.G. Gilbar (ed.), *Ottoman Palestine, 1800–1914* (1990); R. Tourret, *The Hedjaz Railway*

(1989); and William Ochsenwald, *The Hijaz Railroad* (1980). On railways more generally, see W.R. Stanley, 'Review of Turkish Asiatic Railways to 1918: Some Political-Military Considerations', *Journal of Transport History*, 7, November 1966 [published 1970] pp. 189–203.

20 Or Sea of Galilee (or Yam Kinneret).

21 The Druses (or Druzes) are a Muslim sect living predominantly in southern Syria near the town of Deraa and in Lebanon near Mount Lebanon.

22 Jeremy Wilson in his *Lawrence of Arabia: The Authorised Biography* (1990) pp. 423–4 quotes a slightly different version of this telegram at PRO: WO158/634.

23 Brigadier-General (temp) R.G.H. Howard-Vyse (1883–1962), BGGS DMC and GOC 10th Cavalry brigade, 1917–18.

24 A reference to the Inter-Allied conferences on strategy of 25–26 July and 7–8 August 1917.

25 Presumably a reference to Major-General Hon Edward James Montagu Stuart-Wortley (1857–1934). *Who Was Who* also lists a Lieutenant-General Hon Sir (Alan) Richard Montagu Stuart-Wortley (1868–1949) who served in Mesopotamia, 1917–19. The reference could be to either but is probably the former.

26 Presumably a reference to Major-General A.B.E. Cator (1877–1932) who was a temporary major-general in 1917 and Major-General (Lord) E.D. Loch (1873–1942) who was a temporary brigadier-general, 1915–18.

27 Lieutenant R.H. 'Dick' Andrew, Allenby's nephew from the Suffolk regiment, was one of his two ADCs (the other was Captain W.L. Naper – for Naper, see biographical details appendix to this volume).

28 Usually spelt Rarotongan.

29 This seems to be a term of endearment Allenby used for his wife. It reappears as 'Wagglette' in a letter to Lady Allenby on 19 December 1917.

30 The Allenbys' only son, Michael, serving as a subaltern with the RHA, had just been killed on the Western Front. Hit in the head by a shell splinter while walking back to his battery from a detached gun, Michael lived for five hours but never regained consciousness.

31 On the Shatt al-Arab waterway in southern Mesopotamia (Iraq). (Shatt being Arabic for river-bank, landing-place or river).

32 The official histories of the Palestine campaign make no mention of the use of gas at the third battle of Gaza, but there is evidence in the Australian archive to suggest that it was successfully used at the battle: 'Allenby's First Offensive', Gullett papers, AWM, 40/58. The use of gas is also noted in Erickson, *Ordered to Die*, p. 163. For the latest research on the use of gas in the Middle East in the First World War (especially in Palestine), see (in Hebrew) Yigal Sheffy of Tel Aviv University, 'The Gallipoli Campaign and the Introduction of Chemical Warfare to the Middle East' in Zmanim (*Quarterly of the School of History*), Tel Aviv University (Quarterly, 2002–3) pp. 4–17 and 'Chemical Warfare in the Palestine Campaign during the First

World War' in *Cathedra for the History of Eretz Israel and its Yishuv*, 105 (2002) pp. 41–84.

33 See note 18 above.

34 The Italian colony of Libya.

35 This is a reference to a telegram from Allenby on 10 August 1917 requesting gas (up to 2000 cylinders 'White Star') and one gas company (of the Royal Engineers) to operate the gas cylinders (at PRO: WO33/935, p. 237).

36 Ethyliodacentate (75%) and Ethyl Alcohol (25%) = tear (lachrymatory) gas.

37 Chloropicrin = lethal gas. The full stop after 'P.S.' seems to end the sentence.

38 Phosphorous grenades.

39 A type of mortar developed in 1916 by William Henry Livens, an engineer in the Special Companies, later the Special (Gas) Brigade, on the Western Front, to fire chemical projectiles. The projector consisted of a three-foot long steel tube with a base plate. The bomb (or drum) was placed inside the tube on top of a propellant charge, fired electrically by wire. The Livens projectors were used in groups to saturate a given area. The editor is grateful to Dr Yigal Sheffy of Tel Aviv University for supplying the information in notes 36–9.

40 A light narrow-gauge railway line.

41 Wadi el Saba in copy at PRO: WO106/718/169–70.

42 Wadi el Malah in copy at PRO: WO106/718/169–70.

43 Wadi es Sabe/Seba and Wadi Imleih in British OH.

44 Father Knapp was a Catholic Chaplain with whom Allenby developed a close relationship during his time in South Africa during the Second South Africa (or Boer) War (1899–1902) (see Wavell, *Allenby*, pp. 92–3, 105).

45 In David Woodward, (ed.), *The Military Correspondence of Field-Marshal Sir William Robertson* (1989) the date is given as the 16th but as there is an earlier letter on the 10th and none on the 16th – even Woodward has the one on the 10th in his ARS volume – it is more likely that this should read the 10th.

46 Woodward (ibid.) records this as a colon but Allenby rarely used colons, preferring the liberal use of semi-colons and dashes.

47 Major-General George Macdonogh (1865–1942).

48 Haidar Pasha is the main railway station on the Asian side of the Bosphorus; the reference to Stamboul station is a reference to Sirkeci, the main railway station on the European side of the Bosphorus.

49 Riga fell to a hurricane assault by General Oskar von Hutier's German Eighth Army, 1–4 September 1917.

50 St Petersburg was renamed Petrograd when Russia entered the war as the former was considered too German sounding – 'burg' being German and 'grad' being Russian for town or castle (although it seems that the origin of the name St Petersburg was Dutch not German).

51 On 3–4 and 4–5 September 1917, thirteen German Gotha bombers raided Chatham naval barracks, Sheerness, Margate, London and Dover. They dropped 4,375 kgs of bombs, inflicted 318 casualties and caused £50,040 worth of damage, for the loss of one Gotha aeroplane (statistics from Raymond H. Fredette, *The First Battle of Britain 1917–1918 and the Birth of the Royal Air Force* (1966) p. 264).

52 King's Messenger – priority escorted mail service akin to the diplomatic bag.

53 The initial infantry force sent by France was the *Détachement Français de Palestine et de Syrie*, ultimately composed of two battalions of the *Régiment Mixte de Marche de Tirailleurs*, three battalions of Armenians (two of which were formed as the *Régiment Légion d'Orient*) plus a Territorial battalion. Later, France sent a cavalry regiment – the *Régiment Mixte de Marche de Cavalerie* – that was attached to the Australian Mounted Division.

54 A military commission entitling an officer to assume rank above that for which s/he receives pay.

55 Wilfred Edward Bownas Smith (1867–1942).

56 Malaria was a rife among units that had served on the Salonika front. These included the 10th (Irish) and 60th (London) divisions, both of which were moved from Salonika to Palestine in the summer of 1917.

57 Port in southern Italy.

58 On 28–29 September 1917, British forces in Mesopotamia captured Ramadi on the Euphrates river west of Baghdad. See F.J. Moberly, *History of the Great War, Based on Official Documents, The Campaign in Mesopotamia 1914–1918* (1927) vol. 4, pp. 49–59.

59 A huge explosion at Haidar Pasha rail station in Istanbul (on the eastern side of the Bosphorus) on 23 September 1917 consumed Turkish and German military equipment waiting to be railed east (and killed, it is claimed by Wilfred Castle, 1,000 people). It is not clear if the explosion was an accident or the result of sabotage by British agents. For more details, see: Hughes, *Allenby and British Strategy*, 54–5; Wilfred Castle, *Grand Turk* (1943) p. 102; Cyril Cruttwell, *A History of the Great War 1914–1918* (1986) p. 613; Otto Liman von Sanders, *Five Years in Turkey* (1927) p. 184; Archibald Wavell, *The Palestine Campaigns* [1928] (1933) p. 110; and Townley [or Milner?] to Harding, 21 October 1917, Milner papers, OxBod, V/C/363. See also the review of Hauptmann Simon-Eberhard's *Mit dem AsienKorps zur Palästinafront*, 5 January 1928 in Edmonds papers, LHCMA, V/4/1/1.

60 This is probably the image at Allenby papers, LHCMA, 5/33.

61 King Hussein of the Hedjaz (1856–1931).

62 Following Michael's death, Lady Allenby was allowed out to Egypt. The difficulties faced by officers' wives who wanted to come out to be with their husbands in Egypt was a much-discussed topic as the Allenbys finalised Lady Allenby's trip out to Egypt in October 1917.

63 'Cannot' in copy at PRO: WO33/935, p. 388.

64 Telegram of 9 October 1917.

65 Presumably Commandant R. de Saint-Quentin. In 1936, he became French Ambassador to Italy.

66 The *Index Biographique Français* (II, 452, 71–74) lists two possible French diplomats: François Emile Roger Maugras (b. 1881) and François Gustave Gaston Maugras (b. 1884).

67 For confirmation of this Christian calendar date (the year only is pencilled in on the document), the following formula was employed: Islamic (Hijri) date (1336) plus 622 minus the sum of 1336 over 33. This gives the same date of 1917. The month of Moharram (especially with no number supplied for the day) is more problematic as the Islamic year is purely lunar and so does not easily correspond to the Christian (Gregorian) months. But it would seem that 'Moharram 1336' matches up with the period 17–31 October 1917. Moreover, when Moharram (the first month – or new year – of the Islamic calendar) is used (by Muslims) without any particular day mentioned, this usually denotes the first 10 days of Moharram. Thus, a time slot of 17–27 October 1917 is the likely date for this document. For this information, the editor is grateful to the Department of Languages and Cultures of the Near and Middle East, SOAS, University of London and, especially, the Library of the Central Mosque, Regents Park, London.

68 While in and around Gaza little remains of the entrenchments of the three Gaza battles of 1917, parts of the Turkish trench system defending Beersheba are still present to the west of the town.

69 The ALH charge into Beersheba is discussed in Ian Jones, 'Beersheba: The light horse charge and the making of myths', *Journal of the Australian War Memorial*, 3, October 1983, 26–37.

70 Rt Reverend Rennie MacInnes, Bishop of Jerusalem, 1914– (d. 1931).

71 This is a holograph addition in a different hand.

72 Assistant Private Secretary and Equerry to the King, 1910–31.

73 This is a particularly egregious example of Allenby's misuse of the semi-colon.

74 Respectively December 1916 and January 1917.

75 Annotated maps at RA PS/GV/Q 2521/16 (similar to the maps in the OH text volumes).

76 Properly the Imperial Camel Corps Brigade.

77 The reference on the files is RA GV/PS/Q2521/14 with the correct numbering being RA PS/GV/Q2521/14 according to the Royal Archives Forms of Reference leaflet.

78 Or Tikrit. A town 100 miles north of Baghdad on the river Tigris. The home town of the later ruler of Iraq, Saddam Hussein. Also the birthplace of the Muslim military leader Salah al-Din (Saladin) (1137–93).

79 This is possibly the extract at Allenby papers 1/8/21 entitled 'Extract from 16th Division Orders, 29.10.33' detailing how Allenby usually attacked after an intense artillery bombardment. However, in a PS to his letter to Lady

Allenby on 7 November, Allenby also alludes to an enclosure which might be the above extract.

80 Wadi El Hesi in British OH.

81 Unknown. The editor is unable to find personal details for this person.

82 Not here.

83 Approximately 20 miles west of Arras. HQ of Allenby's Third Army from March 1916.

84 The contents of this letter prove that it was written in 1917.

85 The Turkish garrison in Medina refused to capitulate, holding out against Arab forces until the Ottoman High Command in Istanbul ordered its commander, Fahreddin Pasha, to surrender in January 1919. See Wasti, S. Tanvir, 'The Defence of Medina 1916–1919', *Middle Eastern Studies*, 27/4, October 1991, pp. 642–53.

86 At PRO: WO33/946, p. 15 there is a version of this telegram, Allenby to WO (same date), referring to an official not an R telegram. It reads: 'Your No. 45777, cipher, 16th November, received. I quite understand meaning of your No. 44428, 1st November, and No. 45396, 13th November. I realize present situation and bear in mind future possibilities.'

87 Presumably a reference to Sir Harry Lawson Webster Levy, Viscount Burnham (1862–1933), the manager-proprietor of the *Daily Telegraph*, 1903–28. The Monthly Army List for November 1917 (col. 335) lists a Lieutenant-Colonel J.P. Grenfell as GOC the Buckinghamshire Yeomanry (or Hussars); according to the same Army List, the Hon Colonel of this unit was Lord (H.L.W.) Burnham. The 1/1st Buckinghamshire Yeomanry, part of the 6th Mounted Brigade in the Yeomanry Mounted Division, was heavily involved in the fighting at the third battle of Gaza and during the push on Jerusalem. Burnham also worked for the government, including creating the eponymous Burnham scale for teachers.

88 Major the Hon Neil Primrose, formerly Under-Secretary of State for Foreign Affairs. Primrose was the only officer from the 6th Mounted Brigade to die in this attack. See the British OH, vol. 2, pp. 178–80 and The Marquess of Anglesey, *A History of the British Cavalry 1816–1919, Volume 5, Egypt, Palestine and Syria, 1914–1919* (1994) p. 201.

89 2i/c of the Bucks Yeomanry and cousin of Neil Primrose, Major Evelyn de Rothschild died in hospital of wounds received at Mughar (or Maghar). He died assaulting the area near Rishon le Zion (Arabic: 'Ayun Qara), an area of Palestine in which his family had helped to found Zionist settlements.

90 Unknown.

91 In a letter to his wife dated 5–12 September 1917 (LHCMA: Allenby papers 1/8/14), Allenby mentions that Dalmeny had caught a local chameleon (a type of lizard).

92 On Gezira island, one of the two main islands on the Nile in Cairo.

93 The fortress in the east of Cairo constructed in the 12th century (with many changes made over the subsequent centuries).

94 Presumably the Muqattam hills to the east of Cairo beyond the Citadel.

95 In January 1191and June 1192, during the Third Crusade, Richard 'Lionheart', advancing from the coast, got to within a few miles of Jerusalem. Having failed in his endeavour to retake the city, lost to the Muslims in 1187, Richard sailed for home in October 1192.

96 On 24 October 1917, at the 12th battle of the Isonzo (or Caporetto – modern-day Kobarid in Slovenia), an Austro-German force inflicted a huge defeat on the Italians who were forced thereafter to retreat to a new defensive line along the line of the River Piave.

97 Formed in November 1917 to co-ordinate Allied grand strategy.

98 This has been deleted and replaced with a holograph 40,000–45,000.

99 This has been deleted and replaced with a holograph 50,000.

100 Sometimes Bire – *c.* 10 miles north of Jerusalem.

101 This is a draft version of a telegram that was sent as E.A.549 on 28 November 1917 to Chief London. A copy of the final version can be found in IWM: Dawnay papers 69/21/2 'Palestine 1917–18 Battle of Philistia.' In the final version the enemy's fighting strength is given as the original 41,000; some other minor changes have also been made. There are further copies of the 28 November telegram at PRO: WO33/946 and PRO: WO106/718/245–7.

102 Approximately seven miles west (and slightly north) of Jerusalem.

103 His Excellency Sir Reginald Wingate (1861–1953). Wingate was visiting Allenby from 20–22 November (see letters above) and 'His Excellency' is the correct form of address for a High Commissioner: see *Debrett's Correct Form* (1999) pp. 147–50.

104 Luke 24: 13.

105 After the Turkish defeat and loss of Jerusalem at the third battle of Gaza, Jevad Pasha, a Turk, replaced Kress von Kressenstein as commander of the Eighth Army. The latter went on to command forces in the Caucasus in 1918.

106 Allenby was right inasmuch as there was bad feeling between Turkish and German troops that hampered unified command: see 'Correspondence with Talaat Pasha in 1921', Herbert papers, SomRO, DD/DRU, section 56; 'From an intelligent Jew resident in Jerusalem who left that town on the 13th [November 1917?] instant', Dawnay papers, IWM, 69/21/2; and Franz von Papen, *Memoirs* (1952) p. 72. The Turko-German clash was a result of perceived German arrogance versus Turkish pride compounded by differences on strategy. Turkish and German forces in the Caucasus even ended up fighting one another: see W.E.D. Allen and Paul Muratov, *Caucasian Battlefields: A History of the War on the Turco-Caucasian Border, 1821–1921* (1953) pp. 477–8.

107 Not here.

108 Or Bireh.

109 Now the river Yarqon in Israel. There are accounts from EEF soldiers of

their being attacked by crocodiles when bathing in the rivers (such as the Auja) that flowed down from Judæa and Samaria to the Mediterranean Sea through the swampy coastal plain. Indeed, the Nahr el Zarka (now the Nahal Tanninim) just north of Caesarea was also called the Nahr al Timsah (timsah being the Arabic for crocodile). The Crusaders called it 'Crocodile river' (see Jonathan Riley-Smith, *The Atlas of the Crusades* (1991) pp. 38–9), using it as a source of water for their settlement at Caesarea. After the Great War, increased settlement, the draining of swamps and hunting combined to kill off any remaining crocodiles. The behemoth of the Bible (Job 40: 15) might have been a hippopotamus (river horse in Greek) of the coastal swamps of Palestine – again evidence of a once-thriving wildlife in Palestine that included lions, leopards, Syrian bears (hunted to near extinction by German officers in the First World War), roe deer, fallow deer, oryx, Barbary sheep and wild asses. For more on the fauna of Palestine in this period, see F.S. Bodenheimer, *Animal Life in Palestine* (1935) pp. 113–18, 197.

110 In Woodward (ed.), *Military Correspondence of Field-Marshal Sir William Robertson* this is also recorded as 'force'.

111 Church bells across Britain were rung in response to the initial success at the battle of Cambrai by Byng's Third Army on 20 November 1917. The use of tanks and careful artillery preparation by the British (the latter often forgotten due to the interest in the deployment of massed tanks for the first time) made this success possible. A subsequent German counter-attack on 30 November re-took much of the ground won in the initial assault.

112 A newspaper cutting relating how Allenby had outdone Samson who only carried the gates of Gaza.

113 The editor is unable to provide personal details of this individual.

114 While the Jaffa gate (Arabic: Bab al-Khalili; Hebrew: Sha'ar Yafo) is still much as it was in 1917, the tower by the gate, present in photographs of Allenby's entry, has gone (see IWM, photographic archive, reference Q12616). The surrounding curtain wall has also changed since 1917.

115 Or Tower of David.

116 Not here.

117 El 'Azariye – on the road to Jericho.

118 Biblical Moab – to the east across the valley of the river Jordan towards Amman.

119 Colonel P. de Piépape.

120 Lieutenant-Colonel F. d'Agostino.

121 Commandant R. de Saint-Quentin. In 1936, he became French Ambassador to Italy.

122 Commandant Caccia.

123 Presumably Hampson Gary (1873–1952) although the OH does not acknowledge the presence of a US representative.

124 The OH (p. 260) details a Brigadier-General W.M. Borton as Military Governor. The entry in *Who Was Who* lists a Neville Travers Borton

(1870–1938) as Post-Master General in Egypt, 1907–24 (see note 143 below). There seems to be some confusion here, especially as the OH (p. 108) has another Borton (Lieutenant-Colonel A.D.) who won a Victoria Cross in November 1917. Whichever (W.M. or N.T.), Borton was replaced as Military Governor of Jerusalem in late December 1917 by Sir Ronald Storrs (1881–1955).

125 Keeper or custodian.

126 Khalif Omar, the second successor of the Prophet Muhammad, established a mosque, al-Aqsa, on the holy site of the Dome of the Rock (or Haram ash Sharif) (what Jews usually refer to as the Temple Mount atop the Wailing Wall) in Jerusalem. There are two mosques in one on the Dome of the Rock and Allenby's reference to the Mosque of Omar is a reference to the whole area that is of paramount holy significance for Muslims and Jews.

127 Wife of Jacob, mother of Joseph and Benjamin. Rachel's tomb is north of Bethlehem on the road to Jerusalem. Rachel's tomb, along with the Wailing Wall and the Dome of the Rock Mosque, was used as an image for the Palestine postage stamps produced after the war. There were also EEF postage stamps produced during the war but these did not contain any images (in Mesopotamia the British used Ottoman stamps with an occupation force over-print).

128 Wafk translates as agreement or understanding between two or more parties. Not to be confused with waqf (see glossary). When the Khalif Omar captured Jerusalem in the 7th century, he appointed a Muslim family as hereditary guardian door-keepers for the Church of the Holy Sepulchre (known as the Church of the Resurrection for the Greek Orthodox). This family still holds the keys: if one enters the church from the south side and passes through the courtyard (or parvis), one goes through Romanesque doors and, on the left on the ground level, inside the church, is a long wooden bench on which usually sits one or more members of this family (often chatting with Christian clergy). For more information, see Martin Biddle, *The Tomb of Christ* (1999).

129 This telegram (including sub-headings) was sent in response to a telegram of 21 November 1917 from Robertson to Allenby (at PRO: WO33/946, p. 27) pointing out that Lloyd George was planning to make an announcement to the House of Commons on the lines of the sub-headings so Allenby should use this as a template for his announcement. This telegram proves that Allenby faithfully complied with his precise instructions from London on what to do once Jerusalem fell.

130 Robertson to Allenby, 21 November 1917 (received 22 November). In IWM: Dawnay papers, 69/21/2 'Palestine 1917–18 Battle of Philistia', Robertson passed on from the War Cabinet a rough copy of the proclamation that Allenby read out on 11 December. There is another copy of this proclamation dated 21 November 1917 at PRO: WO 33/946, p. 27.

131 Christian tradition, perhaps as early as the second century, identified a cave

in Bethlehem as the site of Jesus' birth. About AD 330, Constantine the Great had a church built over the grotto (and Justinian I reconstructed it in the early sixth century). Properly the Church of the Holy Nativity.

132 Supposedly, the first Gentiles to worship Christ (see Matt. 2: 1–12). Traditionally, these are the wise men (Balthasar, Melchior and Caspar) who came from the east bearing gifts of gold, frankincense and myrrh for the Christ Child. The term 'magi' is an ambiguous one: see, Bruce M. Metzger and Michael D. Coogan (eds), *The Oxford Companion to the Bible* (1993) p. 483.

133 St Jerome (*c.* 345–420) (or Eusebius Hieronymus) settled in Bethlehem in 386 and it is here that he made the Latin Vulgate translation of the Bible. Not to be confused with St Eusebius (see below).

134 St Eusebius, Bishop of Vercelli (d. 371) (feast day either 2 August or 16 December): see Herbert Thurston and Donald Attwater (eds), *Butler's Lives of the Saints* (1956) vol. 4, pp. 569–71. Not to be confused with: St Eusebius, Bishop of Samosata (d. 380) (feast day 21/22 June); the Bishop and Church Historian, Eusebius of Caesarea (*c.* 260–*c.* 340); St (Julia) Eustochium (370–*c.* 419); or the many other Eusebiuses of the early Christian period. For a full list of Eusebiuses, see William Smith and Henry Wace (eds), *A Dictionary of Christian Biography, Literature Sects and Doctrines* (1890) vol. 2, pp. 303–80. See also F.L. Cross (ed.), *The Oxford Dictionary of the Christian Church* [1957] (1997) pp. 574–6. St Eusebius of Vercelli, St Eustochium (and her mother, Paula) and St Jerome are buried in grottoes just outside Bethlehem near the Church of the Nativity and it is these tombs that Allenby is referring to.

135 See note 13 above.

136 7th Indian (Meerut) Division.

137 The Dan spring in northern Palestine (mentioned in the Bible and today located just inside the border of northern Israel by Mount Hermon Jebel ash Sheikh).

138 Or El Maghar.

139 A reference to the fact that the hill of Abu Shushe (or Abu Shusheh) is supposedly the site of the ancient city of Gezer (or Gazara) of biblical fame (see Josh. 16: 10, Judg. 1: 29, 1 Kings 9: 16 and 1 Macc. 13: 43–48).

140 See above note 88.

141 Presumably the road running east–west through the villages of Beit Ur el Foka and Beit Ur et (or 'el') Tahta.

142 Beth-horon of the Bible. Beit Ur el Foka is Upper Beth-horon; Beit Ur el Tahta is Lower Beth-horon.

143 See note 124 above.

144 Judas Maccabæus (d. 161 BC), leader of the Jews in the revolt against the Seleucid king of Syria. In 164 BC, he purified the Temple and restored its worship, and, in 163 BC, he was able to obtain full religious liberty from the Syrian ruler, Antiochus V Eupator.

145 Both upper and lower case 'agreement' are used in this letter. The 'Sykes-Picot Agreement' of 1916 (or Asia Minor Agreement or Anglo-French Agreement of 1916) was a territorial division of Ottoman lands in the Middle East into British, French and Russian spheres of control and influence. Italy received its share of the territorial spoils in the region in 1917. In 1918, the Bolsheviks made public the terms of the Sykes-Picot Agreement (they did likewise with the secret agreement dividing up Manchuria).

Chapter 2

1 A spring at the foot of Mount Hermon by the Golan Heights that feeds the River Jordan.

2 The 7th Indian (Meerut) Division was under orders to go from Mesopotamia to Palestine.

3 Major-General George Macdonogh (1865–1942).

4 Or Beersheba.

5 Presumably a reference to the Balfour Declaration, issued as a letter by the Foreign Office to Lord Rothschild on 2 November and published in *The Times* on 9 November 1917, that outlined (in very ambiguous language) Britain's support for Zionism. For an account of the negotiations leading up to the declaration, see Leonard Stein, *The Balfour Declaration* (1961).

6 Presumably a reference to the Austro-Hungarian and German (non-military) residents of Jerusalem.

7 Organised as a brigade.

8 A Zionist Commission arrived in Palestine in the spring of 1918. Its task was to help organise Jewish settlement of Palestine.

9 After the war, Norman Bentwich wrote several accounts of his time as a legal adviser in Palestine: *England in Palestine* (1932) and *Palestine* (1934).

10 What is now the Hebrew University of Jerusalem. The cornerstone was laid in 1918, with the university officially opening in 1925.

11 Based in Cairo and headed by D.G. Hogarth, the job of the British-run Arab Bureau was to co-ordinate the Arab Revolt. It has been argued (see Elie Kedourie, *In the Anglo–Arab Labyrinth: The McMahon-Husayn Correspondence and its Interpretations 1914–1939* [1976]) that the Arab Bureau acted unilaterally, thus forging a semi-autonomous Cairo-centred policy towards the Arabs. For further information, see Bruce Westrate, *The Arab Bureau: British Policy in the Middle East 1916–1920* (1993).

12 On 30 January 1918, Allenby telegraphed his agreement.

13 This is a reference to Jan Smuts' mission to Palestine (12–22 February 1918). Lloyd George sent Smuts out to the Middle East to put into effect Joint Note 12, agreed by the Supreme War Council in January 1918. Joint Note 12 called for the main offensive punch of the Entente powers in 1918 to be against Turkey. A copy of Joint Note 12 can be found at PRO:

WO106/729 (also in PRO: CAB25/68 dated 19 January 1918). There is a published copy of Joint Note 12 in *History of the Great War: Belgium and France, 1918, Appendices* (1935) appendix 9. For a copy of the conclusions of the Smuts Missions, see 'Report by General Smuts on his Mission to Egypt', 1 March 1918, PRO: CAB24/4/G199. More generally, see W.K. Hancock and J. van der Poel (eds), *Selections from the Smuts Papers* (1966) vol. 3, pp. 612–24.

14 The expression 'for a time' has been pencilled in over 'or retire'.

15 The word 'prevent' has been pencilled in over 'avoid'.

16 General (2nd Baronet and later Baron) Sir Henry Rawlinson (1864–1925) (GOC Fourth Army, 1916) replaced Henry Wilson as Britain's military representative on the Supreme War Council in February 1918.

17 Lieutenant-Colonel Charles à Court Repington was the Military Correspondent of *The Times*. A supporter of the General Staff, he resigned from *The Times* in January 1918 as he was at variance with the paper's support for Lloyd George, after which he wrote for the *Morning Post*. See A.J.A. Morris, *The Letters of Lieutenant-Colonel Charles à Court Repington CMG. Military Correspondent of the Times, 1903–1918* (1999) pp. 36–41.

18 As A.J.P. Taylor wryly noted: 'On 18 February 1918 Robertson read in the morning papers that he had resigned. He was given the command in eastern England – a good joke at the expense of an uncompromising "westerner"' (from Taylor, *English History 1914–1945* [1965] (1990) p. 100). Robertson's dismissal was the result of the long-running dispute over strategy between the CIGS and the Prime Minister, David Lloyd George. Henry Wilson replaced Robertson as CIGS.

19 Accompanying Smuts on his mission were Major-General Webb Gillman, Rt Hon Leo Amery, Brigadier-General J. Stewart (an expert on railways), and Colonel Kirke (Deputy DMO). It is said (see A.P. Wavell, *Allenby: A Study in Greatness* [1941] p. 241) that Smuts and Amery were the 'easterners' with the mission, while Kirke was there to represent the 'westerners'.

20 For a copy of the conclusions of the Smuts Missions, see 'Report by General Smuts on his Mission to Egypt', 1 March 1918, PRO: CAB24/4/G199.

21 A town in the north-west of Persia (Iran), *c.* 150 miles west of Tehran. Operations in Persia, 1914–18, are discussed in full in F.J. Moberly, *History of the Great War, Based on Official Documents, Operations in Persia, 1914–1919* (1929).

22 In which Allenby, following the Russian revolution, outlined his worry about the reliability of Russian Jews serving in the Royal Fusiliers in the EEF.

23 Another Jewish unit that first served on Gallipoli whose exploits are detailed in J.H. Patterson, *With the Zionists in Gallipoli* (1916). For more on the Jewish forces in the EEF, see J.H. Patterson, *With the Judaeans in the Palestine Campaign* (1922); see also Vladimir Jabotinsky, *The Story of the Jewish Legion* (1945).

24 The editor is unable to find personal details for this individual.

25 Presumably General Sir Robert Dundas Whigham (1865–1950). GOC 62nd (West Riding) Division in France, 1918.

26 The only relevant entry in *Who Was Who* is for Major-General Sir Frederick (Barton) Maurice (1871–1951). However, Maurice was DMO 1915–18 and was forced to resign over the 'Maurice letter' in April 1918.

27 General Sir Charles 'Tim' Harington, (1872–1940). Deputy CIGS, 1918–20; GOC-in-C Black Sea, 1920–1; GOC-in-C Allied Occupation Forces in Turkey, 1921–3.

28 General Sir Percy (Pollexfen de Blaquiere) Radcliffe (1874–1934). Lieutenant-Colonel 1916; Major-General, 1918.

29 Presumably a reference to Lieutenant-General Sir (George) Tom (Molesworth) Bridges (1871–1939). Promoted Major-General during the First World War; Military Member of Balfour's Mission to USA, 1917; Head of British War Mission in USA, 1918. Bridges lost his right leg in September 1917 commanding 19th Division. He then, apparently, asked that the amputated leg be fed to the divisional mascot, a lion: see J.M. Bourne, *Who's Who in World War One* (2001) p. 37.

30 Presumably Lieutenant-General Sir Charles Toler McMurrough Kavanagh (1864–1950). In France, commanded the 2nd Cavalry Division, 5th Division, I Army Corps and the Cavalry Corps in September 1916. Kavanagh remained in charge of the Cavalry Corps until the war's end (see Bourne, *Who's Who in World War One*, pp. 151–2).

31 Presumably General Sir William Eliot Peyton (1866–1931). GOC 40th Division in France in 1918.

32 Presumably Major-General Sir Harold Goodeve Ruggles-Brice (1864–1927). Divisional commander and military secretary GHQ.

33 In which Robertson stated that 'British' divisions should be made ready to go to France. In Palestine, 'British' infantry divisions had 12 'white' battalions; 'Indian' infantry divisions had 9 'brown' or 'native' and 3 'white' battalions (to use the terminology of the time).

34 The Germans launched their first Spring 1918 Ludendorff offensives on 21 March against the British Third and Fifth armies on the Western Front; a second attack came on 9 April 1918, again on the British sector of the front (this time against Second Army).

35 This was a very positive telegram sent after Smuts' visit in which the War Cabinet stated that it wanted Allenby to keep up the pressure and attack the Hedjaz railway; also that reinforcements would be arriving from Mesopotamia.

36 For their attack on the dominating feature of Hill 3039, the New Zealanders had just one pack 12–pounder gun for fire support: C. Guy Powles, *The New Zealanders in Sinai and Palestine, Volume III of the Official History of New Zealand's Effort in the Great War* (1922) p. 202.

37 This overly optimistic report ignored the reality of the desperate fight for

Amman in which poorly supplied EEF troops, fighting in inclement weather and lacking sufficient firepower, failed to overcome determined Turkish resistance. See the accounts in Matthew Hughes, *Allenby and British Strategy in the Middle East, 1917–1919* (1999) ch. 5; and Skander Bey, 'The Battles of Salt, Aman [sic] and Jordan from Turkish Sources', *The Journal of the Royal United Services Institution*, 69, May and August 1924, pp. 334–43, 488–98. Communications from the British bridgeheads on the Jordan to Amman were appalling, with roads transformed into muddy tracks by the spring rains. Brigadier-General Granville Ryrie, GOC of the 2nd ALH brigade, wrote to his wife how he had to leave his guns behind 'as the road which had been reported good . . . was an almost impassable goat track . . . I thought sometimes that we would never get through' (letter, Ryrie to wife (Mary), 10 April 1918, National Library of Australia, MS986/485–643).

38 EEF demolition parties never reached the main tunnels and bridges south of Amman, the destruction of which would have seriously interrupted traffic on the Hedjaz railway.

39 The Christian population of Es Salt, which had welcomed the EEF, left with the departing EEF troops and decamped to refugee camps across the Jordan. Anzac troopers did their best to help the Christians of Es Salt in their hasty departure, carrying women and children on their horses and camels on the difficult journey to safety behind EEF lines. In his diary, Lieutenant-Colonel A.J. Mills of the Imperial Camel Corps, retreating from Es Salt, recorded the following about the civilian exodus: 'All along the way we passed the poor unfortunate refugees, trecking [sic], walking, dragging themselves along. Men, boys, girls, old men, babies, all sorts and ages. Poor beggars. Some got a lift in limbers. I took one or two of the kiddies on my saddle . . . Howard had one and many of the boys had kiddies on their saddle' (from diary, 1 April 1918, Mills papers, AWM, 1DRL/501, part 2). For a study of Transjordan and its population in this period, see Eugene Rogan, *Frontiers of the State in the Late Ottoman Empire, Transjordan 1850–1921* (1999).

40 After the first Transjordan raid, the Turks quickly effected repairs to the railway and had their trains running again after just a few days. Wooden blocks fixed to the rails sufficed for temporary repairs to small breaks in the track: see DMC, Operations of A and NZ Mtd Division 23/3–2/4/18, 27 March 1918, PRO: WO157/745, p. 2 (also N.N.E. Bray, *Shifting Sands* (1934) p. 142).

41 From Clayton to the War Office in which he outlined his worry that Feisal might make peace with the Turks. This telegram suggests that there was intelligence that Feisal had been liaising with the Turks. Clayton's telegram stressed the need to cement the alliance with Feisal and that Feisal should visit Jerusalem to meet Allenby and be made a KCB. There is evidence from the Turkish side that Feisal was negotiating with the Turks: see Franz von Papen, *Memoirs* (1952) p. 80.

42 This was a brief message from the WO to Allenby asking about Turkish reports of a local armistice for picking up wounded.

43 Forced labour or conscription.

44 Nine RHA 13–pounders were lost.

45 See Biographical Notes.

46 A line starting 15 miles north of Jerusalem and stretching to the coast ten miles north of Jaffa.

47 Approximately 3 miles south of Ghoraniyeh.

48 Or Na'ur.

49 See OH, vol. 2, p. 352.

50 See the correspondence of 1 May 1918 above.

51 In Egyptian Arabic, mudir translates as manager, head teacher or communal head; mamour translates as sharif or, more specifically, the head of the police station in a village or a police station covering a group of villages; omda is a wise or learned man, the head of a tribe or village, or the head person for an area (something like a village headman). These are references to the local indigenous power structures through which the British authorities in Egypt ruled the country.

52 Unknown.

53 Troops recruited from the North-West frontier region of India (also a term used for tribespeople from Afghanistan).

54 One word indecipherable marked with a pencilled 'x' with the word in question double underlined. Obviously, Wilson was also unable to decipher this word.

55 The railway junction between Nablus and Tulkeram (c. 8 miles west of the former place) (see AOH map 41).

56 In April 1918, Frederick Maurice, the DMO, sent a letter to the press accusing David Lloyd George of deceiving Parliament about the strength of the British army in France. In the subsequent furore, Maurice lost his job as DMO. See David Woodward, 'Did Lloyd George Starve the British Army of Men Prior to the German Offensive of 21 March 1918?', *Historical Journal*, 27/1, 1984, pp. 241–52

57 In a letter of 1 July 1918 (HHW2/33A/9) one of Wilson's staff wrote to Allenby saying that, while the request for tanks would be taken seriously, there was a shortage of tanks in France.

58 Allenby has crossed out this word (possibly the ink has smudged?) making it indecipherable.

59 The coastal plain of Palestine.

60 This is a reference to the 54th Division that Wilson wanted to move to France.

61 On 15 June 1918, the Austro-Hungarians launched an offensive across the Piave. Some of their troops established lodgements on the right bank but were soon pushed back by Allied troops.

62 A reference to Napoleon Bonaparte.

63 Possibly Messudie railway junction between Nablus and Tulkeram.

64 See above note 56.

65 'Subsidy' has been crossed out and replaced with 'gold'.

66 'Require' has been crossed out and replaced with 'want'.

67 'Northern Operations' has been crossed out and replaced with 'Feisal'.

68 A reference to the Turco-German attack at Abu Telal spearheaded by the German 146 Regiment, 702 and 703 Battalions, and the 11th Reserve Jäger Battalion.

69 Spelt Jodhpore Lancers in British OH (sometimes also spelt Jodhpur).

70 Presumably a reference to Lieutenant-General Sir Pertab (or Pratap) Singh, Commmander-in-Chief of the Jodhpore Lancers, part of the Imperial Service Cavalry Brigade. See R.B. van Wart, *The Life of Lieutenant-General H.H. Sir Pratap Singh* (1926) which describes how the Jodhpore Lancers and Pratap Singh were in Palestine in 1918, and that Pratap Singh met Allenby while there (pp. 210–17).

71 Giovanni Ameglio's biographical details in *Dizionario Biografico Degli Italiani* (1960) p. 758 give a date of 9 August for his recall (*rimpatrio*) from Libya.

72 The *DFPS* – see note 53 in chapter one of this volume.

73 Riflemen (i.e. Algerian infantry).

74 The editor has been unable to find personal details for this individual.

75 King's Messenger: secure postal service akin to the diplomatic pouch.

76 For confirmation of Jisr el Mejamie, see the orders detailed in the British Official History (vol. 2, pp. 721–2). Located south of Lake Tiberias near the junction with the Yarmuk river.

77 Nahr el Faliq. This is the Crusaders' 'Rochetaille'.

78 This is recorded as a comma in Brian Gardner, *Allenby* (1965) p. 184.

79 See note 70 above.

80 This sentence is misquoted in Gardner, *Allenby*, p. 185.

81 Presumably the wife of the American Minister (see note 45 above).

82 Unknown.

83 Or El Lajjun. This is the Roman military settlement 1 km. south of the main Megiddo site.

84 This 'went' is a 'met' in Gardner, *Allenby*, p. 185.

85 Major Canaanite and Israelite city in the hill country of Ephraim near the modern-day town of Nablus. It was destroyed in 107 BC by the Hasmonean John Hyrcanus.

86 Present-day Sabastiya.

87 Lacking the proper ellipses, this letter is incorrectly quoted in Gardner, *Allenby*, p. 185.

88 See note 70 above.

89 See above.

90 Attached to this letter and dated 24 September but not copied for this volume.

91 See note 70 above.

92 See note 44 in chapter one of this volume.

93 Muqatta (river of the ford or shallow).

94 In which Wilson laid out British government policy on Syria and provided some quotes from recent correspondence between London and Paris on the subject of Syria. The conclusion of this correspondence was that an Arab administration in Syria would have French liaison officers.

95 The 'Sykes-Picot' agreement of 1916 divided much of the Middle East into Red (British) and Blue (French) zones of control and influence.

96 The date for this letter is given as 3 September 1918 with 'October' written in below the 'September'. Considering the content of the letter, it is obviously a mistake on Allenby's part to have written September (with the correction to October added at a later date).

97 Covering 6,000 hectares in 1918, Lake Huleh was a remarkable area for flora and fauna, especially bird life as Palestine/Israel is astride a major migratory route for birds. In the 1950s, the Israelis drained and reclaimed the malarial Lake Huleh – causing serious environmental problems – leaving today a small wetland nature reserve established in the 1960s.

98 A sketch drawing by Allenby of Mount Hermon is included.

99 There were three 'Djemals' (or 'Jemals') in Syria during the war and they should not be confused. Ahmed Djemal the Greater (Djemal I) (Minister of Marine and Governor of Syria) was one of the triumvirate who ruled Turkey (with Enver Pasha and Talaat Pasha), and who, in December 1917, was recalled to Istanbul. His position as Governor of Syria was taken over by Mohammed Djemal the Less (Djemal II), also GOC of the Fourth Army until Damascus's fall. Mehmed Djemal (III) was GOC of the composite force at Tebuk. The reference here is to Djemal II. See Summary of Hejaz Revolts, appendix D, 30 September 1918, PRO: FO882/7.

100 This letter is misdated by Allenby to 5 September 1918.

101 See note 70 above.

102 Properly Jisr el Mejamie, the railway bridge crossing the Jordan south of Semakh.

103 Provincial governor.

104 Temporary Governor of Damascus; made Governor of Aleppo.

105 As Beirut was to pass to direct French rule, Allenby was quick to stifle this pre-emptive move by the Arabs to occupy Beirut, allowing French marines into the city, so ending the attempted Arab occupation of the Lebanese littoral.

106 A reference to the French and British zones of influence as laid out in the Sykes-Picot agreement.

107 Or Haggett? In Keith Jeffery (ed.), *The Military Correspondence of Field Marshal Sir Henry Wilson 1918–1922* (1985) it is recorded as Huggett. There is no relevant Huggett or Haggett listed in *Who Was Who*.

108 Probably a reference to Ali Riza Pasha el Rikabi, Ottoman general and

someone in secret communication with the Hashemite Arabs, and who became governor of Damascus in October 1918 after the defeat of the Turks.

109 Major-General Sir Richard (Harman) Luce (1867–1952). Director Medical Services Chief, EEF.

110 An Ottoman administrative district equivalent to a province. See the map in Kedourie, *In the Anglo-Arab Labyrinth*, facing p. 80.

111 Former Ottoman general in Syria. Went over to the Hashemites in September 1918 and became Governor (Vali) of Damascus; secretly met T.E. Lawrence in June 1917 (see Lawrence to Clayton, 10 July 1917, PRO: FO882/16).

112 In 1881, the Ottoman Public Debt Administration (OPDA) was created to manage the finances of the ailing Ottoman empire. It was empowered to collect taxes, exploit state revenues and pay creditors. Run by European banks, it allowed the Ottoman empire to re-schedule its debts. A council of seven members (from Britain, France, Germany, Holland, Italy, Austria-Hungary and the Ottoman Bank) ran the OPDA. Income that would have gone to the Ottoman empire went to the OPDA. Later, a separate European-controlled entity, the Tobacco Régie, was established to exploit tobacco profits in the Ottoman empire. The OPDA and the Tobacco Régie formed part of the capitulations regime that afforded Europeans special treatment in the Ottoman empire. The capitulatory regime declined after 1923 and was swept away by the Montreux agreement of 1937.

Chapter 3

1 Presumably King Hussein of the Hedjaz (1856–1931).

2 Or Asir. Located in south-western Arabia, just north of Yemen, Asir was garrisoned by Turkish forces throughout the war (as was Yemen to the south where Turkish troops confronted the British garrison in Aden).

3 The two provinces that made up the Italian colony of Libya. Turkish garrisons in outlying provinces were slow to surrender, partly due to the fear of surrendering to local tribesmen.

4 The editor is unable to find personal details for this individual.

5 With the collapse of Russia in 1917, German troops infiltrated east into Georgia and the Caucasus region, threatening Britain's route to India.

6 Malaria spread among EEF troops as they advanced into enemy territory where the disease was endemic. Prophylactic measures such as oiling and draining stagnant areas of water had helped to eradicate the disease behind EEF lines. Typhoid, influenza and (among the local population) starvation also caused many deaths (some 200,000 local people starved to death at the war's end).

7 On 7/8 November 1918, an Anglo-French Declaration promised representative and indigenous Arab governments in the area conquered by Allenby's forces. For a copy of the declaration, see Jukka Nevakivi, *Britain,*

France and the Arab Middle East 1914–1920 (1969) appendix B. While dated the 7 November, the Declaration, it seems, was issued on 8 November 1917 (see Nevakivi, ibid., p. 81.) This declaration was one of a series of assurances concerning Arab self-determination in the region: viz., the Hussein-McMahon Correspondence of 1915–16, the Declarations issued on the capture of Baghdad and Jerusalem in 1917, the Hogarth Message of January 1918 and the Declaration to the Seven of June 1918. For copies of these declarations and more discussion generally, see George Antonius, *The Arab Awakening: The Story of the Arab National Movement* (1938) (especially, pp. 267–9, appendices A, C, D & E). For a counter-argument to Antonius, see Elie Kedourie, *England and the Middle East: The Destruction of the Ottoman Empire 1914–1921* (1956) and Kedourie, *In the Anglo-Arab Labyrinth: The McMahon-Husayn Correspondence and its Interpretations 1914–1939* (2000).

8 See above note 7.

9 Dated 28/11/18 from DMI to GHQ EEF stating that Zionists felt that Arab needs were met by the Syrian state and that world Jewry wanted a British trusteeship in Palestine where they could build a Jewish commonwealth.

10 For accounts of the Middle East discussions at the Paris Peace Conference, see Michael Dockrill and J. Douglas Goold, *Peace Without Promise: Britain and the Peace Conferences, 1919–23* (1981) ch. 4; H.W.V. Temperley (ed.), *A History of the Peace Conference of Paris* (1924) vol. 6; Marian Kent (ed.), *The Great Powers and the End of the Ottoman Empire* (1996); David Fromkin, *A Peace To End All Peace: Creating the Modern Middle East, 1914–1922* (1991); and Malcolm Yapp, *The Making of the Modern Near East 1792–1923* (1987) ch. 6.

11 See above note 7.

12 There is no day in January 1919 provided for this note.

13 The editor has been unable to discover the content of this protest.

14 Stéphen Pichon, French Foreign Minister (1906–11, 1913, 1917–20).

15 Possibly a reference to a speech made in the French Chamber by Pichon, the French Foreign Secretary, on 29 December 1918, in which he outlined France's historic and legal claim to Syria, Lebanon and Cilicia. See Temperley (ed.), *A History of the Peace Conference of Paris*, p. 143.

16 The armistice with Turkey was signed on 30 October at the port of Mudros on the Aegean island of Lemnos. It was to come into effect the following day.

17 'I the Lord have called thee in righteousness, and will hold thine hand, and will keep thee, and give thee for a covenant of the people, for a light of the Gentiles.'

18 Attached, dated 29 December 1918, and entitled 'The Gallant Dead.'

19 If this is a reference to the white mariana, it is also known as a milk thistle. It grew in Palestine and Syria in this period; in Britain, it would only be on show in Botanical gardens (information courtesy of the Royal Horticultural Society). Could also read narcissi.

20 Cilicia in the PRO: WO33/960 copy of this telegram.

21 Allenby had deployed Armenian troops, part of the French detachment in the EEF (see note 53 in chapter one of this volume), in Cilicia at the war's end.

22 In 1914, when fighting in France with the Cavalry Corps, Allenby was billeted with the Baroness Ernest de la Grange, the *châtelaine* of the Château de la Motte au Bois, near the Forest of Nieppe.

23 Not here.

24 The letter in the Hardinge papers is a copy and considering the content of the letter – such as the reference to a telegram of 26 February – the date must have been noted incorrectly as February rather than March 1919.

25 Properly Dairût. Located approximately 200 miles south of Cairo and home to a large Coptic Christian community.

26 This telegram and others like it deal with the effects of the Egyptian revolt that erupted in the spring of 1919. For more on the struggle for independence in Egypt in this period, see M.W. Daly (ed.), *The Cambridge History of Egypt. Volume 2* (1998) ch. 10; P.J. Vatikiotis, *The History of Modern Egypt: From Muhammad Ali to Mubarak* (1991) ch. 12; Elie Kedourie, *Politics in the Middle East* (1992) ch. 5; Malcolm Yapp, *The Making of the Modern Near East*, pp. 340–5; and Yapp, *The Near East Since the First World War: A History to 1995* (1996) ch. 1.

27 The Egyptian Copts form part of the Oriental Orthodox Churches. Tradition recounts that St Mark the Evangelist founded the Church in Egypt, and Alexandria ranked with Antioch and Rome as one of the chief sees of the early Church. At the Council of Chalcedon in 451 CE, the Copts rejected the Council and its Definition of the two natures in the incarnate Christ, and so became increasingly isolated from the rest of Christendom. The Copts are now said to number some 4 million (F.L. Cross, *The Oxford Dictionary of the Christian Church* [1957, 1997] p. 416), mostly living in Egypt, out of a total Egyptian population (in 2000) of some 65 million. Some authors put their number at 6 million. 'Copt' is a European form of the Arabic 'Kibt', itself derived from the Greek for Egyptian, Αἰγύπτιοι. Led by the Patriarch of Alexandria, Coptic life is, in most respects, indistinguishable from that of Egyptian Muslims (see Vatikiotis, *The History of Modern Egypt*, p. 201) but clashes between Copts and Muslims were (and are) a problem, partly because the former were seen as having a privileged position as a professional class in Egyptian society.

28 Communal head. See note 51 in chapter two of this volume.

29 On the Red Sea coast.

30 From Weizmann (with Zionist delegation Paris) to Wilson, n.d., copy at IWM: Wilson papers HHW2/33B/11. The letter asks if demobilised Jewish soldiers in Palestine could volunteer to remain there for a number of years.

31 Al-Azhar Mosque and University, built in the 10th century, one of the first mosques in Cairo.

32 See note 25 above.

33 Various spellings of Sa'd (or Saad) Zaghlul are employed in the following letters.

34 Movement (upper case) in the holograph copy.

35 Presumably a reference to the proposed Anglo-French-American Commission that was to help decide the future status of the OETA territory conquered by Allenby by conducting a fact-finding tour of the region, during which it would speak to local people. In the end, only the US delegates, Charles Crane and Henry King, went to the Middle East in June 1919, presenting their findings to President Wilson at the end of August 1919. For more information, see Harry N. Howard, *An American Inquiry in the Middle East: The King-Crane Commission* (1963). The French were very reluctant to accede to the idea of a commission that would encourage ideas of self-determination and the British took their lead from the French, saying that if the French refused to send commissioners so would they.

36 The region in Rumania by the Black Sea south of the delta of the River Danube. At the war's end, British troops garrisoned many different localities, often former Central Alliance powers or areas occupied by Central Alliance forces during the war.

37 As early as 1916 there were protests at the forced recruitment of Egyptians into the Egyptian Labour Corps and Camel Transport Corps; also at the forced requisitioning of animals and fodder for the EEF.

38 In the typescript copy at Wilson papers HHW2/33D/2 'dislikes' is replaced by 'disturbs'.

39 Properly Dairût, Located some 200 miles south of Cairo.

40 Presumably Lieutenant-Colonel (George) Stewart Symes (1882–1962) the Private Secretary to Sirdar and Governor General of Sudan during the First World War.

41 Al-Azhar Mosque and University in Cairo.

42 Presumably a reference to the mission headed by Lord Milner sent to Egypt, December 1919–March 1920, to decide its future status. Its report, signed in December 1920 and presented in February 1921, concluded that the Protectorate status for Egypt was not satisfactory. The Milner Mission consisted of Viscount Milner, Sir Rennell Rodd, General Sir J.G. Maxwell, General Sir Owen Thomas, Sir C.J.B. Hurst, J.A. Spender plus, as secretaries, A.T. Lloyd and Captain E.M.B. Ingram.

43 From Curzon to Allenby, dated 7 May 1919, asking whether British women had been raped during the disturbances in Egypt.

44 Laying out the grievances of the men of the EEF and their wish to be demobilised. The men were especially worried about losing jobs at home that had been held open for them by employers.

45 As with No. M.F.A. 37593 of 8 May 1919, this telegram dealt with the pressing need to demobilise soldiers.

46 This letter, addressed 'My dear General', seems to be to Allenby but could

be to Wilson (or even Clayton).

47 This appears to be a letter at PRO: WO106/191/123 from the Zionist Organisation dated 9 May 1919 asking Gribbon to attend a meeting on the 10 May 1919 to discuss the future of Palestine.

48 See above. The second telegram deals with demobilisation and fresh drafts for Egypt.

49 'War' in copy at Kerr papers.

50 'Around' in ARS volume but 'armed' in copy at Kerr papers.

51 Dera'a in ARS volume.

52 Underlined in red. Allenby makes this same point (the one underlined in red) in Allenby to Wilson, 9 May (despatched) 10 May (received) 1919, at PRO:WO 106/191/115.

53 Underlined in green.

54 With a Colonel Nugent.

55 A copy of 539 can be found at IWM: Wilson papers HHW2/33E/3A. It points out that the impasse in the negotiations in Paris on the future status of Syria means that Allenby is in full military charge until a political solution is found. 538 is attached.

56 This seems to be Colonel Nugent.

57 Modern-day Tadmor.

58 See note 27 above.

59 Possibly Allenby to Milner and not Allenby to FO.

60 Not here.

61 This letter was forwarded to Wilson in a letter from Allenby dated 6 June (see below) with a note emphasising the importance of the commission for Feisal.

62 See above.

63 'Sedan' in the Kerr papers copy of this telegram.

64 In the DBFP version of this note it says: 'The French, however, have decided not to send their Commissioners until the relief of British troops in Syria by the French has been arranged.'

65 There is a slightly different version of this telegram at NAS: Kerr papers GD40/17/38/134–5. A slightly different copy of the same telegram, also dated 31 May 1919, is in DBPF p. 259 with prefix of Balfour to Allenby.

66 There is a slightly different version of this reply in DBFP p. 259 – Balfour to Allenby, 31 May 1919.

67 These are the two telegrams from Feisal that Allenby refers to in EA2484 above (Allenby to Balfour, 30 May 1919).

68 A member of the old Egyptian ruling aristocracy, Allenby made Muhammad Said Pasha Prime Minister on 21 May 1919.

69 Horatio Herbert Kitchener, 1st Earl Kitchener of Khartoum and Broome (1850–1916). Agent and Consul-General in Egypt, 1911–14; Secretary of State for War in 1914; drowned in 1916 in the North Sea while on a mission to Russia.

70 Sir John Eldon Gorst (1861–1911). Consul-General in Egypt, 1907–11.

71 Isma'il Sirri, Minister of Public Works.

72 Yusuf Wahba, Minister of Finance.

73 Ahmed Ziwar (1864–1945). Egyptian politician. Opposed to the Wafd party and to Egyptian nationalism generally.

74 Discussing Feisal's views on British unwillingness to accept the League of Nations mandate for Syria.

75 Presumably a reference to the disturbances at Deirut some 200 miles south of Cairo during the Egyptian revolt.

76 The editor has been unable to find personal details for Dunlop, Haines and Pattison.

77 Possibly a reference to Major James Charles Hope-Vere (1858–1933).

78 In the DBFP there is a note here stating that 'The text here is uncertain.'

79 Presumably Perceval Landon (1869–1927). Special Correspondent, *Daily Telegraph* and on staff of the *Daily Telegraph*.

80 The editor is unable to provide personal details for this individual.

81 Presumably Major-General Hubert Ion Wetherall Hamilton (1861–1919). GOC 3rd Division, 1914.

82 Presumably Major-General Sir George Townshend Forestier-Walker (1866–1939), Chief of Staff of Smith-Dorrien's II Corps.

83 On 26 August 1914, Allenby, commanding the Cavalry Division, arrived at II Corps headquartes at Le Cateau. There Allenby told Smith-Dorrien, II Corps GOC, that his cavalry could not cover the retreat of II Corps. Allenby also suggested that II Corps needed to retreat to avoid further attacks. II Corps was in no condition to retire and, while Allenby and Smith-Dorrien were talking over the situation, Hubert Hamilton arrived and confirmed that 3rd Division was unable to retire until 09.00 hours. Faced with a retreat becoming a rout, Smith-Dorrien decided to ignore the order from GHQ to retreat, instead choosing to stand and fight at Le Cateau. Forestier-Walker was II Corps' chief of staff. See Nikolas Gardner *Trial by Fire, Command and the British Expeditionary Force in 1914* (2003).

84 Not here.

85 Presumably Colonel Frederick Dudley Samuel (1877–1951).

86 Detailing Picot's claim that Hussein had asked for French troops for the Hedjaz, a claim that Allenby did not believe.

87 In another letter the Christian name is given as Guiseppe.

88 'The Residency Ramleh' has been crossed out by Allenby.

89 Sir Hamar Greenwood (later Baron and Earl) (1870–1948). Secretary, Overseas Trade Department, 1919–20.

90 Sir Auckland Geddes (later Baron) (1879–1954). Minister of National Service, 1917–19; President, Board of Trade, 1919–20. Not to be confused with his brother Eric Geddes (1875–1937), famous for wielding the 'Geddes Axe' of 1922 that cut British government spending.

91 Nancy Astor (1879–1964) was the wife of Waldorf Astor (who succeeded his

father as 2nd Viscount Astor in 1919). Nancy Astor was the first woman to sit as an MP (Conservative for Plymouth) when she succeeded her husband as MP when he passed into the House of Lords in 1919.

92 Andrew Bonar Law had two daughters – it is not clear which is the one referred to here. If Jane Austen's novels are indicative, the eldest daughter is usually referred to as 'Miss' with any other daughters simply called by their name.

93 This seems to be a reference to the senior French diplomat, Philippe J.L. Berthelot (1866–1934). Not to be confused with General Henri-Mathias Berthelot (1861–1931), the Western Front commander. For Gouraud's details, see biographical index. J.M. Bourne's *Who's Who in World War One* (2001) p. 24 gives a date of birth of 1863 for General Berthelot.

Appendices

1 Led by Chaim Weizmann, the British-sanctioned Zionist Commission arrived in Palestine in the spring of 1918 to help put into effect the provisions of the Balfour Declaration of November 1917 that called for the establishment of a Jewish 'National Home' in Palestine.

2 Presumably Sir Wyndham Deedes (1883–1956), British officer and Zionist, worked with the Arab Bureau in the First World War.

3 Presumably Israel Benjamin Rosov (1869–1948), Russian Zionist leader and pioneer industrialist in Palestine. Nominated for the Zionist Commission but arrived too late to be part of the Commission. Co-opted onto the committee that drafted Zionist proposals to the Paris Peace Conference (1919).

4 This is attached to the letter. See below.

5 In the Cornwallis papers at the Middle East Centre, St Antony's Oxford, there is a letter from Cornwallis pointing out that he was forced to wait in the hall of the hotel while Allenby and Feisal held their meeting in another room on 3 October 1918 (Cornwallis to Wavell [?], 17 May 1939, DS97.58/DR588.4).

6 Mrs Cindy Kingham passed copies of these letters to the Liddell Hart Centre for Military Archives, King's College London, in 2003. Mrs Kingham's uncle was Allenby's first cousin. The handwriting on the letters is not Allenby's but his mother's. Presumably, she copied out the letters from her son. The whereabouts of the original correspondence in Allenby's hand is not known. The fact that the letters have been transcribed might explain the peculiar grammar in parts of the correspondence.

7 A reference to the fact that the hill of Abu Shushe (or Abu Shusheh) is supposedly the site of the ancient city of Gezer (or Gazara) of biblical fame (see Josh. 16: 10, Judg. 1: 29, 1 Kings 9: 16 and 1 Macc. 13: 43–48).

8 Major the Hon Neil Primrose, formerly Under-Secretary of State for Foreign Affairs. Primrose was the only officer from the 6th Mounted

brigade to die in this attack. See the British OH, vol. 2, pp. 178–80 and The Marquess of Anglesey, *A History of the British Cavalry 1816–1919, Volume 5, Egypt, Palestine and Syria, 1914–1919* (1994) p. 201.

9 Neil Primrose, the son of the 5th Earl of Roseberry, had two sisters, Cybil and Margaret, and a brother, Harry. It is not clear to whom Allenby is referring in this letter.

10 Not here.

Biographies

1 The reference to Ameglio comes in a letter from Wingate to Allenby dated 5 August 1918. However, Ameglio's biographical details in *Dizionario Biografico Degli Italiani* (1960) p. 758 give a date of 9 August for his recall (*rimpatrio*) from Libya. There is no mention in his biographical details of why he was recalled from Libya.

2 For more information, see Barrow's account of his life in *The Fire of Life* (1942).

3 Information courtesy of George Newkey-Burden of the *Daily Telegraph* Archive. The notice of Battine's death appeared in the *Daily Telegraph* on 5 January 1949.

4 For more information on Chauvel, see A.J. Hill, *Chauvel of the Light Horse: A Biography of General Sir Harry Chauvel* (1978).

5 This is the information given in *Who Was Who*. However, as Britain had a High Commission in Egypt and not an Embassy before December 1936, this is, it seems, technically incorrect (information courtesy of the Foreign and Commonwealth Office library).

6 For more information on 'Dunsterforce', see L.C. Dunsterville, *The Adventures of Dunsterforce* (1920).

7 For more information on Falkenhayn's period in Palestine, see Cyril Falls, 'Falkenhayn in Syria', *The Edinburgh Review*, 250, October 1929, 272–89.

8 Properly *I-ho ch'üan* – the Righteous and Harmonious Fists.

9 His entry in *Dictionnaire de Biographie Française* (1985) (vol. 16, p. 771) notes that he had both legs broken and he lost his right arm.

10 For more information on Kressenstein's period in Palestine, see Kress von Kressenstein, *Zwischen Kaukasus und Sinai: Jahrbuch des Bundes der Asienkämpfer 1921* (1921) and Kress von Kressenstein, *Mit den Türken zum Suezkanal* (1938).

11 Liman von Sanders outlines his part in the Palestine campaign in his memoir: *Five Years in Turkey* (1927).

12 For more on Meinerzhagen's adventures in the Middle East, see his accounts in: *Middle East Diary, 1917–1956* (1959) and *Army Diary 1899–1926* (1960).

13 The editor is unable to find dates for this individual who has no entry in the *Index Biographique Français*.

14 The distinction in command roles between Piépape and General Bailloud is not clear.

15 For more information on Robertson's remarkable rise through the ranks, see his account in *From Private to Field-Marshal* (1921).

16 For more information on Storrs' time in Palestine, see his account in *Orientations* (1937).

17 After the war, Yale wrote *The Near East: A Modern History* (1958).

Biographical Notes

'Adli Pasha Yakan (1864–1933): Egyptian politician. Descended from family of large land owners; split from the Wafdist movement led by Sa'd Zaghlul in 1919; became Prime Minister, 1921; 'Adli's supporters formed the Liberal Constitutionalist Party.

Ameglio, General Giovanni (1854–1921): Italian general. Fought in the Italian-Ottoman War over Libya (1911–12) as a Major-General; October 1913 appointed Governor of Cyrenaica; made a Senator in February 1917; recalled to Italy, 9 August 1918, where he assumed command of an army corps at Naples.[1]

Bailloud, General Maurice-Chamille (1847–1921): French general. Fought in the Franco-Prussian War (1870–71) where he was badly wounded at the battle of Sedan in the right foot; served in Algeria, Madagascar, Central Asia and China; put on the reserve list in 1912; recalled to service in 1914, commanded France's *corps expéditionnaire d'Orient* in Palestine; went on a mission to Jerusalem after the war.

Balfour, Arthur James, 1st Earl of Balfour (1848–1930): British politician and philosopher. Unionist (Conservative) MP; Prime Minister 1902–5; Foreign Secretary December 1916–October 1919.

Barrow, General Sir George de Symons (1864–1959): British general. Commanded the 4th Indian Cavalry Division in Palestine, 1918; served in India after the war, including during the Third Afghan War, 1919.[2]

Battine, Captain Cecil William (1866/67–1949): British journalist. Military Correspondent for the *Daily Telegraph*, 1911–21.[3]

Bean, Charles Edwin Woodrow (1879–1968): Australian war correspondent and official historian. Responsible for Australia's official history of the Western Front.

Bentwich, Norman de Mattos (1883–1971): Lawyer. With British Army in Middle East, 1915–18; legal adviser to OETA.

Birdwood, General Sir William Riddell, 1st Baron of Anzac and Totnes (1865–1951): British general. Commanded Anzacs on Gallipoli; in supreme command of the Australians on the Western Front, 1915–18, even after becoming an army commander in 1918.

Birkbeck, Major-General Sir William (1863–1929): British general. Commandant of the Cavalry School at Netheravon, 1906–11; Director of Remounts at Army Headquarters, 1912–20; Attorney-General, Palestine, 1920–31.

Bols, Lieutenant-General Sir Louis (1867–1930): British general. Allenby's Chief of Staff, 1917–18; Chief Administrator Palestine, 1919.

Brandeis, Justice Louis Dembitz (1856–1941): US judge. Appointed to the US Supreme Court in 1916; son of non-practising Jews; attended American Zionist conference, 1914; became heavily involved in American Zionist movement thereafter.

Bulfin, General Sir Edward Stanislaus (1862–1939): British general. GOC 60th Division, 1915–17 in France, Salonika and Egypt; commander XXI Corps in Palestine, 1917–19.

Byng, Field Marshal Julian, 1st Viscount Byng of Vimy (1862–1935): British Field Marshal. Commanded Canadian Corps, 1916–17; captured Vimy Ridge, April 1917; commander Third Army, 1917–19; prepared the Cambrai offensive (November 1917) and put up strong resistance during the Ludendorff offensives, March 1918.

Cadorna, General Luigi (1850–1928): Italian general. Italian supreme commander on the Isonzo Front, 1915 until the disaster at the battle of Caporetto (or Kobarid) (also known as the 12th battle of the Isonzo) in October 1917 when the Italians were forced back to the River Piave, after which he was replaced by Diaz; a strict disciplinarian, Cadorna is best remembered for the series of offensives along the lower Isonzo River that gained some ground but at a very high cost in Italian casualties.

Cecil, Edgar Algernon Robert Gascoyne, 1st Visount Cecil of Chelwood (1864–1958): British politician. Minister of Blockade, 1916–18; Assistant Secretary of State for Foreign Affairs, 1918–19; heavily involved in the establishment of the League of Nations.

Chauvel, General Sir Henry George (1965–45): Australian general. Served in the South-African War (1899–1902) as a major with the 1st Queensland Mounted Infantry; helped to re-organise Australian forces prior to the First World War; commanded Australian light horse forces, 1914–15; served on Gallipoli; promoted Major-General in December 1915; elected to remain with the light horse in Egypt as commander of the new Australian and New Zealand Mounted Division; commander Desert Mounted Corps July 1917; August 1917, the first Australian to achieve the rank of Lieutenant-General.[4]

Chaytor, Major-General Sir Edward Walter Clervaux (1868–1939): British general. GOC Australian and New Zealand Division and 'Chaytor's Force', 1917–18.; commandant New Zealand Defence Force, 1919–24; retired, 1931.

Cheetham, Sir Milne (1869–1938): British diplomat. Entered diplomatic service 1894; Counsellor of Embassy[5] Cairo, 1911–19.

Chetwode, Field Marshal Philip, 1st Baron Chetwode (1869–1950): British general. GOC Desert Column in Egypt/Palestine, 1916–17; GOC XX Corps, 1917–18.

Clayton, Major-General Sir Edward Gilbert (1875–1929): British general and military administrator. BGGS Military Operations Hedjaz, 1916–17; CPO, EEF and Military Governor OETA South, 1917–18; Adviser to the Egyptian Ministry of the Interior, 1919–22.

Clémenceau, Georges (1841–1929): French statesman. French Prime Minister, 1906–9, 1917–20); presided at the Paris Peace Conference (1919) where he sought (unsuccessfully) to obtain in the treaty of Versailles a settlement that would preserve France from another attack from Germany.

Congreve, General Sir Walter Norris (1862–1927): British general. GOC troops in Egypt and Palestine, 1919.

Connaught and Stratheam, Duke of (Arthur William Patrick Albert) (1850–1942): British aristocrat and field marshal. Field Marshal, 1902; Governor-General of Canada, 1911–16.

Cornwallis, Sir Kinahan (1883–1959): British administrator and diplomat. Joined Arab Bureau, 1915; directed Arab Bureau, 1916–20; personal adviser to King Feisal of Iraq, 1921–33.

Dalmeny, Albert Edward Primrose (6th Earl of Roseberry) (1882–1974): British soldier. Served as Allenby's Camp Commandant and ADC in France, 1914–17 and then Allenby's Military Secretary in Palestine; remained for a time on Allenby's staff at the Residency (Cairo) after the war.

de Lisle, General Sir Beauvoir (1864–1955): British general. Commanded XIII and XV corps on the Western Front; promoted Major-General and Lieutenant-General in the field.

Derby, 17th Earl of (Edward George Villiers Stanley) (1865–1948): British politician. Minister of War, 1916–18; Ambassador to France, 1918–20.

Diaz, General Armando Vittorio (1861–1928): Italian general. Cadorna's replacement as Italian supreme commander after the Italian defeat at the battle of Caporetto (or Kobarid) in October 1917.

Dunsterville, Major-General Lionel Charles (1865–1946): British general. Commanded 'Dunsterforce' unit that advanced through Persia to the Caspian Sea and then Baku, in September 1918, to block a Turko-German push in the Trans-Caucasus.[6]

Eder, Montagu David (1866–1936): Psychologist and Zionist. Part of the Zionist Commission to Palestine, 1918; on the Executive of the Zionist Organisation until 1929; President of the Zionist Federation of Great Britain and Ireland, 1931.

Edmonds, Brigadier-General Sir James (1861–1956): British soldier and official war historian. Ended the First World war as a Brigadier-General; after the war, made Director Historical Section, CID; compiled the Western Front volumes of the British official history of the Great War.

Falkenhayn, General Erich von (1861–1922): German general. Succeeded Helmuth von Moltke as Chief of the German General Staff in 1914; failure at the battle of Verdun in 1916 led to his dismissal; afterwards commanded Central Alliance forces in Rumania, Palestine (where he was blamed for the loss of Jerusalem and so replaced by Liman von Sanders) and Lithuania.[7]

Feisal, Amir (or Sherif) (later King) (or Faysal ibn Husayn) I (1885–1933): Arab statesman. Son of King Hussein of the Hedjaz; leader of the NAA during the Arab revolt, 1916–18; King of Syria (1920) and Iraq, 1921–33.

Foch, Marshal Ferdinand (1851–1929): French marshal. Entered artillery corps, 1873; professor of strategy *École supérieure de la Guerre*, 1898; commanded XX Corps in 1914; Allied Supreme Commander-in-Chief, March 1918; Marshal of France, August 1918.

Franchet d'Esperey, Marshal LFMF (1856–1942): French general. Commanded the Allied army in Salonika that defeated Central Alliance forces in September 1918, thereafter pushing north on the Danube and east towards Istanbul, forcing Bulgaria to surrender; created a Marshal in 1921; his strong Catholicism made him unpopular with anti-clerical circles in France.

Frankfurter, Felix (1882–1965): US lawyer and judge. Supported Zionist cause in America.

Garioni, General Vincenzo (1856–1929): Italian general. Led Italy's relief force during the 'Boxer' rebellion[8] of 1900; promoted Major-General in 1905; fought in the Italian-Ottoman War over Libya, 1911–12; fought on the Isonzo front during the First World War before being made Governor of Cyrenaica in August 1918 where he was given the job of continuing the pacification of Libyan tribes opposed to Italian rule.

Gary, Hampson (1873–1952): lawyer and diplomat. US Diplomatic Agent and Consul-General to Egypt, rank of Minister. Resident, 1917–20; while serving in Cairo in charge of American interests in Palestine, Syria and Arabia; at the front with Allenby in 1918.

George, David Lloyd, 1st Earl Lloyd George of Dwyfor (1863–1945): British statesman. Liberal MP 1890–1945; Chancellor of the Exchequer, 1908–14; Minister for Munitions, 1915–16; Secretary of State for War, 1916; Prime Minister, 1916–22.

Georges-Picot, François (1870–1951): French diplomat. Consul-General in Beirut before the war (where he left incriminating papers on departure in 1914 that led to the execution by the Ottomans of Arab nationalists); First Secretary at the French embassy in London, 1915; negotiated for France the 'Sykes-Picot' agreement of May 1916; headed French political mission with the EEF, 1917–18; nominal French High Commissioner, 1917; French High Commissioner to Syria, 1918.

Gillman, General Sir Webb (1870–1933): British general. Major-General, 1916. Chief of the Staff of the Mesopotamian Expeditionary Force.

Girdwood, Major-General Sir Eric Stanley (1876–1963): British general. GOC 74th (Yeomanry) Division in Palestine 1917–18.

Godwin, Brigadier-General CAC (1873–1951): British general. GOC 6th Yeomanry Brigade in the advance on Jerusalem, 1917; BGGS of DMC during the advance on Damascus, 1918.

Gough, Lieutenant-General Sir Hubert de la Poer (1870–1963): British general. Commander of Fifth Army, 1916–18; removed from command after the German victory in the first Ludendorff offensive of March 1918.

Gouraud, General Henri Joseph Étienne (1867–1946): French general. In France with the Moroccan brigade in 1914; wounded in 1915; badly wounded commanding French forces at Gallipoli;[9] spent the rest of the war in Morocco and on the Western Front; on 15 September 1919, sent to Syria as France's High Commissioner; commanded the forces that invaded and occupied Syria in 1920.

Grant, Brigadier-General William (1870–1939): Australian soldier and grazier. GOC 3rd (one month only) and then 4th Australian Light Horse Brigade, 1917–18.

Gribbon, Brigadier Walter (1881–1944): British soldier. General Staff, Mesopotamia, War Office and Istanbul, 1914–21.

Gullet, Sir Henry Somer (1878–1940): Journalist, historian and politician. In 1915, appointed official Australian correspondent with the British and French armies in France; 1916 enlisted in the AIF as a gunner; 1917 appointed official Australian historian for the Egypt and Palestine campaign (working under C.E.W. Bean); arrived in Egypt November 1917; briefly first director of the AWM after the war; Australian MP and minister after the war; died in an aeroplane crash near Canberra in 1940.

Haig, Field Marshal Sir Douglas, 1st Earl Haig (1961–28): British field marshal. Entered army, 1885; GOC First Army, 1914–15; C-in-C BEF, 1915–19.

Hare, Major-General Sir Steuart Welwood (1867–1952): British general. GOC 54th Division in Egypt and Palestine, 1916–19.

Harper, Lieutenant-General Sir George Montague (1865–1922): British general. Entered the army, 1884; commanded 51st Highland Division, 1915–18; GOC IV Army Corps, 1918; Lieutenant-General, 1919; turned the 51st Division (a Territorial army unit) into one of the best divisions in the BEF.

Hart, Captain Basil Liddell (1895–1970): Military historian, strategist and thinker; author of many books on warfare.

Henderson, Lieutenant-General Sir David (1862–1921): British airman. Entered the army, 1883; learned to fly, 1911; Director-General of Military Aeronautics, 1913; GOC of the Royal Flying Corps, 1914–17.

Hill, Major-General John (1866–1935): British general. GOC 52nd (Lowland Scottish) Division, 1917–18.

Hodgson, Major-General Sir Henry West (1868–1930): British general. Commanded Australian Mounted Division in Palestine, 1917–18.

Hogarth, Commander David George (1862–1927): Scholar and traveller. Keeper of Ashmolean Museum Oxford, 1908–27; Commander, Royal Naval Volunteer Reserve, 1915–19; Director, Arab Bureau, 1916.

Huddlestone, Major-General Sir Hubert Jervoise (1880–1950): British general. Transferred to Egyptian army, 1910; commanded Camel Corps, 1916–18; Chief Staff Officer under Lee Stack in the Sudan, 1923–24; GOC Sudan, 1925–30. Major-General, 1933.

Hussein, Sherif (later King) (or Husayn ibn 'Ali) (1856–1931): Arab statesman. Sherif of Mecca before 1916; launched the Arab revolt in 1916 and was made the first King of the Hedjaz; defeated by Ibn Saud and forced to abdicate (1924); went into exile in Cyprus.

Ibn Saud (Abdul Aziz ibn Abdul Rahman al Saud) (*c.* 1880–1953): Arab statesman; part of the radical Sunni Wahhabi movement; accepted British protection (1915) and fought against pro-Turkish Arab tribes during the First World War; defeated Hashemites in 1924 and united territory as Kingdom of Saudi Arabia in 1932.

Jellicoe, Admiral of the Fleet John Rushworth, 1st Earl Jellicoe (1859–1935): British admiral. Fought at the battle of Jutland, May–June 1916; First Sea Lord, December 1916; Admiral of the Fleet, 1919.

Joyce, Lieutenant-Colonel Pierce Charles (1878–1965): British soldier. Entered the army 1900; attached to the Egyptian army, 1907–16; served with Hedjaz Operations, EEF, 1916–18.

Kenyon, Major-General Edward Ranulph (1854–1937): British general. Commissioned into the RE in 1874; retired as a Colonel in 1911; re-employed 1914; Chief Engineer IV Corps, 1916; Chief Engineer Third Army, 1916–17; Deputy Controller Chemical Warfare Department, 1918.

Kirke, Major-General Sir Walter Meryyn St. George (1877–1949): British general. Deputy DMO 1918–20.

Kress von Kressenstein, Friedrich Freiherr (1870–1948): German soldier. Commanded Turkish forces at the third battle of Gaza, 1917; blamed by the Turks for the defeat at third Gaza, he was replaced by Falkenhayn; went on to command German forces in the Trans-Caucasus region in 1918; served in the *Reichswehr* after the war.[10]

Law, Andrew Bonar (1858–1923): British (Scottish) statesman. Chancellor of the Exchequer and Leader of the House of Commons, 1916–18; Lord Privy Seal, 1919; Prime Minister, 1922–23.

Lawrence, Colonel Thomas Edward (1888–1935): Soldier and writer. Achieved fame as 'Lawrence of Arabia' leading Hashemite Arab forces during the Arab revolt, 1916–18; Middle East Adviser to the British government after the war; joined the ranks of the RAF in 1922 under the name of J.H. Ross and then the Tank Corps as T.E. Shaw in 1923.

Liman von Sanders, General Otto (1855–1929): German general. Sent to the Ottoman empire in 1913 to help re-organise the Ottoman army; commanded Turkish forces on Gallipoli (1915); replaced Falkenhayn as the German commander in Palestine with the Turks, early 1918; defeated by Allenby at the battle of Megiddo, September 1918.[11]

Longley, Major-General Sir John Raynsford (1867–1953): Joined the army, 1887. GOC 10th (Irish) Division Salonika, Egypt and Palestine, 1916–18.

Lynden-Bell, Major-General Sir Arthur (1867–1943): British soldier. Joined the Buffs, 1885; served in the South African War, 1899–1902; served as Chief of Staff in France and Gallipoli before becoming Murray's Chief of Staff in Palestine; removed from post by Allenby in 1917 and replaced by Bols; Director of Staff Duties, 1918–21.

Macandrew, Major-General Henry John Milnes (1866–1919): British general. GOC 5th (Indian) Cavalry Division, 1918.

MacInnes, Rt. Reverend Rennie (d. 1931): Christian clergyman. Bishop of Jerusalem, 1914; Honorary Secretary Church Missionary Society and the Northern Sudan, 1902–14; Honorary Canon of St George's Collegiate Church, 1909.

Meinertzhagen, Colonel Richard (1878–1967): Soldier and explorer. Commanded Field Intelligence Section, EEF, 1917–18; Chief Political Officer in Palestine and Syria, 1919–20; Middle East Adviser, Colonial Office, 1921–24.[12]

Methuen, Field Marshal Sir Paul Sanford, 3rd Baron (1845–1932): British Field Marshal. Governor and C-in-C Malta, 1915–19.

Milner, Alfred, 1st Viscount Milner (1854–1925): British statesman. High Commissioner for South Africa, 1897–1905; member of Lloyd George's War Cabinet, December 1916–18; Secretary of State for War, 1918; Secretary of State for the Colonies, 1918–21; headed the Milner Mission to Egypt to determine future status of the country, 1919–20.

Money, Major-General Sir Arthur Wigram (1866–1951): British soldier and administrator. Joined Royal Artillery, 1885; served NW Frontier and South Africa (1899–1902); served in Mesopotamia and with the EEF, 1915–19; Chief Administrator with the EEF, 1918–19; Military Governor OETA (South), 1918–19.

Mott, Hon. Major-General Stanley Fielder (1873–1959): British general. In command of mounted infantry in the South African War, 1899–1902; retired, 1911; recalled to duty in 1914; GOC 53rd (Welsh) Division in Egypt and Palestine, 1917–18.

Murray, General Sir Archibald (James) (1860–1945): British general. Director of Military Training, 1907–12; Chief of the General Staff BEF, 1914–15; Deputy CIGS and CIGS, 1915; GOC forces in Egypt, January 1916–June 1917.

Naper, Captain William Lennox (1879–1942): British soldier. ADC to Allenby, 1917–19.

Nugent, Colonel Charles Hugh Hodges (1868–1924): British army officer. Served with mechanical transport services and with Royal Engineers; colonel, 1919.

Ormsby-Gore, Major William George Arthur, 4th Baron Harlech (1885–1964): British politician. Assistant Political Officer in Palestine, 1918; Member of the British Delegation to the Paris Peace Conference (Middle East Section), 1919; British representative on the Permanent Mandates Commission of the League of Nations; Under-Secretary of State for the Colonies, 1922–24.

Palin, Major-General Sir Philip Charles (1864–1937): British general. GOC 75th Division in Egypt and Palestine, 1917–18.

Philby, Harry St John Bridger (1885–1960): British (Indian) civil servant and explorer. In charge of British Mission to Central Arabia, 1917–18; explored Arabian peninsula and became a confidant of the Arab ruler Ibn Saud; retired from civil service in 1925; settled in the Middle East.

Picot (see Georges-Picot)

Piépape, Colonel P. de: French soldier and colonial administrator.[13] Commanded the French *Détachement Français de Palestine et de Syrie*; became French Military Governor in Beirut in October 1918.[14]

Plumer, Field Marshal Sir Herbert Charles Onslow, 1st Viscount Plumer of Messines and Bilton (1857–1932): British Field Marshal. GOC served in France commanding V Corps in 1915, then Second Army, 1915–17; served in Italy, 1817–18; commanded Second Army (again) during the Ludendorff offensives, 1918.

Ribot, Alexandre Felix Joseph (1842–1923): French politician. French Foreign Minister, 1890–93; following Briand's resignation in March 1917, became Prime Minister; resigned as Prime Minister, 7 September 1917.

Robertson, Field Marshal Sir William Robert, 1st Baronet (1866–1933): British Field Marshal. Enlisted in the cavalry as a Trooper in 1877; rose through the ranks to become CIGS, December 1915; dismissed as CIGS, February 1918; transferred to Eastern (Home) Command; GOC Army on the Rhine, 1919–20.[15]

Rushdi Husayn (Pasha) (1864–1928): Egyptian politician. Member of the aristocracy; studied law; served as a judge and became Egypt's Minister of Justice; helped formulate the terms of the British Protectorate, 1914; Prime Minister, 1914; part of the delegation (formed by Sa'd Zaghlul and Wafd party) in 1918 that demanded autonomy for Egypt.

Sa'd (Pasha) Zaghlul (1860–1927): Egyptian nationalist and politician. Lawyer by profession; Vice-President Egyptian Legislative Assembly, 1913; led the delegation (Arabic: *wafd*) after the war to argue for Egyptian independence; deported to Malta (1919) with other members of the Wafd party; allowed to return, partly due to Egyptian revolt, 1919; deported again, 1921; became Wafd Prime Minister, 1924.

Salmond, Air Chief Marshal Sir (William) Geoffrey (Hanson) (1878–1933): British airman. Commanded 5th Wing RFC Egypt, 1915–16; Middle East Brigade, 1916–17; Middle East Command, 1918–21.

Shea, General Sir John Stuart Mackenzie (1869–1966): British general. GOC 60th (London) Division in Palestine, 1917–18.

Smith-Dorrien, General Sir Horace Lockwood (1858–1930): British general. Experienced and able commander of II Corps in the BEF in 1914; dismissed by Field Marshal John French in 1915 after the second battle of Ypres.

Smuts, General Jan Christian (1870–1950): South African soldier and statesman. Member of the Imperial War Cabinet and adviser to Lloyd George during the First World War.

Stack, Sir Lee Oliver Fitzmaurice (1868–1924): British soldier and administrator. Acting Sirdar of Egyptian army and Governor-General of Sudan, 1917–24; assassinated in Cairo, 1924.

Stirling, Walter Francis (1880–1958): British soldier. Served at Gallipoli and in Palestine; chief staff officer to T.E. Lawrence; Lieutenant-Colonel, 1920; governor Jaffa district, 1920–3.

Storrs, Sir Ronald (1881–1955): British colonial administrator. Assistant Political Officer to Anglo-French Political Mission EEF, 1917; Military Governor of Jerusalem, 1917–20.[16]

Sykes, Sir Mark, 6th Baronet (1879–1919): British government adviser and explorer. Responsible for the 'Sykes-Picot' agreement of May 1916; attached to the Foreign Office and employed as Chief Adviser on Middle East affairs, 1917–19; went on various missions to the Middle East, 1916–18.

Tardieu, André Pierre Gabriel Amédée (1876–1945): French journalist, diplomat and politician. Covered foreign affairs for *Le Temps* and *Petit Parisien* before the war. Leading member of the French delegation to the Paris Peace Conference (1919) and a close associate of Clemenceau.

Toynbee, Arnold (1889–1975): British historian and government adviser. Served in the Foreign Office in both world wars and attended the Paris Peace Conference, 1919; Koraes Professor of Modern Greek and Byzantine history at King's College London, 1919–24; Director of the Royal Institute for International Affairs, 1925–55.

Wavell, Field Marshal Sir Archibald Percival, 1st Earl Wavell (1883–1950): British field marshal. Acted as Robertson's liaison officer in Palestine with Allenby; wrote several books on Allenby and the Palestine campaign; served in the Second World War as a senior commander; Field Marshal, 1943.

Weizmann, Chaim Azriel (1874–1952): Chemist, Zionist and politician. Before the First World War, Weizmann worked as a chemist in Manchester, developing a bacterium, *Clostridium acetobutylium*, that helps to plasticize the propellant cordite; during the war, Weizmann worked to promote Zionism with the British government; this came to fruition with the Balfour Declaration in November 1917; in 1948, became the first President of Israel.

Wigram, Sir Clive, 1st Baron Wigram of Clewer (1873–1960): Assistant Private Secretary and Equerry to the King, 1910–31.

Wilson, Field Marshal Sir Henry Hughes, 1st Baronet (1864–1922): British field marshal. British Military Representative on the Supreme War Council, 1917; CIGS, 1918–22.

Wingate, Sir (Francis) Reginald, 1st Baronet and Sirdar (1861–1953): British colonial administrator. Governor-General of the Sudan, 1899–1916; High Commissioner to Egypt, 1917–19 (superseded by Allenby).

Yale, William (1887–1975): US oilman and government special adviser. Worked for SOCONY (Standard Oil Company of New York) before the First World War, training for its foreign service; Special Agent of the US State Department in the Middle East attached to the EEF during the First World War.[17]

Zaghlul (see Sa'd).

Bibliography

A select list of the sources manuscript and printed used in this book. All books published in London unless otherwise stated.

Government Archives

Public Record Office (National Archives), Kew, London
War Office
WO32 Registered Papers General Series
   WO32/5580
WO33 O and A Confidential Printed Papers
   WO33/935
   WO33/946
   WO33/960
   WO33/981
WO95 War Diaries
   WO95/4371
WO106 Directorate of Military Operations and Intelligence and Operations
   WO106/191
   WO106/192
   WO106/718
   WO106/722
   WO106/729
WO158 GHQ Correspondence and Papers: Military Headquarters
   WO158/611
   WO158/634

Cabinet Office
CAB24 War Cabinet Memoranda
   CAB24/20
   CAB24/37
CAB25 Supreme War Council
   CAB25/41
   CAB25/68
CAB44/45 Cabinet Office Historical Section: Official War Histories
   CAB45/78

Foreign Office
FO371 Foreign Office General Correspondence post-1906
    FO371/3715-22
FO882 Arab Bureau Papers
    FO882/7

British Library, Oriental and India Office Collections, London
L/MIL/5
L/MIL/17
L/P&S/10
L/P&S/11

Australian War Memorial, Canberra
AWM4 Australian Unit War Diaries
AWM22 AIF, HQ (Egypt) Central Registry
AWM25 Written Records 1914–18 War
AWM27/252 Library Records
AWM30 POW Statements 1914–18 War
AWM45 Copies of British War Diaries – 'Heyes papers'

Private Papers and Records

Australian War Memorial, Canberra
Charles Bean (1879–1968)
Hon. Sir Henry Gullett (1878–1940)
Brigadier A.J. Mills (b. 1884)

British Library, Manuscript Collections, London
General Sir Horace Smith-Dorrien (1858–1930)

British Library, Oriental and India Office Collections, London
George Nathaniel Curzon, 1st Marquess Curzon of Kedleston (1859–1925)

Cambridge University Library, Department of Manuscripts and University Archives
Charles Hardinge, 1st Baron Hardinge of Penshurst (1858–1944)

Central Zionist Archives, Jerusalem
Z4/170, L3/427, AK207/2

House of Lords Record Office, London
David Lloyd George, 1st Earl Lloyd George of Dwyfor (1863–1945)

Imperial War Museum, Department of Documents, London
Captain C.W. Battine (*c.* 1866–1949)
Field Marshal Sir Philip Chetwode, 7th Bt and 1st Baron Chetwode (1869–1950)
Major-General Guy Dawnay (1878–1952)
Major-General Sir Steuart Hare (1867–1952)
Major-General Sir Walter Meryyn St. George Kirke (1877–1949)
Field Marshal Sir Henry Wilson, 1st Bt (1864–1922)

Imperial War Museum, Sound Archive, London
Trooper L. Pollock (ref: 4220)
General Sir John Shea (1869–1966) (ref: 4227)

Liddell Hart Centre for Military Archives, King's College, London
Field Marshal Sir Edmund Allenby, 1st Viscount Allenby of Megiddo and
    Felixstowe (1861–1936)
Brigadier-General Sir James Edmonds (1861–1956)
Captain Sir Basil Liddell Hart (1895–1970)
Lieutenant-Colonel Pierce Joyce (1878–1965) (formerly the Akaba/Aqaba papers)
Field Marshal Sir William Robertson, 1st Bt (1860–1933)
General Sir John Shea (1869–1966)

Liverpool Record Office and Local Studies Service
Edward George Villiers Stanley, 17th Earl of Derby (1865–1948)

Mitchell Library, Sydney
Trooper G.T. Birkbeck (ref: MSS810)

National Archives of Scotland, Edinburgh
Philip Kerr, 11th Marquess of Lothian (1882–1940)

National Army Museum, Department of Archives, Photographs, Film and Sound, London
Major-General Sir Arthur Money (1866–1951)
7208–14
6309–44
2001–11–125
1990–08–29

National Library of Australia, Canberra
Major-General Sir Granville de Laune Ryrie (1865–1937)

National Library of Scotland, Department of Manuscripts, Edinburgh
Field Marshal Sir Douglas Haig, 1st Earl Haig (1861–1928)
MS.19951 f. 405–9

MS.20249 f. 254
General Sir J.A.L. Haldane (1862–1950)

Oxford University, Bodleian Library, Department of Special Collections and Western Manuscripts
Alfred Milner, 1st Viscount Milner (1854–1925)

Oxford University, Bodleian Library, Rhodes House Library
Diary of Colonel Richard Meinertzhagen (1878–1967)

Oxford University, St. Antony's College, Middle East Centre
Field Marshal Sir Edmund Allenby, 1st Viscount Allenby of Megiddo and
   Felixstowe (1861–1936) GB165–0005
Nina Baird (d. 1919) GB165–0017
Sir Milne Cheetham (1869–1938) GB165–0055
Sir Kinahan Cornwallis (1883–1959) GB165–0064
Brigadier-General Sir Wyndham Deedes (1883–1956) GB165–0079
Prince Feisal (Emir of the Hedjaz) (1885–1933) GB165–0105
J&EM (Jordan and East Mission) Papers Box LX File 1
Willam Yale (1887–1975) GB165–0308
Major Sir Hubert Young (1884–1950) GB165–0309

Royal Archives, Windsor Castle
Colonel Sir Clive Wigram, 1st Baron of Clewer (1873–1960)
RA PS/GV/Q 2521/1–19

Somerset Archive and Record Service, Taunton
Hon. Aubrey Herbert MP (1880–1923)

Staffordshire and Stoke-on-Trent Archive Service, Staffordshire Record Office, Stafford
General Sir Walter Norris Congreve (1862–1927)

Sudan Archive, Archives and Special Collections, University of Durham
Brigadier-General Sir Gilbert Clayton (1875–1929)
General Sir Reginald Wingate (1861–1953)

Film Archive

Imperial War Museum, Film Archive, London
General Scenes of Gaza (IWM 11)
General Allenby's Entry into Jerusalem (IWM 13)
The Occupation of Es Salt (IWM 26)
The Advance through Nazareth and Damascus (IWM 37)

Published Primary Material

Barzilay, Dvorah and Litvinoff, Barnet (eds), *The Letters and Papers of Chaim Weizmann, Volume 8, Series A, November 1917–October 1918* (Jerusalem & Rutgers University, 1977).

Callwell, C., *Field Marshal Sir Henry Wilson: His Life and Diaries* (1927).

Hancock, W.K. and Poel, J. van der (eds), *Selections from the Smuts Papers* (Cambridge, 1966 and 1973).

Handbook of the Turkish Army, Eighth Provisional Edition, February 1916, Intelligence Section Cairo [1916] (Nashville and Stokie, 1996).

Jeffery, Keith (ed.), *The Military Correspondence of Field Marshal Sir Henry Wilson 1918–1922* (The Bodley Head/Army Records Society, 1985).

Mantoux, Paul, *The Deliberations of the Council of Four (24 March–28 June 1919): Notes of Official Interpreter Paul Mantoux* (Princeton, NJ, 1992) trans. and ed. Arthur S. Link.

Meinertzhagen, Richard, *Middle East Diary, 1917–1956* (1959).

——, *Army Diary 1899–1926* (Edinburgh, 1960).

Morris, A.J.A. (ed.), *The Letters of the Lieutenant-Colonel Charles à Court Repington CMG. Military Correspondent of the Times, 1903–1918* (Stroud, 1999).

Papers Relating to the Foreign Relations of the United States: The Paris Peace Conference 1919 (Washington, DC, 1942–7).

Sacher, Howard et al (eds), *The Rise of Israel* (New York and London, 1987).

Sir Archibald Murray's Despatches (June 1916–June 1917) (London and Toronto, 1920).

Statistics of the Military Effort of the British Empire During the Great War 1914–1920 (1922).

Woodward, David (ed.), *The Military Correspondence of Field Marshal Sir William Robertson* (1989).

Woodward E.L. and Butler, Rohan (eds), *Documents on British Foreign Policy 1919–39, First Series, Volume 4* (1952).

Memoirs and Autobiographies

Barrow, George de S., *The Fire of Life* (1942).

Djemal Pasha, *Memories of a Turkish Statesman 1913–1919* (1922).

Kress von Kressenstein, F., *Zwischen Kaukasus und Sinai: Jahrbuch des Bundes der Asienkämpfer 1921* (Berlin-Tempelhof, 1921).

——, *Mit den Türken zum Suezkanal* (Berlin, 1938).

Larcher, M., *La Guerre Turque dans la Guerre Mondiale* (Paris: Berger-Levrault, 1926).

Lawrence, T.E., *Seven Pillars of Wisdom* [1935 and 1926] (1962).

Liman von Sanders, Otto, *Five Years in Turkey* (Annapolis, English translation 1927).

Lloyd George, David, *War Memoirs* (2 volumes) (1938).

——, *Memoirs of the Peace Conference* (New Haven, 1939) (published in 1938 as *The Truth about the Peace Treaties*).

Nogales, Rafael de, *Four Years Beneath the Crescent* (1926).

Papen, Franz von, *Memoirs* (1952).

Patterson, J.H., *With the Zionists in Gallipoli* (1916).

——, *With the Judaeans in the Palestine Campaign* (1922).

Pichon, Jean., *Sur la Route des Indes: Un Siècle Après Bonaparte* (Paris, 1932).

——, *Le Partage du Proche-Orient* (Paris, 1938).

Robertson, William, *From Private to Field Marshal* (1921).

——, *Soldiers and Statesmen* (1926).

Slim, William, *Defeat Into Victory* (1956).

Stirling, W.F., *Safety Last* (1953).

Storrs, Ronald, *Orientations* (1937) (reprinted 1972 as *Memoirs of Sir Ronald Storrs* [New York: Arno Press]).

Official Histories and Unit Histories

Barrett, James and Deane, P.E., *The Australian Army Medical Corps in Egypt* (1918).

Dalbiac, P.H., *History of the 60th Division* (1927).

Falls, Cyril with Macmunn, George, *History of the Great War, Military Operations, Egypt and Palestine* (1928–30) (British Official History) (2 volumes).

Grasselli, Ettore, *L'Esercito Italiano In Francia E In Oriente.* Volume 12 of *Storia Della Guerra Italiana* (Milan, 1934).

Gullett, H.S., *The Official History of Australia in the War of 1914–1918, Volume 7, Sinai and Palestine, The Australian Imperial Force in Sinai and Palestine 1914–1918* [1923] (St. Lucia, 1984) (Australian Official History) (2 volumes).

Hussein Husni Amir Bey, *Yilderim* (Turkish General Staff, n.d.) (Translated by G.O. de R. Channer) (copy in AWM45).

Jones, H.A. (and Walter Raleigh), *Official History of the War in the Air* (Oxford, 1922–7).

Macpherson, W., Herringham,W.P., Elliot, T.R. and Balfour, A. (eds), *Official History of the War, Medical Services, Volume 1, Hygiene of the War* (1923).

Moberly, F.J., *History of the Great War, Based on Official Documents, The Campaign in Mesopotamia 1914–1918* (1923–7) (4 volumes).

——, *History of the Great War, Based on Official Documents, Operations in Persia, 1914–1919* (HMSO, 1929).

Pirie-Gordon, H., *The Advance of the Egyptian Expeditionary Force July 1917–October 1918* (Cairo, 1919).

Powles, C. Guy, *The New Zealanders in Sinai and Palestine, Volume III of the Official History of New Zealand's Effort in the Great War* (Auckland, 1922).

Preston, R.M.P., *The Desert Mounted Corps: An Account of the Cavalry Operation in Palestine and Syria, 1917–1918* (1921).

Biographies of Allenby

Gardner, Brian, *Allenby* (1965).
James, Lawrence, *Imperial Warrior: The Life and Times of Field Marshal Viscount Allenby 1861–1936* (1993).
Savage, Raymond, *Allenby of Armageddon* (1925).
Wavell, Archibald, *Allenby: A Study in Greatness* [1940] (New York, 1941).
——, *Allenby in Egypt* (New York, 1943).

General Books

Allen, W.E.D. and Muratov, Paul, *Caucasian Battlefields: A History of the War on the Turco-Caucasian Border, 1821–1921* (Cambridge, 1953).
Andrew, Christopher M. and Kanya-Forster, A.S., *France Overseas: The Great War and the Climax of French Imperial Expansion* (1981).
Anglesey, The Marquess of, *A History of the British Cavalry 1816–1919, Volume 5, Egypt, Palestine and Syria, 1914–1919* (1994).
Antonius, George, *The Arab Awakening* (1938).
Bentwich, Norman, *England in Palestine* (1932).
——, *Palestine* (1934).
Biddle, Martin, *The Tomb of Christ* (Stroud, 1999).
Bidwell, Shelford and Graham, Dominick, *Coalitions, Politicians and Generals: Some Aspects of Command in Two World Wars* (1993).
Bond, Brian (ed.), *The First World War and British Military History* (Oxford, 1991).
Bonham-Carter, V., *Soldier True: The Life and Times of Field-Marshal Sir William Robertson 1860–1933* (1963).
Bourne, John, *Who's Who in World War One* (London and New York, 2001).
Bowman-Manifold, M.G.E., *An Outline of the Egyptian and Palestinian Campaigns* (Chatham, 1922).
Bray, N.N.E., *Shifting Sands* (1934).
Brémond, Edouard, *Le Hedjaz dans la Guerre Mondiale* (Paris, 1931).
Briscoe-Moore, A., *The Mounted Rifleman in Sinai and Palestine* (Auckland, 1920).
Bruce, Anthony, *The Last Crusade: The Palestine Campaign in the First World War* (2002).
Brugger, Suzanne, *Australians and Egypt, 1914–1919* (Melbourne, 1980).
Bullock, David, *Allenby's War, The Palestine-Arabian Campaigns 1916–1918* (1988).
Castle, Wilfred, *Grand Turk* (1943).
Connell, John, *Wavell, Scholar and Soldier* (1964).
Cross, F.L. (ed.), *The Oxford Dictionary of the Christian Church* [1957] (Oxford, 1997).
Cruttwell, Cyril, *A History of the Great War 1914–1918* [1934] (1986).

Dallas, Gloden and Gill, Douglas, *The Unknown Army: Mutinies in the British Army in World War One* (1985).

Daly, M.W. (ed.), *The Cambridge History of Egypt. Volume 2* (Cambridge, 1998).

Dane, E., *British Campaigns in the Nearer East 1914–1918 from the Outbreak of the War with Turkey to the Taking of Jerusalem* (1918).

Dockrill, Michael and Douglas Goold, J., *Peace Without Promise: Britain and the Peace Conferences, 1919–23* (1981).

Elgood, P.G., *Egypt and the Army* (Oxford, 1924).

Emin (Yalman), Ahmed, *Turkey in the World War* (New Haven, CT: Yale UP, 1930).

Erickson, Edward, *Ordered to Die: A History of the Ottoman Army in the First World War* (Westport, CT, 2001).

Falls, Cyril, *Armageddon 1918* (1964).

Forester, C.S., *The General* [1936] (1979).

French, David, *The Strategy of the Lloyd George Coalition, 1916–18* (Oxford, 1995).

Fromkin, David, *A Peace To End All Peace: Creating the Modern Middle East, 1914–1922* [1989] (1991).

Gammage, Bill, *The Broken Years: Australian Soldiers in the Great War* (Canberra, 1974).

Gardner, Nikolas, *Trial by Fire: Command and the British Expeditionary Force in 1914* (Westport and London, 2003).

Garsia, Clive, *A Key to Victory: A Study of War Planning* (1940).

Gountaut-Biron, R. de, *Comment la France s'est instalée en Syrie (1918–19)* (Paris, 1923).

Hamilton, Jill, *First to Damascus: The Story of the Australian Light Horse and Lawrence of Arabia* (Sydney, 2002).

Handel, Michael (ed.), *Intelligence and Military Operations* (1990).

Hill, A.J., *Chauvel of the Light Horse: A Biography of General Sir Harry Chauvel* (Victoria, 1978).

Howard, Harry N., *An American Inquiry in the Middle East: The King-Crane Commission* (Beirut, 1963).

Hughes, Matthew, *Allenby and British Strategy in the Middle East, 1917–1919* (1999).

Idriess, I.L., *The Desert Column* (Sydney, 1932).

Inchbald, Geoffrey, *Imperial Camel Corps* (1970).

Jabotinsky, Vladimir, *The Story of the Jewish Legion* (New York, 1945).

Jeffery, Keith, *The British Army and the Crisis of Empire 1918–22* (Manchester, 1984).

Karsh, Efraim, *Fabricating Israeli History: The 'New Historians'* [1997] (2000).

Kedourie, Elie, *The Chatham House Version and other Middle-Eastern Studies* [1970] (Hanover & London, 1984).

——, *England and the Middle East: The Destruction of the Ottoman Empire 1914–21* [1956] (1987).

——, *Politics in the Middle East* (Oxford and New York, 1992).

——, *In the Anglo-Arab Labyrinth: The McMahon-Husayn Correspondence and its Interpretations 1914–1939* [1976] (2000).

Kent, Marian (ed.), *The Great Powers and the End of the Ottoman Empire* [1986] (1996).

Khalidi, Walidi (ed.), *All That Remains: The Palestinian Villages Occupied and Depopulated by Israel in 1948* (Washington, DC, 1992).

Lewin, Ronald, *Slim: The Standardbearer* [1976] (1990).

Monroe, Elizabeth, *Britain's Moment in the Middle East: 1914–1956* (1963).

Morris, Benny, *The Birth of the Palestinian Refugee Problem, 1947–49* (Cambridge, 1987).

——, *1948 and After: Israel and the Palestinians* [1990] (Oxford, 1994).

Murphy, C.C.R., *Soldiers of the Prophet* (1921).

Nevakivi, Jukka, *Britain, France and the Arab Middle East 1914–1920* (1969).

Perret, Bryan, *Megiddo 1918: The Last Great Cavalry Victory* (Oxford, 1999).

Presenti, Gustavo, *In Palestine e in Siria Durante e Dopo la Grande Guerra* (Milan: L'Eroica, 1932).

Rogan, Eugene, *Frontiers of the State in the Late Ottoman Empire, Transjordan 1850–1921* (Cambridge, 1999).

Sheffy, Yigal, *British Military Intelligence in the Palestine Campaign, 1914–1918* (1998).

Shepherd, Naomi, *Ploughing Sand: British Rule in Palestine 1917–1948* (1999).

Stein, Leonard, *The Balfour Declaration* (1961).

Strachan, Hew (ed.), *The Oxford Illustrated History of the First World War* (Oxford, 1998).

——, *The First World War. Volume 1: To Arms* (Oxford, 2001).

Tauber, Eliezer, *The Arab Movements in World War I* (1993).

Taylor, A.J.P., *English History 1914–1945* [1965] (Oxford, 1990).

Temperley, H.W.V. (ed.), *A History of the Peace Conference of Paris* (1920–4).

Trumpener, Ulrich, *Germany and the Ottoman Empire 1914–1918* (Princeton, 1968).

Vatikiotis, P.J., *The History of Modern Egypt: From Muhammad Ali to Mubarak* [1969] (1991).

Wart, R.B. van, *The Life of Lieutenant-General H.H. Sir Pratap Singh* (1926).

Wavell, Archibald, *The Palestine Campaigns* [1928] (1933).

Weber, Frank G., *Eagles on the Crescent: Germany, Austria and the Diplomacy of the Turkish Alliance, 1914–1918* (1970).

Westrate, Bruce, *The Arab Bureau: British Policy in the Middle East 1916–1920* (University Park, Pennsylvania, 1993).

Wilson, Jeremy, *Lawrence of Arabia: The Authorised Biography* [1989] (1990).

Woodward, David, *Lloyd George and the Generals* (London and Toronto, 1983).

——, *Field Marshal Sir William Robertson: Chief of the Imperial General Staff in the Great War* (1998).

Yapp, Malcolm, *The Near East since the First World War* (London and New York, 1991).

Zeine, Zeine N., *Arab-Turkish Relations and the Emergence of Arab Nationalism* (Beirut, 1958).

——, *The Struggle for Arab Independence: Western Diplomacy and the Rise and Fall of Faisal's Kingdom in Syria, 1914–1920* (Beirut, 1960).

Journal Articles

Anon., 'The Turkish Operations in Palestine, 19th–23rd September 1918', *The Journal of the Royal United Services Institution*, 66, May 1921, pp. 326–36.

——, 'Notes on Foreign War Books', Review of *Zwischen Kaukasus und Sinai Jahrbuch des Bundes der Asienkämpfer* in *The Army Quarterly*, 4, April 1922, pp. 157–60.

——, 'The Campaign in Palestine from the Enemy's Side', *The Journal of the Royal United Services Institution*, 67, August 1922, pp. 503–13 (partial translation of Kress von Kressenstein, *Zwischen Kaukasus und Sinai: Jahrbuch des Bundes der Asienkämpfer 1921*).

——, 'The Surafend Incident. Why Allenby Ignored The Anzacs', *The New Zealand Returned Soldiers' Association Review*, 15, February 1939, pp. 17–18.

——, 'The Surafend Incident, Further Light on Same', *The New Zealand Returned Soldiers' Association Review*, 15, May 1939, pp. 26–7.

——, 'Notes on Foreign War Books', Review of *Mit den Türken zum Suezkanal* in *The Army Quarterly*, 38, July 1939, pp. 355–60.

Atkinson, C.T., 'General Liman von Sanders on his Experiences in Palestine', *The Army Quarterly*, 3, January 1922, pp. 257–75.

Burne, A.H., 'Notes on the Palestine Campaign', *The Fighting Forces*, 9/1–6 and 10/1, April 1932–April 1933, pp. 67–78 (April 1932), pp. 195–204 (June 1932), pp. 306–14 (August 1932), pp. 452–61 (October 1932), pp. 535–49 (December 1932), pp. 667–74 (February 1933), pp. 64–72 (April 1933).

Elliot, W. and Kinross, A., 'Maintaining Allenby's Armies: A Footnote to History', *The Royal Army Service Corps Quarterly*, 13/1, 1925, pp. 114–28.

Falls, Cyril, 'Falkenhayn in Syria', *The Edinburgh Review*, 250, October 1929, pp. 272–89.

Fewster, Kevin, 'The Wazza Riots 1915', *Journal of the Australian War Memorial*, 4, April 1984, pp. 47–53.

Grainger, John D., 'Subtlety, Misdirection, and Deceit: Allenby's Grand Tactics at Third Gaza', *The RUSI Journal* [formerly *The Journal of the Royal United Services Institution* or *Institute*], 140/2, April 1995, pp. 58–62.

Hughes, Matthew, 'Australians and the fall of Damascus, 1 October 1918', *Journal of the Australian War Memorial*, 26, April 1995, pp. 26–37.

——, 'General Allenby and the Palestine campaign, 1917–18' in Brian Holden Reid (ed.) 'Military Power: Land Warfare in Theory and Practice' (special issue), *The Journal of Strategic Studies*, 19/4, December 1996, pp. 59–88.

——, 'Lloyd George, the generals and the Palestine campaign, 1917–18', *Imperial War Museum Review*, 11, November 1997, pp. 4–17.

Jones, Ian, 'Beersheba: The light horse charge and the making of myths', *Journal of the Australian War Memorial*, 3, October 1983, pp. 26–37.

Larcher, M., 'La Campagne du Général de Falkenhayn en Palestine', *Revue Militaire Française*, October/November 1925, pp. 28–53 & pp. 176–86.

Macdonnell, Norman, 'The British Campaign in Palestine', *Transactions of the Canadian Military Institute*, 22, 1923, pp. 45–58.

Maurice, Frederick, 'The Campaigns in Palestine and Egypt 1914–1918, in relation to the general strategy of the war', *The Army Quarterly*, 18, April–July 1929, pp. 14–23.

Murphy, C.C.R., 'The Turkish Army in the Great War', *The Journal of the Royal United Services Institution*, 65, February 1920, pp. 90–104.

Newell, Jonathan, 'Learning The Hard Way: Allenby in Egypt and Palestine 1917–1919', *The Journal of Strategic Studies*, 14/3, September 1991, pp. 363–87.

Reid, Brian Holden, 'T.E. Lawrence and Liddell Hart', *History*, 70, 1985, pp. 218–31.

Sheffy, Yigal, 'The Origins of the British Breakthrough into South Palestine: The ANZAC Raid on the Ottoman Railway, 1917', *Journal of Strategic Studies*, 22/1, March 1999, pp. 124–47.

Skander Bey, 'The Battles of Salt, Aman [sic] and Jordan from Turkish Sources', *The Journal of the Royal United Services Institution*, 69, May & August 1924, pp. 334–43, 488–98.

Stanley, W.R., 'Review of Turkish Asiatic Railways to 1918: Some Political-Military Considerations', *Journal of Transport History*, 7, 1966 [published 1970], pp. 189–203.

Tardieu, André, 'Mossoul et le pétrole', *L'Illustration*, 19 June 1920, pp. 380–2.

Wasti, S. Tanvir, 'The Defence of Medina 1916–1919', *Middle Eastern Studies*, 27/4, October 1991, pp. 642–53.

Wavell, Archibald P., 'The Strategy of the Campaigns of the Egyptian Expeditionary Force', *The Army Quarterly*, 3, January 1922, pp. 235–49.

Welsch, O., 'Cavalry in the Palestine Campaign' (translation of article in *Militär-Wochenblatt*), *The Cavalry Journal*, 18, 1927, pp. 293–301.

Wheler, George, 'The Capture of Damascus in 1918', *The Cavalry Journal*, July 1935, pp. 444–8.

Willson, Beckles, 'Our Amazing Syrian Adventure, *The National Review*, September 1920, pp. 41–54.

Woodward, David, 'Britain in a Continental War: The Civil-Military Debate over the Strategical Direction of the Great War of 1914–18', *Albion*, 12/1, Spring 1980, pp. 37–65.

——, 'The Imperial Strategist: Jan Christiaan Smuts and British Military Policy 1917–18', *Military History Journal*, 5/4, December 1981, pp. 131–53.

——, 'Did Lloyd George Starve the British Army of Men Prior to the German Offensive of 21 March 1918?', *Historical Journal*, 27/1, 1984, pp. 241–52.

Book Chapters

Divine, Donna Robinson, 'Palestine in World War I', in D.R. Divine, *Politics and Society in Ottoman Palestine: the Arab struggle for survival and power* (Boulder Colorado, 1994).

Lewis, Geoffrey, 'An Ottoman Officer in Palestine 1914–1918', in David Kushner (ed.), *Palestine in the Late Ottoman Period* (Jerusalem, 1986).

Newell, Jonathan, 'Allenby and the Palestine Campaign', in Brian Bond (ed.), *The First World War and British Military History* (Oxford, 1991).

Sheffy, Yigal, 'Institutionalised Deception and Perception Reinforcement: Allenby's Campaign in Palestine', in Michael Handel (ed.), *Intelligence and Military Operations* (1990).

Conference Proceedings

Sheffy, Yigal and Shai, Shaul (eds), *The First World War: Middle Eastern Perspectives. Proceedings of the Israeli-Turkish International Colloquy* (Tel Aviv: Israeli Society for Military History & Department of History IDF, 2001).

Doctoral Theses

David, Philippe, 'Un Gouvernment arabe à Damas. Le Congrès Syrièn (Paris, 1923).

Hughes, Matthew, 'General Allenby and the Campaign of the Egyptian Expeditionary Force, June 1917–November 1919' (University of London, 1995).

Newell, Jonathan, 'British Military Policy in Egypt and Palestine, August 1914 to June 1917' (University of London, 1990).

Websites

Simkins, Peter, review of Matthew Hughes, *Allenby and British Strategy in the Middle East 1917–1919* (1999) in *IHR Reviews in History* at http://www.history.ac.uk/reviews/paper/simkins.html (accessed 20 June 2002).

Index

ARMY RECORDS SOCIETY
(FOUNDED 1984)

Members of the Society are entitled to purchase back volumes
at reduced prices.
Orders should be sent to the Hon. Treasurer, Army Records Society,
c/o National Army Museum,
Royal Hospital Road,
London SW3 4HT

The Society has already issued:

Vol. I:
The Military Correspondence of Field Marshal Sir Henry Wilson 1918–1922
Edited by Dr Keith Jeffery

Vol. II:
The Army and the Curragh Incident, 1914
Edited by Dr Ian F.W. Beckett

Vol. III:
The Napoleonic War Journal of Captain Thomas Henry Browne, 1807–1816
Edited by Roger Norman Buckley

Vol. IV:
*An Eighteenth-Century Secretary at War The Papers of William,
Viscount Barrington*
Edited by Dr Tony Hayter

Vol. V:
The Military Correspondence of Field Marshal Sir William Robertson 1915–1918
Edited by David R. Woodward

Vol. VI:
Colonel Samuel Bagshawe and the Army of George II, 1731–1762
Edited by Dr Alan J. Guy

Vol. VII:
Montgomery and the Eighth Army
Edited by Stephen Brooks